BUSH'S WAR
FOR
REELECTION

BUSH'S WAR
FOR
REELECTION
IRAQ, THE WHITE HOUSE, AND THE PEOPLE

JAMES MOORE

WILEY

JOHN WILEY & SONS, INC.

Published by John Wiley & Sons, Inc., Hoboken, New Jersey.
Published simultaneously in Canada.

For general information on our other products and services, or technical support, please
contact our Customer Care Department within the United States at 800-762-2974,
outside the United States at 317-572-3993 or fax 317-572-4002.

Wiley also publishes its books in a variety of electronic formats. Some content that
appears in print may not be available in electronic books. For more information about
Wiley products, visit our web site at www.wiley.com.

Library of Congress Cataloging-in-Publication Data:

Moore, James, 1951–
    Bush's war for reelection : Iraq, the White House, and the people / James
Moore.
        p. cm.
    Includes bibliographical references and index.
    ISBN 0-471-48385-0 (cloth)
        1. United States—Politics and government—2001–   2. Bush, George W.
(George Walker), 1946—Ethics.   3. Political corruption—United States.   4.
Iraq War, 2003—Causes.   5. Politics and war—Case studies.   6. Iraq War,
2003—Biography.   7. Soldiers—United States—Biography.   I. Title.
    E902.M64 2004
    956.7044′3—dc22

                                                                    2004002218

Printed in the United States of America.

10   9   8   7   6   5   4   3   2   1

for
Mary Lou
forever

In memory of
First Lieutenant Frederick E. Pokorney Jr., U.S.M.C.
Specialist James Kiehl, U.S. Army
Chief Warrant Officer Johnny Villareal Mata, U.S. Army

In honor of their children
Taylor Rochelle Pokorney
Nathaniel Ethan Kiehl
Eric and Stephani Mata

CONTENTS

PART III
COUNTING CASUALTIES

I tremble for my country when I reflect that God is just; that his justice cannot sleep forever.

Thomas Jefferson

AUTHOR'S NOTE

When Saddam Hussein was found, the White House did its best not to gloat. George W. Bush, though, was feeling full of political glory. One of the evil ones had been reduced to a lice-ridden mole. Unfortunately for President Bush, though, he and his Iraqi occupiers had characterized Hussein as the man running the resistance, killing American troops, and leading the insurgency. If Hussein were involved, it was only in an ancillary way, perhaps, as little more than a symbol. He had no communications to run any kind of coordinated battle plan against the United States, and, given his rank cowardice, no courage or vision to do more than suffer through his next day.

Saddam Hussein was still a distraction for the Bush administration. There ought to be great pressure on the White House, as a result of Hussein's capture, to finally discover the weapons of mass destruction. We did not, after all, invade Iraq to get Hussein. Americans raced to Baghdad to conquer the country before weapons of mass destruction could be fired. If Hussein does not tell the U.S. military where those weapons are located, or if there are none, his capture is almost meaningless; except for the value of trying him for crimes against his own people. Of course, the arrest means much to the Bush family. Hussein plotted to kill George H. W. Bush, and the Bush family has been obsessed with the dictator since the days of the Gulf War.

The incontrovertible truth, which is a sour drink for the Bush administration, is that there is no connection between Saddam Hussein and the war on terrorism. His capture will do little or nothing to reduce attacks on American troops occupying Iraq. He was not connected to Al Qaeda. He was not running the insurgency. He was only an icon of Arab extremists, and the White House needed somebody to bring to justice. The American people had to have some kind of action after 9/11. The Bush administration very artfully convinced the electorate of the United States that the best thing to be done was get Saddam. And now we have. But we can expect to slowly learn how he had nothing to do with attacks on U.S. soil, and little, if any, involvement with the resistance inside of Iraq.

The arrest of Saddam Hussein may also set off sectarian warfare. The Shia, repressed for decades by the dictator, may have been exercising restraint, wondering if he might return to power. Hussein's capture removes that variable. The Sunnis, empowered by Hussein, are likely to discover they are now targets of Shia radicals who want both revenge for the way they were treated and power to control the future of Iraq. Iraq's insurgency has been inspired, not just by a desire to kill Americans, but also by the ambition to be in power when the United States leaves.

The attacks will probably increase in number, and, sadly, more American young people will die. In the first few days after the discovery of Hussein, car bombs killed 9 and 10 people in two separate attacks. The White House response was to urge Syria, Pakistan, and Iran to control their borders and stop Mujahideen fighters from crossing into Iraq, but nothing was said about Saudi Arabia, which has the least protected frontier with Iraq. Every Friday night in Saudi Arabia, thousands upon thousands of Wahhabi Imams offer prayers urging young fighters to go to Iraq and take up the Jihad against the Americans. These Imams are paid by the state (which means the Saudi Royal family) to spread the word of Islam. Is this the behavior of an ally?

Stephen Schwartz's book, *The Two Faces of Islam* (New York: Anchor Books, 2003) has given Americans their first exposure to the thinking of Wahhabi clerics. According to Schwartz, Wahhabis, a relatively radical sect of Islam, believe that all Jews, Christians, and even Sunnis and Sufi Muslims are "destined for the fire." Unfortunately, whenever President Bush or other cabinet members are photographed with Arab leaders, they tend to be surrounded by Wahhabis. This is because the administration is connected to the Saudi Royal family and the Royal Family is guided by Wahhabis. No understanding of the terror in the Middle East, or the challenges confronting America in the region, is possible without recognition of Wahhabi influence.

Unlike the Saudis, Saddam Hussein's connections to anti-American ideology have never been a secret. However, he was always willing to do our bidding. Hussein killed about a million people in a war with Iran, urged on by the United States. Weapons he used to attack his own Kurdish countrymen were provided by the American military. He only became our enemy when he failed to do our bidding. If Hussein's trial in Iraq is conducted in a civil court, and attorneys are allowed a process of full discovery, much of Hussein's background will be embarrassing to the United States and the Bush administration. There is a strong legal argument that America gave Hussein a gun, and then urged him to pull the trigger only when we ordered, and only at the target we told him to shoot. Most probably, however, the White House, if it remains consistent with current behavior, will control the trial of Hussein, and a great deal of evidence will not be made public. The trial, though, may be carefully timed to reveal Hussein's evils during the run up to the presidential election in 2004.

None of this, however, will have any true impact on the war on terrorism. Radical Islamist fighters are moving to Iraq from every Arab nation on the planet. The Mujahideen leading the insurgency inside of Iraq are from more than a dozen countries, and they are taking directions from a number of different leaders. Although it is possible that Osama bin Laden is connected to this effort, it is just as likely that he is in the mountains of northern Pakistan plotting yet another attack on America while the Mujahideen kill our young in Iraq. The arrest of bin Laden will not likely have a great impact on terrorism, either. His cause has been taken up by a new generation of terrorists, who have been inspired to kill Americans. Bin Laden has also become iconic. Iraqi fighters in the Jihad against the United States are inspired by him and the convenient location of our troops. An ocean no longer separates them from their enemy, the American infidels. The capture of Saddam Hussein will do nothing to change this painful reality.

What was a more logical response to 9/11? When an enemy attacks, the rational response is to fight the enemy. America did not. The president sent our troops chasing ephemeral weapons of mass destruction (WMD) in Iraq rather than deploying our troops in the mountains of Northern Pakistan. Imagine the improved chances of catching bin Laden if there were 150,000 U.S. soldiers scouring the remote reaches of Northern Pakistan and Afghanistan. Certainly, Hussein was America's enemy, and evil, but he was not an immediate threat. President Bush became impatient with Hussein's refusal to cooperate with U.N. arms inspectors and ordered an invasion. He now asks for patience in the search for WMD, which is exactly what he refused to give the U.N. inspectors. Any potential discovery of WMD after this length of time is certain to lead to accusations from the wider world that the evidence was planted by Americans wanting to justify the invasion.

Nonetheless, the president has difficult choices to make, and they involve moving weapons and troops into a battle. Each soldier is from a family, and it is in families where casualties are counted. The geo-politics of the war, America's need for oil, the fanaticism of terrorists, the failures of the media, the anger of the Mujahideen, and the devotion and commitment of U.S. soldiers has created a deadly mix. The White House needs the simplicity of a good guy versus bad guy battle, but if Saddam Hussein had no weapons of mass destruction, families are asking why it was necessary for their children to die in the act of "regime change." There are a thousand different political dynamics at work in the Middle East, and the Bush administration ignores all of those that do not serve its policies.

Ultimately, the cost of conflict is paid by American taxpayers, families whose children die in combat, ambushes, or terrorist attacks. This book is an attempt to understand that impact. The focus is not meant to be on political discussions inside the Washington Beltway. Whatever prompted the president's decisions, in hindsight, seems less critical than the results. The White House executes a policy, the media interpret and write about that decision, and then the citizen, who is both soldier and taxpayer, must carry out those orders. Whether you are carrying an M-16 in Tikrit, or simply toting your burden of the increased national debt resulting from the costs of the war and rebuilding Iraq, you are involved in Bush's War.

The war on terrorism was not an option. They brought the battle to us, and we had no choice but to strike back. Invading Iraq, though, was a choice, and a bad one. Our failed policies regarding Palestinians and the rest of the Arab world have been compounded by the presence of our troops in Iraq. The president frequently has said that, "If we don't fight them there, we'll have to fight them on the streets of America." In this instance, he is probably right. Iraq has become the battleground in the war on terrorism because the United States dispatched 150,000 troops into the Middle East. They are now convenient targets. Iraq may have had little or nothing to do with terrorist attacks on America in the past, but it has become the center of the war.

There are certain protocols and rituals that take place in each of America's wars. For the fallen, we offer them comfort, and thanks for their family's sacrifice. The bugles blow, flags are folded, tears fall, and pledges of support are made. But America moves into its own future by healing. And we cannot heal by concentrating on those who have fallen. We can only remember them. Unfortunately, after the casket is lowered into the ground and the family is left with a flag in place of someone they loved, they are alone with broken lives to rebuild. The rest of the country has moved on. For each high-profile story like Jessica Lynch, there are hundreds of troops killed in action that America never gets to know; people like Johnny Villareal Mata and James Kiehl of the 507th Mechanized Company, and Fred Pokorney of Charlie Company and the Marines. These are the people I wanted to write about; common citizens like the rest of us, what they did, and how their families are coping.

My goal was to write accurately about the period of time leading up to the war and the months after the invasion of Iraq. I wanted to unravel the connections between presidential decisions, journalism, domestic politics, the economy, and how they affect the lives of our citizenry, whether that is a soldier in the Persian Gulf, or a diplomat in Washington. There is skepticism here about the president's conclusions, and how they were reached, in part, because I believe there has not been enough skepticism in the daily media. Sometimes the facts point only in one direction and to write as if there were another set of facts is irresponsible. Much of what has transpired in our country's recent history might have been avoided if we had all taken our citizenship more seriously and demanded more of ourselves, our leaders, and our democracy.

No one is more serious about citizenship than the soldier. While he or she may not always be politically astute and totally aware of why they are being given a gun, they are committed enough to the republic's future that they will trust their leaders and take the risks believed necessary for our safety. These are the people to whom our obligations as Americans are the greatest. They die for us and do not question the decisions to send them into battle. If we abuse this trust, if we lie to our young about why we have asked them to sacrifice, America will begin its recessional from the grand stage of world leadership. Our soldiers ask us for nothing but we owe them at least one thing: the truth about why they fought, and why some of them died.

I hope I have provided that here.

PART

I

CAUGHT BY
THE CHILL

1

No Guns, No Glory

Anyone who has ever looked into the glazed eyes of a soldier
dying on the battlefield will think hard before starting a war.

Otto Von Bismarck

When the orders came over the radio, both of the
young Marines were worried. First Lieutenant Ben
Reid, and the platoon's other officer, Second Lieutenant Fred Pokorney, talked quietly about the sudden change of strategy from battalion headquarters. A month had
been spent working out a detailed plan to bypass the Iraqi city of Al
Nasiriyah after Charlie Company had crossed the Euphrates River.
Three companies of Marines, Alpha, Bravo, and Charlie of the 1st
Marine Expeditionary Force, were to secure three separate bridges
on the north and south sides of Al Nasiriyah.

Already, though, something had gone wrong.

"If we don't take those bridges now, regiment will give away our
missions." The battalion commander's voice over the combat network
was clear, and distinct. "So, we are going to run the gauntlet. Alpha,
you take the southern bridge. Charlie, you take the northern bridge."

Reid and Pokorney spoke privately, acknowledging their fears to each other, but not their troops. Pokorney, though, had no doubt about what the orders meant.

"We're dead," he told Ben Reid.

Tanks, which were supposed to provide them armored support, had just been called away on a rescue mission, and still Charlie Company was being ordered to go straight up "ambush alley," a main thoroughfare in the center of Al Nasiriyah. Commanders had decided there was no time to wait for the return of the tanks. Al Nasiriyah needed to be controlled by the Americans, and neither Pentagon planners nor the White House was exhibiting much patience for a more calculated approach to battle. There was tremendous political pressure to prove that a small invasion force had the strength to move quickly and decisively on to Baghdad.

The stretch of road in front of Charlie Company was known to be occupied by Iraqi irregulars and Saddam Hussein's Fedayeen fighters, who had set up firing positions, were hiding in buildings, and waiting to attack. This information was the reason leadership had chosen a strategy of skirting the city after taking the southern bridge over the Euphrates. Alpha and Charlie Companies were then expected to close on the two northern bridges across the Saddam Canal.

A few hours earlier, Ben Reid and Fred Pokorney had gotten their first look at combat. Charlie Company, positioned at the rear of a column advancing up the main supply route, had moved northward as part of the 2nd Marine Expeditionary Brigade at 3:00 A.M. Around first light, the two young men saw Iraqis firing at the approaching Marines.

"From what I remember," Reid said. "First contact with the enemy was a few mortar rounds the Iraqis were shooting at us from the rooftop of a building. The front of the column also came into contact with machine guns, and I remember the anxiousness of the Marines in contact to employ their weapons systems."

As he listened on the radio, Reid gathered information on enemy positions, unfolded his map, and marked Iraqi and friendly positions with blue and red dots. Information off the combat network radio led him to believe the Marines out front were doing a good job of hitting their targets. Reid was encouraged. In the middle of the night on the Iraqi desert, while his platoon was preparing to move out, Ben Reid had spoken with several soldiers in a huge convoy moving through his own company's lines. He was surprised to learn that none of the personnel, junior officers, or senior staff noncommissioned officers had any maps of the area in which they were being deployed. Reid was pleased that he and Pokorney seemed to be more prepared for the coming challenges.

The morning of March 23 was already expected to be significant in the military career of Fred Pokorney. Not only was he getting his first combat experience, the 6 foot, 7 inch Marine was scheduled for promotion to First Lieutenant. Ben Reid had told his friend to plan on a brief ceremony acknowledging Pokorney's rise in rank, after they had accomplished their mission of taking the northernmost bridge over the canal.

Pokorney and Reid had become friends on the long ocean voyage from the United States to Kuwait. The two had shared a stateroom on the ship with several other junior officers. Pokorney was with Bravo Company and had been attached to Charlie Company to serve as an artillery forward observer in an infantry rifle company. Standard Marine procedures, these types of rotations are designed to give officers experience in a number of different military disciplines. Pokorney might have remained with his artillery unit and been relatively safe in the rear, but he asked for a change of orders.

His wife, Chelle Pokorney, did not learn of her husband's plans until he was preparing to leave for the Persian Gulf.

"After September 11, Fred was very eager, and willing to do something about what had happened to our country," she said. "But he didn't tell me he was going over with the infantry until the last minute. He was in the infantry before he became an officer and joined the artillery."

If the Marine Corps' advertising agency had ever stumbled across Fred Pokorney Jr., they might have used him as the new, national poster board Marine. Pokorney's dark eyes conveyed the kind of determination Marines have used to accomplish history's most difficult military goals. A photo during his days as an enlisted Marine showed him kneeling in front of three officers holding the company banner on a guidon. Pokorney's size and command presence, even from a ground level, dominate the picture and diminish the natural resolve of the officers arrayed behind him at attention.

Discipline was not what Fred Pokorney was looking for in the Marines. He already had that characteristic. Born with a hardened will, no one had ever heard him indulge in remorse or self-pity. Things were just what they were, he believed; you learned how to deal with circumstance, not make excuses, and if you were determined enough, you excelled. Pokorney was probably hoping the Marines would become his family. As a child, his existence was disrupted by the divorce of his parents and the nomadic nature of his father's work. Fred Pokorney wanted a permanent home.

After a promising basketball career was ended by an injury during his freshman year in college, Pokorney went to work in the silver mines of Tonopah, Nevada, where he had attended high school. In a few years, he enlisted in the Marines; his focused self-discipline and rigorous attention to detail brought him a quick promotion to sergeant. In Pokorney, Marine commanders knew they had a natural, and they offered to pay for his college education, which, ultimately, qualified him to become a commissioned officer after attending Officer Candidate School (OCS).

Wade Lieseke, a decorated Vietnam veteran who became Pokorney's adopted father, was worried about his son joining the Marines.

"I remember when Fred said he was gonna be an artillery officer, I was thinking, 'Oh God, at least he'll be safe.' The artillery is in the rear. It never occurred to me they'd have an artillery forward observer. In my day, airplanes did that.

"But he wanted to be a Marine," Lieseke said. "He said they were the best and he wanted to be part of the best."

Before the Marines sent him off for an education at Oregon State University, Fred Pokorney was stationed at the Bangor

Marine Barracks in Washington State, a submarine base. He met Carolyn Rochelle Schulgen (Chelle), a nursing student, and they married. Around the time he earned his degree in history and political science, the Pokorneys learned they were going to be parents. After Chelle pinned his officer's bars onto his shoulder at a commissioning ceremony, the young family, Fred, Chelle, and their daughter Taylor, went east to the Fleet Marine Force at Camp Lejeune, North Carolina. He spent more than a year in OCS and artillery training. Upon completion of those courses, Fred Pokorney became a "Mustang," an enlisted Marine who had earned the rank of officer. He had finally achieved the stability that had been missing from his childhood; the honor and pride of the Marines fortified his already strong personal character. The Marines were his family, and his devotion to the corps took him away from Chelle and Taylor.

During the two hundred kilometer roll from northern Kuwait to the Jalibah Airfield south of Al Nasiriyah, where the Marines were to encamp, Pokorney frequently brought up the subject of his wife and daughter to Lieutenant Ben Reid. Inside the amphibious assault vehicle, as the tracks ground against the desert sand and the rank smell of diesel filled their lungs, Fred Pokorney was sharing pictures of his girls playing in the snow back in the Carolinas.

"Here we are, advancing on the enemy, and he's showing us all pictures of Chelle and Taylor," Reid said. "He was so proud of them and loved them so much. Fred was a great husband, and the most honorable guy you could ever meet. He had good, strong values. This was the kind of guy you would want your own daughter to meet and marry."

He was also the kind of Marine that Reid wanted in his unit as they approached enemy fire. Up ahead, the tanks from Marine Task Force Tarawa had been sent forward to rescue soldiers from the 507th Mechanized Company, a maintenance and technical support group from Fort Bliss, Texas, which had lost direction and had fallen victim to an Iraqi ambush. Lacking adequate communications, with their automatic weapons jammed by desert sand, the mechanics were pinned down by withering Iraqi fire until the Marines pulled them out for evacuation to the rear. A series of wrong turns had led the 507th to disaster.

On the combat radio network, Reid heard a voice claiming that the 507th was attacked by Iraqi soldiers faking surrender. The description of events indicated the Iraqis had been waving white flags to lure the Americans into a position where they were easy targets for machine guns and rocket-propelled grenades. Although there is no evidence or narrative testimony to prove the deception actually occurred, the information was repeated by battalion communications headquarters, picked up by embedded journalists, and dispatched to the United States as fact. Before the day of March 23 had concluded, the story was also used to explain what had happened to the fifty-four man platoon commanded by Lieutenant Ben Reid. But nothing of the sort ever happened to either the 507th or the Marine companies. Neither the Army nor the Marines offered any understanding of where the story originated, or why it was never clarified.

"I still don't know where that came from," Reid said. "It was just on the comms net, and the reporters started broadcasting it. A lot of stuff that's been in the media about what happened to us and the 507th, is wrong. It needs to be cleared up."

As Reid and Pokorney's unit edged up the road with their company just south of Al Nasiryah and the Euphrates River Bridge, they saw Cobra helicopters and F-18 Hornets making passes near the city. The helicopters fired at a tree line, and red smoke from the trail of their Zuni rockets floated across the sky. Reid, the fire support team leader, wanted to know who or what was being engaged by the aircraft, and radioed battalion for information. The positions of the targets might be valuable when he began to coordinate his own combat fire. Although he reached commanders on the combat network, Reid got no answers. Just short of the bridge over the Euphrates River, Charlie Company came upon burning T-55 Russian tanks. A few, unmanned, also appeared untouched. Several vehicles belonging to the

Army's 507th Mechanized were in flames. A ball of fire consumed a large, armored truck used for logistical support.

Alpha Company, which had taken the Euphrates Bridge, had set up in a herringbone position to protect their location, and as Reid and Pokorney's Marines moved through their ranks to cross the river, sporadic small arms fire was audible on the edge of the Iraqi city. Original orders for Charlie Company were to follow Bravo Company to the east and avoid "ambush alley." Unfortunately, visual contact with Bravo had been lost, and simple radio communications failed.

"I hate to say this, sir," Ben Reid explained. "But you gotta remember, our radios were built by the lowest bidder. We had all kinds of problems with our combat comms network. And once all these different companies started taking fire, there was an unbelievable number of people trying to talk on that one combat net. Anything you wanted to say kept getting stepped on by other people jumping on the air."

As a result, Reid's company commander had no idea what had happened to Bravo after it had crossed the Euphrates. If Bravo was stuck in the mud off to the east, Charlie was certain to jeopardize the mission of securing the northern bridges by taking the same route. Everyone might end up bogged down, immobilized, and exposed to Iraqi attack. Reid was told by his commander that it was likely Bravo had made a run up "ambush alley" to get to their objective of the first canal bridge. But he didn't really know what maneuver had been executed by Bravo. Immediately, Reid knew what that meant and when new orders from battalion command passed over the net confirming his fears, Charlie Company began moving into the city of Al Nasiriyah, making a direct course up "ambush alley."

Very quickly, Reid and Pokorney's men encountered small arms fire. Their ten amphibious assault vehicles (referred to by Marines as amtracks, or tracks) and two Humvees were armed with .50 caliber machine guns and nineteen 40-millimeter grenade launchers. Returning fire, the convoy hurried through the crude urban reaches of Al Nasiriyah. Bullets pinged off the side of the Americans' tracked vehicles, and enemy fire dramatically intensified the further north they traveled into the city. While the Marines configured their armor in a combat-oriented position, on their right, to the east, they saw modest, low structures, mud huts uncommon in more developed cities. The other side of the road was lined with office buildings, and architecture slightly more typical of the commerce of a mid-sized city, though few structures rose to more than four or five stories in height. Iraqi gunners had set up fields of fire from hidden posts inside of mud huts, and the more modern, small office structures.

Ramp doors at the rear of some of the tracks were partially open. Lieutenant Fred Pokorney, and the mortar men, who would not be active until the convoy stopped, were using their M-16s to return Iraqi fire. Pokorney called out that a track, just to the rear of the one in which he and Reid were traveling, was hit by a rocket-propelled grenade, and caught fire. Four Marines were wounded. But the platoon kept pushing up through Al Nasiriyah. Exposed through the open door, Pokorney was hit in the right arm by a bullet and fell to the floor.

"Hey, I'm hit," he yelled to Reid over the intercom. "Hurts like hell. I'm fine. I'm fine. I was just nicked. I'll be all right. Don't worry about it."

Still under attack from RPGs and small arms weaponry, Reid's platoon crossed the two northern bridges over the canal. In the center of the road, 200 meters north, a track was burning. Reid's own track #C-208 stopped between the bridge and the burning vehicle. The remaining vehicles in his platoon quickly parked in a combat position on either of the road. As Reid hastily jumped down, he saw dusty agricultural fields and drained swampland spread beyond the canal and the raised roadbed. Iraqis were directing machine guns and rocket-propelled grenades at his platoon from a few nearby buildings.

Reid and Pokorney, like the men serving at their side, had little intelligence about the military strength of their enemy. Political pressure from the White House had led commanders of the U.S. invasion of Iraq to portray an excessively optimistic and expeditious campaign. Briefings in advance of the attack on Al Nasiriyah indicated the operation to secure the bridges and control the city was expected to take about six hours. Instead, fighting went on for eight days before the Marines were able to take complete control. Intelligence was supposedly unclear on Iraqi troop numbers in the region, and whether the soldiers were Saddam Hussein's Fedayeen fighters, Republican Guard, or Iraqi irregulars and citizens, who often acted as observers or carried bombs.

Foreign intelligence sources later reported the Americans were battling an estimated 40,000 troops of the Iraqi 3rd Army Corps. Armaments deployed against U.S. soldiers, most of them oblivious to what they were confronting, included 250 tanks, approximately 100 mortars and 100 artillery, as well as 1,000 rocket-propelled grenade launchers and anti-tank guided missiles. In terms of sheer troop strength, the Iraqis doubled the number of American soldiers approaching from the south in the U.S. 3rd Motorized Infantry Division, though the U.S. offensive was supported by considerably more armor; 200 tanks, 150 artillery pieces, and 600 armored vehicles. By doctrine, U.S. military planners always try to have a three to one force ratio against an enemy. In this case, the Americans were simply outnumbered.

Grabbing the maps he had marked and his flak jacket and helmet, Reid threw them to the ground as he jumped. The ramp at the back of the track was still up and he banged loudly to order his men out of the vehicle to take cover below the roadbed along the canal. Reid began linking up his mortars to return fire on enemy locations. Using the guns on the tracks first, he got one of them to focus on a huge building near the T-intersection on the east side of the road. The two other weapons mounted on the track were pointed back to the southwest in the direction of Al Nasiriyah, where Reid assumed most of the heaviest fire was originating. Over the noise of explosions, he shouted at his Marines to pick up the pace of their fire.

The mortars began to hit the targets Reid had selected. But there was trouble with the fire support team on the track.

Radio communications were not working.

"We've got no comm. on arty conduct of fire or our 81s," Pokorney told Reid.

"Okay," Reid answered. "Let's forget those nets. Take a look at this map." Lieutenant Reid pointed at spots he had marked. "We need suppression or duration suppression on these positions. See if you can pass them over the battalion net."

"Got it," Pokorney answered.

"I'm going to fight our 60s," Reid said, as he left the safety of the track. "They're all we've got right now."

Outside, Reid moved along the road, trying to find targets. One of the Marines in his platoon pointed out a group of vehicles, and Reid ordered all the guns on the tracks to try to take them out of the fight. Directed fire from the Americans did not appear to reduce the intensity of the Iraqi attack.

Staff Sergeant Phil Jordan ran up the road to talk to Reid.

"Sir, Torres has been hit," Jordan said.

There was no way Reid might have prepared himself for such news. His first time in combat, the young lieutenant was stunned by word that one of his men was down. Briefly, Reid admitted, he lost his focus. Jordan, who must have seen the shock on his commander's face, offered reassurance as RPG explosions and rounds from small arms filled the air.

"Don't worry, sir," Jordan said. "I've already killed two or three Iraqis, so we're even."

"Okay, Staff Sergeant," Reid answered, regaining his composure. "I need you to run and get the fifty cals focusing their rounds back into the city. Have them fight the close fight. I'll get the mortars to take on targets 2,000 meters and beyond."

As Jordan ran off to find machine gunners, one of Reid's forward observers was coming down the road with the radio. Another platoon had called asking for fire support because they were taking incoming rounds from Iraqi mortars. On the radio, Reid said he had all of his weapons in the fight, and he was doing everything possible. Seconds after the Marine had left with the radio, Reid found himself on his back, looking up at small arms rounds cutting through the air.

"Get the fuck down," Fred Pokorney screamed. "You're getting us all shot at."

Reid had been tackled by Pokorney, the Tonopah, Nevada All-Star football player. Before leaving to call in the artillery missions, Pokorney had noticed that Reid was standing up and seemed almost oblivious to the danger he was attracting to himself and the rest of the Marines.

"I was glad Fred told me I was being an idiot," Reid said. "He probably saved my head from getting blown off."

Only seconds after Pokorney had rolled off of Reid, Phil Jordan returned to ask his commander how they might be able to improve their combat posture. The two Marines agreed their mortars needed to be more widely dispersed.

"Espinoza, come up here and take my place spotting," Reid yelled. "I'm going to take Garibay's gun south."

Reid ordered Corporal Jose A. Garibay's mortar crew to follow him down toward the canal, a spot about sixty meters south of their present location, but still north of the bridge. Staff Sergeant Phil Jordan followed with two cans of ammo. As they ran, Reid failed to notice their positions were being bracketed by Iraqi RPG gunners. One round landed long. The next fell short. The subsequent explosion was long, but closer to the Americans. The Iraqis were walking their shots onto target by adjusting off of each previous explosion.

As Reid and his men set up the mortar, they realized they did not bring a wiz wheel, which was needed for calibrating the range of their targets. A Marine ran back to grab the device while Reid put in the aiming stake. His men, however, were unsure of shooting without precise calculations from the wiz wheel. Reid told the mortar crew to estimate an elevation based on previous missions fired. The lieutenant grabbed a round and dropped it in to sink the base plate. Down range, they spotted the location of the explosion, and Reid dropped two more rounds into the tube to make corrections on the targets based on where the previous rounds had landed.

"I guess that was kind of stupid," Reid said later. "I had no idea really where those rounds were going to land. But I wanted to get a round out there quickly and adjust off of it. Besides, I didn't want to just sit there and do nothing, while we were under fire, other than wait for a wiz wheel."

When the Marine returned with the wiz wheel for the mortar, he was trailed by Fred Pokorney. Most of the gun crew was provided protection in a partial defilade around the mortar. Reid was up near the aiming stake, spotting the mortar rounds. Iraqi RPG explosions were coming closer, each concussion registering more powerfully on the Marines' eardrums.

"I got those nine arty missions passed over the battalion net," Pokorney yelled to Reid.

"Are they the positions I gave you?"

"Yeah."

A few seconds after Pokorney had spoken, an explosion knocked Ben Reid back onto the road. The force of the blast was felt in his arm, which Reid thought had been blown off. When he saw his arm still hanging at his side, Reid assumed it had been broken by the explosion. The lieutenant lay in the road waiting for the ringing in his ears to cease.

The first words he heard were devastating.

"Sir, Buessing is dead."

Ben Reid, the young Annapolis graduate, in his first combat command, had suffered an initial death among his men. Turning, Lieutenant Reid saw Lance Corporal Brian R. Buessing and recognized from the wounds that his Marine had been killed instantly. Buessing died serving in the same Charlie Company mortar squad in which his grandfather had won a Silver Star during the Korean War.

Reid was uncertain what to do next, both fear and responsibility for the rest of his men racing through his head. Two other bodies lay not far from where Buessing had fallen. Reid ran to the nearest and rolled the Marine over to see who it was. Staff Sergeant Phil Jordan was also dead. The other man down was Second Lieutenant Fred Pokorney, his hulking frame lay twisted near where the round had exploded. Reid assumed Pokorney had also been killed.

"I didn't go check on Fred," Reid said. "I just assumed from the way he was laying, he was dead. I know he wasn't moving. But I couldn't see any physical injuries. I know he was at least injured by that round. I just made an assumption about Fred. Maybe it was a bad assumption."

In a moment of doubt, Reid worried that his men had been hit by his own improperly calibrated mortar rounds. On the road, the men were slightly down range from the mortar positions, though they were considerably offline from the guns' directions. Reid also feared that he had given Pokorney the wrong coordinates of Iraqi targets to radio into artillery operations.

"I don't think that was it, though," Reid explained. "If an artillery round had landed there, it would have killed all of us. And I know I wasn't off by five kilometers on the coordinates. There's no way I could have missed by that far."

What Reid described as a "magic round" had also wounded three of this other men, including Coporal Garibay, Corporal Jorge A. Gonzalez, and Private First Class Tamario D. Burkett. Uncertain of the extent of injuries to his troops, Reid ordered Garibay to keep everyone in place until he returned with medical assistance. RPG rounds were consistently exploding closer and closer to Reid's platoon. Crouching down, he turned and ran in the direction of his track.

In the low sky to the north, an American A-10 Thunderbolt jet, known as the "Warthog," and the "tank killer," made a turn and lined up for a gun run down the raised canal road where Reid's men had fallen.

2

A Beautiful Lie

Truth is beautiful, without doubt; but so are lies.

Ralph Waldo Emerson

The newly elected president was greeted in the Oval Office by the departing incumbent. A few words were spoken, good wishes exchanged as the "exit interview" was concluding. Usually this tradition affords the retiring office holder a moment to provide advice to the successor. As William Jefferson Clinton was leaving the White House, he shared some of his insights with George Walker Bush. Clinton assumed his eight years in office might be of some value to Bush in confronting the nation's lingering challenges, not the least of which, in Clinton's assessment, was terrorism.

The former president told close friends he listed five priorities for his administration, which President Bush ought to consider.

"First," he said, "There is bin Laden. He is angry, and we have intelligence that indicates he is coming after us, somehow. We've put together a plan to deal with terrorist threats, and my people will brief you and your staff on its details. I consider this the top priority.

Secondly, I'd say do not leave the Israelis and the Palestinians to their own devices. You are going to want to stay involved in that process. Then there's North Korea. Their leadership is questionable, and they are not that far away from getting a nuke. Next, I'd say keep your eye on Pakistan and India. They've both got nuclear weapons, and they hate each other. Lastly, I'd watch Saddam Hussein very closely. He's got oil money and anger against the U.S."

The new president thanked his predecessor, and then provided his own clue as to what was in the future for America.

"I think you've got your priorities wrong," Bush said. "I'm putting Saddam at the top of the list."

In the story repeated by President Clinton's friends, and later confirmed by the former president, George W. Bush was dreaming of an assault on Iraq the day he took office. Clinton, of course, cannot be expected to speak publicly of a private conversation between presidents. Nonetheless, the exchange was one more piece of anecdotal evidence that Bush had no intention of using a policy of containment on Saddam Hussein. Even though Hussein had not demonstrably acted against the interests of the United States since he was chased out of Kuwait, the Bush administration immediately began to plot a move on the Iraqi dictator. Senior advisors to Bush knew what they wanted to accomplish before the candidate even became the president. They needed only a pretext for military action and a method for building political support.

At least one of those essential elements was delivered by Al Qaeda terrorists, most of whom were from Saudi Arabia, when they flew passenger jets into the World Trade Center, the Pentagon, and a farm field in Pennsylvania. Suddenly, the Bush White House had nothing more complicated to execute than a business proposal for marketing and branding a political cause. While there remained a substantial body of information that the White House had been warned repeatedly about a possible attack like September 11, beginning with Clinton's admonition, what the Bush administration has done in the aftermath of that tragedy is more illuminating with regard to its craven distortion of facts to serve a political agenda. Using the taxpayer's money, their own government's institutions to advance those politics, and a compliant media often acting as nothing more than a stenographer for the White House's revisionists, the Bush presidency has filled the air of America with the rank odor of history's greatest democracy entering early stages of decomposition.

And it began only hours after the great New York towers fell.

According to notes obtained by CBS News, Defense Secretary Donald Rumsfeld immediately saw the terrorist attacks as a rationale for going after Saddam Hussein, not just Osama bin Laden. Aides who were with Rumsfeld in the National Command Center at 2:40 P.M. on September 11, 2001, were ordered to find justification in the airliner attacks for creating an American plan to target Saddam Hussein and Iraq. The instructions from Rumsfeld, scribbled down by his staffers, were unmistakable in their intent.

"Best info fast. Judge whether good enough to hit S.H. [Saddam Hussein] at same time. Not only O.B.L. [Osama bin Laden] Go massive. Sweep it all up. Things related and not."

Unless Rumsfeld had an inspired moment while the rest of the nation was in shock, the notes are irrefutable proof the Bush administration had designs on Iraq and Hussein well before the president raised his hand to take the oath of office. The network news report meant that all of the president's representations to the world that he was being patient with Iraq and Hussein were, at best, disingenuous, and at the extreme, nothing more than a step in a choreography leading to war. Further, when the president spoke to the United Nations, he did not do so because he believed in the U.N.'s charter and purpose; nor was he or his cabinet concerned about the United Nation's backing of an invasion of Iraq. Advisors simply wanted the president to appear as a reasonable and circumspect leader seeking approval from the international community for the invasion. This moment, too, had been blocked out by the senior staff in charge of the White House's stagecraft.

Hussein's mere existence was so irritating to George W. Bush that he was not always capable of containing his emotions. Undoubtedly, the president has never been able to countenance the idea that the Iraqi dictator plotted to kill his father, George H. W. Bush, during a 1993 visit to Kuwait. While he will never admit such a thing, George W. was also annoyed that geography and destiny had combined to plop Hussein atop what many geologists believe is the world's largest oil reserves, greater, even, than those of the Saudis. This only meant that Hussein had the resources to be a presence in the Persian Gulf for as long as he lived, and U.S. companies were unlikely to ever develop the production of Iraqi crude. If the opportunity presented itself, therefore, President Bush was going to eliminate the Iraqi dictator and not make the strategic error historians have assigned to his father after the first Gulf War.

The president's cowboy machismo on the subject of Saddam Hussein, it turned out, was irrepressible. According to a *Time* magazine article one year before American guns began to sound in Iraq, Bush stuck his head into a meeting being conducted by National Security Advisor Condoleeza Rice. Three U.S. Senators were conferring with Rice over using the United Nations, or Middle East allies, to deal with Hussein. The president, hearing their conversation, waved his hand dismissively.

"Fuck Saddam," he said. "We're taking him out."

The war was still a year away on the day the president slipped into the lexicon of a posturing fraternity boy. In the coming months, Bush sought hard to position himself as a patient man, who was willing to let weapons inspectors do their job, a leader disinclined to capricious, emotional decisions.

But he had already made up his mind.

There was a rational argument for confronting Saddam Hussein. But George Bush never bothered with it. Honesty apparently involved more political risk than obfuscation. If the president had told the American people that our nation's future, indeed, even the economy of the planet, might soon be at risk because a madman was astraddle the largest supply of oil in existence, he might have been surprised by the influential power of the truth. This argument was easily buttressed by intelligence reports that Hussein was killing uncountable numbers of innocent people for their religious and political beliefs, paying thousands of dollars in cash bonuses to families of suicide bombers, and that he was illegally circumventing the United Nations' oil for food program by running unmarked tankers along the coast to Syria. No one ever lost an argument, either, by suggesting Middle East peace was impossible as long as Saddam Hussein sat in the center of the region, threatening both Arabs and Israelis.

Of course, no one wants to send a son or daughter to war over oil, regardless of the nation's practical interests in securing the Iraqi oil fields. Bush advisors did not believe honesty was a viable strategy. Americans are willing to die for principles, not practicalities. We have always tried to serve greater purposes than our own well-being. Acceptable losses are defined by the cause in which they are accumulated. No president can survive the political storm that might come from parents losing children in combat to assure cheap tanks of gasoline for housewives running errands in Chevrolet Suburbans and Toyota Sequoias. That's why the president avoided any attempt to persuade Americans there were important economic causes behind the war.

A more elegant, principled rationale was required.

The Bush administration tried to deliver a logical explanation by talking about weapons of mass destruction. But the war was only marginally about anything other than oil. In fact, public admission about the motive for the invasion came from Deputy Defense Secretary Paul Wolfowitz a few months after American troops began their uneasy occupation of the country. Wolfowitz, who was speaking to an Asian security summit in Singapore, took a few questions from reporters of German newspapers *Der Tagesspiegel* and *Die Welt.*

"Why," the reporters wanted to know, "was a nuclear power like North Korea being treated differently from Iraq, where hardly any weapons of mass destruction had been found?"

"Let's look at it simply," Wolfowitz explained. "The most important difference between North Korea and Iraq is that economically, we just had no choice in Iraq. The country swims on a sea of oil."

The White House, clearly, had a problem with its message. Evading oil questions was essential. Using the contemporary business marketing technique of "positioning," Bush senior strategist Karl Rove re-framed the argument over attacking Iraq. The president began to speak of weapons of mass destruction and Hussein's unproved ties to Al Qaeda terrorists. No one in the administration ever referred to Iraq's vast natural resources. Rove kept the cabinet and staffers on message. Psychologically, Americans were being told, in plain language, "Some bad Muslims attacked the United States, and now the United States is going to attack some bad Muslims." For simplification of argument, Muslims, either by design, or inadvertently by association, were all connected and somehow this was going to reduce terrorism.

When he met with reporters just prior to the onset of combat operations, the president mentioned 9/11 more than a dozen times during questions and comments, and constantly referred to his constitutional obligation to protect America. A CNN/Time/Gallup Poll, which proved this strategy worked, revealed at the time of the invasion that more than 70 percent of Americans believed Saddam Hussein and Osama bin Laden plotted together to attack the United States on 9/11. Months after the invasion, polls showed the deception lingered with almost the same percentage of Americans.

Even neophyte analysts and intelligence operatives knew that allegations of connections between Saddam and bin Laden were specious and unsupportable. In bin Laden's worldview, the Iraqi dictator was only slightly less despicable than the United States. Hussein's greatest sin was to run a secularist, non-Islamist government. A whiskey-drinking, cigar-smoking, fornicating Hussein came to symbolize the lapse of Islamism in the Muslim world. Bin Laden has always wanted Allah to be involved in every aspect of Muslim life, including the creation of government policies and leadership. Saddam Hussein appeared to be glorifying himself, rather than Allah, through the accumulation of wealth and power.

Nonetheless, there were, undoubtedly, Al Qaeda terrorists moving through Baghdad and, in some cases, working out of remote camps in the northern regions of Iraq. In the north, Saddam had lit-tle control over his own country, but there is no western intelligence that he was ever in league with the handful of Al Qaeda operatives inside of his own country. In fact, the White House's own report on Hussein and Iraq, *A Decade of Defiance and Deception*, posted in Septem-ber 2002, indicated he harbored terrorists working with Abu Nidal, the Palestinian Liberation Front, and was paying rewards to families of suicide and homicide bombers, but it made no mention of Al Qaeda connections. Information in the report, curiously, dated back to the 1980s, a time when Iraq was a U.S. ally because Hussein was willing to serve American purposes in his war against Iran. The con-clusion ignored by the Bush administration was that Hussein and bin Laden did not, and probably never had, joined forces against the United States.

Fundamentally, they hated each other.

A former diplomat from the region, who has years of experience as an envoy in Pakistan, Syria, Iraq, and Iran, said Arabs accepted the antipathy between Hussein and bin Laden as basic, conventional wisdom, and so did American Middle East analysts. Bush advisors simply chose to avoid facts contradicting their premises.

"He [bin Laden] has said Saddam is the infidel," the diplomat ex-plained. "We have no love for Saddam the infidel. And we have fought him well, and for longer than the U.S. However, this war is not about Saddam. It's about Iraq and oil."

As the case against Saddam Hussein and Al Qaeda began to gen-erate more skepticism than anger and public support, Bush advisors adroitly retailored the emperor's clothes. Ideologically, the neo-conservatives driving the White House's policies have always be-lieved there was a strong tier of logic holding up the proposition that America needed to depose Saddam Hussein. Backing terrorism as a tactic, and criminal treatment of the Iraqi population, however, were never sufficient cause for U.S. military action. Something bigger was needed. Also, any argument for war demanded simplification for both the international community and the domestic political discourse.

During a magazine interview, Deputy Defense Secretary Paul Wolfowitz unknowingly lifted the administration's strategic skirts and offered an embarrassing peek at what lay underneath.

"The truth is," he told writer Sam Tannenhaus, "That for reasons that have a lot to do with the U.S. government bureaucracy, we settled on the one issue that everyone could agree on, which was weapons of mass destruction as the core reason . . ."

When the subsequent article was published, predictably, Wolfowitz howled that his words were taken out of context. Tannenhaus did omit the secretary's comments about terrorism and violence against the Iraqi citizenry being secondary to weapons of mass destruction. Including those remarks, however, does nothing to change the revelatory conclusion offered by Wolfowitz. The White House was going to push weapons of mass destruction as the reason for going after Saddam because the message was readily accessible to various government agencies and Congress, which were needed to supplement the arguments, and, more critically, taxpayers grasped the idea without much effort. More politically significant was that this approach meant the nation's "petro-lust" was relegated to the status of a non-issue.

The Department of Defense (DoD) recorded the telephone interview between Tannenhaus and Wolfowitz, and the entire transcript was later posted at a DoD Internet address. The implications of some of the text of that conversation, startlingly, suggested that a part of Wolfowitz's thinking relative to the invasion was driven by a desire to placate Osama bin Laden, and take heat off of the Saudis. If, eventually, the United States was an occupying force in Iraq, Wolfowitz indicated that American armed forces could be removed from Saudi Arabia, an issue that had animated bin Laden and other terrorists for years.

Wolfowitz's words almost sounded as if he was meeting the demands of the terrorists.

"Their presence there over the last twelve years has been a source of enormous difficulty for a friendly government," he said.

"It's been a huge recruiting device for Al Qaeda. In fact, if you look at bin Laden, one of his principle grievances was the presence of so-called crusader forces on the holy land, Mecca and Medina. I think just lifting that burden from the Saudis is itself going to open the door to other positive things."

Why he thought that turning Iraq into a U.S. military base might lessen antagonism of Islamists has never been clarified. At least with American soldiers stationed in Saudi Arabia, bin Laden had to be more careful about his attacks because the Saudis were the source of much of his funding. Also, the Saudis did not want anything to happen that might too deeply anger the United States because Americans are the world's largest market for oil products. Neither bin Laden, nor any other terrorist organization, was likely to feel such restraint with Saddam Hussein ousted and U.S. soldiers walking the streets of Baghdad. This was the battleground they had dreamed of. Live, American targets were sitting right in the midst of the Arab world. Strangely, though, Wolfowitz told Tannenhaus that getting rid of Saddam Hussein was certain to stabilize the Middle East.

He was about to get that terribly wrong.

But first Wolfowitz had to help the Bush administration convince the world that Saddam Hussein was hiding weapons of mass destruction (WMD).

And surprisingly, the White House discovered the WMD sales job wasn't going to be too difficult.

The timing was a thing of pure political beauty. President George W. Bush was only a few days away from speaking to the United Nations' General Assembly about Iraq's renewed efforts to acquire banned weaponry. And, in a month, the president was going to Congress to seek a resolution approving of a war against Iraq. A Sunday morning story, September 8, 2002, in the *New York Times* made the U.N. speech and the congressional debate much easier for the White House. Under the headline, *"Threats and Responses: The Iraqis; U.S. Says Hussein Intensifies Quest for A-Bomb Parts,"* a 3603 word story by Michael

R. Gordon and Judith Miller detailed the administration's case against Saddam Hussein related to weapons of mass destruction.

America was about to be scared.

Citing "administration officials," "Iraqi defectors," and "intelligence sources," Gordon and Miller wrote that Iraq had attempted to buy the type of aluminum tubes needed for the construction of a gas centrifuge to develop nuclear materials.

"In the last 14 months," they reported, "Iraq has sought to buy thousands of specially designed aluminum tubes, which American officials believe were intended as components of centrifuges to enrich uranium." According to the newspaper's report, the specifications, including diameter and thickness, had persuaded American officials that the tubes were meant for Iraq's nuclear program. The duo ticked up the national pulse rate with the news that, "Iraqi defectors who once worked for the nuclear weapons establishment have told American officials that acquiring nuclear arms is again a top Iraqi priority."

If, however, what Gordon and Miller's sources had told them was true, and the shipment of tubes had been intercepted in "recent months," a contradictory opinion on the tubes might have saved them from relentless criticisms, and spared America unnecessary angst. It might have also helped to stop a war.

"I had no reason to believe what I reported at the time was inaccurate," Judy Miller said during an extensive interview. "I believed the intelligence information I had at the time. I sure didn't believe they were making it up. This was a learning process. You constantly have to ask the question, 'What do you know at the time you are writing it?' We tried really hard to get more information and we vetted information very, very carefully."

The claims in the *Times'* story, however, were not able to be independently corroborated at the time of publication. Miller and Gordon wrote that officials told them that, "the aluminum tubes were intended as casing for rotors in centrifuges, which are one means of producing highly enriched uranium." While senior administration officials insisted to the two journalists that the specifications of the tubes, length, thickness, and number, indicated they were destined for use in a gas centrifuge, those specifications were not included in the story the pair filed for the paper. The *Times* reported that the sensitivity of the intelligence kept the officials from divulging where the tubes came from, or where they were intercepted.

The truth about the scary tubes wasn't easy to access. The *Times* finally began to acquire contradicting information a few days after their first story was published. Correspondent Judy Miller said she and Michael Gordon made numerous calls in an attempt to get differing opinions on the tubes from the intelligence community prior to publishing their original report.

But no one was willing to talk.

"We made many, many calls," Miller explained. "All of these intelligence analysts and operatives said the same thing, 'We are not having this conversation.' Someone had ordered them not to talk. This [story] was a hot one, and they weren't going to talk about it. Nobody was willing to speak until after we published the first piece on the tubes."

According to a story in the *Washington Post*, published almost a year later, the senior administration officials speaking to Gordon and Miller appeared to be talking about a shipment of 3,000 aluminum tubes intercepted in Jordan, bound for Iraq. In July 2001, exactly fourteen months before the *Times* printed its front page exclusive, a CIA operative, working with Australian intelligence, discovered the tubes going to Baghdad from China. Even though the timing of the delivery coincided with the fact that Iraq had depleted its supply of rocket body tubes, the operative set about trying to convince analysts the tubes were part of an Iraqi scheme to build a gas centrifuge. The *Post's* Barton Gellman and Walter Pincus wrote that missile assembly lines in Iraq had thousands of crated rocket motors and fins awaiting arrival of the tubes at the Nasser factory north of Baghdad. But that information was not reported in newspapers until long after American citizens had been convinced the tubes proved Saddam Hussein was chasing a bomb.

During the late summer of 2002, however, when journalists were first learning of the aluminum tubes, Gellman had trouble finding someone to disagree with the administration. Contradicting science on the purpose of the tubes was gathered between the fall of 2002 and the spring of the war. Throughout the course of this work, government scientists refused to speak with journalists.

"The scientists who disagreed with the White House were effectively silenced," Gellman said. "The intelligence types were told to keep their mouths shut all the way up to the end. I heard from a lot of people that they weren't authorized to talk and they weren't going to, even though there was strong disagreement with the White House over what these tubes were for."

Judy Miller, who broke the story, encountered the same politically enforced silence.

"We tried to get other intell types to talk," Miller added. "I went all over looking for data. The White House knew we had been working on this for weeks. And remember what it was like at that time. The drums of war were already beating. But the White House manipulating the *New York Times* is just bullshit. The timing was ours, not theirs. But they may have worked with it. I mean, if you were the administration, wouldn't you have used that tubes story for your cause?"

That is exactly what happened.

Knowing that the war effort required coordinated information and messaging, Bush chief of staff Andrew Card organized the White House Iraq Group in August. The strategists on that team included the president's senior political advisor, Karl Rove, who had sharpened his media manipulation skills during the Texas gubernatorial terms of George Bush, and a tough presidential campaign. Karen Hughes, communications counselor and Bush confidante, and Mary Matalin, Republican media expert, also worked with National Security Advisor Condoleeza Rice, and Vice President Dick Cheney's chief of staff, I. Lewis Libby. Stephen J. Hadley, deputy to Secretary Rice, was also a part of the assembled big thinkers.

Convinced that the war's promotional effort required a constant message campaign, the White House Iraq Group (WHIG) coordinated with senior staffers in Tony Blair's administration in the United Kingdom, and was in constant contact with U.S. military officers in Kuwait, who were conducting briefings each day during America's morning network newscasts. The aggressive approach drove the daily news cycles and editorial content of the media. Rove and Hughes, two of the best practitioners there have ever been at "gaming" the media, guided the WHIG. The president's two closest advisors, Hughes and Rove are masters of an evolutionarily new version of media relations, which they practically invented. The method pitches political interpretation as fact, even in governmental, nonpolitical environments.

And they were all so confident of their skills; the WHIG members chose to let Americans know what was coming. Two days before the *New York Times'* story on the tubes of terror, Andy Card was quoted in the paper, explaining why talk of Iraq and the war had diminished during the summer months.

"From a marketing point of view," he explained. "You don't introduce new products in August."

Sunday morning, though, the product was delivered on the front page of the nation's most influential newspaper, and the story carried the White House's message of fear, invoking the image of a mushroom cloud over America. The long article offered no voices of dissent on administration claims that Iraq had accelerated its pace of nuclear development. The journalistic coup, however, was by White House design, and not a failure of the *Times'* writers. The WHIG had sent out word to the government intelligence and scientific communities that no one was to dispute administration claims about the aluminum tubes.

Husain Haqqani, a Pakistani and Middle East scholar with the Carnegie Endowment for International Peace, identified a pattern of reportage in U.S. journalism during the war, which served the administration's purposes.

"The media keeps creating enough doubt for people who are not going into enough depth," he said. "How many people read the

3,000 words in one article in the *New York Times*? The majority doesn't. The majority has these photo images. Then you have things like, for example, all of the lies of the Iraq war. All of the things that have turned out to be incorrect have come from the coalition and not from the Arabs."

This particular lie was in danger of being revealed.

The White House was in a hurry to give the story some validity because, in the intelligence community, the allegations about the tubes had already been discredited, if not publicly. When journalists finally spoke with scientists about the discovery, they were certain to learn the administration's charges about Saddam Hussein and the aluminum tubes were, either uninformed, or blatant lies.

To create the beginnings of war hysteria and nuclear phobia, the White House Iraq Group had planned to immediately execute a tactic that created a media echo chamber. The same Sunday morning that the tubes story was splattered on the front page of the *Times*, the Bush administration dispatched the vice president, the national security advisor, and the secretary of state, to elevate the buzz on the network talk shows. A false story had been planted, was given credibility by a leading publication, and then the people who benefited from the one-sided information appeared on national television to corroborate the value of their bad evidence.

On NBC's *Meet the Press* with Tim Russert, Vice President Dick Cheney warned Americans that Hussein was taking all the steps necessary to end up with a nuclear warhead, and he made it sound as if the question of the aluminum tubes was not subject to verification by science.

"And what we've seen recently that has raised our level of concern to the current state of unrest, if you will, if I can put it in those terms," Cheney told Russert. "Is that he now is trying, through his illicit procurement network, to acquire the equipment he needs to be able to enrich uranium to make the bombs."

"Aluminum tubes?" the moderator asked, having read the Sunday *Times*.

"Specifically, aluminum tubes," the vice president explained. "There's a story in the *New York Times* this morning, this is, I don't, and I want to attribute the *Times*. I don't want to talk about, obviously, specific intelligence sources, but it's now public that, in fact, he has been seeking to acquire, and we have been able to intercept and prevent him from acquiring through this particular channel, the kinds of tubes that are necessary to build a centrifuge. And the centrifuge is required to take low-grade uranium and enhance it into highly enriched uranium, which is what you have to have in order to build a bomb."

Even Secretary of State Colin Powell, who cannot hide his discomfort when nuclear explosions are mentioned, went on Fox News and mentioned "specialized aluminum tubing," and referred to the *Times'* piece with the words, "We saw in reporting . . ."

The strongest assertions were on CNN's *Late Edition with Wolf Blitzer,* where National Security Advisor Condoleeza Rice insisted that the tubes were "only really suited for nuclear weapons programs, centrifuge programs," and she argued that Hussein was "actively pursuing a nuclear weapon." Almost astonishingly, Rice parroted words the reporters had used in their story in the *Times,* raising immediate suspicion she was one of the unidentified sources of the story.

"We don't want the smoking gun to be a mushroom cloud," she said.

The smoking gun to prove that these tubes were not for use in a gas centrifuge was likely an Internet address. According to *Newsweek* magazine, Iraq's purchase order for the aluminum tubes was posted on the Web. The White House surely did not think Hussein wanted the United States to get advance notice he was working on a nuclear bomb. Clearly, a vast intelligence network was not essential for the Bush administration to learn about the tubes. Hussein had put the information on the Internet.

Regardless, a frenzy of follow-up stories covered front pages of newspapers and filled the broadcast and cable news shows for days. In some cases, reporters did not even bother with attribution for claims about the tubes. Andrea Mitchell of NBC News, in her nationally broadcast story the next day, flatly stated, "They were the kind of tubes only used in a centrifuge to make nuclear fuel." Her colleague, White House correspondent Norah O'Donnell had already called the tube news, "An alarming disclosure." By the time President Bush stood before the United Nations' General Assembly later that week, the aluminum tubes had slipped into the national collective consciousness as indisputable proof Saddam Hussein had his finger on a nuclear trigger.

There were several resources in a position to discredit the Bush administration's allegations about Iraq's aluminum tubes after the original story had broken in the *Times*. Andrea Mitchell must have failed to order her producer to make a call to the International Atomic Energy Agency; had she done so, she was likely to have been told the specifications of the aluminum tubes meant they were going to be used in rocket production. An Italian rocket, the Medusa 81, used body tubes that matched down to the fraction of a millimeter those being pushed by the White House as proof of a nuclear weapons' gas centrifuge under construction in Iraq. All of the dimensions and the type of alloy were precisely the same as those needed for Iraq to create copies of the Medusa 81. Further, U.S. analysts in Iraq had taken a photo of one of the tubes, which appeared to be identical to those intercepted. The logo of the Italian manufacturer of Medusa was on the side, and, clearly visible, was a label: "81mm rocket."

When he spoke before the United Nations, however, Secretary of State Colin Powell tried to deflect the idea that the tubes were meant for rocket production. He argued several batches of tubes had been intercepted and that they showed a "progression to higher and higher levels of specification, including in the latest batch an anodized coating on extremely smooth inner and outer surfaces."

"Why," Powell wondered, "would they continue refining the specifications, go to all that trouble for something that, if it was a rocket, would soon be blown into shrapnel when it went off?"

Unwittingly, the secretary of state had confirmed that the tubes were not for a gas centrifuge, though neither journalists nor the wider world happened to notice. Anodized coating helps aluminum resist corrosion, and rusted rocket bodies had ruined most of Iraq's previous arsenal. More specifically, according to scientists later quoted by the *Washington Post*, the anodized coating had to be removed for the tubes to be used in a gas centrifuge. What the White House also knew from intelligence reports, but refused to share with the American public, was that Iraq had two blueprints for a gas enrichment centrifuge. Those plans had been stolen somewhere in Europe, and required a hard steel alloy, not aluminum, for the rotors. The specs for the other stolen design listed carbon fiber rotors. In fact, aluminum rotors had not been used in centrifuge construction since the 1950s, and the shipment being touted as evidence of Iraq's nuclear ambitions were too long, the walls excessively thick, and the tube diameters too narrow.

These conclusions had all been reached by scientists after the details of the intercepted tube shipment had been circulated through the U.S. Department of Energy's Oak Ridge National Laboratory, a year earlier. Their unanimous findings were supported by Houston G. Wood, III, who founded the Oak Ridge centrifuge physics department. Considered to be the world's expert on the subject matter, Wood said, "It would have been extremely difficult to make these tubes into centrifuges. It stretches the imagination to come up with a way. I do not know any real centrifuge experts that feel differently."

Wood's scientific conclusion, and those of his colleagues, was known to the White House almost a year before the story about the tubes appeared in the *New York Times*. The White House Iraq Group, however, had managed to suppress dissenting opinions within the government's scientific community to the point that none were available when Miller and Gordon were making calls for their initial report. Not surprisingly, either, no one bothered to include Wood's opinion in the National Intelligence Estimate, being prepared for the White House as the tubes story was playing out in the media. Eventually, in front of the United Nations, Colin Powell included the esteemed scientist in the same category with the Iraqis.

"Most U.S. experts," Powell said, "think they [tubes] are intended to serve as rotors in centrifuges used to enrich uranium. Other experts, and the Iraqis themselves, say the tubes were really for rockets."

Powell, whose reputation for integrity was unparalleled in Washington, was either easily hoodwinked by government bureaucracies, or he simply lied. The vast majority of scientists with expertise in the development of nuclear material disagreed with the White House about the tubes.

In the *Post*, Wood described Powell's statement as a "personal slam at everybody in the DOE." [Department of Energy]

"I've been grouped with the Iraqis, is what it amounts to," he said. "I just felt that the wording of that was probably intentional, but it was also not very kind. It did not recognize that dissent can exist."

The Institute for Science and International Security was busily dissenting, regardless. Based in Washington, the organization had prepared a report analyzing the White House's allegations related to Iraq's nuclear potential. The lengthy treatise, written by nuclear physicist David Allbright, an Iraqi arms inspector during the 1990s, concluded the Bush administration's claims about the aluminum tubes were without merit. Allbright, who had been a member of a team sent to Iraq by the International Atomic Energy Agency, interviewed a number of researchers and analysts for his October 9, 2002, report.

The findings showed that the anodized coating of Saddam's tubes was the surest sign that they were not designed for use as parts in a gas centrifuge. The coating had to be machined off before they were installed in any kind of uranium separator. Allbright had also spoken with scientists at Oak Ridge's Lawrence Livermore Laboratories in California, who strongly disagreed with the White House's analysis of the tubes, and they told Allbright they had been ordered by the Bush administration to keep quiet.

"This is the problem with reporting on the intelligence community," Judy Miller said. "You can only write what you know. And if no one else will give you contradicting information, you try to give your readers a sense of where the information is coming from that you are using. The naysayers on that [the tubes] story did not come out of the closet until afterwards."

London's authoritative International Institute for Strategic Studies, though, also issued a report about the same time as Allbright's organization. The data was counter to the paranoia the White House Iraq Group was selling to the public.

"Iraq does not possess facilities to produce fissile material in sufficient amounts for nuclear weapons. It would require several years and extensive foreign assistance to build such fissile material production facilities," the report stated.

The absolute refutation of the aluminum tubes story was already more than a year old when Michael Gordon and Judith Miller broke the aluminum tubes story in the *Times*. Apparently, though, they were unable to immediately find opinions divergent from the "administration sources" and "intelligence analysts," whose frightening assessments of the tubes meant that, if we did not act, there were certain to be "mushroom clouds" in America. Presumably, the reporters contacted nongovernmental organizations in Washington that monitor nuclear weapons issues, as well as government agencies.

Miller and Gordon, who were later accused of being used by the administration, found themselves in a tough spot. Over the course of several weeks, they had been developing sources that had told them the tubes were a part of an attempt by Hussein to build a uranium enrichment facility. But they did not come up with sources to refute that allegation. Ethically, were they supposed to not report this information if they were unable to find a different scientific opinion? The most brutal criticisms came from people who argued the two simply did not try hard enough to find other perspectives.

When Judy Miller was asked if she had contacted any of the nongovernmental organizations about scientific data on the aluminum tubes, she demurred.

"I'm not about to discuss whom we called," she wrote in an August 2003 e-mail. "That would get into sources, the protection of which is sacrosanct as far as I'm concerned."

But Washington was supposedly filled with people who knew those aluminum tubes had nothing to do with nuclear proliferation.

One of them was Greg Thielmann. He was retiring as the head of the State Department's Office of Strategic Proliferation and Military Affairs. According to Thielmann, "The most knowledgeable people in the U.S. government believed that this was not the kind of aluminum that the Iraqis would have been seeking to use in centrifuges for uranium enrichment."

Drama-driven, oh-my-God journalism, had, however, taken root, and fear was selling newspapers and cranking up television newscast ratings. By the end of the week, the President was before the United Nations' General Assembly, adding White House authority to the fable that the confiscated tubes were for making nuclear fuel.

"Iraq," he told the world, "has made several attempts to buy high-strength aluminum tubes used to enrich uranium for a nuclear weapon. Should Iraq acquire fissile material, it would be able to build a nuclear weapon within a year."

Reporters covering the president's trip were given what was labeled as a "fact sheet," detailing claims made in the president's speech. In it, White House analysts said Saddam Hussein was trying to make chemical weapons, biological agents, and was pursuing a nuclear program. Less than a week from their story that had launched the aluminum tube hysteria, Judith Miller and Michael Gordon were once more reporting what they were told by the Bush administration. In a piece about a third as long as their previous Sunday expose, they did acknowledge that there was a debate about the purpose of the aluminum tubes. Unfortunately, the reporters did not include anyone in their story who disagreed with the White House's version of reality. A "senior administration official" told them that it was a "minority view" among intelligence experts that Iraq had acquired the aluminum tubes to construct a multiple launch rocket system.

Karl Rove, who has always insisted on being referred to as "a senior administration official," and his White House Iraq Group were running so fast that the truth did not begin to get real traction until December, even though Miller and Gordon did write some lower profile pieces questioning the Bush administration's claims on the tubes. Bob Simon of CBS's *60 Minutes* interviewed David Allbright, the weapons inspector whose findings had strongly contradicted the president's charges against Iraq. According to a transcript of the interview, Allbright indicated there was almost no support for the administration's suspicions of the tubes as parts of a potential centrifuge.

"People who understood gas centrifuges," Allbright told Simon, "Almost uniformly felt that these tubes were not specific to gas centrifuge use."

"It seems that what you're suggesting," the correspondent said, "Is that the administration's leak to the *New York Times*, regarding aluminum tubes, was misleading?"

"Oh, I think it was. I think it was very misleading."

Judith Miller vehemently denied she was a recipient of a White House leak.

"We worked our asses off to get that story," she said. "No one leaked anything to us. I reported what I knew at the time. I wish I were omniscient. I wish I were God, and had all the information I had needed. But I'm not God, and I don't know. All I can rely on is what people tell me. That's all any investigative reporter can do. And if you find out that it's not true, you go back and you write that. And I did that. You just keep chipping away on an assertion until you find out what stands up."

Actually, if Miller had spoken to one of the various scientific organizations when she wrote the first story, including the leading groups in her own country, she would have learned there was almost no chance the tubes were going into a centrifuge. Her list of interview subjects needed to include contradictory voices and opinions on the uses of the aluminum tubes. There were certainly plenty of them out there. Working in Iraq, with limited, intermittent communications, undoubtedly hampered Gordon's and Miller's ability to do more comprehensive work, utilizing sources in the states. Editorial assistance from the *Times'* foreign desk might have added dimension to her reportage. But it's just as possible the architecture of modern, electronic journalism is not prepared to offer timely, balanced reporting from a war zone, especially on questions of intelligence. How does a reporter in a Persian desert call a Washington think tank to get a response to a White House allegation, especially when the country where that journalist is working has no electricity or functional communications?

There is also the confounding matter of a journalist's obligation to report. Presented with authoritative sources making claims that an enemy dictator is trying to build a uranium gas centrifuge to make a nuclear weapon, the journalist is compelled to deliver that information to the public. In a story of this nature, the assertions may be too significant to be withheld until a skeptical source can be developed. This reasoning, though, often creates misleading impressions. If a reporter writes only what they know at the time and that data comes only from a source with one perspective, a reader or viewer can readily conclude they have just experienced fact. A refutation, in the form of a follow-up story, often does not receive the same prominence or promotion, and that results in the original report having greater veracity.

Either way, in the case of the aluminum tubes story, it was too late.

The story was alive, and it was never completely retracted or repudiated by the prominent newspaper that had initially put it in front of the American public. A few days after Judith Miller filed her story about a "minority" of scientists protesting the belief that the tubes were for nuclear development, the *Washington Post* wrote in great detail about David Allbright's research, and how it scientifically contradicted the Bush administration. Miller and Gordon's inability to find a divergent opinion in a city full of political minds, scientists, and think tanks, has remained a perplexing mystery among their colleagues.

But the words of war had been written. And more were coming; equally flawed, potentially lies. A claim by President Bush that Iraq had tried to acquire uranium from Niger was to split apart the institutions of U.S. government, while the White House turned to the new tactic of talking about biological and chemical armaments, which Saddam Hussein supposedly possessed.

The White House had mixed up journalists' ambitions with misleading intelligence and created a myth that yielded a powerful national belief in its illusion. A political Sasquatch, the aluminum tubes story was the first to begin banging the drums of conflict.

The truth, finally, was tortured until it was no longer recognizable.

And the sons and daughters of America were sent marching off to war wearing the boots of a well-told lie.

3

BOYS AT WAR

The greatest blunders, like the thickest ropes, are often compounded of a multitude of strands. Take the rope apart, separate it into the small threads that compose it, and you can break them one by one. You think, "That is all there was!" But twist them all together and you have something tremendous.

Victor Hugo

Maybe it was something his father had said. Or, perhaps his stepmother. Either way, James Kiehl had been thinking about getting baptized. Besides, he was about to be part of an invasion force entering a country with a well-bred hatred of Americans. And James Kiehl stood out as a target. He was a giant, Redwood of a man at 6 feet, 8 inches in height, and bullets flying over the heads of everyone else were likely to hit him.

James' father, Randy Kiehl, was relieved when he got word that his son had decided to be baptized in the northern Kuwaiti desert.

"Janie [James' stepmother] and I approached James in discussions of Christianity. We talked about it. It wasn't one of those passing subjects. And I didn't hammer it into him because that's a decision each person has to make on his own. We tried a couple of times to cajole him a little bit but something always seemed to come up that it didn't work."

A computer and systems technician, James Kiehl was part of the 507th Mechanized Company from Fort Bliss, Texas. According to his friends, Kiehl was "scary smart," and was able to take apart computers, figure out problems, and then reassemble them to full functionality. In the air defense artillery operations, which were supported by the 507th, Kiehl did everything from keeping vehicle systems operational to maintenance and deployment of computerized launch systems for the Patriot Missile Company.

Kiehl was only a few days away from crossing over the Iraqi frontier as part of the U.S. military's invasion force, and his mind was on unsettling possibilities. The persistent words of his father and stepmother, urging him to consider his spiritual life, were gnawing at James Kiehl's consciousness as he faced war.

Baptism presents, of course, a special problem in the desert. The shortage of water creates certain restrictions. Military chaplains required a minimal number of soldiers interested in an immersion baptism before precious water resources were used to create a pool. Unfortunately, only two soldiers, Kiehl and Sergeant Lewis Baldrich, had expressed an interest in the religious rite. The chaplain, Captain Scott Koeman, did not know if he'd get permission to conduct the ceremony because of water shortages.

James Kiehl, however, was determined. He told a television reporter traveling with his unit that he realized his "hour of need" had arrived.

"My hour of need was having my own stepmother to ask me to think about the path that I was on," he said during an interview. "It was something I was thinking about, and I kept putting it off. Is that something I wanna do right now? But I kept thinking about it and just putting it off. And I put it off for so long it was time for a reality check."

Kiehl, like thousands of young Americans camped in the northern deserts of Kuwait, was confronting his own mortality. Married
for only about eighteen months, James Kiehl had left under orders
for the Persian Gulf with his wife seven months pregnant. At 5
feet, 2 inches, Jill Kiehl is a foot and a half shorter than her husband, a man she described as a "big, goofy, lovable kid." Initially,
the couple worried a child was likely to affect their plans for James
to use his military benefits to attend college and get a degree in
computer programming. Barely out of their teens, James and Jill
were slightly intimidated by the responsibilities of parenthood.

"At first, of course, he was nervous and scared," Jill said. "But
after a while he was just as excited as I was, and especially after he
found out he was having a boy. He said he didn't care either way,
but I know he wanted to have a son to be able to do all the guy stuff;
cars and the hunting and fishing and wrestling around and sports
and everything."

During his time at Camp Virginia in northern Kuwait, before the
U.S. invasion of Iraq, James Kiehl did, however, reveal other anxieties about his future. He convinced the chaplain, Captain Scott
Koeman, to baptize him and Sergeant Baldrich, even though no
other soldiers were ready for the commitment. Baptized just over a
week before he crossed into Iraq with the 507th Mechanized, Kiehl's
imagination was already working through a fateful reckoning, which
he seemed to sense.

A television crew from KTVT-TV, Dallas, who were among the
journalists embedded with the unit, came across the baptismal rites
by accident. During an interview they taped with Kiehl, he sounded
as if he knew what lay ahead for him on the road to Baghdad.

"You always have the threat of something new here every day,"
he said. "And every morning, you wake up, and then you think the
next morning you may not wake up. I look at it that if it's my time to
go, it's my time to go. But if I can leave here, leaving something behind, saying, you know, I was here. . . ."

The water for the baptism did not come from the Army's tanker trucks. Soldiers donated their own rationed bottles of water to fill the plastic-lined pit where Kiehl and Baldrich were to cleanse their souls. In the desert sand, in the midst of the Muslim world, American soldiers dug a hole to accommodate the broad frames of Kiehl and Baldrich. Unconcerned about the great spiritual conflict or the perceived cultural insult to Arabs, the pit was lined with plastic, and the bottles of drinking water were poured into the hole. Accompanied by a guitar, the troops stood and sang hymns of praise to their God, asking his protection from harm. On the other side of the border, Iraqis were petitioning Allah with the same request.

As the soldiers gathered around the small pool of water, Chaplain Koeman turned their private thoughts into his public hopes.

"Our danger lies to the northwest," he said. "We do not know what we are going to face when we cross the border. And it is possible that when we get across into Iraq, not a shot will be fired and not one single Patriot will have to be launched. We'll turn in all of our ammo, and that will be great. Amen?"

The last word had the inflection of a question, as if the chaplain was trying to convince them of his optimistic vision. But he acknowledged, just as the troops did, there was an alternate possibility.

"However, on the opposite end of the scale of things that could happen, we know that it is possible we could get hit," he told the soldiers listening to his brief sermon.

The men were silent as Koeman called forward Kiehl and Baldrich, asking them a question Christians have answered with nothing more than their faith for two thousand years.

"Do you believe that Jesus Christ is your only Lord and savior?"

Both men answered, "I do."

"Therefore," Koeman continued, "Go and make disciples of all nations and baptize them in the name of the Father, the Son, and the Holy Spirit."

Kiehl and Baldrich took off their desert camouflage field jackets and wore olive drab tee shirts, combat boots, and pants into the baptismal pool. Individually, they sat in the foot-deep water, and lowered themselves backward as the chaplain cradled their heads to dip them beneath the surface. Kiehl smiled as his boyish face was covered with water.

"I baptize you in the name of the Father, the Son, and the Holy Spirit," Koeman said, loud enough for the other soldiers to hear.

The two Americans stepped up from the water, their clothing drenched, as the other troops applauded.

"Praise God," Chaplain Koeman intoned.

Dripping, James Kiehl and Lewis Baldrich moved among their friends, accepting congratulations. Baldrich proudly shook hands while the massive Kiehl leaned over and hugged everyone whom he greeted.

"James never wanted to have things done in a good-mannered way," his father Randy Kiehl explained. "He always left things until the last minute. Homework, learning a solo piece on his horn, learning basketball, always the last minute. But we always knew when the time was right he would make the right decision."

A few days after James Kiehl's baptism, Muslim clerics, during Friday night prayers at mosques throughout Iraq, asked Allah's assistance in turning back "the American crusaders." Exactly one week later, as Iraqis knelt before their God, U.S. bombs were already falling on Baghdad. The 507th Mechanized Company was also part of an almost unimaginably huge convoy that had begun to race across ancient deserts and into the heart of the land where civilization began.

And whatever came of the attack on Iraq, James Kiehl, the towering basketball star of Comfort, Texas, was as prepared as he knew how to be.

On the grounds of the White House, President George W. Bush was taking a quiet walk, collecting his thoughts, after authorizing an attack on the nation of Iraq. He had come from the Situation Room, where various commanders had appeared on teleconference screens, and the national security team had been assembled around a table. The president had given orders to General Tommy Franks to proceed with Operation Iraqi Freedom. After asking for God's blessing on the assault, the president saluted Franks, who returned the salute to his commander-in-chief.

The war, according to the U.S. president, was being conducted on orders from God. Bush, who had already told friends and advisors that he felt "guided" in his war on terror after September 11, 2001, apparently had reached the point where he was hearing directly from the Almighty. During a trip to the Middle East to attempt to implement the Road Map to Peace, Bush met with the new Palestinian Prime Minister Mahmoud Abbas, also known as Abu Mazen, and Israeli Prime Minister Ariel Sharon. Later, when Abbas gathered with other Palestinian factions to detail the Road Map, and his meeting with the American and Israeli leaders, Abbas told the group that President Bush had claimed to have been spoken to by God.

According to the minutes of the meeting, Bush said: "God told me to strike at Al Qaeda, and I struck at them, and then he instructed me to strike at Saddam, which I did, and now I am determined to solve the problem in the Middle East. If you help me, I will act, and if not, the elections will come and I will have to focus on them."

The text of the president's words came from the Israeli newspaper *Haaretz*, and the *Moscow Times*, which published excerpts from minutes of the meeting between Abbas and other Palestinian organizations. As appealing as it is to dismiss the story, the deeply held religious connection Bush asserted, and the guidance he has felt, suggested there was credence to the report that God had told him to strike at Al Qaeda and Saddam Hussein. The concluding note, also, was fitting with the president's political character; as important as peace might be in the Middle East, getting reelected remained more critical.

God was not, however, in charge of tactics. Donald Rumsfeld was. Shortly after the president's stroll around the White House, the secretary of defense called the Oval Office, and told the president that plans needed to be changed. Intelligence sources had informed the U.S. military commanders of the location of Saddam Hussein and his two sons, Uday and Qusay. Reassembling his national security advisors, the president listened as CIA operatives described the information on Hussein's whereabouts, and made the case for launching an early bombing run on a particular bunker in Baghdad.

"I was hesitant, at first," the president told NBC's Tom Brokaw. "To be frank with you, because I was worried that the first pictures coming out of Iraq would be a wounded grandchild of Saddam Hussein, but Saddam Hussein, who was not there at the time we started making the decision, would never show up, that the first images of the American attack would be death to young children."

Interestingly, the president did not express concern about the actual deaths of children; only that the images of their dying might hurt public relations for the American invasion of Iraq. Certainly, this was a moment for the veteran broadcaster Brokaw to interrupt, and ask Bush questions about innocent civilian deaths as a result of the attack. Brokaw, however, chose to let the president continue a soliloquy about "ordnance packages" and how difficult it was to quickly reprogram missiles for their launch. A chance to humanize the war had been lost, and Americans were able to retain their clinical, almost antiseptic visions of how neatly Baghdad had fallen.

According to what the president told NBC, the intelligence source was supposedly on the ground in Baghdad as the bombs fell, and he felt like the attack had hit when Hussein was inside the facility. If Hussein's sons were in that same structure, as the source had indicated, they had not been harmed. Uday and Qusay were later surrounded and killed by U.S. troops, many weeks after the initial bombing of Baghdad. Still, the source fed information to the White House that he was convinced Saddam Hussein, if not killed, was severely wounded.

Who was this source? And why did U.S. commanders place so much trust in what he was telling them? According to an intelligence operative with years of experience in Saudi Arabia, the White House was relying on information being relayed from a few Iraqi generals in Saddam Hussein's army. The intelligence was supposedly being passed from them through connections in Jordan then on to Saudi Arabia and Washington. The analyst said the Saudis were trying to be helpful to the Bush administration, and ease political pressures on them from America, which had resulted from Saudi Arabia's connections to Al Qaeda.

"That was the Saudis in touch with Jordanian intelligence," the operative said. "And they got played. That was my take. They got played by those generals. They [the Saudis] might have offered the [Iraqi] generals some money, or U.S. citizenship, through the Jordanians, for the information, but I don't think any of it was accurate. They [the Saudis] had no U.S. citizenship to offer. Anyway, the generals just played them, that's all. They might have just wanted the U.S. to harm civilians to hurt domestic political support for the war."

The president's interview with NBC, the first he conducted after the war had begun, was important for transitional language unveiled by Bush. Instead of insisting Saddam Hussein had actual weapons of mass destruction, the president began to clarify, telling Brokaw he was "pretty confident" America was going to discover a "weapons of mass destruction program." A program, of course, was different than an actual weapon. It only meant Hussein was trying to develop that which American political and military leaders claimed he already possessed, and possessed in mass quantities.

A "program" wasn't the reason America went to war.

If Tom Brokaw had been an aggressive interviewer, he might have asked the president about the overwhelming list of weaponry that Colin Powell had told the United Nations was in Saddam Hussein's possession. Since that tally included 500 tons of mustard gas and nerve gas, 25,000 liters of anthrax, 38,000 liters of botulinum toxin, 29,984 prohibited munitions capable of delivering chemical agents, several dozen Scud missiles, gas centrifuges to enrich uranium, 18 mobile biological factories, and long-range unmanned aerial vehicles to dispense anthrax, Brokaw missed an opportunity to read that list to the president, and then ask how it was possible that such vast quantities of weapons and materials were not easily discovered, especially since Vice President Dick Cheney had insisted the United States knew most of these weapons were in and around Tikrit.

Brokaw's questioning appeared more calculated to make the president squirm on matters of social import than it did to discover the logic behind important conclusions related to why Bush had taken America to war. The anchorman wanted to know if the president was going to invite French President Jacques Chirac to his ranch in Crawford, Texas. When Bush answered that his first postwar guest was to be Australian Prime Minister John Howard, Brokaw pressed again, and asked, "What about President Chirac, though?" On Middle East peace, Brokaw inquired as to whether the president intended to invite new Palestinian Prime Minister Abu Mazen [Mahmoud Abbas] to the White House, and later, when the subject turned to dissenting voices on the war, he wanted to know if Bush planned to invite the Dixie Chicks to the White House.

Brokaw also ignored chances to ask the president about alleged connections between Al Qaeda and Hussein, letting Bush get off with his tough guy talk of, "We're on the hunt." The interviewer broached the subject of the tax cuts, but did not press the president on why he thought they would help the economy when most economic models showed increasing dangers from an enormous federal deficit, nor did he confront Bush with the fact that the wealthy benefited the most from the president's tax policies. Instead, Brokaw wanted to know what parts of the war the president watched on television, if he sought advice from his parents, and if he talked with Laura about things. The collegial tone of the interview made the viewer wonder if NBC News had agreed, in advance, to ground rules in order to bag the interview ahead of competition.

Too many questions went unasked by too many journalists.

Allegations, suspicions, accusations, diplomatic impatience, imperialism, and even poor journalism were all contributing factors to the launch of a massive American military convoy across the Iraqi border with Kuwait. On the morning of March 20, 2003, five lanes of vehicles, their headlights pointing northward, wended for miles across the sands of Persian Gulf deserts. Thirty-three vehicles of the thousands in the procession belonged to the 507th Maintenance Company of Fort Bliss, Texas. The sixty-four soldiers in the 507th portion of the convoy were deployed to support the vehicles and launch systems of the Patriot Missile battalion, considered a vital element of U.S. armaments to be used against Iraq.

Though they had no way of knowing, the soldiers of the 507th were in danger even before they moved out. Their commander, Captain Troy King, had been given an orders brief that included both a CD-ROM, and a 1 : 100,000 scale map showing the various routes troops were to follow. King was also provided a handheld Global Positioning System (GPS) that gave him a readout of directional signals and distance. If he got lost, the GPS displayed an arrow pointing the convoy to its proscribed route, and the distance it needed to cover to get back on course. Additionally, as a backup, he had the map with the route of travel. Unfortunately, King had highlighted it incorrectly. King was also quoted as telling a few of his troops that his GPS had jammed, affecting directional readings.

According to the Army's preliminary report of what happened to the 507th, King was to take his company up a course designated as Route Blue (Highway 8) turn onto Route Jackson (Highway 1) and then return to Route Blue, thus avoiding the city of Al Nasiriyah. On his map, however, only Route Blue had been highlighted. An error of this magnitude is easily corrected during what military planners call "briefback," a session where the officer explains to his commanders his own understanding of the orders he has been issued. King, though, was not asked to participate in a briefback session. The army has not explained why there were no briefbacks on orders, though perhaps, under pressure to deploy quickly, Lieutenant Colonel Joseph Fischetti, commander of the 5th Battalion, 52nd Air Defense Artillery, had not ordered briefbacks for officers.

The young wife of one of the 507th's soldiers was astonished by the lack of logic among officers readying for the attack. After meeting with army investigators, Jill Kiehl was dumbfounded by their findings, and their shortage of detailed information or answers.

"I don't even know who did the original briefing," Jill Kiehl said. "They should have given him [King] a map that was highlighted and said, 'This is your route,' not just said, 'You know where you're supposed to go, right? Right.' Okay, that's stupid. Right there, that was the first thing to go wrong. They tried to find a scapegoat, which was Captain King, and blame it all on him. I was saying, 'Yes, but what about everyone else who took part in it? What about them?' There were errors on a lot of people's parts."

Jill Kiehl's husband, Specialist James Kiehl, and Specialist Jamaal Addison were riding in a five-ton truck, pulling a small supply trailer as the 507th moved through the darkness of an early desert morning. Kiehl was an unlikely warrior, almost too encumbered by his great size to be in the military; a friend described him as both "the class clown and the silver voice of reason, at the same time." Back in El Paso at Fort Bliss, Kiehl was known as a tech-head and prankster, who once taped a video camera to a radio-controlled toy car and raced it around the base motor pool, laughing at the reactions of soldiers as they realized they were being spied on by a remote camera. Raised in the rocky Texas Hill Country, Kiehl, like thousands of other soldiers, had enlisted in the military to earn money for a college education.

Kiehl might have been remembering the last conversation he'd had with his father over the telephone the day he deployed. Only halfway intended as a light-hearted recommendation, Randy Kiehl told his only child how to avoid harm.

"I said, 'Son, you get over there, and dig yourself a foxhole about seven feet deep.' He said, 'Why seven feet deep, dad?' You're six foot, eight. I said, 'put four inches of sand above you.' He said, 'You're right, dad.' You can reach up above that and fire an M-16, or whatever you're carrying. Start shooting. You'll probably get somebody. But you dig that foxhole to seven feet.' Never had that opportunity."

The 507th Maintenance Company never stopped long enough to dig any foxholes.

Because some of the heavy trucks and armor needed in battle were expected to get stuck in the Iraqi sands, the 507th had large tow trucks needed to recover stranded vehicles. In one of them, Chief Warrant Officer Johnny Mata stared at the string of lights leading toward Baghdad. This was the kind of service to his country Mata had long dreamed about. The Pecos, Texas, native had told his wife that, if he did not ever get to go into combat, he would "feel like I cheated my country during my years of service." In his little town on the northern edge of the Chihuahuan Desert, Johnny Mata was famous for his athletic skills and his ability to fix cars. While his wife, Nancili, and their two children waited in their new house near the Franklin Mountains in El Paso, Johnny was finally realizing his ambition to serve America in a war.

Nancili Mata had no ability to envision what was about to happen to her husband.

"Too many mistakes," she said. "Too many. Too many. Way too many. I started researching on my own and looking at letters and reports, and archive material in that report when they did everything. I came to the conclusion that there were four or five mistakes. Usually, a person gets killed for just one mistake."

At the tail end of the great chain of military vehicles, the 507th also included Jessica Lynch, who was to become a national figure because of her controversial rescue, and an eighteen-year-old private, Ruben Estrella Soto Jr., whose mother had to be convinced to sign the papers for him to enlist in the army. His father, who distrusted the military, tried until the end to convince his son not to join. Engaged to Sonia Romero before he left for the Persian Gulf, Ruben Estrella-Soto Jr. had told friends he wanted to be famous, and to bring together his family, which was spread out across Texas and Mexico.

Moving to the northwest, military planners had picked map positions, referred to as objectives Dawson, Bull, Lizard, and Rams, where the convoy was to stop, rest, and prepare for the coming battles. The trip was largely without incident as the 507th moved to Attack Positions Dawson, Bull, and Lizard. At Bull, the unit was linked up with the 3rd Forward Support Battalion. Leaving their last stop in the early evening, the heavy trucks and vehicles spent much of their time off-road, navigating soft sand. What the army described as "poor trafficability" and mechanical problems caused the 507th to break into two smaller groups. Darkness and blowing sand led to a number of drivers being confused. Eventually, several trucks broke down, while others simply settled into the soft, grainy earth.

The 3rd Forward Support Battalion's vehicles continued moving northward, and Captain Troy King made the decision to split the 507th. Vehicles still functioning, which were able to keep pace with the larger convoy, kept going under King's command. Tow trucks, vehicles bogged down, and those with mechanical problems became the responsibility of First Sergeant Robert Dowdy. While King's smaller group traveled through the night to arrive at Attack Position Lizard just before sunrise, Dowdy's team worked to free the second group of trucks, which had become stuck and to repair those that weren't mechanically functional. Eventually, Dowdy's convoy caught up with Captain King's. Arriving more than twelve hours after King's, however, mechanical failures and trapped vehicles caused Dowdy's team to spend twenty-two hours covering only eight kilometers of desert. They were tired, sleepless.

While waiting for First Sergeant Dowdy to arrive with the trailing vehicles, Captain King contacted his battalion commander to let him know of the 507th's circumstances. King was informed by 3rd FSB's staff that the overall plan of movement, including route, was unchanged, and King indicated he understood his instructions. He was also told that the larger battalion was planning to move out on schedule, and was not able to wait for the trailing convoy. When he learned of his commander's intentions, Captain King ordered his executive officer, First Lieutenant Jeff Shearin, to gather the thirty-two soldiers and seventeen vehicles already at Attack Position Lizard, and depart with the larger 3rd FSB convoy.

As the main group was leaving Lizard, Robert Dowdy radioed Captain King, who was waiting for him, to tell him he was only ten to twelve kilometers away. Dowdy reported that he had all of the 507th's remaining trucks either running, or in tow. He was also being accompanied by two more soldiers, tow truck operators from the 3rd FSB, who had been left behind to pull fuel tankers out of the sand. Sergeant George Buggs and Private First Class Edward Anguiano were using their wrecker to pull a disabled five-ton truck belonging to the 507th.

Only three and a half hours after Dowdy's group reached Attack Position Lizard, Captain King had reorganized them into an eighteen-vehicle, thirty-three soldier convoy, and ordered them to pull out. King seemed determined to catch up with the larger convoy of the 3rd Forward Support Battalion (FSB). Because he was unable to reach commanders in the 3rd FSB via radio, Captain King decided the only way to rejoin the main group was to take a direct line across the open desert to intersect Highway 8, the assigned route of all the vehicles driving north toward Baghdad. Although there were only fifteen kilometers of distance between his location and the paved road, the rough terrain caused many vehicles in his convoy to become stuck. Five more hard hours elapsed before the soldiers were able to cover the short distance, and most of King's troops had now gone almost two days with no more than a few hours of sleep.

Back on his assigned route, Troy King moved his parade of vehicles westerly along the hardtop road designated Highway 8, which was also known to military planners as Route Blue. After a short distance, King's convoy came to an intersection with Highway 1, referred to on his map as Route Jackson. Mistakenly, King had assumed he was to proceed all the way to the next attack position by traveling along Route Blue, when all tactical planning had called for convoys to move onto Highway 1, Route Jackson, to avoid Al Nasiriyah by skirting the city to its southwest. The intersection where King had just arrived was expected to be confusing for drivers, and the army had stationed soldiers there to provide directions for traffic. Unfortunately, King's convoy was hours behind the battalion leaders, and the troops, who had been directing traffic at the intersection, were gone. A small contingent of Marines was present at the spot where the two roads came together, and Captain King asked them if he was on Route Blue, which was confirmed for him by the Marines. Wrongly assuming he was to continue on Route Blue, up Highway 8, King failed to direct his soldiers to make a left turn onto Route Jackson, Highway 1. The arrow on his GPS, pointing generally northward, affirmed his decision, and the 507th Mechanized Company began driving up the wrong road, toward the city of Al Nasiriyah.

Nancili Mata, the wife of the 507th's Chief Warrant Officer Johnny Mata, has been unable to accept the idea that the Marines did not steer Captain King onto the correct road, a mistake she first discovered when she was briefed about the incident by the U.S. Army.

"The Marines are at a checkpoint, and they see so many Americans going through that checkpoint in one way, and then all of a sudden one comes the other way? They just let them pass," she said. "When Captain King got there, he asked, 'Is this Route Blue?' The Marines said, 'Yes, it is.' So they kept going, even though they should have said, 'Okay, Captain King, why are you going this way? It's not secure over there.' So that was another mistake."

The misstep by King, however, was not unexpected by many of the people who served in the 507th. Troy King worried the soldiers who were under his command. A former dental assistant, King had been in the Army for about a decade and had only recently received his captain's bars. He had never before been in combat.

Laura Cruz, a reporter for the *El Paso Times*, who has written extensively on Fort Bliss and the soldiers of the 507th, had heard numerous criticisms of King's abilities.

"The soldiers of the 507th have mentioned that they didn't trust him," she said. "I don't know if they'll tell you on the record that they didn't trust him, but it is one of the things they told me, and I've heard it from other people, as well. I've also heard a lot of the POWs say they didn't have any respect for him, and they weren't convinced Captain King would make a good commander."

Months after the incident, Troy King had still not spoken to reporters about his role in the tragedy that befell the 507th. He was
under strict orders at Fort Bliss to remain silent and was not allowed
the opportunity to defend his command decisions publicly.

The army's preliminary report, however, states "soldiers fight as
they are trained to fight . . . the soldiers of the 507th upheld the
Code of Conduct and followed the Law of War."

As King pushed his convoy up Route 8, lights began to shimmer
in the distance. Talking to his first sergeant, Robert Dowdy, on the
radio, the two concluded they were looking at an industrial complex
or an oil refinery, and King chose to continue. Another intersection
lay ahead, however, and if King had understood the road markings,
he might have yet avoided the disaster awaiting the 507th. Just
south of Al Nasiryah, Highway 8 turned west, while Highway 7/8
followed a northerly course across the Euphrates River and into the
city. If King had made a left turn, the 507th would have missed ambush alley, and might have safely passed Al Nasiryah to the west.

But the lights kept coming closer. And King's troops were optimistic that what they were seeing up ahead was the main convoy of
the 3rd Forward Support Battalion. A mechanic in the 507th, Joe
Hudson, was beginning to feel relieved.

"I thought it was the convoy in front of us," he said. "That we
were catching up to them. Then all of a sudden, a town appeared out
of nowhere, buildings just started popping up everywhere. Wow,
we're in a town, and what was running through my mind: hope this is
a friendly town."

Communications for vehicles in the 507th's convoy were inadequate. Only five drivers had SINCGARS (Single-channel Ground
and Airborne Radio System) and some soldiers had been equipped
with walkie talkie radios. Batteries in most of the handheld radios,
however, had been depleted because of the amount of time they had
been used during the previous two days. Several sources have also
said soldiers in the 507th used their own money to buy additional
radios for their unit because they did not feel their communications
capabilities were sufficient. Why no additional batteries, battery

chargers, or handheld radios were supplied to the 507th, is an issue not addressed in the army's report on the 507th's combat engagement at Al Nasiriyah.

Al Nasiriyah is built up to the banks of the Euphrates River, and the 507th was immediately into the urban center the moment it crossed the bridge. Ahead, Iraqi soldiers had established a checkpoint, but they made no attempt to stop the convoy nor did they show any hostile intent toward the Americans passing through their city. Many of the Iraqi soldiers were in uniform, while others were armed civilians. The 507th reported seeing a few pickup trucks with Iraqi civilians manning machine guns, which had been mounted in the back. Regardless, none of them fired on the U.S. vehicles or troops. They simply waved, and the trucks rolled past a crude sign saying, "Welcome."

But Specialist Joe Hudson was growing worried.

"We passed them," he said. "They're waving at us. I'm like, you know, something doesn't feel right. I mean, these are uniformed Iraqi soldiers."

An anonymous letter from one of the 507th's soldiers, quoted by ABC News, described what it felt like to enter the foreign, hostile city.

"At about 5:30 or 6, we started driving through the city of Nasiriyah. It seemed like a peaceful town. Most of the town was still asleep. We crossed over the Euphrates River and drove all the way through town. We then pulled over to the side of the road and turned around. We later figured out the group we were looking for wasn't where they said they were. At about this time, we started seeing more traffic. The information we had been given was that the Iraqi soldiers would be giving up. We were also told that the Iraqi soldiers would be keeping their weapons. So we were nervous."

While the failures of Captain Troy King may have been partially responsible for placing the soldiers under his command inside of a hostile enemy city, so was the flawed planning of the U.S. military, which was instrumental in leading the 507th to this dangerous spot. Determined to reach Baghdad quickly, under political pressure from the Bush administration for a speedy, low-casualty, low-cost victory, the Department of Defense laid out a plan of attack that used a light and fast movement into Iraq. The plan, however, was certain to leave behind any maintenance company as vehicles broke down or got stuck in desert terrain. The main convoy would be moving off while the impaired vehicles were being recovered. Catching up had to be considered impossible for the heaving tow trucks of the maintenance company.

"The 507th Maintenance Company was placed in a terrible predicament by the wanton desire of its command structure to race to Baghdad," wrote the Reverend Tandy Sloan, in a letter to CNN. Sloan, the father of Private Brandon Sloan, believed that what happened to the 507th was, "a tragedy, which is preposterous in nature, and unheard of in proportion."

"It seems to us that these events were brought about by unpreparedness [sic] of our military in this conflict," he added. "In their view, [they] could not afford time to cover their ranks as they went, or even to slow down for unforeseen complication, such as heavy trucks stalling or becoming bogged down in the sands of the desert they knew they had to cross."

The army did not make accommodations for this inevitability. With hundreds of trucks and Humvees, there were certain to be breakdowns in the desert. But, in many ways, the maintenance company troops were left to fend for themselves. They were not provided any kind of combat infantry support, even though the 507th's soldiers had received only standard training in combat.

"They left us there," one unidentified soldier told ABC News. "They were supposed to protect us, and they didn't. We were all alone with no protection. That is not supposed to happen. We are always supposed to be protected."

One of the U.S. commanders in Iraq, who has fifteen years of experience in foreign operations, including the Gulf War, described what happened to the 507th as "doubly frustrating."

"Because," he said, "we train against precisely that scenario. It's called a contemporary operational environment. As the enemy realizes they are defeated, those kinds of assets, like logistical support provided by the 507th become soft targets. They're easier to hit. That's the only means they [the enemy] have to strike back. It makes no sense to send those guys out without support. We train against that. We know better than that. Sending those guys out without proper combat support was a calculated risk and a decision that was made, but I don't think it was a good one. Like I said, we sure don't train like that to send out our logistical support unsecured."

In fact, many of the soldiers did not even expect to encounter hostile Iraqis. The political spin from Washington, which was being fed to troops and reporters, was that Iraqi soldiers were likely to greet them with "happy fire." Washington was so confident of friendly treatment for American troops that soldiers were informed that surrendering Iraqis were to be allowed to keep their weapons. The 507th was not ready, mentally or professionally, for what it was about to confront.

The troops in the 507th were certainly not considered marksmen or experts in small arms warfare, though they were capable of defending themselves. While the soldiers of the 507th were issued a basic combat load of ammunition prior to their departure from Camp Virginia, having infantry or armored support attached to their company was likely to have improved their odds of survival. But they were abandoned as the main convoy raced to Baghdad.

Darrell Cortez, a Fort Bliss soldier who lost his best friend in the ambush of the 507th, thinks someone needed to find a better plan.

"I personally disagree with the leave-them-behind, they-can-catch-up-later mentality," he said. "I don't know how we could do it better, though. Stopping a three-hundred vehicle convoy for one vehicle that is broken could delay the entire mission.

"Stopping? You put four or five people in eminent danger versus the complete mission. In the military sense, crass to say, they don't mean as much as completing the mission."

After passing through a second Iraqi checkpoint without incident, and crossing a canal bridge just north of Al Nasiriyah, the 507th came to the end of Highway 7/8. The road made a "T" intersection with Highway 16, and Captain King took his convoy west, to the left. A short time later, King was faced with a similar decision when Highway 16 reached a "T" intersection with Highway 7. Choosing to go northward, in the general direction of Baghdad, King had the convoy follow him through a right turn. A few kilometers down Highway 7, King began to believe he was off course and brought all trucks and Humvees to a stop.

While King checked his GPS handheld device to find where the correct route was located, a number of Iraqi cars passed the stopped Americans. Soldiers of the 507th had noticed the same vehicles as they traveled through the city. A few members of the company began to worry they were being scouted by the enemy. King's GPS showed that the main route of the convoy was due west, across more open desert. After all of the difficulties his unit had experienced in going off road, he decided to turn around his convoy and retrace its route through Al Nasiriyah. As King issued an order for the U-turn, more Iraqi vehicles came into view. Everyone in the 507th, including Captain Troy King, knew their moves were now being scrutinized by the enemy. Troops were nervous, worried about driving back through the Iraqi checkpoints and becoming targets. Matthew Rose, a 37-year-old supply sergeant for the unit, was one of a few soldiers in the 507th who grabbed his M-16, and established a defensive perimeter. A pickup truck carrying a machine gun sped past.

Combat seemed even more unavoidable when King issued an order to get prepared. They were simple, frightening words, which signaled to the soldiers they were in danger, in a foreign country, and some of them might soon die.

"Lock and load."

4

A FEW YOUNG MEN

To save your world you asked this man to die;
Would this man, could he see you now, ask why?

W. H. Auden

I n his comfortable home, set on a ridgeline above Tonopah, a surprise awaited Sheriff Wade Lieseke as he returned from his duties in Pahrump, Nevada. Three days of the week, Lieseke lived out of a motel room in Pahrump. Though his home was in Tonopah, on the other side of Nye County, Pahrump was the biggest city in the nation's second largest county. To do his job, the sheriff needed to spend a lot of time away from his family. All 18,400 square miles of Nye County, the endless, hazy distances of the Great Basin Desert, were a part of his law enforcement jurisdiction.

On the right hand wall as he entered the house on this particular evening, a shadow box had been hung. In perfect rows, his medals for military service in Vietnam had been placed behind glass, centered on a folded American flag. Lieseke had lost track of the location of his combat decorations. He wasn't ashamed of his service, but it wasn't exactly a time that had given him great happiness, either.

The medals had been put away for a reason. Soldiers don't like to be reminded of war.

"I looked at that thing on the wall," he said. "And I knew right away it was Fred. You could just tell he had done it by the perfect rows he had hung the medals in. It was all just so precise, so Fred."

Lieseke's adopted son, Fred Pokorney Jr., had come home from the Marines for a few days. When he arrived, he had asked Suzy Lieseke where he might find Wade's medals from Vietnam.

"Where'd you get those?" Lieseke asked Pokorney.

"Suzy and I dug them out."

"Why? I had those put away. I never really think about them any more."

"I know," Pokorney answered. "But that's where they need to be. Right there where people can see them. You need to be proud."

Wade Lieseke looked at the commendations he had received as a gunner on an attack helicopter. He had served in four of the war's major campaigns, and had been decorated with a National Service Medal, Vietnam Service, Vietnam Campaign, the Army Commendation, an Air Medal, the Purple Heart, and the Vietnam Cross of Gallantry with a Palm Leaf bestowed by the government of South Vietnam. Lieseke knew something of war. Hundreds of Viet Cong had died from his accuracy during fourteen months of flying combat missions. War was not something Wade Lieseke celebrated. He hated it as only a soldier can.

But he was moved by his son's thoughtfulness.

"That's pretty nice," he told Pokorney. "I appreciate you thinking of me like that."

Pokorney smiled. "Yeah, there's just one thing wrong with it."

"Oh? What's that?"

"That."

Pokorney pointed his finger at the U.S. Army insignia near the top of the shadow box. He had positioned it above a shoulder patch, which he had given to Lieseke, designating the sheriff's military unit; "282nd Assault, Alley Cats Helicopter Company."

"What's wrong with the Army insignia?" Lieseke asked.

"It oughta be the Marines," Pokorney explained. "You should have been a Marine because they're the best."

Fred Pokorney Jr. did not come into the world as Wade Lieseke's son. Lieseke, whose physical presence in a room demands almost most as much attention as the six foot, seven inch Pokorney's, first met the future Marine while Fred was dating Lieseke's daughter, Angie. During his high school years, Fred Pokorney had come to Tonopah with his father. They were living with Fred's aunt, while Fred Pokorney Sr., worked construction in the mining town. When his aunt died, Fred's father decided to look elsewhere for work. The younger Pokorney, however, did not want to leave Tonopah.

Wade Lieseke invited the young man to come live with his family.

"Sure, you think about what you are doing when the kid is dating your daughter," Lieseke said. "But with Fred, that just wasn't an issue. You just met the kid and you knew he was different, very special. You were in the presence of someone outstanding, and you knew it. You just knew it. Him dating Angie was never a worry. We had our discussions. He knew the kind of behavior I expected. And that's the way he acted. I never had the slightest reason not to trust Fred."

In Tonopah, Fred Pokorney was noticeable. Tall, with green eyes and dark hair, he was a natural athlete. Classmates say he never struggled to fit in with his peers, and became a leader, even though he was quiet, not what many students considered outgoing. On the football team, Pokorney was a big target as a receiver for the quarterback, and a daunting obstacle for running backs to get around when he played defensive end. A teammate said Fred was "always good for at least one touchdown a game." Basketball, though, appeared to fit more closely his physical skills. Whenever the Tonopah Muckers competed, Fred Pokorney always seemed to be in the middle, underneath the basket, clearing out rebounds or dropping in two pointers. During off-season, he spent his time in the high school gymnasium, lifting weights, trying to "put on size" to help attract the interest of college recruiters.

Rarely, if ever, did Fred Pokorney speak of his birth parents. He had told Suzy Lieseke that the last time he saw his mother was at age six, after she had left him abandoned in a shopping mall near Lake Tahoe, and police turned him over to the custody of his biological father. Many people in Tonopah assumed Pokorney's parents were Wade and Suzy Lieseke, even though Fred had lived with them as foster parents. The Lieseke's never formally applied to adopt Fred because, according to Wade, he never felt he needed "a piece of paper to make him my son."

"That's just what he was," Lieseke said. "He was my son."

He was born, however, to a construction worker named Fred Pokorney Sr., who moved around the West, and his first wife. Around the time he was entering kindergarten, Fred Pokorney's parents divorced. No one in Tonopah ever heard him speak of his mother.

"We always just assumed Fred's birth mother was dead," Suzy Lieseke said. "He never once mentioned her to us, and we didn't pry."

Whatever his childhood hardships were, Pokorney was reluctant to share the experiences even with his closest of friends, and he did not let the past burden his teenage years. Fred Pokorney excelled in sports, was a fine student, and worked two jobs, at the Mizpah Hotel and in an open pit mine. He went about the business of building his own life.

"He was a pretty independent guy," said former high school teammate Mike Grigg. "Rather than sitting and pissing and moaning about it, he was working two jobs. He didn't expect anyone to support him, even in high school. What happened . . . happened, and he seemed more than confident he could take care of himself."

Grigg, who is a Nevada State Trooper in Tonopah, came across Pokorney during Marine boot camp. They spoke only briefly, but long enough for Grigg to realize Fred Pokorney was driven into the Marines by the same focus he'd had in high school.

"He was far beyond my maturity level when I was going to school," he said. "Most kids tend to be carefree and not pay any attention to the kind of things Fred was dealing with, like work and responsibility. He was down to earth and hardworking. His work ethic was outstanding."

No one admired Fred Pokorney's determination more than Wade Lieseke. Until he was shot and critically wounded by a Utah prison escapee, the sheriff had not missed a single game in which Fred played football or basketball. The one contest he was unable to attend was the East-West Sertoma Classic in Reno, an All-Star game for high school seniors put together by the Sertoma Club of Reno. In a Las Vegas hospital, Lieseke lay recovering from the damage done by a bullet; a ripped diaphragm, torn lung, and ruptured spleen. When he got out of his patrol car, the flash of the convict's gun prompted Wade Lieseke's adrenalin to stir his combat instincts, and he fired several rounds, killing his attacker. The 1989 incident was later featured on a national, prime time television broadcast.

Many weeks later, after he had been released from the hospital, one of the people he depended on the most while his wife Suzy was at work, turned out to be Fred. Pokorney spent his first summer out of high school in Tonopah saving money from his two jobs to help pay for his freshman year in college and assisting Wade Lieseke in his recovery. Pokorney's goal of attending college and playing basketball had been achieved. After an injury during his freshman year, however, Pokorney did not return to the University of Nevada at Las Vegas. He stayed in Tonopah, working construction and the silver mines.

Wade Lieseke noticed Fred had begun talking about joining the military, in particular, the Marines.

"I just kept trying to talk him out of it," Lieseke said. "I wish to hell I had tried harder. I told him if he wanted to join up he should join the Air Force or the Navy, not the Army, and surely not the Marines. It's just too damned dangerous."

As he spoke, Wade Lieseke was having breakfast at a small casino on the north side of Tonopah. The road outside, Veterans' Memorial Highway, sloped north toward Reno, and then down from Tonopah's altitude of 6,100 feet. Behind the casino's restaurant, on a small plateau, desert wind blew dust across Logan Field; a modest patch of green where Fred Pokorney had run to glory in high school football.

Above the conversational clatter of the restaurant, the ping and rattle of slot machines were heard, even during the early morning hours. The air in the lobby was thick with the putrid tang of cigarettes and alcohol, as if small town desperation had become a stench. Lieseke's big hands curled around his coffee cup, and he looked out the window as he spoke, almost too softly to be understood.

"I said, 'Fred, my problem is that the Marines are always the first ones in there,' and he said, 'That is the tradition and the history.' And I told him, 'You also have the first opportunity to get killed.'"

Pokorney's determination served him well when he joined the Marines. On visits to Tonopah, Wade Lieseke became convinced that the young man, who had brought an additional, unexpected happiness into his home, was certain to become the first four-star Marine general who had not graduated from Annapolis. Fred Pokorney loved being a Marine. He was a part of an organization that appreciated and understood his kind of personal strength, the independence and will that men need to do great things. Fred had cultivated these characteristics within himself, and nothing pleased him more than being around people who valued what he had created.

He was home.

After commissioning as an officer, he was stationed at Camp Lejeune, North Carolina. Neither he nor his wife, Chelle, had ever been East. And once they had settled into the little beige house near the base, their first excursion to explore the East Coast was a trip for a Memorial Day visit to Arlington National Cemetery. Fred had always had a desire to stand in the sacred spot where American soldiers lay in honor. Chelle's grandfather, Air Force Colonel William Schulgen, who had served in World War II, was buried in Arlington, and they wanted to see his grave and offer their respects.

May 28, 2001, was also the first day for new President George W. Bush to deliver Memorial Day remarks at the national cemetery. After laying a wreath at the Tomb of the Unknowns, the president addressed a crowd spread beyond the seating capacity, standing among the tombstones and markers of the dead, listening, as their president tried to convey a context for the loss and sacrifice marked by rows of dead filling the hills along the Potomac River. Out of uniform that day, Fred Pokorney was erect, his chin up above the crowd, as his commander-in-chief spoke.

"It is not in our nature to seek out wars and conflicts," President Bush said. "But whenever they have come, when adversaries have left us no alternative, American men and women have stood ready to take the risks and to pay the ultimate price. People of the same caliber and the same character today fill the ranks of the Armed Forces of the United States. Any foe who might ever challenge our national resolve would be repeating the grave errors of defeated enemies."

Undoubtedly, Fred Pokorney believed his president was talking to him. He was ready. He loved what he was doing. Serving his country in the Marines was the greatest job anyone could ever have. Fred trusted his president. He knew if he ever got orders to go into combat, it was because America was at risk, and he was willing to put his own life up to protect his country. If a Marine cannot trust in his commander-in-chief, he cannot fight in combat. Fred Pokorney believed in America; its principles, its leadership, its unrelenting truths. And he had just heard the president make a solemn vow that America was not going to be seeking out any wars or conflicts. If war came, it was certain to be the result of another nation's aggression.

After the ceremony, Fred and Chelle lingered among the veterans. Many were wearing their combat decorations; gray and changed by death they had seen, the soldiers were, nonetheless, proud of their service. They had done what their country said needed to be done for freedom. Fred Pokorney spoke with many of the veterans. Hearing their stories made him feel a kinship, a connection to something holy. As he walked among the monuments, stood before the gravestones, and listened to the old soldiers, Fred Pokorney felt as though he were among his own kind.

"I want to be buried here someday," he told Chelle. "It's important. And you can be buried on top of me."

After the holiday, back at the base in North Carolina, life for the Pokorney's settled into the daily rituals of work and household. On September 11, 2001, however, Fred, Chelle, and Taylor's days together began to grow tense. America had been attacked, and Fred was a Marine. The consequences of those two facts were obvious, and needed no discussion in the Pokorney house. Months passed, and they heard the talk from Washington about Iraq, and aluminum tubes to build a reactor. Eventually, there was a report in the president's State of the Union speech that Saddam Hussein had tried to acquire uranium from an African country. Even when they attempted to avoid the newspapers and television newscasts, they still heard about Iraq giving assistance to terrorists, maybe even some of those who had attacked the World Trade Center and the Pentagon. The Pokorneys did not dissect the news. They simply knew what it all meant to Fred.

"We aren't real political people," Chelle Pokorney said. "Fred was just doing his duty. I do wish the country had agreed more going into it. I heard about most of this from my husband. Those people needed help, I guess. And we were there for that. I just hope they get whatever it was they wanted from us, freedom or whatever it was."

Back in Tonopah, however, the rhetoric of war was making Wade Lieseke sick with anger. Iraq looked like Vietnam without the trees. Americans would go in, fight and die, and then, ultimately, leave. Iraq was likely, in Lieseke's estimation, to return to the mess it was before the United States invaded. He'd seen it in Vietnam. Lieseke wasn't political as a young man, either. When the government said it needed soldiers to help stop the spread of communism, Wade Lieseke believed in the cause.

"What I know now is that it was all a lie," he said. "I mean, if you're gonna do that, then do it. We got a lot of guys killed, 60,000, and I'm counting the POWs and MIAs that were never heard from. Whether you wanna believe it or not, they're gone. That's over 60,000 killed."

Lieseke has scars on his body from wounds received in Vietnam, and there are others in his head that no one can see but him. He admits to being dark, too often depressed, thirty-three years after leaving Vietnam. There are memories he'd rather not have, the kind of experiences he hoped Fred would be able to avoid as a Marine. The experts call it post-traumatic stress disorder. Wade knows what he is dealing with, though, and often, it is just anger over the lies that sent him to war.

"If we are gonna let the place fall to communists, why in the hell didn't we do that in the first place?" he asked. "Why did all those U.S. soldiers die? After all these years, what really was the mission? What did you witness all of this death and destruction for? Why did you become a part of this death and destruction? If nothing was gonna change?"

Pretending that attacking Iraq was going to reduce the terrorist threat was just another government deception, as far as Wade Lieseke was concerned. More kids were going to be killed. Nothing was going to be accomplished. The president just needed a war to distract from all of his other problems. Washington leaders always made choices based on factors that had nothing to do with the people who would suffer.

"They've got no feeling or compassion or anything like that, when they make these decisions," Lieseke said, his voice raspy with anger. "They just don't care. Bush says, 'We know we're gonna suffer casualties.' What a cold statement to make. I know that my decision's gonna get a bunch of people killed, but, oh well. And people like that, I say screw you. They view our kids as cannon fodder. That's all. They just don't give a damn."

"Now, you're talking about the president?" he was asked.

"President on down, and all of these elitists he has making these decisions, like Dick Cheney, and the super fucking multimillionaires sending people into harm's way. Bush has never had a hard day. His children have never known hardship. But it's okay. Those aren't his thoughts when you are getting other peoples' kids killed. It's not a thought when they are getting other peoples' children killed. It's just not a thought."

Fred and Chelle Pokorney had different beliefs than Wade Lieseke. They were convinced Fred's service as a U.S. Marine was going to make a difference in the lives of oppressed Iraqis and maybe even stop terrorism. Fred Pokorney's convictions did not falter.

"Fred did believe in what he was doing," Chelle said. "And I never doubted my husband. Never doubted him as a Marine or as a man. He was one of the great ones. He so loved what he was doing. That's all I know how to say. Once you knew Fred, you just knew him, and you trusted him."

The big Marine, though, was human, and he had his own fears. On a February morning of 2003, Fred and Chelle drove through the Carolina pines to the buses, which were to take him and other Marines to ships bound for Iraq. He tried to be light-hearted, issuing Chelle her own set of orders, "Take care of Taylor and don't wreck the car." When they held each other to say goodbye at the base, Fred's broad frame was quivering. Chelle did not know if it was the chill air, or apprehension at what lay across the ocean. She said she had never seen her husband shake before. As he boarded the bus, she had the recognition of something awful, which she wanted to deny and push out of her mind.

"I did have this feeling," she said, "that I was never going to see him again."

The tanks had been ordered to move off on a rescue mission. Survivors of the 507th, a maintenance company, were under heavy Iraqi fire and armor was needed for their protection and evacuation. The tanks, however, were expected to be part of the plan to protect the amphibious assault vehicles of Charlie Company as they ran through Al Nasiriyah's ambush alley. Originally, all of the Marine companies were supposed to circumvent the city proper. But Bravo Company had bogged down in the mud to the east, and Alpha and Charlie suddenly got orders to take two bridges over the Saddam Canal on the north side of the city.

Sergeant William Schaefer of Charlie Company thought he had heard wrong.

"Say again," he said into his radio.

The orders were repeated. Schaefer had not been mistaken. He, like all of the other Marines in Charlie Company, was worried. They felt very vulnerable without the tanks. Their amphibious assault vehicles, known as "tracks," were made of heavy aluminum, and were susceptible to rocket propelled grenades and artillery attacks. The design of tracks, which was thirty years old, allowed for protective armor plating to be attached. But there was none available when the Marines arrived for preparations in Kuwait. The Pentagon, and the White House's plans for a light, cheap, fast-moving assault, was about to leave the men of Charlie Company unnecessarily exposed to their enemy. Circumstance was also conspiring against the Marines when the tanks were dispatched to rescue the 507th. The tank company had already performed its rescue operations and had returned to the rear for refueling. As it moved up ambush alley, Charlie Company passed burning U.S. and Iraqi vehicles left from the fight to save 507th's soldiers.

In one of the vehicles behind Schaefer, First Lieutenant Ben Reid and Second Lieutenant Fred Pokorney were dodging fire from the warren of buildings in Al Nasiriyah. Body parts of Iraqis were strewn across the road in front of the tracks. They saw no one in uniform. Women and teenagers were pointing weapons at the Americans. RPG rounds and machine gun fire poured in from the small structures lining the narrow streets. Pokorney had taken a flesh wound in the arm. The overwhelming diesel smell made the anxious breathing of the men inside their tracked vehicles even more labored and difficult.

After they crossed the bridges over the Saddam Canal, three miles through the city, the battle intensified when they dismounted from their tracks. Close air support appeared, and American A-10 Thunderbolts, the Warthog jets were dropping bombs on enemy locations while strafing other positions. An Iraqi RPG, however, hit close enough to Ben Reid and three of his men that two of them were instantly killed, and the third, Fred Pokorney, was laying immobile. Reid, who had been knocked into near unconsciousness, got up and discovered the two had fatal injuries. He did not turn over Pokorney, assuming he had suffered the same fate. But there were no external signs of massive, fatal trauma.

Before Reid went for help, he told one of his injured men, Jose Garibay, to keep everyone located in one spot. Reid began to run and an explosion, ten to fifteen feet in front of him, threw the young lieutenant into the air. When he landed, Ben Reid was staring at the dirt and saw a lot of blood dripping from his face onto the ground.

"I was scared," he said. "I thought that was it for me. I almost stayed where I was. I thought about it, anyway. But I got up and continued to run toward the track."

In the back of the track, Reid found two of his men, Elliot and Trevino, breaking out packs of ammo. He issued them orders to move to where Garibay and the rest of the wounded were waiting for assistance. They were to get the wounded to the battalion aid station south of the Euphrates River, back through ambush alley. Reid jumped out of the track, and looked to the north, trying to see the two mortar crews he had placed in that spot. They were gone. He had no idea where.

"I felt really alone," Reid said. "Then I looked south and saw some guys down by the canal in the prone."

Small arms fire and RPG rounds were filling the air around Reid. He decided to return to Garibay and the wounded troops and give them orders to retreat. Reid crouched as he ran down to the canal to tell Garibay a track was coming over to pick them up, and get everyone to the battalion aid station. His orders to Garibay were to load all of the wounded, no matter how much it hurt. Reid intended to find some help for Garibay and the injured men.

He moved in the direction of the Marines he had seen lying along the canal. An explosive thud of some kind knocked him backward, slightly. Reid said he didn't think anything of it. His gunnery sergeant and several other Marines were staying low, off of the elevated road, to avoid being hit by intensifying Iraqi fire. Reid, who must have seemed disoriented, and in shock, was pulled to the ground by Gunnery Sergeant Blackwell.

"See if my eye is still in my head," he asked Blackwell.

"Yeah, I think so. Looks like it," he was told. Initially, none of the troops recognized Reid. The Marines broke out their first aid kits and began to treat the lieutenant.

"I guess I started doing a sanity check on myself," Reid said. "I realized I had no Kevlar or gas mask, guess they had been blown off. I also had lost my maps and binos. Don't know what happened to those. I noticed right then they [Blackwell and other Marines] were worried about something."

The gunnery sergeant saw the A-10 first, according to Reid. The jet, designed for close combat support, made a strafing gun run along the canal and the elevated road, and opened up with its 30-millimeter cannon, which are capable of firing 3900 rounds per minute.

An American aircraft was firing on American Marines.

"It's the first time any of us have been in combat, sir," Ben Reid explained. "And remember, we don't train together [with Air Force]. They probably thought we were an enemy mechanized force. They probably saw our injured going south through the city, and assumed we were Iraqis. I'm not sure."

The A-10 had made other passes through the area, and Gunnery Sergeant Blackwell and the men gathered with him along the canal were very nervous. Even in his own battered state of consciousness, Reid was aware of that much. He saw the men had "kept their attention focused up in the air."

"I remember gunny [Gunnery Sergeant] being very worried about the Air Force support in the area," Reid recalled.

As the plane made its run, Reid looked in the direction of where he had left his injured troops. They did not get hit by the A-10's hail of cannon fire because they were gone, evacuated, he hoped, to an aid station. But Fred Pokorney, who might have still been alive, and the two others who had been killed in action, were lying out in the open.

"Fred was not put on a track," Reid explained. "He was still on the ground, and I assume still up in that area. I'm not saying he got hit by the A-10. I don't know, and I don't know if he was still alive or not."

One thing Reid did know, however, when he had looked at Pokorney before running for assistance, was that he did not see any massive trauma to the Marine's body. At least two published reports suggested Pokorney had been hit in the chest by a rocket propelled grenade. If so, Reid was certain to have seen extensive physical damage to Pokorney. But he did not. Ultimately, Pokorney's wounds were determined to be so traumatic that his family did not view his body. Much of his torso was reportedly gone, as was an arm, and part of his face and head. These are the types of massive wounds Reid was certain to have noticed, if they had happened when the RPG round landed, apparently injuring Pokorney, and killing two others. Since Pokorney showed no visible external wounds when Reid saw him after the RPG explosion, he might have still been alive. He was almost certainly riddled with 30-millimeter bullets from the A-10 as he lay on the ground. Either way, Fred Pokorney, who had put himself at risk to call in artillery rounds on a radio with poor reception, in a defective military communications network, was now killed in action.

"I saw the A-10 come in from the north to the south," Reid explained. "And I saw it fire up the east side of the road, about 85 meters from where I was with the gunny. I remember seeing the big, green tracers skipping off some of the parked tracks. The A-10 also dropped a bomb on a building several hundred meters to the east of us."

Reid stumbled to the other side of the road and was placed inside of a track for treatment of his injuries. A bullet entrance wound, but no exit, was visible in his shoulder. Reid had no memory of being shot. Captain Dan Wittnam stuck his head in the track where Reid was being bandaged, and ordered the Marines to get back on the east side of the road. Wittnam, along with another Marine, set up with the M249 Squad Automatic Weapons, and the wounded stumbled between their suppressing fire to reach safety. Reid, who said he had "a rough time seeing and was pretty tired," was helped across the road by Corporal Pedersen. Another amphibious track arrived and Reid was placed in the back with a number of other injured Marines.

All of the Marines were in shock from being shot at by their own Air Force.

Wittnam, a 33-year-old who was a Charlie Company commander, said, "The earth went black from dirt being kicked up. And a feeling of absolute, utter horror and disbelief."

The A-10, though, had not completed its mission. Corporal Jared Martin heard the jet and watched it approach.

"He was low. He was coming right toward us. The next thing I know, I'm feeling a lot of heat in my back."

Martin's right hand and left knee began bleeding. He had a piece of shrapnel stuck below an eye, and his fingers didn't feel right, as if they were "just dangling."

Martin, and Lance Corporal Edward Castleberry, was not far from Lance Corporal David Fribley, who was next to his track.

"I'm turning around screaming at him, telling him to get in," said Castleberry, who was the driver of the track. "He was trying to climb in, he's got one arm trying to get in, and he just takes a huge round directly through his chest, and it blew out his whole back."

Twenty-six-year-old Lance Corporal David Fribley was killed instantly. Flesh and viscera from the fallen Marine flew onto Jared Martin's clothing.

"I wore what was inside of his body on my gear for a couple of days," Martin said.

Finally, the tanks that had been dispatched to rescue soldiers of the 507th Maintenance Company returned to the north bridge over the Saddam Canal and began firing their 120-millimeter cannons at the Iraqis. Malfunctioning pumps had delayed their refueling, which was cut short when word came that Charlie Company was pinned down in a firefight. The armored tanks with their big guns, the weapons that were originally supposed to protect Alpha and Charlie Companies as they took the bridges over the Saddam Canal, had, at least, showed up to help some of them escape with their lives.

The Iraqi attack was suppressed, and helicopters were allowed into the area to medevac the wounded. Lieutenant Ben Reid, who had been lying in the back of a track for thirty minutes and talking to other injured soldiers, vaguely remembered being loaded onto a CH-46, the giant twin rotor helicopter that took him back to a shock trauma hospital in Jalibah. The bodies of the dead, including Lieutenant Fred Pokorney's, were removed after the wounded.

Pokorney's father, Wade Lieseke, will tremble with anger all of his life.

"I'm not an emotional person on a lot of things," he said. "But this is just such total bullshit. This is just such a horrible waste, and it didn't need to happen, and that's the frustration of this. He's a young man who didn't need to die. We didn't need to waste all of his talents on fuckin' Iraq, and he's blown to bits.

"But that's the worst memory, knowing how he died. This beautiful person that we knew, was blown apart, literally blown apart, and for what? He died that horrible death and left all these things behind; his beautiful daughter, his beautiful wife, a life that would have been nothing but success. They'd had a good life, and now there's nothing."

Lieseke snapped his fingers.

"And now it's over."

Everything had ended for Fred Pokorney, and brutally. But for his family, the horror of George W. Bush's war was just beginning.

"Fred died a hero," Wade Lieseke said. "But he's still dead."

5

PIONEERS OF A
WARLESS WORLD

One owes respect to the living; but to the dead one owes nothing but the truth.

Voltaire

An eighteen-vehicle convoy does not easily make a U-turn. After Captain Troy King had passed the word to all of his soldiers to "lock and load" their weapons, he ordered the string of vehicles to head back through the city they had just left. Iraqi civilians had been tracking the 507th Maintenance Company's convoy as it drove north, out of Al Nasiriyah, and King must have begun to worry about attack. His soldiers were properly armed, each with 210 rounds for their M-16s, a thousand rounds had been acquisitioned for the M-249 Squad Automatic Weapon, and 45 rounds for an M-9.

But King had made a mistake.

The 507th had been equipped with what are known as "crew served" weapons, larger guns for attacking a heavily armored enemy.

These included the .50-caliber machine gun and a 40-millimeter MK-19, but also hand grenades, pyrotechnics, and AT-4 anti-tank weapons. Possibly, because they did not expect to be passing through hostile territory, Captain King had not distributed the more lethal weapons and ammunition to the troops of the 507th. According to the Army's draft report on the incident, King had ordered pyrotechnics, hand grenades, and the AT-4 anti-tank weapons "consolidated and secured," which meant they were located in one vehicle. This decision was to contribute to the deadliness of what happened to the convoy.

Darrell Cortez, a Fort Bliss soldier who considered James Kiehl of the 507th his best friend, was baffled by the fact that those weapons were not in the hands of the troops.

"No soldier was issued grenades or rockets," Cortez said. "Those, at that point, were still secured. I've not seen a report as to why that was the case. I don't know whose decision it was to keep them locked. I don't know if it was Captain King or someone higher up who decided, at this time, we will not need these armaments."

Whoever it was, they turned out to be very wrong.

As the convoy began to make a loop to return in the direction opposite of what it had been traveling, a ten-ton wrecker ran out of fuel, and there was no longer any reserve fuel in the tanker truck accompanying the 507th because the company had been moving for three straight days. King ordered all vehicles to stop; the wrecker was refueled using five-gallon cans, emergency fuel carried on each truck and Humvee. Iraqis in personal vehicles, and talking on cell phones, watched the refueling from a relatively close distance for the next forty minutes. A few of them drove past the stopped Americans.

Finally, refueled, the 507th headed back to the south, and turned left at Highway 16. First Sergeant Robert Dowdy, who was in the last vehicle, radioed Captain King to report they were beginning to take small arms fire. King ordered all trucks and Humvees in the line to accelerate, as trained, to get out of the ambush. At this point the convoy began to break into smaller groups because of the varying size and acceleration rates of the vehicles. In the front of the column,

Captain King was racing eastward to lead the 507th out of the gun-fire. Probably because of a high rate of speed, or simple confusion caused by combat, King missed the intersection with Highway 7/8, where he was to take the convoy back to the south.

Sergeant Dowdy radioed his commander to inform him he had passed the critical turn. In the middle of the string of big trucks, Specialist First Class Anthony Pierce told his driver, Specialist Tim-othy Johnson, to speed up so they could catch Captain King and give him directions back to the intersection. By the time this had happened, all of the vehicles had passed the turnoff to Highway 7/8, and the fierceness of Iraqi fire on the passing column began to build.

Specialist James Kiehl of Comfort, Texas, sat in the passenger seat of a slow, five-ton truck with a trailer, being driven by Special-ist Jamaal Addison. Bullets pinging off the side were hardly heard over the noise of the straining engine. Kiehl, like all the others in the 507th, had not expected this kind of danger. Soldiers in the maintenance company had told their families not to worry about them because they were "in the rear with the gear." Kiehl and Addi-son had to be wondering where they were going and what was hap-pening. The limited supply of walkie-talkie radios and batteries left most of the soldiers without information on convoy movement. But Kiehl knew enough. He was in combat now, a completely unex-pected assault, and neither he, nor most of the others in the 507th, were really prepared to fight.

"These people were technicians, mechanics," Kiehl's father Randy explained. "Did you ever hear them say the words 'combat specialists'?"

They were isolated, and alone. No combat infantry had been pro-vided for the maintenance soldiers who, by design, were certain to be left behind as the entire war machine hurried toward Baghdad. Mili-tary planners apparently believed that by the time the maintenance crews passed through an area that it would have been secured by the army advancing in front. The decision not to attach a combat unit may have also been a result of cost-saving pressures from Defense Secretary Donald Rumsfeld, who envisioned Iraqis greeting U.S.

troops as their liberators. Instead, James Kiehl and the rest of the 507th were being met with a wall of gunfire.

Back in Des Moines, Iowa, Kiehl's wife, Jill, who was seven months pregnant with the couple's first son, was already beginning to confront the possibility that the president may have misled the nation into an unnecessary war. Her husband, however, had no choice but to serve, even if his unit was exposed by bad planning, nor did it matter that the president may have been less than truthful about the reasons for invading Iraq.

"It's his commander-in-chief. It's his head boss," Jill Kiehl explained. "You don't question what he said. You just do it, whether you like it or not, for personal reasons. If it is true that a lot of the evidence that they based the war on was made up, it's gonna upset me a lot. All of this could have been prevented and I could have had a normal life with my husband."

As the lead vehicles began to pull away, a five-ton tractor trailer became disabled, most likely by Iraqi weapons fire. A private, Brandon Sloan, was driving and Sergeant Donald Walters was his passenger. They were being followed by a truck pulling a water tank. While under fire, the two soldiers in the trailing vehicle, Private First Class Patrick Miller and Sergeant James Riley pulled up alongside of Sloan's truck and executed a "moving combat pickup" of Sloan. Walters, on the far side, did not get into the rescue vehicle, and the U.S. military has no definitive information about his fate.

The Army's draft report only added mystery to that part of the 507th's story:

> It is unclear whether Sgt. Walters was picked up by others in the convoy or remained in the area of the disabled tractor-trailer. There is some information to suggest that a U.S. soldier, that [sic] could have been Walters, fought his way south of Highway 16 toward a canal and was killed in action. Sgt. Walters was, in fact, killed at some point during this portion of the attack. The circumstances of his death cannot be conclusively determined by available information.

Still taking fire as they moved eastward, Captain King appeared to be searching for a flat, open space along the highway, where the big rigs could be turned around. The convoy had to travel three kilometers past the missed intersection before there was enough room to execute a U-turn. A wrecker, which was pulling a five-ton supply truck, very quickly got stuck in the sand. George Buggs and Edward Anguiano, the wrecker crew who had helped the 507th retrieve some of its trapped trucks a day earlier, were left behind as the rest of the convoy made an arcing turn and headed back to the west.

"This is where we start splitting up into different groups," explained Sergeant James Riley, a thirty-one-year-old machinist. "Because you can't afford to sit there and wait while somebody else turns around. No, you don't do that."

First Sergeant Robert Dowdy, at the tail end of the column, had his Humvee pull up next to the stuck wrecker, and Buggs and Anguiano jumped in. Privates Lori Piestewa and Jessica Lynch were also in Dowdy's vehicle. Piestewa, who was driving for Dowdy, and Lynch had been traveling in the supply truck being towed by Buggs and Aguiano before it had become disabled. Dowdy keyed his radio and told Captain King he had picked up the two men. Incoming fire was bristling up and down the sides of their vehicles. Dowdy urged King to get the convoy out of the city as fast as possible. Out the back of the Humvee, either Buggs or Anguiano, Dowdy wasn't sure which one, had picked up the M-249 Squad Automatic Weapon and began returning fire at the Iraqis.

King was down to fifteen vehicles, and with bullets and tires kicking up dust, there was increasing confusion. The differing speeds with which the big trucks and smaller Humvees had turned around and their varying acceleration rates had caused large gaps to appear in the convoy. The distance between them and the rest of the convoy was expanding very quickly for Joe Hudson and Johnny Mata, who were driving the 507th's remaining wrecker and towing a giant tractor-trailer rig. They had too much weight and not enough horsepower to close ranks with the rest of the column. Forty-five miles per hour was about their maximum speed.

Just a few months earlier, Johnny Mata had moved his wife and their two children into their first new home. Built on the morning side of the Franklin Mountains in El Paso, the Matas were still unpacking boxes when Johnny, a chief warrant officer, got his orders to Kuwait, and then onto Iraq. In front of him, Mata saw the convoy was breaking into three groups because of the discrepancies in size and speed of the trucks and Humvees. There was nothing to do but for him and Hudson to go as fast as possible and hope the fifteen tons of steel and rubber they were driving might keep up.

But they did not.

When Nancili Mata, Johnny's wife, was briefed by the Army about what happened to the 507th, she was astonished to learn her husband had no way to speak with the soldiers in the other vehicles who were outrunning his rig.

"Those devices, they didn't have enough," she said. "They only had five, the walkie-talkies. The soldiers went out and bought some extras out of their own pockets. They told us that at the briefing." She turned her palms upward, and lowered her chin, angry at the absurdity of American soldiers using their own modest earnings to equip themselves for war.

"I can't remember, but they had five in total for the whole 507th, and the soldiers themselves went and bought some more, and that was one of the mistakes they were going to correct, and they said it themselves, they were going to correct it."

Out front, Captain King and his driver, Private Dale Nace, led two of the 507th's trucks on a dangerous run back down through the heart of Al Nasiriyah. Behind King's Humvee was a five-ton tractor trailer with Sergeant Joel Petrik and Specialist Nicholas Peterson. Specialist Timothy Johnson and Specialist First Class Anthony Pierce were in the next vehicle back, a five-ton truck with an attached trailer. Most of the Iraqi fire they received was coming from the west side of the road, and Peterson, Pierce, and King were returning fire out the passenger side of their vehicles. Cars and debris had been positioned in the middle of the road to slow the

Americans, and make them easier targets. Nace, Petrik, and Johnson drove with one hand through the obstacles, while shooting out the window with their M-16s, when they were able to get their guns to function.

Several times, the soldiers found themselves unarmed when their weapons jammed. The Army report blames the malfunction of the M-16s on "inadequate individual maintenance in a desert environment." This was possible. The 507th was a maintenance company, and the soldiers very likely did not expect to see combat action. However, there had not been more than a few minutes since they had crossed the Iraqi border during which they might have taken a break to clean a weapon, and their hasty run through the Iraqi deserts had stirred up constant clouds of sand and dust. By the time their weapons failed, the troops in the 507th had been on the move for three consecutive days. They might have reasonably complained that they had been equipped with weapons by their commanders that were not meant to function in a desert battle.

Captain King and his small group made it back through Al Nasiriyah without injuries. South of the intersections of Highways 8 and 7/8, King came upon tanks from Task Force Tarawa of the U.S. Marines 8th Tank Battalion. He told them the 507th had been split up in an ambush, and most of his soldiers were under deadly Iraqi fire. The Marines immediately moved their heavily armored tanks northward on Highway 8 to rescue the 507th. Unfortunately, those same tanks were originally supposed to provide the armored protection for the Marine's Alpha and Charlie Companies in their mission to take the two bridges on the north side of Al Nasiriyah, which crossed the Saddam Canal. The two Marine companies, later that morning, faced a brutal assault from the Iraqis, and there were no tanks to assist them in the battle.

Before the tanks had reached them, enemy fire appeared to dramatically increase on the second group of vehicles. The three tractor trailers, one large fuel truck, and a Humvee with a trailer, were twisting and weaving their way through the Iraqi obstacle course on

Al Nasiriyah's main street. Numerous rocket-propelled grenades and unceasing small arms fire was now coming in a consistent volley from both sides of the road. In one of the tractor trailers, Corporal Damien Luten jumped up to man the 507th's only .50-caliber machine gun, mounted on top of the truck's cabin.

The weapon failed.

"I was up there, and I think of it now, kind of thinking of the movie *The Matrix*," he said. "And you see the bullets flying. And it, it seems like it's slow motion. The bullets were flying. I can actually see them, as they pass me, uh, over my head, back in front of the vehicle. It seemed like they were going that slow."

Without the protection of the larger gun, Luten reached down for his M-16, and was shot in the knee. Trying to fire the automatic weapon, Luten discovered it jammed. The weapon, he said, had been cleaned every time the convoy had stopped. Luten, though, never fired either his M-16 or the larger machine gun. Both had failed him in combat. Private First Class Marcus Dubois pushed the bob-tailed rig forward, sweeping between old cars and truck tires strewn across the road. At one point, the Iraqis had pushed a bus in front of the Americans.

Ahead of Dubois, a similar truck took numerous hits from the Iraqis and rumbled to a stop in the oppressive gunfire. Specialist Jun Zhang, who had been driving, jumped out and ran back to climb onboard Luten and Dubois' rig. Curtis Campbell, the sergeant who had been riding with Zhang, grabbed Zhang's M-16, and struggled with the weapon, trying to get it to fire. He was shot in the hip and went down briefly, before a Humvee crew snatched him from the street. Staff Sergeant Tarik Jackson, inside the Humvee, had already been wounded as he returned fire, and he suffered further injuries while rescuing Campbell. The Humvee, with a man identified by the Army only as "CW3 Nash" at the wheel, was disabled by Iraqi fire not far from where it had stopped to pluck Campbell from potentially deadly Iraqi attacks.

With Nash, Jackson, and Campbell stranded in the Humvee behind them, Zhang, Dubois, and Luten turned around in the midst of the firefight. They had crossed the Euphrates River Bridge, and a few kilometers away the wavy silhouette of Captain King's parked Humvee and two trucks were visible. The three men were determined, being that close to safety, they were not going to leave behind the other three soldiers in the disabled Humvee. As they struggled out of their doors, Matthew Rose, the supply officer and a father of six children, was making a serpentine run, taking his truck through RPGs, debris, and other large obstacles. Corporal Francis Carista, shooting out the passenger window with an M-16, was struck in the heel by a piece of shrapnel. Rose's rig, battered by the assault, sputtered to a stop near the Humvee, where the other six soldiers had gathered to seek protection.

"My vehicle was being hit. It was blowing smoke everywhere, and at least one of my tires was flat. I didn't expect to be in that position," Rose said. "Proper military doctrine says that if you're in an ambush, drive out of the ambush. I just prayed and drove. I kept saying, 'Lord, I don't want to die. I want to see my kids.'"

Miraculously, the gargantuan fuel truck driven by Private First Class Adam Elliot also made it through ambush alley. James Grubb, a specialist, had been struggling to return fire out the tanker's window with his jammed M-16 and was wounded in both arms by the time the fuel truck lumbered up next to the other soldiers of the 507th, just south of the Euphrates River Bridge. After his truck had crossed the river, Rose, who had once served as an Army medic, began to lead the other medically trained soldiers in treating the seriously wounded. Limping and dragging each other, the soldiers made it into a ditch as Iraqis directed more fire at them from behind sand berms and nondescript buildings.

"When the mortar fire started to get closer," Rose explained, "We tried to get all the people off the road. Corporal Luten couldn't walk, so I tried to carry him but couldn't, so I actually dragged him from the road. I was dragging him when the Marines arrived."

Down off the road, as they waited, the ten soldiers of the 507th heard the immediately recognizable clanging sound of approaching tanks. Earlier in the day, they had passed Iraqi T-55 tanks on the side of the road, their turrets facing away, and they suddenly feared those tanks were rolling up to end their lives. Instead, they turned out to be the Marines from Task Force Tarawa, who rotated their turrets in the direction of a few buildings where Iraqi fire had been concentrated. After those structures were blown up by the tanks, the Marines were able to evacuate the 507th's wounded, but not without suffering a few of their own men being killed.

At the rear of the 507th convoy, however, things were much worse.

The soldiers driving the larger trucks had experienced a great deal of difficulty in executing the final U-turn and had slipped well behind the two groups leading the convoy. As Specialists Edgar Hernandez and Shoshana Johnson approached the intersection to take them back south through Al Nasiriyah, their five-ton tractor-trailer came under heavy Iraqi fire. The Iraqis had put a truck in the road to block passage, and Hernandez, who was driving, swerved to go around it and lost control of his rig when he veered to the right and went off the road. Hernandez had been ducking beneath the dashboard to avoid flying bullets, and apparently was unable to prevent jackknifing his truck, leaving the trailer protruding into the road.

"I got stuck in the mud," he said.

First Sergeant Robert Dowdy, who had remained with the slower trucks to lead them back to safety, ordered his driver to race ahead and catch the vehicle carrying Private First Class Patrick Miller and Sergeant James Riley. Over his radio, Dowdy called out to Miller to "increase speed and keep moving." Dowdy had his driver, Private First Class Lori Piestewa, push their Humvee to near maximum speed as every enemy gun along the road appeared to be tracking their path.

Joseph Hudson, in the wrecker with Johnny Mata, saw the Humvee "fly past."

"Machine gun fire," he remembered. "There were people firing at the Humvee. And there were, everywhere you looked, somebody was firing. There was return fire from the Humvee, and they just disappeared into the distance."

According to Miller, the Iraqis had set up an ambush on the corner of the highway's intersection, and they were "unloading on anything that turned at their corner." Somewhere, in one of the trucks, was the weaponry that might have ended the ambush. Dowdy had to be wondering why the pyrotechnics, rocket-propelled grenades, and the anti-tank weapons had been "consolidated and secured." If he'd had the heavy ordnance, he and the soldiers at the back of the convoy might have been able to take out the guns being leveled at their trucks. But they had no access to those weapons, and their best hope for survival was to run. The Army's report of the incident did not address this controversial question of weapons consolidation.

Moments later, the Humvee, in which Dowdy was riding with four other soldiers, was hit by Iraqi weapons fire and slammed into the back of Hernandez' stalled tractor-trailer at a high rate of speed. The impact was loud and forceful, and was another indication to the young soldier that he might not live much longer. Hernandez, who'd only barely worked up the courage, before he left for the war, to ask his eighteen-year-old high school sweetheart to "be his girlfriend," was facing death.

"There was one point where I just gave up," he said. "I thought, 'This is where I am going to die.' I remember during the fight, I was holding my arm because I got shot and my weapon got jammed. That's when I thought I was going to die. I thought, 'What will my parents say after they find out I'm dead?' In those last minutes, I just gave up. I was praying."

The jolt of the Humvee colliding with his truck's trailer interrupted Hernandez' contemplation of his mortality.

"And all of a sudden," he said, "Somebody hit us from behind. And the whole truck moved. I turned back, and then I saw the Humvee."

Dowdy's Humvee, with Lori Piestewa at the wheel, Jessica Lynch, George Buggs, and Edward Anguiano as passengers, was crushed beneath the trailer. Buggs and Anguiano were, essentially, victims of their own kindness. They had remained behind their own group, the 3rd Forward Support Battalion, to help pull the 507th's stranded trucks out of the sand a few days earlier. The Army was unable to provide details of how they died, but, if they had not assisted the 507th, they would have never ended up in the deadly ambush and collision that took their lives.

Edgar Hernandez and Shoshana Johnson saw that there was "no movement whatsoever" by any of the people inside of the Humvee. Johnson, who was later captured by the Iraqis, said she felt "heartbreak 'cause you just knew that they were all gone."

Still out on the road, Joe Hudson and Johnny Mata were pushing through the fog of bullets and rocket-propelled grenades (RPGs), their truck becoming more and more debilitated by Iraqi guns. Mata, trying to make his jammed M-16 work, was attempting to return fire from his position in the passenger seat, while Hudson struggled to stay on the road. He wanted to get the SAW, the Belgian-made M-249, to work, hoping he might shoot as he drove. This weapon also failed to operate. Sometime during their scramble, Mata stopped firing, though Hudson was unable to say when the Chief Warrant Officer was killed. He was too busy trying to get them out of the death trap.

"At this point," he said, "I probably had four of my eight tires shot out by that time. There's just smoke just flying everywhere, rubber flying everywhere."

Fairly quickly, Hernandez' and Mata's big rig came to a full stop. The Iraqis quit firing, walked up, opened the door of the truck, and pulled out Hernandez, taking him prisoner. Johnny Villareal Mata, whose wife, sixteen-year-old son and seven-year-old daughter were in El Paso settling into their new home, had been killed in the combat service he had sought.

His family was uncertain exactly how Mata had died.

"After he got shot in the leg," Mata's wife, Nancili said, "They told me he got shot in the back of the head, and like in the back of one of the shoulders, and a lot of the shrapnel. And the autopsy report has a lot more detail that I really don't understand about the neck and the head."

Patrick Miller, James Riley, and Brandon Sloan found themselves riding in the last vehicle at the back of convoy, and they were taking the heaviest fire. Using the dashboard to protect himself, Miller popped his head up, from time to time, to make sure he was still on the road. Bullets were bouncing off the hood, the persistent sound of the attack filling the cabin of the truck.

"Just pop, pop, pop, pop," Miller said. "And I saw one guy jump out in the road and aim at me. And I ended up hitting him."

The transmission on his rig, though, was shot out, and the truck ground to a halt. Sloan, killed by Iraqi fire, was left behind in the cab of the truck as Miller and Riley ran through the rain of bullets to get to the wrecked Humvee and tractor trailer, about four hundred yards distant.

When they arrived at the crashed Humvee, Riley reached into the wreckage in an effort to recover Dowdy's M-16, hoping to get his hands on a functional weapon. Miller, however, was trying to determine if any of the five members of the 507th inside the Humvee had survived the accident. He leaned into the crumpled vehicle.

"Is anyone alive?" he screamed above the din of the battle. "Is anybody alive?"

There was no answer. Jessica Lynch's foot was twitching, but Miller assumed it was nothing more than the reaction of nerves after death.

Riley's M-16, meanwhile, was not working, and his survival, as well as the soldiers still alive, depended on a weapon. Unable to free Dowdy's gun from the wreckage, Riley got M-16s from Johnson and Hernandez, who were both wounded, and he tried to shoot back at the enemy.

"At this point," Riley said, "The weapons are jamming up. They're, uh, we're experiencing some malfunctions. You could hear the bullets winging by your head and impacting on the concrete around us."

Without useful weapons, Miller ran off to try and commandeer an Iraqi truck to get them away from the ambush. From beneath the crashed Humvee, Riley, seeking protection with Johnson and Hernandez, tried to provide covering fire for Miller. The Iraqis were becoming braver, moving into the open, and stepped up the level of their assault on the stranded Americans.

"Trying to take cover and taking fire from RPGs, which are rocket-propelled-grenades," Riley recalled in a nationally televised interview. "Some, I don't know what they were, an improvised explosive, like a great big pipe bomb. 'Cause you could hear it hit the asphalt and go, dig, dig, boom, as it blew up."

Miller was unable to reach the Iraqi truck. According to the Army's investigation of the incident, Miller found a sand berm above the road and began to single-handedly take on the Iraqis with his faltering M-16.

"I seen [sic] a group of Iraqis setting up a mortar pit," he said. "And as one of them tried to load the round into the tube, I shot him and he fell over and he dropped the round. They did that like about five or six more times. And never got the round loaded."

Undoubtedly, Miller's actions affected whether the other three soldiers remained alive. A well-placed mortar round on the wrecked Humvee and tractor-trailer was certain to kill Riley, Johnson, and Hernandez. After he had taken the mortar out of combat, Miller turned around to shoot at an Iraqi running past carrying an AK-47 automatic weapon. By the time he turned back in the direction of the mortar, he found himself surrounded by Iraqis, who then gang tackled him. (Miller was awarded the Silver Star for his heroic actions during the ambush.)

Riley, in the refuge of the wreckage with Johnson and Hernandez, also knew there was no point in further resistance.

"None of the weapons were functioning," he explained. "I've got two wounded, Miller's already been surrounded and captured, and they've got us totally in . . . pretty much encircled and pouring fire in. So the choice was taken away . . . that's part of the code of conduct. You resist until you no longer have the means to resist, and at that point we didn't have the means to resist. It was a choice of die now or die later."

The Iraqis removed the dead and wounded Americans from the crumpled Humvee. Lori Piestewa and Jessica Lynch were still alive. They were later given medical treatment, and Lynch survived. Piestewa, however, became the first Native American woman in history to die in combat under the U.S. flag. In this new U.S. Army, women had earned the privilege of serving alongside men, and firing their faulty guns out windows at the enemy in combat, even if they had ended up there inadvertently. They had also earned the right to die while fighting.

When Riley, Johnson, Hernandez, Miller, Piestewa, and Lynch were all being taken prisoners of war, another 507th tractor trailer and a five-ton truck had almost reached the edge of Al Nasiriyah. The Army's report said Howard Johnson and Ruben Estrella-Soto, and Jamaal Addison and James Kiehl had "maneuvered several miles under fire."

As the guns hammered at the side of his truck, Kiehl probably did not have time to think about a light-hearted request he had made of Captain King's wife before he left for Iraq. According to Cynthia King, James Kiehl was concentrating on his unborn child before he deployed to the Persian Gulf.

"He came up to me one day," she said. "And he said, 'Mrs. King, Mrs. King, would you put in a good word for me and ask your husband to move me to rear detachment until my wife has the baby and I promise to go the next time?' He was half joking and half serious, but we knew it wasn't going to happen. But he had to try."

At the intersection of Highways 8 and 7/8, where Captain Troy King had first lost his way, Addison and Kiehl's truck had overturned. Evidence indicated it was hit by "either direct or indirect fire." Just south of where the five-ton truck was upturned, Johnson and Estrella-Soto's rig had come to rest. Structural damage to their tractor-trailer looked like it had come from colliding with the barrel of an Iraqi tank. Kiehl, Addison, Johnson, and Estrella-Soto were all dead. The U.S. military has said it has no real details on their deaths.

As a result, Estrella-Soto's mother, Amalia, refused to believe her son was dead.

"The Estrella-Soto family is very angry with the military," said Laura Cruz, a reporter for the *El Paso Times*. "They despise it, actually, because from their perspective, they still don't know what happened to their son. The military had told her, 'We have your son's body but we can't return him right away because we are missing a piece of it.' So, she said they told her to have a closed casket, and she signed paperwork saying, 'I will not see my son's body.' So, she got the casket, and ever since then, she's been absolutely hysterical. She never got to see him, and because of that, she thinks he's still alive. She never got to see the body."

The Army's report of what happened to the 507th states, "fatigue, stress, the asymmetric nature of the threat, and the environment contributed to the events leading up to and during this attack." The report concludes, "every soldier performed honorably and each did his or her duty."

At Fort Bliss in El Paso, the Army's report of what happened to the 507th was not given much credibility by soldiers. All of them were afraid to criticize it publicly, but several dismissed its findings.

"Soldiers that are in 552nd and 507th know what happened," one Fort Bliss junior officer said, "and they look at the report, and go, 'yeah, whatever.' I think the ones that are there they see the discrepancy, and they know what happened. They just let it go. Because they have to. They work for the United States government, and there are channels to take it all up in."

"But they don't," he was asked. "Even though they don't buy into the report?"

"No."

"Is that because if you take it up through official channels, you bring attention to yourself?"

"Absolutely."

James Kiehl's wife, Jill, who was pregnant with the couple's first child when he died, had to deal with her own anger caused by her husband being unable to protect himself because of all the jammed up M-16s identified in the report. She refused to accept the Army's explanation that the soldiers of the 507th were at fault because they did not properly clean and maintain their weapons.

"They just said because of the sandstorms and everything, that's why they were jamming, and I don't know if they had time to clean them, or if they did clean them, because the location they were at was all sand, and it was impossible to keep them from jamming. They also had to have time to do that, if they are keeping them busy with all of this other stuff, when are they gonna find time to do that, while they are sleeping?"

In his hometown of Comfort, Texas, Kiehl was one of six young people who were serving in the war with Iraq. His high school basketball coach, Colin Toot, said the giant Kiehl was the "kind of kid who was more interested in protecting the girls in his class than he was in dating them." His protective instinct, Kiehl's friends said, was also a part of the undercurrent that led him to serve in the military, and guided him during the war. Kiehl, of course, will never know his son's face, or name, and the boy will grow up staring at pictures and monuments, wondering about his father, knowing him only as an abstraction, rather than a large, comforting, physical presence. Nathaniel Ethan Kiehl was born just weeks after his father had been killed in a war.

James Kiehl had told his own father, Randy, he believed in the fight against Saddam Hussein. James had said he did not want to raise his own child in a world where people have to worry about terrorism. He believed in President George W. Bush's explanations for the war, and, before he died, he made sure the world knew that he also believed in Christianity, and that Jesus Christ was the son of God, come to save him.

On a country road across the highway from the school where James Kiehl played basketball, his father Randy sat at a table in his home. An all-night production manager of a bakery, Kiehl had raised his son to strive for importance and contribution. Although he knew James believed in the president's call for the war, Randy Kiehl was beginning to wonder about the countless questions suddenly being raised about the Bush administration's politics. Raw from the loss of his only child in a war of uncertain purpose, he placed his faith in higher powers than the White House.

"God has a reason," he said. "We may not like it. We may not agree with it. But in the bigger scheme of God's plans, there is a reason he took James home. It's just like his being baptized eleven days before the ambush. 'Cause God made him ready."

And softly, Randy Kiehl began to cry.

6

THAT AWFUL POWER

If you don't want to work, become a reporter. That awful power, the public opinion of the nation, was created by a horde of self-complacent simpletons, who failed at ditch digging and shoe making, and fetched up in journalism on their way to the poorhouse.

Mark Twain, Connecticut Evening Dinner Club, 1881

Judith Miller, of the *New York Times*, stood at a distance. A man in "nondescript clothing," wearing a blue baseball cap, emerged from a military vehicle, and walked into the Iraqi desert. As he pointed to the ground in several locations, the man was watched by American soldiers of the Mobile Exploitation Team Alpha (MET Alpha). According to Miller, the unnamed individual was an Iraqi scientist with more than a decade of experience in Saddam Hussein's chemical and biological weapons programs. Supposedly, he was showing the U.S. troops where he had buried deadly compounds and other agents.

Three days later, Miller, in a front page story for the U.S.'s most influential newspaper, wrote a fourteen hundred word story entitled

"AFTEREFFECTS: PROHIBITED WEAPONS; Illicit Arms Kept Till Eve of War, an Iraqi Scientist Is Said to Assert." In her lead paragraph, Miller said that she and the MET Alpha team members had discovered the proof of weapons of mass destruction (WMD), a Bush administration argument for invading Iraq.

"A scientist who claims to have worked in Iraq's chemical weapons program for more than a decade," Miller wrote, "has told an American military team that Iraq destroyed chemical weapons and biological warfare equipment only days before the war began, members of the team said."

Based on what the MET Alpha team had related to Miller, she reported that the scientist had led them to the site south of Baghdad because it was where he had buried evidence of an illicit weapons program. Her story also included the mysterious scientist's charges that Hussein had transferred illegal weapons to Syria and was cooperating with Al Qaeda. She suggested that the discovery supported charges from the White House that Iraq was developing such weapons and had lied about it to the United Nations. Miller also quoted the commanding officer of the 101st Airborne Division, Major General David Petraeus, who said the findings were likely the "major discovery" of the war, and of "incalculable value."

The story did not reveal, however, if Judith Miller spoke to the scientist.

Her report did not include quotes from the man. Nor is there any indication she saw his face, or if she was told his name. There was no evidence Miller was permitted to learn where the scientist lived, or worked. Every piece of information she delivered to the front page of the *New York Times* appeared to come from secondary sources, the soldiers serving on the MET Alpha squad. Nothing showed independent confirmation, or corroboration, and Miller disclosed as much in her narrative.

"Under the terms of her accreditation to report on the activities of MET Alpha, this reporter was not permitted to interview the scientist or visit his home. Nor was she permitted to write about the discovery of the scientist for three days, and the copy was then submitted for a check by military officials. Those officials asked that details of what chemicals were uncovered be deleted. They said they feared that such information could jeopardize the scientist's safety by identifying the part of the weapons program where he worked," Miller wrote.

The scientist, if, in fact, he was a scientist, had come to the attention of the U.S. occupation force when he handed soldiers a note saying he had information on weapons. A part of Miller's justification for writing her story appeared to be this handwritten message. Penned in Arabic, she was shown the document by an officer of MET Alpha. Although Miller does not speak or read Arabic, the note, seemingly, lent the scientist's assertions some credibility. If it was translated for Miller, she did not say in her alarming story.

"I had an independent translation," she said in a later interview. "There were at least two separate translations of that letter, and I couldn't use either one of them because it would tell you who he [the scientist] was, and he was living in a hostile neighborhood that was filled with Ba'ath Party officials. He would have been in danger."

In Miller's narrative, there was no report on the text of what the scientist had written. Nonetheless, Miller did write that the scientist had led the Americans to a "supply of materials that proved to be the building blocks of illegal weapons," even though she never gave any more proof of those allegations than to the unidentified man pointing at a bare spot in the Iraqi desert. She also offered as fact that material unearthed over the course of three days had proved to be precursors to toxic agents, which had been banned in Iraq by the United Nations. At no point did Miller say she was shown these materials or provided evidence that they were, in fact, deadly elements to chemical or biological weaponry.

Even Judith Miller's editor, Andrew Rosenthal, seemed unaware of how the story had been acquired. In an e-mail exchange with Russ Baker of the *Nation*, Rosenthal said that the article "made clear that Judy Miller was aware of his [the scientist's] identity and in fact met him, but was asked to withhold his name out of concern for his personal safety." Actually, the report failed to clarify how close Miller came to the scientist, making an unusual journalistic confession that the correspondent was not allowed to interview the actual source of her news report.

"I have a photograph of him," Miller explained. "I know who he is. There's no way I would have gone forward with such a story without knowing who my source was, even if I got it from guys in my unit. You know, maybe it turns out that he was lying or ill-informed and what he said cannot be independently verified. He did say he worked in a security lab in Baghdad, and he took MET Alpha there and retrieved materials."

The commander of MET Alpha, Chief Warrant Officer Richard Gonzales, said the scientist was an Iraqi insider with important knowledge.

"In terms of information that I had access to, up until the time I handed him over to another operation, I considered it important," Gonzales said. "It helped us to understand everything that was taking place, and allowed us to realize some things that we just didn't recognize until we hooked up with this guy. You know, until that point I was looking for stockpiles of WMD. For me, he represented the turning point on how we needed to proceed with the entire operation. His intell was hugely important. It changed everything on how we were to proceed."

Judy Miller was clearly convinced of the scientist's credibility. On the same day her story was published, April 21, 2003, Miller appeared on Fox News to talk about her reportage, and the next day, on PBS Television's *The NewsHour with Jim Lehrer.* During Lehrer's program, the correspondent was interviewed by Ray Suarez, who asked a tenaciously, obvious question: "Has the unit you've been traveling with [MET Alpha] found any evidence of weapons of mass destruction in Iraq?"

Miller's response was even more affirmative than her *Times* story.

"Well, I think they found something more than a smoking gun," she told Suarez. "What they've found is a silver bullet in the form of a person, an Iraqi individual, a scientist, as we've called him, who really worked on the programs, who knows them, firsthand, and who has led MET Alpha people to some pretty startling conclusions."

Although the "startling conclusions" had not been proved, the story written by Miller began to live in a greater fullness across the entire spectrum of American media. On the Fox network, Bill O'Reilly used Miller's writing to argue the war had been justified.

"Reporter Judith Miller of the *New York Times* does believe the weapons are there," O'Reilly said on his popular, nationally broadcast program. "She spelled out the weapons yesterday."

Of course, what a journalist "believes" is not relevant. The issue must always be what a journalist knows, and Miller did not know the compounds had been buried at the site she visited with MET Alpha. No proof was ever offered. She only knew that a scientist had told MET Alpha where they were located, and MET Alpha had told her.

In an extensive analysis of Miller's story, conducted by the *American Journalism Review*, Charles Layton described how the bad information was undergoing a mutation on cable television. Interviewed on MSNBC, Paul Leventhal of the Nuclear Control Institute had turned the one, unnamed scientist into a plural, lending further credibility to the allegations printed by Miller.

"The *scientists* [emphasis added] told the *New York Times*," he said, "That they had buried the chemical weapons."

Another reporter, cited by Layton, Brett Baier, wrote about Miller's appearance on Fox television. He, too, had made the jump to multiple scientists, implying the information in Miller's story was completely open-sourced.

"In an interview with Fox today," Baier wrote, "Miller talked about the importance of the information the *scientists* [emphasis added] had provided."

The transcript of Miller's appearance on *The NewsHour* showed that she was, at least, partially culpable for creating the impression there was more than one scientist.

"But those stockpiles that we've heard about," Miller told interviewer Ray Suarez, "Well, those have either been destroyed by

Saddam Hussein, according to the *scientists*, [emphasis added] or they have been shipped to Syria for safekeeping."

Going even further, almost endorsing Bush administration policies, the reporter used the plural a second time when Suarez asked if her story confirmed the White House's belief that Iraqis would start talking as soon as they had been freed by American forces.

"And that's what the Bush administration has finally done," Miller replied. "They have changed the political environment, and they've enabled people like the *scientists* [emphasis added] that MET Alpha has found to come forth."

According to *American Journalism Review*, Bush advisor, former CIA Director James Woolsey distorted Miller's language even more dramatically during an appearance on CNN. Woolsey told interviewer Lou Dobbs, the scientist said, "He had been ordered to destroy substantial shares of nerve gas." Miller, obviously, had written nothing related to nerve gas. Her story described only "building blocks" or "precursors" to chemical and biological weaponry. Dobbs, though, was apparently not informed sufficiently enough to correct Woolsey.

Just as had happened with Judith Miller's initial page one scoop about aluminum tubes, the story of the Iraqi scientist was running away to live on its own. In what has become conventional process for American journalism, the details and limited facts were tortured by cable television's talking heads until the original spare substance of the report was unrecognizable. The tenuous information provided by Miller's work was constantly reframed by pundits to give it greater political weight and purpose, and as legitimate local newspapers, subscribers to the *New York Times* wire services reprinted the story, its allegations began to seep into the American consciousness. The United States had found proof of weapons of mass destruction in Iraq. The president was correct. War was justified.

The *New York Times* plays an unparalleled role in U.S. journalism. Each morning, editors from television networks, major metropolitan daily papers, producers for cable talk shows, and local broadcast and print editors, scan the pages of the *Times* in their own efforts to determine what news is. Additionally, the *Times* distributes much of its editorial content via a subscriber wire service to publications around the world. In the case of Miller's WMD story, reprints appeared all across the American landscape.

In the *Rocky Mountain News*, an edited version was published with the unmistakable headline: *"Illegal Material Spotted."* Distorting even further, the subheading claimed, *"Iraqi Scientist Leads U.S. Team to Illicit Weapons Locations."* The hyperbole of the *Seattle Post-Intelligencer* was even more blatant. The headline, *"Scientist Says Iraq Retained Illicit Weapons,"* was completely overshadowed by the disturbing subheading, which asserted: *"Outlawed Arsenals Destroyed by the Iraqis Before the War."* Although they are only two examples of communities where the story found great purchase, there was barely a statement of fact in any of those headlines.

Numerous analysts suggested the *Times* had failed to adhere to the most fundamental of journalistic standards. On the Globalvision News Network, Miriam Rajkumar of the Carnegie Endowment for International Peace, very quickly identified the ramifications of the newspaper's reporting by suggesting Miller offered "politically potent use for those who wanted to justify and validate the allegations made before the war regarding Al Qaeda and WMD. Anything that validates that will be pounced on."

And, of course, it was.

Suddenly, the *New York Times*, often accused of being the publishing arm of America's progressive-liberal thinkers, was assisting the neo-conservative cause. Talk show host Rush Limbaugh burned up nine minutes of air time on Miller's story, calling it "a big, huge, very important story." On his web site, Limbaugh argued, "If this appeared anywhere other than the sainted *New York Times*, many liberals would be out there pooh-poohing it. Since it appears there, what are they going to say?"

People like Jonathon Tucker, a former U.N. weapons inspector, who was with the Monterey Institute of International Studies at the

U.S. Institute for Peace, said the story ought not to be regarded as serious journalism.

"It's very vague and not corroborated," he said. "I don't view it as definitive. It's pretty thin on the evidence."

The executive director of the Arms Control Association, Daryl Kimball, blamed management of the *Times* as much as he did Miller for an editorial lapse.

"What's surprising and I think disappointing is that the *New York Times*, not just Judith Miller," he said, "chose to take at face value the initial assessments of a U.S. investigations team that certainly has a vested interest in finding WMD in Iraq."

Regardless of any accuracy questions, Judy Miller's reporting was feeding into the national discourse. Miller also got attention for something else she had done, which some editors and writers felt had troubling implications for journalism. Her disclosure that she had agreed to "terms of accreditation" set off whorls of dismay in the profession. "Terms of accreditation" was an anomaly in reporting. Journalists don't accept terms. They report information they are able to acquire and independently corroborate. Any source offering terms, regardless of what kind of information they might deliver, has, historically, been ignored. Miller, however, accepted ground rules laid out for her by the U.S. military and the MET Alpha team when she wrote about the alleged Iraqi scientist. Furthermore, she turned over the copy she had drafted so the military was able to scrutinize her language, and whether, in fact, they accepted her version of events.

"You have to accept terms to get to be an embed with a unit like MET Alpha," she explained. "No reporter could have gone with them without agreeing to protect the unit's work, and not expose them or their sources to danger. That's just the way it was. Lots of reporters agreed to terms of accreditation when they became embeds with combat operations. I was certainly not the only one. But I had to talk my head off to get into this unit. I was not wanted there."

The same day Miller's disclosure of her terms was published, Jack Shafer of *Slate* savaged the decision of *Times'* editors to allow their correspondent to make deals with the military.

"Most pungently," Shafer wrote in his *Pressbox* column on the media, "She consented to prepublication review—oh, hell, let's call it censorship!—of her story by military officials. Did the 'military officials' who checked her story *require* her to redact parts of the story, or did she do so on her own accord? Were any other 'terms of accreditation' imposed on Miller? Other levels of censorship? Are other *Times* reporters filing dispatches under similar 'terms of accreditation'? When and where were the terms of accreditation negotiated? Where are they stated?"

While not quite as acidic, *Editor and Publisher* magazine decried the odor Miller's work was dispersing through journalism, and it referred to several other stories she had filed, including a later discredited report that mobile biological labs had been found by the United States.

"Surrounding this whole saga," William E. Jackson Jr. wrote, "there is the smell of compromised reporting, using and even colluding with tainted Iraqi sources, while essentially surrendering detached judgment to the Pentagon. The *Times* has a serious obligation to scrutinize Miller's reporting, and editors' editing, on the threat that was widely advertised as the primary reason for sending American and British soldiers off to war."

A Pulitzer Prize winner, Judith Miller is an elite, international journalist at the nation's most prestigious newspaper. Her published resume and her body of work show her to have expertise on the Middle East. She has written best-selling books on the region and its politics. Miller is also recognized as a specialist who writes with authority about germ and biological warfare. Six months after her controversial reports on aluminum tubes, and the unnamed "baseball-capped" scientist, Miller had spoken publicly only to *American Journalism Review* about the professional fury generated by her work.

In a later interview about the controversy surrounding her work, however, Miller said she believed she was the victim of petty jealousy and competitiveness from the *Washington Post.*

"Bart Gellman [*Post* reporter] tried as hard as he could to knock down my scientist story," she said. "But he couldn't. If he has been beaten every day in the field, what would you expect him to report? My response wasn't to try to knock him down when he beat me. I just find this whole thing with the *Post* to be really ugly lately. Their reporting has been nothing short of reckless. It was spiteful, bitter, and wrong."

A talented correspondent with a discerning eye for facts, Bart Gellman of the *Washington Post* is a bit baffled by Judy Miller's charges. According to Gellman, his trip to Iraq was timed to take place after the fall of Baghdad, as the search began for weapons of mass destruction, and he had no choice but to write about Miller's bombshell piece on the "baseball-capped" scientist.

"I did not come to debunk her stories," Gellman said. "And, in fact, I made only one reference to any of her stories. That was about the scientist and the baseball cap. Of course, I was asking about that. Before I had arrived, she reported that Iraq had destroyed a whole arsenal of weapons, which was a very obviously a big story. No one would know that. You have to ask the basic questions as to how we know that. She was not allowed to identify the scientist or name the program he claimed to work in. She said he showed investigators precursors to WMD. But she couldn't say what precursors or what weapons. And independent experts can't determine credibility of those claims without knowing those two things. I don't think I ever made any other reference to any of her stories beyond that."

Refusing to back off from her belief that the *Post* was out to prove her wrong or incompetent, Miller believes the main reason Gellman traveled to Iraq was to rebut her work. Gellman finds such an assertion to be absurd.

"Did she really say that?" Gellman asked. "I'm not sure how any journalist can feel like a competitor on a huge running story would travel five or six thousand miles to write about her, instead of the story. I wrote about what I saw, and what was important. She did the same. All of my quotes were on the record. And look, I wasn't writing about the same unit she was reporting on. I can't imagine she thinks those stories I published were about her. I guess I can't imagine Judy Miller thinking I came to Iraq to report on her. I came for weapons stories. People should judge for themselves whether my stories hold up. And I'm not interested in talking about her stories."

As for Miller's stories and their longevity, she tried to persuade some critics that her story about the "baseball-capped" scientist was proof that there were no weapons of mass destruction. "To me, it was world-class news that the stockpiles [of Hussein's forbidden weapons] probably did not exist. Those giant stockpiles, that were going to create anthrax clouds and nuclear clouds over our cities, did not exist."

Miller did not, however, make any such statements in her copy. A reader needed to extrapolate from what she wrote that, if the Americans were chasing "precursors" and "building blocks" of WMD, there probably weren't any finished weapons. Nonetheless, she insisted, the findings of the MET Alpha team, if there actually was a discovery, provided proof of a WMD *program* [emphasis added], and, therefore, according to Miller, "offered some vindication of what the administration had been saying." The inference to be easily drawn by her critics is that she almost appeared to be seeking to "vindicate" the Bush White House.

As scrutinized as Miller's writing has been, how she got her information was a matter of as critical importance as what she did with it. By her own admission, the majority of stories she wrote about WMD came from Ahmad Chalabi, the exiled leader of the U.S.-backed Iraqi National Congress. Chalabi, who had not lived in Iraq for four decades, was a convicted Jordanian embezzler. According to a military court in Amman, Chalabi embezzled $70 million from the Petra Bank, which he founded in the 1970s. The case was tried in absentia after Chalabi had fled the country. Friends said Chalabi was framed by Jordanians who were political allies with Saddam Hussein because Chalabi was trying to fund a resistance effort to overthrow the Iraqi leader.

He was persistent in his attempts to remove Hussein. Chalabi was a capable lobbyist and convinced the U.S. Congress in 1998 to pass the Iraq Liberation Act, which was the first formal call for "regime change." Funded out of the State Department, Chalabi was given $4.3 million dollars of American taxpayers' money to promote this cause. Unfortunately, a state department audit of his spending revealed that more than half of that figure was not properly accounted for. After his bookkeeping skills were shown to be lacking, Chalabi's financial provider became the Pentagon, and he reportedly burned through an estimated $100 million dollars to fund his dream of an American assault on Iraq.

Often described as an abject military failure for his absurdly designed plans to invade Iraq, Ahmad Chalabi served the purposes of the Pentagon and the Bush administration. Consistently, the Iraqi exile fed both the White House and military intelligence operatives the kind of information they needed to politically justify moving U.S. troops into Iraq. The CIA, however, considered much of Chalabi's information to lack credibility, and constantly warned the Bush White House to be skeptical of its value. Chalabi's knowledge of Iraq's armaments, which ought to have been perceived as less than objective by American leaders, was the beginning of the Bush administration's tactic of cooking intelligence reports, and pressuring operatives who disagreed with Chalabi's assessments. Chalabi's reports almost always turned out to be wrong. He was, after all, the individual who had convinced Vice President Dick Cheney that Iraqi citizens were certain to greet U.S. troops as liberators, and that hardly any resistance was to be expected. Chalabi first made the claim on ABC News.

There is also proof that Ahmad Chalabi was the primary source for some of Judith Miller's reporting on weapons of mass destruction, and that proof came from Judith Miller. Another *New York Times* Pulitzer Prize winner, Baghdad Bureau Chief John Burns, had become angered at Miller over a story she had written about Chalabi. Burns had not assigned the piece to Miller, and sent her an e-mail chastising her for stepping in front of another correspondent.

"I am deeply chagrined at your reporting and filing on Chalabi after I had told you on Monday night that we were planning a major piece on him, and without so much as telling me what you were doing," Burns wrote. "We have a bureau here; I am in charge of that bureau until I leave; I make assignments after considerable thought and discussion, and it was plain to all of us to whom the Chalabi story belonged. If you do this, what is to stop you doing it on any other story of your choosing? And what of the distress it causes the correspondent who is usurped? It is not professional, and not collegial."

The electronic note, which had been obtained by media critic Howard Kurtz of the *Washington Post*, was published in his column, including Miller's response to Burns, which amounted to a confessional.

"I've been covering Chalabi for about ten years," Miller told Burns, "and have done most of the stories about him for our paper; including the long takeout we recently did on him. He has provided most of the front page exclusives on WMD to our paper." Miller went on to explain to her boss that she had been traveling with the Army's Mobile Exploitation Team Alpha, which "is using Chalabi's intell and document network for its own WMD work. Since I'm there every day, talking to him, I thought I might have been included on a decision by you."

When Howard Kurtz published Miller's e-mail in the *Washington Post*, he appeared to be launching a war within the war. Media arguing over the quality of competing reporters' work, undoubtedly, added further complications and confusion to the process of getting stories correct from the war zone. Miller's pieces tended to be first, if not as comprehensive as critics might have wanted, and Kurtz and the *Post* were consistently beaten. However, the *Post*'s articles often had elements and independent voices not included in Miller's reports from the war zone. The *Post* also was egregiously wrong, in many cases. After being told an inspiring tale about the bravery of Private Jessica Lynch, the Washington paper ran a narrative of how the diminutive soldier gallantly fought to the end, was stabbed by Iraqis, and resisted until overwhelmed. None of that, of course, was borne out by facts. Lynch was unconscious and debilitated in a deadly vehicle accident, which killed several other people in her military company. The *Post* never retracted the story.

Exposing Miller's e-mail and showing her as someone who worked with Chalabi and the Iraqi National Congress appeared to be the *Post*'s attempt to prove she was playing into the White House's hands. Chalabi clearly had an agenda, and the *Post*'s reporting was an effort to associate Miller with him and the Bush Administration.

"Of course, I talked with Chalabi," Miller said. "I wouldn't have been doing my job if I didn't. But he was just one of many sources I used while I was in Iraq."

There was also a good chance Chalabi and the White House were working *on* Miller, even though, as a seasoned correspondent, she was an unlikely candidate for manipulation. A former CIA analyst, who has observed Miller's professional products and relationships for years, said he had no doubt of how the lines of communication were operating.

"The White House Iraq Group had a perfect deal with Miller," he said. "Chalabi is providing the Bush people with the information they need to support their political objectives with Iraq, and he is supplying the same material to Judy Miller. Chalabi tips her on something, and then she goes to the White House, which has already heard the same thing from Chalabi, and she gets it corroborated by some insider she always describes as a 'senior administration official.' She also got the Pentagon to confirm things for her, which made sense, since they were working so closely with Chalabi. Too bad Judy didn't spend a little more time talking to those of us in the intelligence community who had information that contradicted almost everything Chalabi said."

Miller's style had been to grab headlines and front page placement with alarming allegations. Deeper into the pieces, she offered lines of skeptical copy, though rarely, if ever, did she quote authoritative voices who scoffed at what was asserted in her story's lead. She did that in follow up stories, which frequently did not get the same prominence in the newspaper. In some reports, the only consideration Miller gave doubters was to quote unnamed White House sources who told her "skeptical scientists were in the minority." This may have been caused by logistical challenges or the fact that many people in government who disagreed with the administration were ordered to keep quiet. Intimidation of sources might have affected editorial balance in many of Miller's reports, which were filed before she was able to find skeptics to quote.

After writing her front pager, *"Illicit Arms Kept Till Eve of War, An Iraqi Scientist Is Said to Assert,"* on April 21, Judy Miller appeared on PBS television the next day and called the scientist "more than a smoking gun" and a "silver bullet" in America's quest for Saddam Hussein's WMDs, and said MET Alpha had made "the most important discovery to date in the hunt for illegal weapons."

Oddly, the story she filed the day after these claims on *The NewsHour with Jim Lehrer,* basically, said what she had written about the scientist and his allegations, just two days earlier, was, suddenly, obsolete information. Headlined, *"Focus Shifts from Weapons to People behind Them,"* Miller did her best to explain a "paradigm shift," which apparently had taken place almost overnight, as she slept, and after she had been on PBS. The story, however, had to have already been written the same day she was on PBS, or, perhaps, right after she filed her original piece on the baseball-capped scientist, otherwise it would have never made the next day's paper. In any case, the paradigm shifted sometime between Monday and Wednesday. Whenever it shifted, Miller was on top of it. The same MET Alpha soldiers who had told her the scientist had led them to buried chemicals may have told her the paradigm was shifting, possibly as soon as a few hours after they had taken her to the site, simply because they checked and found nothing sinister under the ground where the baseball-capped enigma had pointed. If that's the case, what was the value in Miller writing the first story when she knew she was very quickly, in less than two days, writing another piece, which invalidated the first report? Perhaps this change in perspective actually occurred more slowly but appeared to be a few days because Miller's original piece on the scientist was held for three days by the U.S. military before it was released for publication.

Again relying on unnamed sources inside of MET Alpha, Miller wrote that America's WMD strategies were in a constant state of flux. Originally, the source told Miller, U.S. troops were looking for the vast stores of WMD, which had been detailed in Secretary of State Colin Powell's presentation to the United Nations Security Council. After finding nothing in half of the 150 targeted locations, they began to seek "building blocks" and "precursors" to those weapons. That effort, too, proved fruitless, and now, Miller's MET Alpha source informed her, their focus had shifted to finding scientists, like the one she had written about two days earlier, to prove there was, in fact, a WMD program.

Miller's copy sounded to some like a tinny rationalization for her blockbuster from earlier in the week. "Based on what the Iraqi scientist had said about weapons being destroyed or stocks being hidden, military experts said they now believed they might not find large caches of illicit chemicals or biological agents, at least not in Iraq."

That was how Miller clarified the "paradigm shift."

Slate's Jack Shafer, who had led the critical charge against the correspondent's work, was indignant at the sudden change in her editorial slant.

"Paradigm shift, my ass!" he wrote in his column. "[U.S. Secretary of State Colin] Powell's intelligence report insisted there were tons of WMD and now the military—and Miller—are preparing us for their complete absence. That's what I call the most important discovery to date in the hunt for illegal weapons!"

The *Washington Post*'s Howard Kurtz was also critical of Miller's closeness to the MET Alpha team, stepping up the professional antipathy between the two newspapers. Quoting a half dozen military officials involved in the operation, Kurtz said that the *New York Times*' reporter, according to what he had been told, turned MET Alpha into a "rogue operation," or as one source suggested, "a Judith Miller team." MET Alpha, which was a part of the 75th Exploitation Task Force, was integral to the U.S. military's attempt to find WMD. A senior staff officer with the 75th Exploitation Task Force, quoted in the *Post* article, said, "It's impossible to exaggerate the impact she had on the mission of this unit, and not for the better."

The commander of MET Alpha was incensed when he read Kurtz's story.

"That really pissed me off," said Chief Warrant Officer Richard Gonzales. "She had absolutely no influence on any of my decisions. Anybody who knows me knows that's not the way I operate. I saw [Bart] Gellman [*Post* reporter] come in and it was patently clear the animosity he had for Judy Miller and the *Times*. He didn't come in to get a story about MET Alpha or WMD. What he was doing was very personalized. They [the *Post*] already had their thesis statement and they were trying to prove it. That's what I saw unfolding. It was strange. Kurtz wrote his article without ever having been over there and all of it was second-hand information. I think he was just looking for support from a third party to back up his position about Judy and that's why they sent Gellman over."

Gellman, who sounded as though he had not heard of Miller and Gonzales' accusations, said they were totally without substance.

"I don't know how either of them could think they know those things," he said. "I spent maybe four or five minutes in conversation with Judy. Mostly just pleasantries. About the same with Gonzales, who did not want to be interviewed. I did ask XTF [Exploitation

Task Force] headquarters if I could go over on several missions. But I was not allowed to go. I asked to interview those MET Alpha guys. But that never happened either. They considered Judy's arrangement with them to be exclusive. But he [Gonzales] wasn't hearing me ask questions while I was there, and neither was she."

Kurtz wrote that Miller had influence on leadership's decisions about how to use MET Alpha troops. He did not, however, speak with the commander of the unit, Chief Warrant Officer Richard Gonzales. Kurtz said he had been unable to reach Gonzales. According to the commander, though, no attempts had been made to ask him for an interview.

"Let me just tell you," Gonzales said. "He [Kurtz] did not speak to me. I was not contacted. And no one ever tried to contact me. They said I'd refused to comment. That's nonsense. He wrote this story that completely distorted everything, and was almost completely factually wrong. The picture it painted was really distorted. I didn't even know who Howard Kurtz was until I read that story."

Kurtz argued his case for Miller's influence by publishing a note she had sent to MET Alpha senior officers. On the same day that her story on the "baseball-capped" scientist appeared in the *Times*, MET Alpha was ordered to withdraw to a small town in southern Iraq. The United States may have thought there was less value to the scientist's claims than did Miller's editors. The correspondent, however, was described by Kurtz as upset, and she sent a handwritten note to two different public affairs officers, which sources interpreted for Kurtz, as a veiled threat.

"I see no reason for me to waste time (or MET Alpha, for that matter) in Talil," she wrote. "Request permission to stay on here with colleagues at the Palestine Hotel til [sic] MET Alpha returns or order to return is rescinded. I intend to write about this decision in the *NY Times* to send a successful team back home just as progress on WMD is being made."

"Essentially she threatened them," an officer told Kurtz. "She would publish a negative story."

One Army officer said Miller was not subtle about her control and connections. According to Kurtz's sources, Miller often referred to her relationships with Secretary of Defense Donald Rumsfeld, and others at the Pentagon, including Undersecretary Douglas Feith.

"Judith was always issuing threats of either going to the *New York Times* or to the secretary of defense," the officer said. "There was nothing veiled about that threat,"

Miller refused to talk to Kurtz because he had published her internal e-mail to John Burns. Her editor, however, Andrew Rosenthal, defended her performance in Iraq.

"We think she did some good work there," he said. "We think she broke some important stories."

"Singling out one reporter for this kind of examination is a little bizarre," he later added. Rosenthal also argued that characterizing Miller's note to the public affairs officers as a threat was a "total distortion of that letter."

Regardless of the *Times* protestations, some conclusions from events are unavoidable. According to Kurtz, Miller went to the commander of the 101st Airborne, Major General David Petraeus, and asked that the order sending MET Alpha to the southern Iraqi town be rescinded. Colonel Richard McPhee, who commanded the 75th Exploitation Task Force, did not report to Petraeus. He did, however, pull down his orders for MET Alpha's withdrawal from the field. Miller got what she wanted.

Miller's version of events in her interview with *American Journalism Review* was that Gonzales did not want her to write about the "baseball-capped" scientist, but she "put her foot down," and made plans to return to New York to write the story "in defiance of the Army." She insisted that she was pressured by her editors to stay and negotiate a compromise, and that is when she chose to go to Petraeus to get a quote. His words, she argued, are what convinced MET Alpha's Gonzales that it was okay for her to publish the story.

MET Alpha commander Gonzales said Miller's interpretation of what happened is factual, not the *Post's*.

"I'll tell you this, too," he said during a lengthy telephone interview. "There was huge heartache that Judy's story [about the scien-
tist] even got printed as it was. The fact that she was able to print as
much as she did was a direct result of her own persistence. This was
a serious, dedicated woman. And I took her wishes to tell her story,
and I went directly to General [David] Petraeus about what we
could release without jeopardizing security. We sure weren't going
through and editing her work. But we were making sure she wasn't
harming operational security. She was privy to a great deal more information than she published, and she wasn't happy about the fact
that she couldn't release more than she did."

The record of MET Alpha's actions, nonetheless, may also reveal
the nature of Judith Miller's relationships with the commander of the
unit and Ahmad Chalabi. When Chief Warrant Officer Richard L.
Gonzales, who was the leader of MET Alpha, was promoted, Miller
was involved in the ceremony. An eyewitness related to the *Post's*
Kurtz that she had pinned the bars to his uniform, and that Gonzales thanked Miller for her contributions. Kurtz claimed that he was
unable to get Gonzales to comment on the claim.

"If he'd ever bothered to ask me about this," Gonzales said, "I
would have told Mr. Kurtz exactly what this ceremony was about.
Any time you spend three months in the field with people, you become friends. But Judy's relationship with Colonel McPhee, [Com-
mander of Exploitation Task Force] was not good because he didn't
want her out there with us. This ceremony was near the end of our
operation. I thought it would be a good idea to have McPhee there,
along with Judy, to show my guys some closure. She was very important. She was telling the entire world about what we were doing.
This was just a chance to reconcile a relationship with McPhee,
which had been a mess from the beginning. I had him pin one bar
on one side and Judy pinned on the other one on the other side."

In at least one instance, Kurtz's attack on Judy Miller appears to
be without any factual basis.

In his report, *"Embedded Reporter's Role in Army Unit's Actions Questioned by Military,"* he wrote that the officers he interviewed said

Miller acted as a middleman between MET Alpha and Iraqi National Congress' leader Ahmad Chalabi. Kurtz cites, as a powerful example, the turnover of Saddam Hussein's son-in-law to MET Alpha by Chalabi. According to his sources, Jamal Sultan Tikriti was delivered to Gonzales' team, and was interrogated as Miller sat in on the questioning. The officer who talked to Kurtz about the Tikriti incident said his name could not be used because he was not an authorized spokesperson. But he insisted Miller's increasing influence, which he claimed led to the meeting with Chalabi and Tikriti, endangered MET Alpha's mission.

"This was totally out of their lane, getting involved with human intelligence," he said. "This woman came in with a plan. She was leading them. She ended up almost hijacking the mission."

However, according to both Judy Miller and MET Alpha commander Gonzales, she had nothing to do with the surrender of Tikriti. Both say she was nowhere near the location where Tikriti was being interrogated, nor did she have anything to do with his briefing or his transfer to the United States from the Iraqi National Congress.

"These so-called facts in the *Post* were made up," Miller said. "I was never in a debrief with anyone. That would have been crossing the line. I didn't do it. And I didn't write a letter threatening anyone, either. [General David] Petraeus says the whole version of Kurtz isn't true, either. That's not what was going on. I just feel like Howard Kurtz has been so scurrilous, so used."

Miller's version of how events transpired is corroborated by Colonel Ted Seel, the U.S. Army's liaison officer with Ahmed Chalabi and the Iraqi National Congress. In a letter to the *Washington Post's* ombudsman, Seel said Miller was not involved in any way with the transfer of Saddam Hussein's son-in-law, or the son-in-law's cousin. According to Seel's letter, Miller was not connected to the intelligence process, and he had never seen MET Alpha do anything that was outside the scope of its mission.

"I don't know why Mr. Kurtz chose to publish this story," he wrote, "without checking the facts with the personnel still present with the INC [Iraqi National Congress]. I can understand his not contacting me since I am no longer 'in theater,' but others are, who could have told him that what he was about to publish was false and inaccurate information. I think at the very least he owes Judith Miller an apology and that it should appear in print, under his by-line, as did the article with which he smeared her."

No such apology was forthcoming from Howard Kurtz or the *Washington Post*.

In the *American Journalism Review* article, Miller claimed MET Alpha's Gonzales was anything but comfortable with her presence because he did not want her having access to classified information. Gonzales later concurred with that assessment. The *Times'* management strongly protested any claims their reporter was involved in the movements or tactics of MET Alpha, to the point of even calling such a statement "an idiotic proposition."

"She didn't bring MET Alpha anywhere," *Times* editor Rosenthal told Kurtz. "It's a baseless accusation. She doesn't direct MET Alpha, she's a civilian. Judith Miller is a reporter. She's not a member of the U.S. armed forces. She was covering a unit, like hundreds of other reporters for the *New York Times*, *Washington Post*, and others. She went where they went to the degree that they would allow."

Gonzales, too, sent the *Post* a blistering letter of complaint, which was not part of any follow-up article, but was printed on a letters to the editor page:

> Howard Kurtz' article on 'embed media' is filled with errors of fact, distortions, slanderous assertions about my leadership of MET Alpha, my relationship with the 75th XTF, [Exploitation Task Force], and the role of embedded media.
>
> I think readers can draw their own conclusions about your sloppy reporting and decision to publish a smear on her [Miller] without bothering to talk to the commander of the unit with whom she spent the most time.

Zaeb Sethna of the Iraqi National Congress also charged Kurtz with unsavory journalistic tactics in a letter to the *Post's* editor.

Sethna said, "Your article makes several false allegations concerning the handover of Saddam's son-in-law. . . . Mr. Kurtz quotes me as saying that the idea of transferring [him] originated with Ms. Miller. That is not true and I did not say it.

"It is always dangerous to base a story entirely on sources who did not witness the events they allege and then refuse to be named. It is even worse to misquote and selectively use quotes to fit the story. Unfortunately, the *Post* has done both of these things."

On a critical issue, Sethna's perception is unerring. The individual who accused Miller of getting involved in the debriefing was a protected source. Kurtz had agreed not to reveal that person's name. If this source had a grudge against Judy Miller, this was an extremely safe way to exact revenge without being exposed, and there had been many grumblings from public affairs officers about having to deal with Miller and her aggressiveness.

Although he refused to talk directly about the work of Howard Kurtz, the *Post*'s Barton Gellman said Kurtz was approached by officers who had worked with Miller, who offered him the story. Kurtz then asked Gellman to verify the legitimacy of the sources who had called, and Gellman did.

"But I did not put those people in touch with Howie," he said. "And I did not spend my time in Iraq reporting on Judy, and I had nothing to do with the generation of Howie's stories on Judy. That's just wrong."

Miller, though, has been unable to escape constant attention.

When a journalist's stories begin to cause some readers to believe the reporting is serving a political agenda, however, the reporter's personal background becomes a matter of considerable scrutiny. Miller's work seemed to frequently corroborate Bush administration warnings about Iraq, whether she was writing about aluminum tubes, mobile germ labs, or discoveries of building blocks of weapons of mass destruction. The perception of a political cant to her reportage prompted intense analysis of Miller's beliefs, and there was an abundance of material, which generated even more controversy and led to accusations she was anti-Islamist.

The most confusing connection the *New York Times* correspondent has had appeared to be her association with an organization known as The Middle East Forum. Founded by Daniel Pipes, the group has openly advocated attacking Iraq and deposing Saddam Hussein. In an article co-authored for *Front Page Magazine* in August of 2002, Pipes challenged Bush family friend and long time advisor Brent Scowcroft. According to the narrative, Scowcroft was wrong about a measured approach to dealing with Hussein. Pipes wrote that it was time for America to launch a military invasion.

"Saddam Husayn [sic] poses no less of a threat to American and global security than Osama bin Laden," Pipes wrote, "yet for more than a decade, Washington has jockeyed and yammered for the right moment, the right place, the right opportunity to depose him. The time for prevarication has passed. The time to attack is now. Saddam must be overthrown, and soon."

In keeping with the Bush White House's strategy to use American outrage over 9/11 to advance a political agenda, Pipes added, "Today, with Americans mobilized, is exactly the right moment to dispatch him."

A regular contributor to the *New York Post*, Pipes was also by-lined in an editorial a few months after 9/11, which argued that Hussein had potential nuclear weapons; that the Iraqi dictator was involved in terrorist attacks on America's Twin Towers; he was likely a part of the Anthrax scares in Washington, and that Ahmad Chalabi's Iraqi National Congress was poised to install a democratic government in Baghdad as soon as America removed Saddam Hussein.

Pipes and his Middle East Forum have been accused of being Zionist, and blatantly anti-Muslim. As far back as 1990, writing in the *National Review,* he expressed fears over what he described as a "Muslim influx" into western cultures.

"West European societies," he argued, "are unprepared for the massive immigration of brown-skinned peoples cooking strange foods and not exactly maintaining Germanic standards of hygiene."

A former employee of the state and defense departments, Pipes was nominated by President Bush to serve on the U.S. Institute of

Peace. The choice of Pipes was subject to senate confirmation, and the *Washington Post*, whose editorial pages had supported much of the Bush policy regarding Iraq, immediately editorialized against Pipes. The paper urged the president to withdraw Pipes' name, or for senators to block the nomination. Not surprisingly, Pipes has close relationships with Douglas Feith, an undersecretary at the Department of Defense, right-wing conservative U.S. Senator Jesse Helms, and neo-conservative leader Richard Perle.

The Middle East Forum (MEF) also offers expert speakers on its web site. Among them are people like Bernard Lewis, a professor emeritus of Princeton, who gave a speech for MEF, which was entitled, "Today, America's Interests are Oil and Israel." Lewis, who achieved international acclaim as a scholar of Middle East history, was described by Judy Miller as a mentor during her days at Princeton University's graduate school, which may explain how she ended up being associated with the Middle East Forum. Under a heading on the MEF web site, entitled, "List of Experts on Islam, Islamism, and the Middle East," for as long as two years, the organization promoted Judith Miller as someone capable of speaking on, "Militant Islam, Biological Warfare." When her reporting from Iraq began to draw fevered criticisms, Miller's name was pulled down from the site's links.

Daniel Forbes of the Globalvision News Network confronted both the *New York Times* and the MEF about the unseemly association between an organization with a pure political agenda, and a journalist, who is expected to maintain objectivity in her writing. When he contacted Daniel Pipes, Forbes asked the MEF founder if he felt it was appropriate for Miller to be listed as an expert on his web site.

"If I didn't think it was appropriate," Pipes answered. "Why would she be on our on our web site?"

Pipes refused to answer Forbes' questions about whether Miller received fees for speaking, and when he pressed the issue of the reporter's affiliation with a politically motivated group, Pipes hung up the phone, according to Forbes' published narrative of the conversation, *"Pulitzer Prize-Winning Reporter Crosses the New York Times' Line of 'Strict Neutrality.'"* The persistent Forbes called back, and, pushed the questioning further, inquiring of Pipes whether he thought Miller's objectivity might be tainted by being connected to the Middle East Forum.

"I'm declining to answer," he said. "All this is none of your business, whether we paid her or not. Did I call you up and ask about your business?"

Undaunted, Forbes asked Pipes about his nomination to the U.S. Institute of Peace, and Pipes hung up the phone a second time.

Forbes' comprehensive reporting included a comment from Bob Steele, director of ethics for the Poynter Institute, a widely respected journalism think tank in Florida. Steele left little doubt that such a relationship ought to be examined.

"My question would be," he told Forbes, "Is it a leap of logic that they are ideological soulmates? I would want to ask the reporter why she is on the site, and find out the level of connection."

As a minimum, the level of connection included the promotion of Judith Miller's books, which several critics have interpreted as anti-Muslim. Daniel Pipes confirmed that the Middle East Forum held a launch party for the release of her 1996 book, *God Has Ninety-Nine Names*, (New York: Simon and Schuster, 1996). Apparently, she also appeared at a 2001 MEF forum regarding another one of her books. *God Has Ninety-Nine Names* was also excerpted in the organization's publication, the *Middle East Quarterly*.

Miller's objectivity was assaulted in a review of *God Has Ninety-Nine Names*. In the *Nation* magazine, the book was vilified by the late Edward W. Said, Columbia University's Professor of English and Comparative Literature. Although her own newspaper and the *L.A. Times* gave her favorable notices, Said's review accused Miller of trading in "the Islamic threat" and advancing her thesis that "militant Islam is a danger to the West." The review suggested Miller, and other anti-Islamist writers and thinkers appeared to be accomplishing their goal.

"The Islamic threat," he wrote, "is made to seem disproportionately fearsome, lending support to the thesis (which is an interesting parallel to anti-Semitic paranoia) that there is a worldwide conspiracy behind every explosion."

Said, though, was not a writer without controversy, either. During a confrontation on the Lebanese-Israeli border, he was photographed throwing stones at an Israeli guard post. Said, who, like Miller, was the author of several books on the Middle East, was on the board of the Palestinian Advisory Council until he felt betrayed by Yassir Arafat's signing of the 1993 Oslo Accords. In a less than conventional obituary of Mr. Said in the *Wall Street Journal*, the newspaper said he "will go down in history for having practically invented the intellectual argument for Muslim rage." In the obit, he is accused of "routinely twisting facts to suit his political purposes." Said is charged, after death, with blaming all of the ills of the Muslim world on "imperialists, racists, and Zionists," and that they were what was preventing the Arab world from being great once more.

Said was, fundamentally, a literary critic whose best-selling *Orientalism* (New York: Vintage, 1979) served to politically justify much of the Arab world's violence toward the west. When he took on Judy Miller's logic in her book *God Has Ninety-Nine Names*, Said offered a scathing deconstruct. Said wrote that the publication was a "weapon(s) in the contest to subordinate, beat down, compel, and defeat any Arab or Muslim resistance to U.S.-Israeli dominance." Although she has lived in the Middle East for twenty-five years, Said chastised Miller for having little knowledge of Arabic or Persian languages, arguing that she was woefully unqualified to write as an expert, and that Miller would not be taken seriously as a reporter with expertise if she were lacking linguistic skills on assignment in Russia, France, Germany, or Latin America. He said Miller does not view such language capability as necessary because she interprets Islam as a "psychological deformation," and not a real culture or religion.

Miller was also accused in the review of perceiving Mohammed as the founder of an anti-Jewish religion, laced with violence and paranoia, while not directly quoting one Muslim source on Mohammed.

"Just imagine a book," he asked, "published in the United States on Jesus or Moses that makes no use of a single Christian or Judaic authority." Said claimed *God Has Ninety-Nine Names* is a conglomeration "not of arguments and ideas but of endless interviews with what seems to be a slew of pathetic, unconvincing, self-serving scoundrels and their occasional critics."

Miller was also blamed for factual errors in the book. According to Said, she misidentified "her friend" Hisham Sharabi as a Christian, even though he is a Sunni Muslim. Also referred to as a Muslim by Miller, Badr el Haj, is actually a Maronite Christian. Name-dropping appeared to consistently backfire on Miller, in Said's estimation. The *Times* reporter said she was "grief-stricken" over Jordan's King Hussein's cancer diagnosis. Said took her to task for not offering any perspective on the fact that Hussein ran a police state where people were tortured, disappeared, and unfairly placed in prison. According to Said's analysis, Miller "perfectly exemplifies the *New York Times*' current Middle East coverage, now at its lowest ebb."

Undeterred, Miller believes that her reporting has stood the test of historical scrutiny.

"You know what," she offered, angrily. "I was proved fucking right. That's what happened. People who disagreed with me were saying, 'there she goes again.' But I was proved fucking right."

Ultimately, though, Said completely dismissed *God Has Ninety-Nine Names* and its author. "Miller is, in short, a shallow, opinionated journalist whose gigantic book is too long for what it ends up saying, and far too short on reflection, considered analysis, structure, and facts."

Miller's perspective, which has probably been more widely disseminated than Said's, has been spread through American culture with constant mass media appearances on programs like *Oprah* and *Larry King Live*, and her numerous presentations at various symposia and forums, as well as the pages of the *New York Times*. Each of her major front page stories on the war in Iraq did, eventually, take steps away from the story's original characterizations. Miller's greatest transgression, however, according to her critics, the one which brought scorn from her colleagues, was the story about the baseball-capped scientist. If it had been a collegiate class assignment, one journalist complained, Journalism 101 professors were likely to have sent the paper back to the student, and ordered a complete rewrite, or a spiking of the story, unless new sources and corroboration were found. Constantly, Miller wrote in the piece about what "this reporter" was allowed to see, and terms accepted by "this reporter," though she never delivered substantiation of anything alleged because of restrictions placed on her by MET Alpha.

Inevitably, Judith Miller's work became the subject of satire. Writing for *Scoop.com*, Dennis Hans, an essayist, whose work has appeared in the *New York Times* and the *Washington Post*, ridiculed Miller's tactics by turning her into a sports reporter writing about the Super Bowl, without ever being allowed to watch the game.

"A respected accountant who is a member of the Sausalito chapter of the Oakland Raiders Fan Club has told a friend who told his cousin who told this reporter that he (the respected accountant) has provided evidence to the National Football League that the Raiders nipped the Tampa Bay Buccaneers in the 2003 Super Bowl.

"Based on that evidence, which this reporter and her editors have not yet seen, the *New York Times* has decided to retract earlier stories filed the night of the game that proclaimed a Bucs victory."

Hans' piece had Miller being locked into a basement room without a television while the fan club watched the game on television in another part of the house. Unable to accept that the Raiders actually lost the game, they decided to convince Miller of a different outcome, when she met with them the next day.

"That morning, this reporter spoke to the cousin of the friend of the accountant/fan who had evidence of a Raiders victory. The cousin accompanied the reporter to a flower bed by a window that provided a clear view of a large recreation room. The cousin pointed to a silver-and-black sofa, where he said the accountant had viewed the game from the left-most cushion and jotted down in a silver-and-black notebook details on every scoring play, including the Raiders' game-winning touchdown pass, caught by someone named Jerry Rice, as the clock expired."

Miller, though, regardless of the professional degradations she has endured, has continued to exhibit the relentlessness that allowed her to talk her way into the MET Alpha team.

"It didn't occur to me that people would act like this," Miller said. "I just don't hang out a lot with journalists. I'm not a part of that club. I think a lot of what was directed at me was a result of an institution's anger [The *Washington Post*]. I think all of this stuff started because certain people viewed me as being a softie for the administration, and I was constantly beating the competition on stories. These lies all just get regurgitated. You know, I can spend my time doing my job, or waste it on talking about this nonsense."

But burgeoning criticisms of Judith Miller's work have gone beyond the story of the baseball-capped scientist to question both the timing and the standards of her journalism, as well as public traces of her own politics. However, the MET Alpha team's mysterious scientist has brought her the largest amount of ridicule from media critics. Probably, the most incisive, painful assessment of that report came from one of Miller's own colleagues in the *Times* news room, who was quoted by a columnist in the *New York Observer*: "It was," he said, "a wacky-assed piece."

Even wackier, though, was what the entire institution of journalism did to affect the most profoundly important political decisions in America.

PART II

JUST WALK AWAY

7

REWARDS OF SERVICE

Right is still right, even if nobody is doing it. And wrong is still
wrong, even if everybody is doing it.

Texas Ranger saying

Bill Burkett thought he was dying. Each heart beat, the rise
and fall of his pulse, registered in his head as a hard blow
to the skull. Everything he saw was rotating, spinning
through a dizziness that tilted all of his perceptions. Burkett's skin had become so acutely sensitive he was unable to wear
clothes. Walking was impossible, and, eventually, he was unable
to get himself to the bathroom. Body temperatures hovering between 101 and 104 degrees triggered recurring convulsive attacks.
Whenever sleep came, he was sitting nearly upright in a recliner.
Lying down pressed a dreadful weight on his brain and sent him to
the verge of unconsciousness.

A knock at the door dragged the career military man from his
haze of pain. Burkett's wife, Nicki, who had been nursing him
through the illness, had left him alone while she went to the drug-
store to fill a prescription. Because he could no longer walk, Bill

Burkett pulled himself across the floor, an agonizing crawl to see who might have knocked. Possibly, it was important. Family and friends knew that he was too ill to answer. Maybe it was someone with good news about clearing up a conflict over his health care at Dyess Air Force Base in Abilene. By the time he made it to the door, however, the visitor, whoever it was, had disappeared.

But something more frightening than even his disease was about to enter the Burkett household.

"There is no confirmed connection to what happened that day, but this was a strange event within the day, that I instinctively believe may be related," he said.

It was mid-afternoon, and Burkett noticed that his wife had not retrieved the day's mail. After he pulled himself up, and lifted the letters out of the box, he heard a metal on metal clinking sound. The mailbox at the Burkett residence was a common type made of a tin and painted a flat black. At the bottom, there were drainage slits, approximately ⅜-inch wide. After reaching his hand in to feel along the entire length of the box, Burkett's fingers came upon a .45-caliber Winchester bullet. It had been taped to a piece of paper. Holding it up in the West Texas daylight for examination, he saw there was nothing written on the slip of paper. Burkett studied the bullet closely. Etched into the side, in black ink, he saw his own name.

"LTC Burkett."

Lieutenant Colonel Bill Burkett tried to rub off the letters. The ink did not dissolve.

"I was sick and scared," Burkett said.

This was not the first threat his family had received. The previous week, one of their cars, which had been parked on the street in front of the house, had two holes shot into the driver's side of the windshield. Bullets were found lodged in the seat back cushion. Struggling to simply get through a day without pain, Burkett did not know how to deal with the mysterious dangers confronting his family.

"I was so sick and scared at that time that I waited until five or six days later to report the threats," he explained.

A phone call threatening his wife was what finally prompted Bill Burkett to get the police involved in investigating who was terrorizing his household.

"Nicki got a call," Burkett said, "from a male voice that told her she 'better check the brakes on that blue car before you go to work this afternoon. Wouldn't want you to have a fatal accident.' At that point, we knew they knew too many details about our schedules and habits to be safe."

Although he did not want to follow his mind where it was leading, Bill Burkett had a very distinct idea about who was making his miserable existence even worse. He had been the Senior Plans Officer with the Texas National Guard in Austin, and was the leader of a comprehensive analysis on the readiness of the state's military force. Burkett's findings were disturbing. In his estimation, the Texas National Guard, under Governor George W. Bush, was not capable of performing any valuable missions to assist the U.S. military. Further, there was a culture of deceit and corruption, which led to falsifying troop numbers, cheating on officer exams, and keeping "ghost soldiers" on rosters in order to maintain federal funding. People without credentials, but with political connections, were being promoted without merit.

General Daniel James, who had been appointed to command the Texas National Guard by Governor George W. Bush, had sought the expertise of Lieutenant Colonel Bill Burkett, a Texas Guardsman and noted strategic planner and consultant. James wanted a "work-out strategic plan" for the state, and Burkett, who, at that time, had 25 years in the Guard, and experience in the areas of plans, operations, and intelligence, was recommended by senior Guard staff with the concurrence of Bush associates. During the Gulf War in 1991, Burkett had conducted training and planning for troops deploying out of Fort Hood, Texas. As part of the 49th Armored Division's War Plans cells in the Texas National Guard in Austin, Burkett's background made him a natural fit to assist in the Simulation Center at Fort Hood.

When he was called to conduct his examination of the Texas National Guard, Burkett says he was given unobstructed access to General James.

"I kept asking him, 'What's important to you? How do you see this operation developing?' I wanted to know how he wanted things to work. I needed to know his vision for the forces. And I always asked him, 'What's your boss [Governor Bush] telling you?' I couldn't get much accomplished without knowing what he viewed his mission to be. I found out later that [Governor Bush's Chief of Staff] Joe Allbaugh had told a number of officers, 'The mission Danny James has is to keep this son-of-a-bitch out of the newspapers.'"

During her administration, Texas Governor Ann Richards had seen the Texas National Guard supply helicopters for a federal government raid on a religious sect outside of Waco. Those helicopters were taped by television cameras as they delivered armed support for agents from the Bureau of Alcohol, Tobacco, and Firearms when they stormed the wooden walls of the Branch Davidians' home at Mt. Carmel. A failure by Richards' office, and the Guard's commanders, to adequately explain the state's involvement in the deadly assault harmed the reputations of the governor and the Texas National Guard. A drug task force within the Guard had not kept Governor Richards' office informed of details of its participation in the ATF operation. Television and newspaper reports about the tragic conflict, and the Guard's complicity in the events leading to the deaths of more than 80 people, were perceived to have angered the generally conservative Texas voters.

The Bush team did not want any political complications caused by the Texas National Guard. In fact, there were opportunities to use the Guard's shortcomings as political fodder as soon as the presidential campaign was launched. Improving the Texas Guard would take away specific political arguments about military readiness under the administration of President Bill Clinton. No one in the governor's office in the Texas capitol building in Austin had any interest in making the Guard a better military force.

Either unaware or unconcerned of the political dynamics at work when he was summoned to assist, in April of 1996, Bill Burkett created three teams of experts to intensely scrutinize the Texas National Guard. By September, he was delivering his brief, the most extensive in the history of the state's military operations, to General James. Within his report, there was great detail on the shortcomings of the Guard's readiness process and the results of those failures, as well as other potential complications that might arise. This summary led to the drafting of a strategic plan, and Burkett was asked by James to remain with the Guard and implement recommended changes.

As his work drew him deeper into the function of the Texas adjutant general's department [a state agency], and the Texas National Guard [a federal military force], Burkett encountered what he later described as "major scandals and absolute violations of law and regulation." According to Burkett, the command structure began to resist Burkett's findings, refusing to accept the evidence. When he tried to implement his recommendations, Burkett discovered officers were fighting all attempts to improve the Texas National Guard.

Apparently, nobody wanted to hear what Bill Burkett had to say.

"They first got mad at me," he said, "when I clearly identified a full case that the leadership of the Texas Air National Guard was marginally successful; doing less than they should and not abiding by either the stated objectives of the departments of the Army and Air Force, or the very needs and objectives they had established themselves. They got madder when I pressed the issue that technically they were failing to meet required funding objectives based upon contractual obligations to the federal funding agency. They got madder when I pressed the overall readiness issue. Got even madder when I uncovered the [ghost soldiers and promotion] scams."

Political pressure on Burkett was building from within the Guard's officer ranks. "He was a very hard-working man," General Danny James said. "I think he even worked himself into bad health. But he didn't seem to have much tolerance for people who didn't agree with his ideas." Nonetheless, General James must have believed in Burkett's efforts because he ordered his chief of staff to find a permanent position for Burkett at the rank of Lieutenant Colonel.

Burkett's promotion was blocked by the chief and director of personnel, in spite of the General's recommendations. His quality analysis, though, continued, and Burkett pressed, unsuccessfully, for changes in the Guard's operations, structure, and overall preparedness to perform military missions. Eventually, he submitted a second report to General James that identified further military shortcomings, and other "serious and catastrophic shortfalls." James signed it.

"I took twelve former senior commanders into a work room, working sixteen-hour days for eleven days, and we totally took the Texas Army National Guard apart, piece by piece, and rebuilt it. When we took it apart, we saw [sic] all of the stench," Burkett explained.

Perhaps, because of increasing internal resistance to Burkett's determination to improve the Texas National Guard, General James, under new orders, dispatched Burkett to Ft. Clayton, Panama, as a Quality Site Team Chief to review the transfer of Ft. Clayton to the Panamanian government.

"This happened only because I refused to falsify readiness and information reports," Burkett claimed. "I confronted a fraudulent scheme that kept 'ghost soldiers' on the books for additional funding, and I refused to falsify personnel records of Governor Bush."

Burkett knew he had angered the command structure of the Guard, and the political establishment in the offices of Governor George W. Bush. A series of special projects for the Army, though, also suited Burkett's skills, and his eleven-day assignment in Panama was successful.

On the long flight back northward, Burkett began to feel discomfort, a rising nausea, and physical unease he was unable to identify. The rigors of work, or travel, he thought; possibly even a digestive bug contracted in the tropical environment. Nothing to be overly concerned about. He made it to the airport in Abilene before he passed out.

Initially, Bill Burkett believed he had been hit by the flu while in Panama. Some of the symptoms pointed in that direction. Both his pulse and temperature were elevated, and he had dizziness, a ringing in his ears as well as a tenderness to touch. Slowly, though, he began to lose some of the sensation on his right side. Within nine days of his collapse, he was no longer able to walk because of the severe dizziness and failing muscular function.

After recovering consciousness at the Abilene Airport, Burkett was taken home for bed rest, convinced, as was his family, he had picked up the flu from a fellow passenger on one of his crowded international flights, or, perhaps, in the tropical airs of Panama. Recovery, though, did not come. If this was the flu, it was persistent, lingering in Burkett's body in a way no disease ever had. He tried a number of over-the-counter drugs, and nothing seemed to make his affliction abate. After five or six days of agony, Burkett made a request to be treated at Dyess Air Force Base's military hospital near his home. As an active duty Lieutenant Colonel in the Texas National Guard, and while under orders for Panama from the department of the Army, he was eligible for medical care from any military facility. All he needed was authorization from one of his superior officers.

According to Burkett, none of his supervisors at Camp Mabry Headquarters of the Texas National Guard would take Bill Burkett's calls. He called every day to report his status.

"They were mad at me," he said. "Remember, I had confronted their whole sort of culture of corruption. I refused to participate in a process of falsification of troop readiness and failing equipment status reports. Worse than that, I challenged their scam promotions of political cronies. Remember, I consistently, but professionally commented about actions (not embarrassingly within the meeting setting, but one-on-one after the meeting setting), about the inconsistencies of information being sent forward in reports, and the facts that we knew to be true. They got mad at me for inferring they were liars, and thieves, I guess, in a nutshell."

Burkett had been relentless. After his team's initial analysis and report, he helped lobby Congress and the Pentagon to provide resources to modernize the Texas Army National Guard. On April 15, 1997, the Army chief of staff under the Clinton administration, General Dennis Reimer, who was in Austin on other business, made a courtesy call on Governor George W. Bush. General Reimer offered to "modernize the force and structure" of the Texas Army National Guard and make it more relevant and useful within the total force structure, and provide the equipment, training, and funding necessary to accomplish most of the suggestions made by the panels of senior officers formed by Burkett. Although the Guard had been reduced in troop strength by 8000 in the first three years of Bush's initial term as governor, the Texas governor refused the help from the U.S. Army.

"This was the thing that would have legitimately improved readiness and increased funding and training and modernized equipment," Burkett said. "I guess I threw a bit of a fit when they just tossed that all away after we had worked so hard to get the offer. The force structure just wasn't relevant and, therefore, of limited value to a fight in Iraq, Syria, Iran or other places, and it's not of much use in peacekeeping, either."

After spending his entire career in the military, Bill Burkett understood the influences of politics on soldiers, commanders, and the government. Even if he only realized it in retrospect, Burkett learned that Governor George W. Bush was not interested in force readiness. Already quietly planning for a presidential bid, Bush and his staff intended to make the Clinton military a lead issue in the campaign for the White House. Accepting the Pentagon's offer of money and other resources presented by General Reimer would have diminished political claims by Bush that the Clinton administration was not concerned about the U.S. military.

Criticism of Bush was growing, though, because of the chronic problems within the Texas National Guard. No other governor in the United States had complete control of an entire division. In order to fade political heat on weaknesses in the Texas guard, 300 troops of the 15,000 in the 49th Armored Division were trained as a command and control unit for deployment in Bosnia. Taxpayers spent $4 million on their training. The move was perceived as entirely political, a tactic to fade the heat off Governor Bush for low readiness levels in the Texas National Guard.

When George W. Bush launched his presidential campaign in the summer of 1999, his first policy speech was about the failings of the U.S. military under the leadership of Bill Clinton and the Democratic party. In a speech delivered at the storied military academy The Citadel, Bush denounced Clinton for allowing the military to become slow-moving and burdened by an antiquated force structure. These were, of course, the precise problems Bill Burkett had identified in the Texas National Guard during Bush's tenure as governor. As Bush walked through the palmettos to speak to cheering cadets at The Citadel, he was the commander of the slowest moving and least ready National Guard division in the United States.

Not a single reporter wrote of the hypocrisy.

Pointing out all of these flaws, apparently, did nothing to increase Bill Burkett's popularity among his fellow officers.

"I view him as a guy who wanted access to power," said Gen. Danny James, who hired Burkett. "And when things did not work out the way he wanted them to, he didn't take it very well."

Struck down by a mysterious disease while on duty, Burkett, nonetheless, expected to be provided appropriate health care, a benefit enjoyed by every soldier serving their country. Because he was only on temporary duty with the Army, and was an officer of the National Guard, his treatment at a U.S. military base required clearance by his commanders in Austin. Unfortunately, according to Burkett, no one at Camp Mabry, Austin headquarters of the Texas National Guard, was willing to talk to him. Almost delirious, Burkett worked his way down the list of his superior officers, hoping he might get a formal approval of health care, which was, by federal law, his right. No one gave him authorization, nor even got on the phone to hear his anguished pleas.

James, again, discounted Burkett's version of events. "That makes no sense, and he knows it. He had active duty orders. All he had to do was contact the nearest military base, and he would have been given health care. We didn't deny that to him. We couldn't even if we wanted."

Burkett considered James' characterization incomprehensible, especially considering evidence entered into a lawsuit Burkett had filed against his commanders.

Regardless, Burkett said he hesitated to run to an emergency room, constantly believing he had to be on the verge of recovery. Also, as a rancher, his finances were suffering as a result of a five year drought. An emergency room visit would be expensive, and he did not feel he should pay for critical care when he had earned it through his military service. Every day, he kept thinking he'd get better, or get care at the base, before he decided to call a doctor.

Pain and desperation were overwhelming Bill Burkett. His fever soared to near fatal levels, and nothing his wife found in the local pharmacy, or a doctor recommended over the phone, provided relief. Nine days had passed, and there was no word from Austin on getting medical clearance. Owning a cattle operation, Burkett had a small inventory of drugs he used on his animals. Assuming he had a severe case of the flu, he decided to use some of the dosages of cattle penicillin. Bill Burkett gave himself Procaine Penicillin G by approximating his weight level against the drug's potency on animals. Initially, the fevers were not checked, and Burkett finally gave himself a dosage that was three times the recommendation for his body mass.

"We found that the fevers were relieved somewhat with the penicillin," he explained. "I went from convulsive fevers at 104 degrees to 102 and then 101 when we used that penicillin. None of this was done under a doctor's care or knowledge."

As drastic as this decision was, a doctor later told Burkett the self-prescribed animal penicillin almost certainly saved him from death.

Bill Burkett's difficulties, though, were just beginning. There were months of struggle ahead of him, not just to stay alive, but to get the military health care that was rightfully his. Whatever disease was destroying his health, he assumed he had contracted it in

Panama while serving in the U.S. Army, as an active duty officer of the Texas National Guard. He was entitled to treatment.

Burkett had to wonder, though, if there wasn't something else in his way. Inadvertently, he says, he had found himself in the midst of conversations with Bush advisors and Guard officers about Governor George W. Bush and his years in the Texas Air National Guard. According to Burkett, the governor's office had called General Danny James to inquire about details in Bush's service file. In three separate incidents, Burkett said he had witnessed discussions about removing "embarrassments" from the governor's files.

Bill Burkett may have become a man who knew too much.

8

BIRD OF PRAY

A man's dying is more the survivor's affair than his own.

Thomas Mann

On top of a bunker, Chuck Dean and Richard Cunnare [kuh-nair] sat and stared at the South Vietnam sky. Dean, who had been flying his AH-1G Cobra attack helicopter in combat all day, was frustrated. In August of 1972, U.S. ground troops were no longer conducting combat operations in South Vietnam. Americans were flying air support for Vietnamese ground troops. Pilots like Dean and Cunnare were, essentially, getting briefings and intelligence from commanders in the Army of the Republic of Vietnam (ARVN). And things were not going well.

"Hey Chuck," Cunnare said. "Look at that."

Dean, who was on his second tour of duty as a helicopter pilot, tilted his head farther skyward in the direction Cunnare was pointing.

"What's that look like to you?" Cunnare asked, afraid of the obvious answer.

"A skull and crossbones," Dean said. "You know what it looks like."

The cloud, drifting through the heavy tropical air of Southeast Asia, might have been a warning for Chuck Dean and Richard Cunnare.

"I might not be able to take this much longer, Chuck."

"Yeah, I know what you mean," Dean replied. "I don't think I'm going to make it through this."

Both men had been flying combat for months; up to five days in a row before they were given time off to rest. In between their duty rotations, though, they were expected to keep track of what was happening on the battlefield. Both aviators knew they were at greater risk than before American ground forces had been pulled out. Cunnare, in fact, had flown the last extraction of U.S. soldiers, the 196th Light Infantry, which were ordered off the field no later than D-Day, June 6, 1972, by President Richard Nixon. Cunnare was providing cover in his Cobra as Hueys withdrew the final Americans. One hundred and twelve thousand U.S. troops had been ordered home from Vietnam by August of that year.

Combat hardened by his first tour as a medic and crew chief in the 45th Medical Evacuation Air Ambulance Company, Cunnare liked aviation enough to return to the states for pilot training in order to go back to Vietnam as an aircraft commander. He did not really begin to worry about flying in combat until his fellow pilots started being sent home. Experience in battle was being tossed away, and that was deadly.

"Our top twelve pilots left our unit all in one day. All of a sudden, I am lead Cobra aircraft commander without any experience there with me any more. All of a sudden, all of that going to school on the enemy we had was gone," Cunnare said.

The war needed fire-tested pilots and troops. The North Vietnamese Army (NVA) regulars had launched what came to be known as the Easter Offensive, a six-month long battle to capture the Imperial City of Hue. NVA commanders were trying a military maneuver to split the country into three separate battlefields. Nixon had ordered the bombing of Hanoi and Haiphong in retaliation for the new North Vietnamese offensive. But American gun ships were continuing to be flown in support of the ARVN in South Vietnam. As the North Vietnamese Army moved through the Demilitarized Zone and on to the cities of Quang Tri and Hue, attack helicopters were, for the first time, deployed into a mid-intensity battlefield.

On the jungle floor below them, U.S. pilots like Cunnare and Dean saw troops in trenches, anti-aircraft emplacements, heat-seeking missiles, and surface-to-air missiles.

"The stress level on a battlefield like that," Cunnare explained, "is so much more intense than anything we had done in helicopters. We ended up getting orders to destroy the enemy from the field with fire from the air. That was one of the first times that orders like that had ever been given to helicopter crews."

According to Cunnare, Chuck Dean had just flown through a very dangerous day in the Easter Offensive. Command and control had broken down, and "a bunch of guys got shot up pretty bad." Dean's Cobra had also been damaged in the fight, and neither he nor Cunnare felt that any of it should have ever happened. When Cunnare looked at his friend, he saw a "thousand yard stare" in Dean's eyes.

"Rich, you need to leave me," Chuck Dean said. "I'm going down."

"No, I'm not. And you aren't going down, either."

In fact, Dean had already gone down once. His first time in Vietnam, he had flown C-model gun ships and had taken a large caliber bullet through the top of his leg. After being sent home, Dean had opened up a crop dusting service in Searcy, Arkansas, north of Little Rock. His marriage, though, was deteriorating. When his wife won custody of their infant daughter in a divorce, Chuck Dean picked up the phone and called the Army and asked if they needed any Cobra pilots. He had been a courageous pilot, constantly taking chances, and had saved uncountable lives. Dean was probably drawn back to the war because it made him feel useful, and it was something he was very good at. But combat was beginning to exact a psychological toll on Dean.

On top of that bunker, perceiving dark omens in tropical cloud formations, Lawrence Charles Dean had become convinced he was soon to die.

"He just said his time was here," Cunnare recalled. "And he knew it. When a guy starts doing that, you don't want to fly with him. You really don't. You need to get him to a doctor. Get him sedated. Get him down for a while. Evaluate him. Whoops. There wasn't anybody else to do the job. They sent all of these other guys home."

Cunnare tried to talk Dean into grounding himself, but he refused. He also persisted with his dark, fearful talk of death. Dean was unable to run as a result of the loss of muscle tissue after he had been shot, and he constantly told Cunnare, or anyone else who flew with him, if they went down, Dean intended to stay behind while his co-pilot escaped. Eventually, Richard Cunnare began to believe in Dean's troubling vision.

"He knew. I knew. I felt it," Cunnare said.

While they watched the clouds pass and awaited new orders, Chuck Dean told Cunnare that he had just written what he assumed was his last letter to his daughter. In the late summer of 1972, she was preparing for kindergarten. Dean had tried to explain to his daughter that he would always be with her in spirit, even though he would not be present physically, to put his arms around her, and watch her grow into an adult. Dean wrote his daughter that he would always love her.

"I just had this feeling," Cunnare explained. "If I got into an aircraft with Chuck, something was gonna happen. I would not have made that choice to fly with him, if I could. I thought everybody knew how bad Chuck was. And I was flying with another guy the night before, and they pulled the switch out of my co-pilot."

Cunnare had been on a different five-day shift than Dean and did not expect to fly with Dean again until their schedules were changed. Because of the pilot shortage, however, crews were often allowed to fly beyond their five-day shifts and overlap into the flight sequences of other helicopter teams. Dean, who was beginning to appear oblivious to combat dangers, walked up to Cunnare just as his Cobra had finished being rearmed and refueled on the pad. After flying four consecutive hours of missions from 1:00 to 5:00 A.M., Cunnare was tired. When he had finished an external check of the aircraft before going back into combat, Cunnare looked up and saw Chuck Dean.

"Ya know, he gets into the aircraft and hands me an omelet sandwich. I love omelet sandwiches. And he has one of these little things of orange juice. He says, 'I'll fly. You eat something.' So, I eat the sandwich and we're talking and everything going up there, and we get our first mission of the day."

Orders had come over the radio to go back into a region Cunnare had been scouting twice during the previous day. Intelligence had reported that the North Vietnamese Army's 325th Infantry Division was working its way along a river tributary in an effort to resupply the attack on Quang Tri City. With Dean as aircraft commander of the Cobra, and Cunnare on the weapons systems, they flew from the coastal plains to the foothills, searching for signs of the enemy.

They found evidence quickly and easily.

Thick bundles of communication wires were running along the river bank, and huge stacks of gear were visible in the clearings. Cunnare spotted a trampled path, worn and muddy, which indicated that hundreds of troops had passed along the jungle trail during the previous night.

"The hair's going up on the back of your neck," Cunnare recalled.

The purpose of the reconnaissance mission was to draw enemy fire. ARVN commanders and their U.S. advisors were trying to determine a "box" where the NVA division was located. B-52 bombers were orbiting overhead and were set to scour the location with massive ordnance. As Chuck Dean guided the helicopter to a higher altitude after their first pass over the site, the enemy opened up on the

Cobra from all sides. The two men expended all of their ammunition, 76 rockets, and 40-millimeter mini-guns in less than three minutes while escaping.

Cunnare was angry. After two similar flights the day before, he had provided coordinates of the NVA division. He did not understand the rationale behind conducting the risky operation again. Unfortunately, Dean and he had been given direct orders, and there was no way to avoid the flight. The fact that they had just been through the concentrated attack and had not received a hit left both men thinking they were safe and done with the assignment.

"I was euphoric," Cunnare said. "We had gotten away with it again, ya know? I told Chuck, you know, those are the lousiest goddamned shots I have ever seen. They oughta be ashamed of themselves. We were bantering back and forth that way."

Cunnare knew a bit about combat danger. His first time in Vietnam, he had served as a crew chief on a medical evacuation "Dust Off" helicopter, while also being trained as a medic. Generally, several times a day, Cunnare and the men he flew with were sent into the midst of deadly firefights to airlift out the dead and wounded. In 1968, he had been shot out of the sky four times. While trying to rescue troops in a valley near Song Be, the Huey helicopter on which he was working suffered more than eighty bullet holes. The aircraft commander had a massive part of one leg blown off. This was the first day of the Tet Offensive by the Viet Cong, and Cunnare's crew had already lifted out a half dozen American grunts.

Cunnare remembered the enemy shooting at his Huey from a distance of ten feet as they flew in directly at a ridgeline. When he looked down, he saw a North Vietnamese soldier armed with a rocket-propelled grenade launcher (RPG). The pilot stood the Huey on its tail, pulling up sharply to avoid the RPG. The maneuver caused the aircraft to stall, and the commander dropped altitude, diving back through the landing zone, where the battle was raging, to gain airspeed and rise out of the fight. As they passed through the landing zone, machine guns raked the side of the Huey. The ship limped back to the airfield at Song Be and crashed. Cunnare, however, avoided serious injury.

Less than a month before Dean and Cunnare had received their orders in 1972 to find the "box" for B-52s, Cunnare was part of a mission that went so badly he was extremely fortunate not to have been killed. He was using his Cobra in a combat cover support role as a huge, twin rotor Chinook moved in to drop a sling and airlift a helicopter, which had been brought down by the North Vietnamese the previous day. Cunnare, piloting the Cobra, began flying expanding concentric circles over the area, scouting for approaching enemy. The Cobra serving as his wingman stayed directly off Cunnare's right side.

As the flight circles widened, Cunnare believed he had moved into a safer range, which was away from the helicopter retrieval operations. An RPG, however, rose up from the jungle and slammed into his ship's left, inboard rocket pods. The impact knocked out two of his rockets, but the RPG had been fired at Cunnare's Cobra from such a close range that it had not had time to arm, or was simply a dud. There was no explosion, but the entire left side of his aircraft was quickly covered by flames. In the other helicopter, Cunnare's wingman screamed at him over the radio to get his burning Cobra on the ground.

Under power, Cunnare managed to land his ship. Unfortunately, he was in the middle of Viet Cong troops. Rocket motors in the launch tubes were running, but they had not released. If the rockets armed and exploded, Cunnare and his co-pilot, Billy Holmes, would die. Panicking, both young men stumbled out of the helicopter. One of them, however, hit the collective, a handle between the seats that is used to control flight. Before Cunnare was free of the burning Cobra, it began to lift back into the air, and he fell fifteen feet to the ground. Landing on his shoulder, Cunnare also discovered that his leg was injured. He struggled to get away from the burning Cobra, the rockets, and approaching Viet Cong.

An OH-6A Scout chopper swept down to rescue Cunnare and Billy Holmes. On approach, the smaller ship was gunned down by Viet Cong. Whirling blades passed within a few feet of Richard Cunnare's head, and the wreckage settled about fifteen feet from where he was standing. When the Scout hit, it caught fire, and Cunnare pulled the two crew members free while telling them their helicopter was burning. They clambered past him and ran to safety to avoid any potential explosion. Eventually, a Huey settled into the landing zone, and pulled out all four of them before the VC were able to close in for a kill. Cunnare spent a week in Da Nang, recovering, before he was able to return to flight duties.

Images of those narrow escapes lingered in Richard Cunnare's memory, vividly, and fueled the euphoria he was feeling as he and Chuck Dean returned from their mission of scouting the movement of the North Vietnamese Army's 325th Infantry Division. They had gotten away with something again. Every day seemed to be more and more dangerous. The ARVN commanders, and their American advisors, were just learning how to concurrently fight the air and land battle. Combat rules had changed overnight, and no one, especially not the Army of the Republic of Vietnam, truly understood close air support tactics on the mid-intensity battlefield.

Relieved that they were done for the day, Dean and Cunnare put their Cobra down at Landing Base Sally. Cunnare had already flown a full shift, and assumed that if there were other missions, they were certain to be less risky than the one he had just concluded with Dean. If they were to go back out again, he figured it would be for a bomb damage assessment after the B-52s had dropped their payloads in the box. That type of job was fairly safe.

Before their turbines had stopped whining, an American colonel, who had been advising the Vietnamese, approached Cunnare and Dean on the pad.

"Gentlemen," he said. "I think we're going to have to rely on your professionalism."

To Cunnare, this meant only one thing.

"It's just another way of saying you're gonna have to go out and get killed. I'm sorry. And he gave us a direct order to go back out to that area and parallel the ridge where we got the heaviest fire. Personally, I objected. You do not parallel. That's committing suicide."

A fourth run through that region made no sense to Richard Cunnare. A "box," coordinates for the B-52 bomb strike, had already been established after the first two passes. The third, when they had nearly been shot down, was confirmation. Cunnare was astounded by the orders to return.

"We already knew the box," he insisted. "I was trying to explain that to the Colonel. You can't be a yes man as a pilot. You had to say things like, 'Well, sir, if you want us to do that, I can't accept direct responsibility because this is suicide. Give me a direct order, and I'll do it, sir.'"

"Did you say that?"

"I didn't say it that time. I wish I had."

When he looked at Chuck Dean, Cunnare said his friend's eyes had "glazed over."

"I had never been so scared in all my life," Cunnare said. "Chuck had reached that point of just being a warrior, and he didn't care. He didn't care about a thing, and when a man does that as an aviator, you just get a feeling."

Cunnare thought about the absurdities he was confronting. He had already lived through more than he had ever expected to endure, and now they were adding more chaos. The whole Easter Offensive battle seemed so ridiculous. Twenty-five thousand troops had already been killed on both sides. American officers and advisors to the Army of the Republic of Vietnam (ARVN) kept trying to convince their pilots that the South Vietnamese soldier was fighting extremely well. But ten divisions of NVA regulars had come south and the ARVN were routed from Quang Tri. Cunnare and Dean didn't see much of a will to fight among ARVN troops. In fact, he saw great reluctance. Every time Cunnare flew re-supply missions, ARVN soldiers tried to climb onboard his helicopter to get out of the battle. One aircraft commander, who was dropping off ARVN Rangers, turned around to see an American door gunner try to force the Vietnamese soldier out of his helicopter and into combat. The ARVN Ranger shot off the American's head.

The desperation of the Easter Offensive prompted the South Vietnamese to use brutal methods to instill the desire to fight into their troops. Timid soldiers were often imprisoned in deep pits, without water or food. If they refused to return to combat, they might be shot while sitting in the hole. Summary executions were frequently used to send a message to other men unwilling to face the enemy. Richard Cunnare had walked past several of these open pits and had seen dead soldiers covered in blood.

In the states, young men who did not want to fight the war, or support it in any way, were considered protestors. College students were granted deferments, and children of the rich and politically well-connected got into the National Guard to avoid combat. Cunnare's own brother was protesting against the war on his college campus. Cunnare also knew there were sons of congressmen, who managed to avoid Vietnam by using their family influence to be jumped into the National Guard ahead of long waiting lists. None of that bothered Richard Cunnare. In many ways, he did not view the war in a political context. He was simply doing his job. His first time in-country, as a dust-off crew chief and medical assistant, Cunnare was dedicated to getting wounded grunts out of firefights, regardless of the risk. Dust off was a special kind of aviation, flying medical evacuation, usually landing or hovering in the midst of a battle to take out the injured and dead. Going back to Vietnam as a pilot, he found himself providing covering fire for the reluctant South Vietnamese warrior.

But he had no interest in seeing protestors or sons of congressmen serving at his side. "These were men who didn't have the psychological ability to control their fear. All of these bugaboos happen

in their minds. And if you're in a pitched battle, and they're screaming for their mothers, you know what happens when that happens?
You're dead."

Richard Cunnare and Chuck Dean did not have options available to college students and the sons of congressmen. They were
flying back into fire.

Two OH-6A Scouts joined Cunnare and Dean's Cobra, and
their wingman commanding a second Cobra, Terry Overton. Before
liftoff, Overton had made his own assessment of Dean, and he decided to take the lead on the flight. Dean agreed without argument
to fly "chop 2." Both Cobra commanders had flown this type of mission many times. Their biggest fear was always the SA-7 shoulder
held rocket used by the North Vietnamese. To avoid becoming easy
targets, the ships came in low with their skids just above the tree-
tops, flying in a wingover position. The goal was to keep terrain in
the helicopter's background because the missile launcher was unable
to obtain an infrared lock on its target without a clear sky behind
the helicopter. The Cobra pilots allowed themselves three to five
seconds to find the enemy. One second longer gave a missile
launcher the time needed for a lock on target.

As they approached the ridgeline about fifteen kilometers south
of Quang Tri, Cunnare was watching Terry Overton in the lead helicopter. Overton continued flying past the objective because the plan
was to separate their routes, come back on both sides of the ridge,
and pass each other while directing suppressing fire, if needed, down
into the jungle. When they reached the end of the ridgeline, the two
Cobras were to pull away from each other in a tactic designed to ex-
pand the battlefield. No one was to fly over the same location twice.

But Chuck Dean was out of patience.

"We don't have to do this," he said.

Dean lowered the nose of his Cobra, and dropped his ship directly at the ridgeline. He had not radioed the maneuver to Terry
Overton in the lead helicopter. Cunnare, trying to man the weapons
systems, was stunned by the decision.

"Without saying a word, we are now at a point parallel to the ridge," he explained. "Here we are. Here's the ridge. Instead of going down and making our split, and coming around, Chuck just, ah, broke for the ridge. And he never called it, so we didn't have a wingman."

"So they've got a full shot at the side of you?" Cunnare was asked.

"Yeah, and they see us coming," he said. "And everybody gets on their guns, and they were just salivating."

The OH-6A Scout choppers were nearby in a running gun battle with a bunker complex their pilots had discovered. Their intended role, as smaller, less-armed aircraft, was to provide rescue and additional attack support. In the lead Cobra, commander Terry Overton knew he was out of position. But it was too late. As soon as Overton and his co-pilot, John Bridgers, got the nose of their Cobra reoriented, they saw Dean and Cunnare taking hits from large caliber machine guns.

"There were three big machine guns," Cunnare remembered. "And they got us in a triangulation and the aircraft got hit pretty hard."

Working the gun turret, Cunnare began firing the 40-millimeter cannons. Very quickly, the three hundred rounds began to tear into the jungle canopy.

"I'm hyper-focused, trying to direct my fire. There's all kinds of limitations with weapons systems. So you're super concentrating doing that. The next thing I know is I start hearing hits on the aircraft."

Three hundred feet above the ground, doing 160 miles an hour, Richard Cunnare saw fire coming out of the air conditioning vents. RPMs on the rotor were bleeding down, which meant the engine had been damaged, and the turbines were failing. The main rotor quickly separated from the engine to allow autorotation, a technique for maintaining lift by controlling the pitch of the freely spinning blades. Inside the cockpit, the intercoms and radios had also been shot out.

Cunnare was yelling at Dean.

"Are you on the controls, Chuck? Are you on the controls? Have you got it?"

A low RPM audio warning began wailing at them as the turbines wound down. More shells were hammering the side of the Cobra.

"Going down," Chuck Dean yelled. "Going down."

Richard Cunnare looked over at Chuck Dean and saw that he was not moving. Doing just as he had been trained, Cunnare began conducting emergency procedures. In a matter of seconds, the helicopter would be slamming into the jungle. An expanse of ever-widening green filled the cockpit bubble in front of Cunnare. He reached into his flight vest and clicked on the emergency locator radio. Frantic but focused, Cunnare grabbed the collective, the flight control lever that had been in Dean's hands a few moments ago. He pulled hard, trying to find pitch in the blades, and enough lift to lessen his speed of impact. But there was nothing there. The Cobra had taken rounds in the transmission, and the rotor pin was gone.

The helicopter was falling, not flying.

In an instant, on August 15, 1972, Richard Cunnare prepared himself to die.

9

THE GHOST SOLDIER

I think people need to be held responsible for the actions they take in life. I think that's part of the need for a cultural change. We need to say that each of us needs to be responsible for what we do.

George W. Bush, first presidential debate, October 3, 2000

August 15, 1972, the day that Richard Cunnare and Chuck Dean were shot down in Vietnam was a difficult time for George W. Bush, too. Word had reached him that verbal orders had been issued suspending him from flight status in the Texas Air National Guard. Bush was living in Montgomery, Alabama, at the time he learned of the disciplinary action. He was working on the Republican senatorial campaign of his father's friend, Winton "Red" Blount. Although there were almost two years left of his six-year obligation to the National Guard, Bush had failed to appear for his annual flight physical. After only twenty-two months of flying, he was permanently grounded.

And that's just one of the mysteries related to George W. Bush's military record.

In May 1972, Bush's National Guard file shows he stopped reporting for duty at the 111th Fighter Interceptor Squadron at Ellington Air Force Base near Houston. He had already moved to Alabama a month earlier, even though he had not yet sought permission to perform similar Guard duties in another state. The future president must have presumed his request for a transfer was certain to be approved. On an Application for Reserve Assignment document, dated May 24, 1972, Bush formally asked to serve in the 9921st Air Reserve Squadron in Montgomery, Alabama. Trained to fly the F-102 Delta Dart interceptor fighter, Bush's last flight at the Ellington air wing was recorded on April 16, 1972. The application to leave Houston can be interpreted to suggest he had no intention of continuing his responsibilities as pilot because he had applied for transfer to a postal unit in Alabama. Either way, Bush left for Alabama before he had requested transfer or received approval.

"We met just one week night a month," said Colonel Reese H. Bricken, who agreed to let Bush join the 9921st. "We were only a postal unit. We had no airplanes. We had no pilots. We had no nothing."

Nonetheless, responding to Bush's application only two days later, Bricken signed off on the transfer, but with an advisory. "The continuation of this type of unit is uncertain at this time and we may last three months, six months, a year or who knows! With this in mind, if you are willing to accept assignment under these circumstances, welcome! We're glad to have you."

Why Bush's commanders in Houston approved the transfer is baffling, almost as much as why they let him disappear from April to November without a reprimand. Federal taxpayers had invested almost a million dollars in training Bush to pilot a missile-equipped jet, and suddenly he was being cleared to leave for a Guard postal operation in Alabama. Bush's six-year hitch in the Guard did not expire until May 26, 1974, and he was allowed, according to regulations, to be transferred only to a Ready Reserve position. The Alabama postal unit was not in that category. The department of the Air Force, Headquarters Air Reserve Personnel Center in Denver denied the application for transfer by declaring, "He is ineligible for assignment to an Air Reserve Squadron."

Bush did not, however, hurry back to Texas from Alabama.

In fact, from May until September, when Bush finally wrote a second time asking for a transfer, and while technically still on duty with the Texas Air National Guard, no record exists to show George W. Bush did anything for any Guard operation. No one in the Texas Air National Guard command structure appeared to know the lieutenant's whereabouts. What was he doing during this time period when he had taken an oath and sworn to defend the United States? When the summer had passed, Bush wrote to his commander in Houston, Colonel Jerry Killian asking permission to perform equivalent training with the 187th Tactical Reconnaissance Group in Montgomery, a nonflying support organization. This was his second request.

"This duty," Bush wrote, "would be for the months of September, October, and November." The letter was dated September 5th, which meant it was likely no one had heard from Bush since his previous transfer was denied in late May.

Like the postal unit in Alabama, the commanders of the 187th Tactical Recon appeared happy to have the son of former Texas Congressman George H. W. Bush (who had become chairman of the Republican National Committee) ask to be placed on their roster. George W. Bush had already missed the 187th's Unit Training Assembly for the month of September, but his approval of transfer included orders that he appear "7–8 Oct 72 at 0730–1600 and 4–5 Nov 72 at 0730–1600."

"Lieutenant Bush should report to Lieutenant Colonel William Turnipseed, DCO, to perform Equivalent Training," the approval letter indicated. "Lieutenant Bush will not be able to satisfy his flight requirements with our group."

But Bush never showed up.

"I'm dead-certain he didn't show up," said retired Brigadier General William Turnipseed during the 2000 campaign. "Had he reported in, I would have had some recall, and I do not. I had been in Texas, done my flight training there. If we had had a first lieutenant from Texas, I would have remembered."

Turnipseed, who gave money to the Republican National Committee and described himself as a Bush supporter, suggested in 2004 that Bush might have performed drills in Alabama. Turnipseed, however, had no recollection of Bush on base.

Captain Kenneth K. Lott, director of the personnel branch of the Alabama National Guard, has also said he has no memory of Bush training with the 187th. Regardless of the recall of his commanders, Dan Bartlett, who became a spokesman for the Bush presidential campaign, said Bush did serve in Alabama.

"Governor Bush specifically remembers pulling duty in Montgomery and respectfully disagrees with the Colonel," [Turnipseed] said Bartlett. "There's no question it wasn't memorable, because he wasn't flying."

But why wasn't he flying? Who gave him permission to stop?

As a candidate and president (with the exception of a few questions on *Meet the Press*), Bush has refused requests to be interviewed on his time in the Guard, so any clarification he might offer as to what he did, or didn't do, in Alabama, has remained generally unavailable. He has said only that he did perform drills, but he can't exactly remember when, or what they were. Bush gave a vague response on his time in Alabama when he was asked about it while campaigning for president in Tuscaloosa. His response to NBC interviewer Tim Russert was, essentially, the same, unaltered message.

"I was there on a temporary assignment and fulfilled my weekends at one period of time," he claimed. "I made up some missed weekends."

In fact, there is no irrefutable National Guard record, nor any document of any kind, which has proved George W. Bush reported for drills in Alabama, as ordered, nor is there anyone in the 187th Tactical Recon unit who has come forward to say they witnessed Bush on duty. The *Air Force Times* reported during 2000 that the Bush

campaign was trying to find members of Bush's unit who might testify that he had been on duty. In spite of that effort, and a reward of
$1,000 offered by former members of the 187th for proof of Bush's
service as well as another offer of $2,000 by a former Guard pilot,
neither narrative testimony nor documentation has ever been produced that George W. Bush followed orders to appear at Dannelly
Air Field, Maxwell Air Force Base. *Interceptor Magazine*, the monthly
National Guard publication, which is distributed nationally, ran regular advertisements from former Guard members trying to find anyone to give testimony that they had seen Bush on duty in Alabama.
This, too, was unable to turn up a witness to back up Bush's story.
More critically, in both Texas and Alabama, not a single member of
the guard has ever said they remember doing weekend drills or summer camp with the congressman's son, who later became the president of the United States.

Albert Lloyd Jr., who handled personnel issues for the Texas
Guard during Bush's years of enlistment, initially admitted such con-
firmation does not exist, and that there was no way of knowing if
Bush appeared at the 187th Tactical Recon.

"If he did, his drill attendance should have been certified, and
sent to Ellington [Bush flight wing in Houston] and there would have
been a record. We cannot find the records to show he fulfilled the requirements in Alabama," he told Walter Robinson of the *Boston Globe*.
Lloyd later helped the Bush campaign try to figure out the candidate's
Guard records.

One of the people who first brought Bush's absence from duty to
the attention of journalists is a former railroad brakeman and a farmer
in Clinton, Iowa. Martin Heldt, who used the long layovers on the
railroad to read and educate himself, acquired all available National
Guard documents through the Freedom of Information Act. After
studying the materials extensively, Heldt decided that there were
several things that simply did not make sense then, or now.

"Bush is supposed to have orders," Heldt explained. "You can't
just get up and leave. But he did. And he got away with it. That letter

back to Killian has always bugged me. Killian knows that's not where Bush is supposed to be, over in Alabama. I mean, Killian had to know he [Bush] was gone since he was the one who had been dealing with him in the letters. I can't figure out why he let him get away with that."

Whatever Bush was doing in Alabama, he was apparently too busy to report to take his flight physical in Houston, scheduled for sometime during the three-month period preceding his birthday on July 6, 1972. He also did not seem to impress everyone in the Winton Blount campaign for U.S. senate. According to a full-time senior staffer within Blount's campaign, who did not want to be identified, Bush was "worthless" and "not dependable" in any of his work for Blount. This source, who was personally close to Bush, said he was "rarely available" to conduct campaign business, and that he never asked his supervisors for time off to attend any Guard duty. The Blount campaign staffer said "the Guard was the last thing on Bush's mind," and that he did not pack any uniforms, materials, or equipment for his time in Alabama. If Bush's behavior in a senatorial campaign were lax, it is unlikely he acted any differently with regard to his responsibilities in the National Guard.

That also may explain why he did not return to Texas for his physical.

The penalty for not being checked out by a military doctor was to lose his flight status. Verbal orders grounding First Lieutenant George W. Bush were made official by Major General Francis S. Greenlief, chief of the National Guard Bureau, on September 29, 1972.

"Reason for suspension: Failure to accomplish annual medical examination."

The suspension became an issue during the presidential campaign in 1999 and 2000, and it was not handled well by the Bush team. Dan Bartlett of the Bush campaign, who was given the task of talking to reporters about the sketchy National Guard performance of candidate Bush, originally claimed Bush did not appear for his physical because the Bush "family physician was unavailable" in Houston during that time period. Physical exams for Air National Guard pilots, however, are only conducted by qualified Air Force flight surgeons.

Bush's rationale for not taking his flight physical has never been adequately explained. Since he was living in Montgomery, Alabama, the location of Maxwell Air Force Base, it was a simple matter for Lieutenant Bush to schedule an examination with one of the flight surgeons on the base. However, Bush was away from Texas without orders, and his application to join the 9921st in Alabama had been turned down. If he were to report for a flight physical as required before his birthday on July 6, it ought to have been Ellington Air Force Base, where he was still on the flight duty roster. Approval of his transfer to the 187th Tactical Recon at Dannelly Air Field on Maxwell Air Force Base was still three months distant. No one had authorized him for any service or drills in Alabama, and he was expected to report to a flight surgeon in Houston.

After Dan Bartlett was informed that the Bush family doctor did not have authority to conduct the exam for the National Guard, he told the *London Times* that Bush did not "technically" need to take his physical.

"You take that exam because you are flying, and he was not flying," said Bartlett. "The paperwork uses the phrase 'suspended from flying,' but he had no intention of flying at that time."

Bush seemed to have unilaterally decided he was no longer going to perform his duties as a pilot. This was an odd interpretation of military conduct and discipline. After taxpayers had spent close to a million dollars training him to fly a highly technological aircraft in defense of the United States, Bush simply chose to stop two years short of completing his full six-year obligation, and no one in command intervened. Bartlett later tried to explain the suspension as nothing more than a bureaucratic complication caused by Bush's transfer to Alabama, and the fact that his paperwork was processed too slowly.

"It was just a question of following the bureaucratic procedure of the time," according to Bartlett. "He knew the suspension would have to take place."

The order to suspend Bush because of "failure to accomplish annual medical examination" was left open to interpretation because of an absence of detail. The language can be perceived to mean Lieutenant Bush simply never showed up for his exam. It can also be interpreted to suggest that he took the physical and did not pass, though that does not appear to have happened.

On December 31, 1969 the Pentagon announced plans to begin random drug and alcohol testing of U.S. military personnel. The new program did not begin to be implemented until April 1972, and many states failed to institute the testing until early in the 1980s. However, 1972, was the first year George W. Bush might have been exposed to the possibility of testing his blood for drugs and alcohol. "Failure to accomplish annual medical examination" can imply that Bush did not show up, or he was examined, and a foreign substance was discovered in his blood.

Bush was not oblivious to the Pentagon's orders for random testing. The military had made a point of spreading the word to each officer and enlisted person in the United States and overseas. Making everyone in the service aware of the risks they ran for substance abuse was the tactic for eliminating the problems caused in the Armed Forces by drugs and alcohol. Substance abuse was at crisis levels among U.S. troops in South Vietnam, and the Pentagon decided to test random samples of servicemen and women. The National Guard was not exempted from the new rules. Bush, like everyone else in the military, had to know about the new random testing policy. His commanders were required to inform all of their personnel.

A retired National Guard mission pilot, First Lieutenant Robert A. Rogers, was convinced that the September 29, 1972, order suspending Bush after the verbal orders in August, revealed Bush's personal conduct while in the Guard. Rogers worked closely with farmer Martin Heldt in acquiring Bush's Guard records, and in offering analysis of the documents. In his estimation, the suspension memo was a "smoking jet."

Rogers wrote that the memo "points to a potentially devastating interpretation: that Bush stopped flying two years short of his obligation because of substance abuse, either directly, because he failed his physical exam, or indirectly, because he refused to take it out of fear that he would fail it."

One of Bush's supervisors in the Texas Guard has said that the lieutenant did not fail the physical exam. "His flying status was suspended because he didn't take the exam, not because he couldn't pass," according to Colonel Bobby Hodges, Bush's commanding officer at Ellington.

But the question of why he didn't take the exam remains unanswered.

Self-described as a "hard partier" during his twenties and thirties, Bush has admitted to drinking excessively, though he has never acknowledged any use of illegal drugs. Originally, reporters were unable to get Bush to answer the question of whether he had ever used drugs. Eventually, though, when asked if he were able to qualify for a federal job under the government's drug usage guidelines during his father's administration, Bush responded affirmatively. By extrapolation from the date the question was posed, and the number of years required of nondrug use on a federal job application, some journalists reached the conclusion Bush was saying he had not used anything illegal since 1974. He was drinking, though, and sometimes too much. During the 1972 Christmas holidays, he took his younger brother Marvin out partying, and knocked over garbage cans with his car on the drive home. Upset, Bush's father confronted his eldest son, who was both drunk and angry enough to ask his dad if he wanted to go "mano a mano" outside of the house.

Among the documents obtained through FOIA by Martin Heldt, and Lieutenant Robert Rogers, there are three that offer evidence about George W. Bush's conduct, prior to joining the Texas Air National Guard. Bush's Enlistment Contract for the Armed

Forces of the United States asked a number of questions about his background. Item number 19, on the second page of the document, was, "Have you ever been arrested, indicted, or convicted for any violation of civil or military law, including minor traffic violations?" The blank space left for answering, which is the largest provided on the page, has been completely redacted. Of course, if Bush had not had anything to declare then that space would have been left blank, and there would have been no need to black out an entry. Instead, there is a half-inch wide swath of black where his answer must have been written. (If anything had been in this space, there was a chance it related to his arrest in New Haven, Connecticut for a college prank of stealing a wreath off of a fraternity house.)

Another official form identified as Statement for Enlistment in the National Guard, dated May 27, 1968, posed a series of four questions about criminal behavior. In a column next to the alphabetized questions, there are "yes" and "no" boxes for the enlistee to check. They, too, have been redacted with a black marker. The initial question asked, "Have you ever been arrested, charged, or held by Federal, State, or other law enforcement authorities for any violation of Federal Law, State Law, County or Municipal law, regulations or ordinance?" The other questions want to know if Bush had been convicted of a felony or any other offense, or if he had been imprisoned under the sentence of any court. The final one inquired as to whether he had been on parole, suspended sentence, or probation. Under item "e" the document said, "Enter full explanation for those questions answered 'Yes.'"

Below item "e," there are four columns for providing details of any offense. They are listed as "Reference Item," "Offense," "Date and Place," and "Disposition." Bush had apparently written something under each of those columns because the space below each listing is also redacted by black ink.

He had also given details of an incident on the second page of his "Request and Authorization for Active Duty Training/Active Duty Tour." Number 17 on that questionnaire asked, "Have you ever been arrested, indicted, or convicted for any violation of civil or military law including minor traffic violations? If 'Yes' explain stating nature of offense, date, name and place of the court and disposition of the case." Bush used up three lines of the seven provided in delivering his explanation. However, all of the information has also been redacted by black ink or marker.

Unless George W. Bush allows complete, unrestricted access to a printout of the entire microfiche record of his service from military archives in Denver and St. Louis, there will be no way to ever know if these incidents were patterns of behavior that led to his suspension, or if he simply lost flight status because he did not show up for his physical examination. Either way, the available evidence showed Bush was clearly unconcerned about the disciplinary action because he did not return to Houston and make any attempt to seek reinstatement as a pilot. Just over a month after the verbal suspension order was issued in August, Bush was still in Alabama, still working on the Blount for Senate campaign, when he finally asked, on September 5, 1972, to perform equivalent duty with the 187th Tactical Recon at Maxwell Air Force Base.

Although Bush claimed that he went back to Houston after Blount lost the election, records contradicted him and indicated he did not report to Ellington Air Force Base. In his annual Officer Effectiveness Report for the period May 1, 1972, to April 30, 1973, his commanders checked "Not Observed" on all 55 different categories in which they were asked to assess Bush's performance.

The two names on the report are Jerry D. Killian, whom Bush has identified as a personal friend, and William D. Harris Jr. Both Lieutenant Colonels. Killian, the same officer Bush wrote requesting the transfer to the 187th Tactical Recon unit in Alabama, was apparently under the impression, as was Harris, that Bush was doing his drills and regularly reporting for duty in Alabama.

"Lt. Bush has not been observed at this unit during the period of report. A civilian occupation made it necessary for him to move to Montgomery, Alabama," the two officers wrote in their annual report.

"He cleared this base on 15 May 1972, and has been performing equivalent training in a nonflying status with the 187 Tac Recon Gp., Dannelly ANG Base, Alabama."

Harris and Killian are deceased. However, retired Colonel Rufus G. Martin, director of personnel at Ellington during Bush's service period, has been reported as saying he was under the assumption that Bush had completed his required drills in Alabama during that missing year.

Bush's disappearance from Guard duty was confirmed in his discharge papers. A chronology in the military tenure of Lieutenant Bush showed that there was no record of any duty between May 26, 1972 and October 1, 1973. The May entry gave Bush twenty-two days as a First Lieutenant with the 111th Fighter Interceptor Squadron at Ellington. The next listing on the time sequence was his transfer to Denver reserve status on October 1, 1973, which was essentially a record keeping procedure that did not involve duty. If Bush had served any duty time between those two dates, it ought to have been reported on that chronology, and it was not.

In October of 1972, Bush's fighter group in Houston had been placed on a standby alert. Normally, this meant that pilots alternated turns sitting in the cockpit of their jets at the end of a runway. Also, F-102 pilots were in short supply during this latter stage of the Vietnam conflict, which made it even more of a mystery as to how Bush's commanding officers at Ellington Air Force Base might have lost track of a pilot who had twenty-two months of flying, and hundreds of hours at the controls. Bush should have been taking his turn, sitting for the four-hour shift, putting his F-102 in position for a take off roll, awaiting orders to fly on an intercept.

"That's the part I sure don't get," said Lieutenant Robert Rogers, a retired National Guard pilot. "During the Cuban missile crisis I spent a lot of time in a jet at the end of a runway, waiting to fly on a mission. I don't understand how they let this guy just stop flying, when they trained him, and they needed him. There wasn't any punishment, though. It doesn't appear that there were even any questions."

For most soldiers, National Guard duty had been considered secondary to the enlistee's civilian life. During times of conflict, however, service had been more closely scrutinized, and drills were mandatory because there was an increasing probability of being called to active duty in one of the U.S. armed services. A relaxed military culture in the Guard outside of war time, however, resulted in many cases of soldiers and airmen failing to report for their obligated training or duties. The Department of Defense decided to deal with this problem by adopting a policy that provided an option for ordering National Guard members or reservists to two years of active duty. Active duty generally meant being sent to the Army, going through basic training, and then getting shipped out to South Vietnam. The penalty was often applied not just against those who failed to show up for drills, but also anyone who "fails to perform satisfactorily."

And the penalty was used. But not against George W. Bush.

Bill Burkett spent three decades involved in the National Guard, and was an officer during the Vietnam War era. He finished his career as the state plans officer for the Texas National Guard while George W. Bush was governor. The men serving under Burkett who did not report for assigned duties during the Vietnam era were severely disciplined, not ignored.

"We didn't let anyone off of the hook. If I had a man over twenty minutes late for a drill, I sent out an arrest warrant, and the local police would pick those people up, even if they simply overslept (as was the case twice). Once, the police hauled in a guy who was having sex with his wife when they knocked on the door. Those were serious times for most of us."

And most malingerers were punished.

A Riverside, New Jersey reservist, who missed seven training days in 1967, was called for draft induction. Fred Goldstein, who was twenty-four years old at the time, argued unsuccessfully before the U.S. Court of Appeals for the Third Circuit that he had a valid medical reason for not appearing for drills. A similar case in San Diego, California, involved Marine Private Paul V. Winters. After

missing reserve drills, Winters was ordered back to active duty status, and he had filed an appeal with the U.S. District Court in San
Diego. The twenty-three-year-old lost his legal argument and was
ordered reactivated.

George W. Bush missed twenty-four sessions of National Guard
drills between 1972 and 1973, and no one said a word. His commanders had both the military authority, and Bush's own legal commitment to the Guard, as justification for issuing punishment. When
he joined the 111th Fighter Interceptor Group, he signed a separate
document affirming his awareness of laws that might send him to
combat for failure to perform his Guard drills.

"I understand that I may be ordered to active duty for a period
not to exceed 24 months for unsatisfactory participation as presently
defined in Chapter 41, AFM 35-3. Further, I understand that if I am
unable to satisfactorily participate in the ANG, [Air National Guard]
and have an unfulfilled military service obligation, that I may be discharged from the State ANG and assigned to the Obligated Reserve
Section (ORS), AF Reserve, Denver, Colorado, and subject to active
duty for a period not to exceed 24 months considering all previous
active duty and active duty for training tours."

A statement of understanding, which also bears Bush's signature,
explained what ought to have happened to him for being gone for a
year. Paragraph F said that his voluntary enlistment "will override any
classification for which I may be eligible under the Selective Service
System." This language, of course, meant that Bush was avoiding the
draft. The subsequent paragraph, however, was the one that empowered his commanding officers to turn him over to his local draft
board for having run off to Alabama without a transfer authorization,
and for not performing duty during his "missing year."

"If I fail to participate, I may be involuntarily ordered to perform
forty-five days active duty and/or be certified for induction." The
Texas Air National Guard commanders had every reason they
needed to make Bush available for induction in the draft.

Instead of punishing Lieutenant Bush, however, his commanders
did nothing more than write on his Officer Effectiveness Rating

Report that he had "not been observed" at his home base for an entire year. Had they ordered him to active duty, odds were quite good Bush would have spent time in the jungles of South Vietnam.

Retired Guard officer Bill Burkett said the "not observed" comment was as caustic a statement as Colonels Killian and Harris were able to write without putting their own military stature in jeopardy.

"When the two commanders simply said the man was not available for that rating period," Burkett explained, "they were saying the very most damaging things that can be said within an official OER. [Officer Effectiveness Rating]. Don't kid yourself. I know first-hand when those comments were first filed, several personnel experts up the chain of command called those two commanders and asked the very suggestive question, 'Are you sure you want to say it this way?' Again, I've been there, I know."

"Those were comments of anger and frustration of a commander," Burkett added. "You just don't make those kind of comments unless you have tried, failed, and the guy has rubbed your nose in it. Those were comments about—Who's in Charge? They were really 'career-enders.'"

During the presidential campaign in 2004, one torn, mysterious sheet of paper was supposed to prove George W. Bush did Guard duty for his last two years. First public reference to this document occurred in July 2000, as the Texas governor was taking the title of Republican Party presidential nominee. Jo Thomas, a reporter for the *New York Times*, got the candidate to agree to an interview about his younger days, which had been spent in Houston. Campaign officials clearly believed this softer, feature story was a good place to release evidence that Bush had reported for drills in Alabama. They provided the journalist with the controversial document, which was a list of points for dates served in the National Guard. (A later version of the document, without the tear, was released by the White House in February 2004. But it is unclear if that copy or the torn page was given to Thomas.)

In her narrative, reporter Thomas considered the document a legitimate confirmation. "National Guard records provided by the

Guard and by the Bush campaign indicate he did serve on November 29, 1972, after the [Alabama senatorial] election," she wrote.

The November 29 reference has appeared in the Bush military record only once, and it has never been unequivocally verified. Knowing that candidate Bush was certain to face daunting questions about his "missing year" in Alabama, the campaign produced an ARF statement of points earned. It purportedly showed Bush had served one day in the Alabama National Guard, on November 29, 1972, after working in the failed U.S. senate campaign of Winton Blount. This points statement, however, was torn along the left side, and it showed only the number "29," but not the month associated with that date. The tear occurred just to the left of the number, which was precisely where the abbreviation Nov., which was used by the National Guard on similar documents, was supposed to be visible. Unless she had a different record provided by the Bush campaign, reporter Jo Thomas of the *Times* appeared to have taken the word of Bush officials that the 29 was a reference to November of 1972.

There were several reasons not to take the points statement seriously. The left side tear ran a ragged course up a list of nine sets of numbers, which the Bush campaign said were dates associated with the days the points were earned by the young lieutenant. A letter "N," however, was the closest anyone came to determining a specific month to connect to one of the dates. Essentially, the document provided nothing more than a row of nine numbers. Also, the name on the top of the sheet, which was the simplest method for determining who earned these Guard points, had been torn away. Only the letter "W" remained. Bush officials have said, even though the months and name were not visible because of the tear that this document still proved Lieutenant Bush served at least one day in Alabama, and made up other missed duties. Bush told reporters in 2000 that he remembered making up his time on November 29, 1972. The only strength in this assertion was that the numbers on the torn document, which were supposed to be the dates, corresponded to an April 23, 1972, order listing days Bush was to report for "certain duty." That has also raised suspicions that the document was created to fit with the dates on his orders. Unfortunately, a copy of the April 23, 1973, orders was not included in his FOIA file. However, the campaign did provide those orders to a few reporters during the presidential campaign, raising questions about whether the full file was being delivered when requested under federal laws.

The torn points sheet, referred to as "Document 99" in Bush's file was discovered by Albert Lloyd. A supporter of Bush's, Lloyd was a personnel official with the Texas National Guard from 1969 to 1995, and helped the presidential campaign "make sense" of the candidate's service record. Lloyd said that Document 99 had Bush's social security number across the top.

"I had his social security number," Lloyd said. "They gave me a letter to present to the Guard so I could go in and look at his records. The social security number on the top of that paper is George Bush's. I know. I saw it and compared them."

Independently, though, no one has been able to corroborate this because the space for Bush's social security number was redacted by black ink. The only evidence of Bush's ownership of the points on the page was the letter "W." Pay records, such as check stubs or W-2 statements, which could verify earnings for the days claimed, were missing and not released in original FOIA files.

When Marty Heldt of Clinton, Iowa received his package of Texas National Guard documents under FOI laws, Document 99 was included. Lloyd said he found the points sheet some time around the middle of 1999, approximately a year before it arrived in Heldt's shipment of Guard files. Lloyd said it was found in a separate box of materials, which were not a part of the Bush official records file.

"I found it in a general orders file," Lloyd explained. "It wasn't a part of his personnel file. These were general Guard records, not Bush's records."

If true, Document 99 was inserted into Bush's official files. Although Lloyd said he discovered the document, he said he did not put it into the file. He turned it over to the campaign. Sometime after that, it was inserted into Bush's official record. Otherwise, it would not have been distributed to Heldt, and others who filed FOIAs. This mere addition to Bush's military record was "very unusual," according to several sources in the National Guard. Changing, or adding to a serviceman's record, almost thirty years later, is not done unless that soldier or airman has filed a formal petition before the Air Force Personnel Records Corrections Board. Bush has never made such a request. As a result, an unsigned, undated, and partially mutilated sheet of paper was submitted as a reason for skeptics to drop questions about his time in the Alabama and Texas Air National Guard. In fact, Bush's file record showed no activity at all from 1973, his date of release, until 1999, when he began his run for president. Suddenly, documents were dropped into Bush's military records personnel jacket as he prepared to run for the presidency. Prior to his campaign for the White House, Bush made no attempt to get his record corrected.

"This is a story that just really smells," said Marty Heldt, the Iowa farmer who attempted to get at the facts surrounding Bush and the Guard. "I think it's pretty obvious he skipped out for a year, and then all this time later they are trying to cover it up. They're embarrassed. The Guard's embarrassed. I don't see why anybody should take this thing [Document 99] seriously."

The United States military ought to be especially skeptical. Given the number of signatures needed on most records, detailed routing instructions and chain of custody requirements, verification and authorization of important dates, and other qualifications and protocols before any document is accepted, it is confounding that this partial piece of paper was allowed to be slipped into the Bush Guard files. Almost no information of value is available on Document 99, yet the military culture, which runs on command structures and audits, allowed the ripped piece of paper into an official record. One possibility is that there was an effort to fix Bush's background before it caused him trouble in the presidential campaign.

Credibility of Document 99 was also diminished when two of them were discovered in circulation. The second version has handwritten notations, which appear to clarify the numbers, and what they represent. First posted on the web site of *George Magazine*, the annotated copy of Document 99 included writing that totaled the points earned figures. This tally appeared to be an attempt to prove that the "W" on the top of the page had performed duty for late 1972 and early 1973. Unlike similar points statements, there is no heading on the bottom of Document 99 that reports total points. The cursive writing added to the version posted by *George* had a heading "Active Duty," which was underlined. Beneath that headline was the notation "9 days AD" [active duty], "32 days IADT" [Inactive Duty Training], and "15 Grat," which was a reference to the "Gratu-itous Points" that are granted to all Guard members who serve out their annual time. These figures are then summed as "56 points," which Bush needed to satisfactorily complete his annual service. His annual period of duty was charted from May, the month he entered the Guard. In the lower right hand corner of Document 99, printed in block letters rather than composed in cursive, and with a different color of ink, was the notation, "May 1972–1973."

Whoever wrote on this version of Document 99 seemed to have an interest in giving "W" credit for these service points, in spite of the fact that there are no months connected to the days and points, nor even a year. Who did the writing?

"Yeah, that's my handwriting," Albert Lloyd said. "I'm pretty sure I added up those numbers on the paper so that we could all figure out his duty days."

The numbers, however, don't add up. There are an unexplained additional 15 points on that page, which Lloyd appeared to grant "W," and there is not a listing of total points at the bottom of the document. A number should have been recorded next to the head-ing, "Total Points Accrued."

Thus, the only evidence that George W. Bush served any duty at all in the National Guard in Alabama and Texas between May 1972 and May 1973 was provided by a man who wanted to see Bush elected president, and who volunteered his time to help the cam-paign understand Bush's records. Albert Lloyd worked closely on the project with Dan Bartlett, the future White House communications director.

The annotated version of Document 99, however, does not show up in FOIA applications for Bush's file. The blank, virtually meaningless copy is included. Even if this piece of torn paper is a true and accurate depiction of Lieutenant Bush's service, as a minimum, it confirmed that he was in violation of a direct order to report for four "certain duty" days with the 187 Tactical Reconnaissance Group in Alabama. Those orders were for "7–8 Oct. 72" and "4–5 Nov. 72," not the 29th, which Document 99 claimed Bush served. Substantiation of this document, if it were possible, would provide certain corroboration that Lieutenant Bush was absent from all duty from the time he left Houston in April of 1972 until November 29 of that same year, the date he allegedly performed a day's worth of drills in Alabama.

At least one other factor challenged the veracity of Document 99, and it is not a minor consideration. Records at state National Guard offices have historically been kept within those particular headquarters. National operations of the Guard are, by design, decentralized, and were even more so during the Vietnam era. If Lieutenant Bush had actually served in Alabama on November 29, 1972, the time and points would have been on a record provided by the Alabama National Guard. No such document exists. Instead, a solitary number, "29," at the top of a list of other numbers, on a torn, redacted sheet of paper from Texas, rather than Alabama, was supposed to confirm that Bush did a day of duty with the 187th Tactical Recon.

"We don't even know that 29 refers to November," Marty Heldt said. "I don't know how we're supposed to believe that it proves he was doing duty in Alabama. They've tried to say it was for time served in Alabama. Well, what's it doing in the Texas records then, on a piece of paper that records Texas time? That's not supposed to happen. That's one of the reasons I'm pretty suspicious."

At the U.S. Air Force Selection Boards Branch in July 1973, Master Sergeant Daniel P. Harkness must also have been suspicious. Harkness was charged with overseeing the filing and completion of

Officer Effectiveness Rating Reports in his Denver office of the Air Force Reserve Personnel Center. After he got the report from Bush's commander in Ellington that he had "not been observed" and that Bush had "cleared this base," Harkness was apparently confused by the incomplete information. He sent a form, identified as a "Notice of Missing or Correction of Officer Effectiveness Training Report" to Bush's commanding officer at Ellington Air Force Base in Houston. In the remarks space of the form, Harkness was specific in demanding information on Bush's whereabouts, and his duty record:

> Ratings must be entered on this officer in Sections V & VI. An AF Fm 77a should be requested from the training unit so that this officer can be rated in the position he held. This officer should have been reassigned in May 1972 since he no longer is training in his AFSC or with his unit of assignment.

Harkness wanted Bush's commanders in Houston to provide a report on the lieutenant's progress at the 187th Tactical Recon Group, which he was supposed to be training with in Alabama, or whatever unit Bush was assigned to beginning in May 1972. Obviously, Major Rufus G. Martin was unable to deliver any information because Bush had not reported for duty. If Bush had shown up at the 187th on November 29, 1972, as Document 99 claimed, there ought to have been some report available by June 1973, which Martin could have sent to Harkness. But there was nothing.

"Report for this period not available for administrative reasons," Major Martin wrote. Above that line he had reconfirmed Bush's absence from Ellington. "Not rated for the period 1 May 72 through 30 Apr 73."

There is one way to validate Document 99. If Lieutenant Bush had actually served any duty or training days, they were most likely to be listed on the chronology included in his discharge papers. They are not present. His discharge has no record of service for Bush between May 26, 1972 and October 1, 1973. Document 99 was probably the campaign's effort to fill in this blank.

Although George W. Bush has said he made up his missed Guard time in a nonflying capacity when he returned to Houston in the late fall of 1972, there is still no one who has ever said they saw him at the 111th Fighter Interceptor Squadron's headquarters after he disappeared in April of that same year. According to Bush, this was because he was doing his duty in an office, not as a pilot. Nonetheless, a pilot is generally a high-profile individual in an Air Guard wing, and it would have been difficult for Bush to go unnoticed as an obscure administrator, particularly since he had been described by one of his superiors as being in the top 5 percent of all pilots flying out of the base. Also, Bush was, after all, a congressman's son when he enlisted, and the number of pilots serving in the pool was generally only around two dozen. In addition to the natural notoriety of his family name, Lieutenant Bush had been used as a poster boy by commanders at Ellington. His father had shown up for a photo op when Bush became a pilot, and the 111th press office had issued a news release on Lieutenant Bush and how he "doesn't get his kicks from pot, hashish, or speed. Oh, he gets high, all right, but not from narcotics," but because he was the pilot of an F-102.

This was the profile of the pilot who said he existed so anonymously during the summer camp at Ellington in 1973 that no one saw him. And if he was hiding out in a back office, why? While running for president Bush said he stopped flying when he got back to Houston because the 111th Squadron was switching to a new jet, the F-101, and there was no point in retraining him to fly the more advanced aircraft because he was nearing his discharge date. This, too, was yet another inaccuracy, or a simple lie. The 111th continued to fly the F-102 for a full year after Bush had left for Harvard Business School.

"If Bush had come back to Houston, I would have kept him flying the 102 until he got out," said Major General Bobby Hodges, who has called himself a Bush admirer. "But I don't recall him coming back at all."

Hodges testimony is narrative confirmation that Bush had violated his second direct order in less than a year to report for duty on specific days: orders to appear at the 187th in Alabama and a May 1,

1973 order for nine days duty in Houston between May and June of that year. If Bush had attended the ordered May and June days, his commanders would have filed an Officer Effectiveness Rating report for 1973–1974, but none has ever been found in his file.

A misunderstanding of the Bush military record may have developed from reporters with nonmilitary backgrounds attempting to understand arcane government records. When the experts examined released documents, however, the picture did not improve for Bush. Journalists have generally given the president credit for 36 days on duty between May and July 1973, as though someone alerted him to his dereliction, and he took the warning seriously and went back on duty. However, the only proof of any service time during that span of three months in 1973 is an unsigned and undated one page listing of 35 inactive Reserve temporary duty credit days from May 25, 1973 to July 30. Retired National Guard pilot Robert Rogers, who has spent years deconstructing the Bush military file, has written an argument that the inactive Reserve document did not verify Bush attended drills as he had been ordered.

He said it proved the opposite.

"This document," Rogers wrote, "is a paper confirmation that Bush did not actually report for duty in person at the Texas Air National Guard on any of these days. Bush was credited with 35 'gratuitous' inactive Air Force Reserve points—in other words—nonattendance inactive Reserve credit time. The proof that this time was 'gratuitous' is the absence of any Bush duty time on his official Texas Air National Guard record all the way from May 26, 1972, entry of 22 pilot days the previous year. This is because 'gratuitous' time does not count as scheduled Texas Air Guard duty. This leaves Bush without a single, legitimate Texas Air National Guard service day for his fifth and sixth years of service to his discharge on October 1, 1973— a critical fact that has been misunderstood in several previous reports of this period of Bush's service."

A few days before the presidential election, correspondent Jo Thomas of the *New York Times* wrote another story that tried to clarify the Bush Guard history. In her piece, *"Bush's Guard Duty Is Questioned and Defended,*" Thomas wrote that, "Mr. [Dan] Bartlett pointed to a document in Mr. Bush's military records that showed credit for four days of duty ending Nov. 29 and for eight days ending Dec. 14, 1972, and, after he moved back to Houston, on dates in January, April, and May." She did not seem to be making a reference to Document 99 because that record showed only one day of service, which the campaign had claimed was November 29, 1972, even though only the number "29" and not the month was visible on the torn sheet. It is unknown how Thomas, or the campaign, arrived at the conclusion that Document 99 proved four days of service on November 29, 1972, if they were looking at Document 99. Taken at face value, this controversial sheet of paper only affirmed one day of attendance on November 29, though there are numbers purportedly showing Bush served in Texas on several other days.

Thomas' narrative further confused matters by identifying a set of orders that were not then in public records. "The May dates correlated with orders sent to Mr. Bush at his Houston apartment on April 23, 1973, in which Sgt. Billy B. Lamar told Mr. Bush to report for duty on May 1–3 and May 8–10." The April 23 orders, which have been referred to as fact by journalists, were not released in the initial FOIA to researcher Marty Heldt. If such orders were issued, as appears to have been the case, the document ought to have been contained in Bush's released Guard file, and it was not. Martin Heldt has never seen it. Further, the Bush campaign asserted to Thomas that the papers she was shown proved he had been on duty in Houston May 1–3 and May 8–10 in 1973. However, if Bush had attended those drills, his commanders would have filed an Officer Effectiveness Rating for 1973–1974, which would have included assessment of Bush's performance on those May dates. They did not file such a report.

Under political pressure to clear up the president's record, in February of 2004, the White House added to the confusion by providing reporters with an untorn copy of Document 99. This third version appeared to contradict the president's memory that he served on November 29, 1972. The month associated with the number 29 on this complete copy is October. If the dates are correct, it means that Bush decided to do guard duty just days before the election he was working on for Winton Blount. This new document, without a rip up the side, was used by the White House to insist the president was paid for days of duty in the fall of 1972 and the spring of 1973. However, Bush has not released pay stubs, W-2 forms, or income tax filings to corroborate his staff's interpretation of the numbers. Also, no explanation was given for why this document was not included in FOIAs when the president had said everything was released in 2000.

An essential contradiction was left unexplained by the White House press secretary when he shared the new materials with journalists. The dates on the sheet contradict the conclusions of Lieutenant Bush's commanding officers back in Houston. If the numbers are correct, they would confirm that the president was on duty in Houston for days in January, March, and April of 1973. If that were the case, though, his commanders would have reported as much when they filed their Officer Effectiveness Rating in May of 1973. Instead, they wrote that Lieutenant Bush "has not been observed" and that he had "cleared this base." Were the commanders oblivious to the famous young lieutenant doing several days of duty at Ellington Air Force base? Is it possible Lieutenant Bush was getting paid even though his commanding officers never saw him?

A number of conclusions can be drawn from the new and uncorroborated Document 99. The commanders who let Bush disappear without orders, and never called him to account, might have chosen to create a political cover for the congressman's son. In Houston, the "champagne" unit, filled with the sons of the wealthy and well-connected, was already controversial. If Bush had gotten privilege to get into the Ellington air wing, and then abused that privilege by capriciously walking away, it would have caused trouble for the officers who gave him special treatment. It is not improbable that Lieutenant Bush was simply given gratuitous points on his record to avoid attracting unflattering attention to the unit and the pilot with the famous family.

The historical truth of George W. Bush's National Guard years is probably most accurately revealed by what remains missing from his public file. His suspension as a pilot, as an example, was not a minor event. The nation was in a long and ghastly war, and it was costly to train pilots to fly combat fighter jets. Pilot training in the National Guard was a very coveted assignment, regardless of the risks involved in learning to fly a jet. The U.S. military did not have a reputation for signing pilots to six year commitments, investing time and tax money in their training, and then just letting the pilot walk away. When Lieutenant Bush was suspended from flight status, there ought to have been a board of inquiry to examine the causes of his failure, or some kind of a written reprimand and report. This was considered standard procedure. No record has ever been produced to show a board met, or that Bush's suspension was considered a serious matter. A report of the board's findings, if it had convened, probably existed, and can serve to explain how Bush was able to leave for Alabama without authorization, never to fly again. A grounding related to any ongoing physical problems would have also produced a medical record for the Bush file. The president limited the release of medical records from that time.

Bill Burkett, the Texas National Guard State Plans Officer during Bush's tenure as governor, said that a complete service file on Bush will provide explanations.

"If a full file had been furnished by the campaign or by the FOIA, then the answers would have been clear," Burkett explained. "The fact that those 'retained record' files were purged, sorted, or otherwise filtered only became an issue to me when the official files were forwarded under FOIA with tremendous gaps and holes in them. It's like the several minute gap in the Watergate tapes."

According to Burkett, Lieutenant Bush's file ought to include pay records, which are the simplest method for determining how many days he actually did duty. The other critical document is the official federal release form, which shows Bush did not serve after May 1972. Burkett said that needs to be compared to the points records offered by the campaign, and the final "roll up" report on total retirement points. Finally, he said, Bush's service can be clarified by backing out all administrative service points he was awarded, and his education points. When those are removed from his total, the final figure is his actual number of service points. These can then be corroborated with pay records, if they were made available.

"Pay records are kept in a separate location and file," Albert Lloyd explained. "Somebody will have to decide to release those. They aren't a part of the service record files."

Bill Burkett, a former Guard unit commander, has said investigators are all looking for the facts in the wrong location. "As I've tried to point out to everyone, don't look at what is *in* the file, look at what is missing, and it gives you the major answers."

No one can get those answers because the full George W. Bush file now exists only on microfiche at the Air Force Reserve Personnel Center in Denver and the National Personnel Records Center in St. Louis. According to the director of the St. Louis facility, Charles Pelligrini, there is no record that the president's National Guard microfiche file has undergone any corrections since his discharge in 1974. Any changes would require a formal appeal before a board, and none has ever been made. A full release of the microfiche file at the Air Reserve Personnel Center in Denver along with a similar authorization to disclose the St. Louis microfiche is the best method for determining the president's service record. Additionally, the Defense Finance and Accounting Service in Colorado, which provided the White House with master payroll records, should also be able to deliver pay stubs and receipts. Bush can validate these by asking the IRS to release any existing tax records from the relevant time period. The president can gain credibility and end the controversy by providing release authorization to those federal facilities and allowing the files to be delivered directly to reporters who have requested them under Freedom of Information laws rather than having them first go to the White House for scrutiny.

Obviously, there is precedent for this kind of a procedure. During the 2000 presidential campaign, political rumors were circulated about Bush Republican primary opponent U.S. Senator John McCain of Arizona. Attributed by journalists to Bush strategist Karl Rove, the spurious information prompted McCain to release his entire military file to the public. Stories about his mental health disappeared. Although Bush might end the mystery of his Guard years by authorizing the release of his own records, he is also likely to reveal evidence he was coddled, and treated with privilege, even by military commanders.

So only some of the documents have been released.

And the file available for public review has had all of the embarrassments removed. Nobody knows that better than Bill Burkett.

Because Bill Burkett was there when it happened.

[For an examination of George W. Bush's National Guard records, see the chapter appendix that begins on the following page.]

George W. Bush's National Guard Records

> Reason for suspension: Failure to accomplish annual medical examination.

AO S7, DAAF-NGC, dated 29 September 1972

CAPT BRIAN M LEIDING
                                    IL

CAPT EDWARD L SHARP
                                    IN

CAPT WILBUR J LATHAM JR
                                    IA

CAPT JAMES H RENSCHEN
                                    PA

Hq 182 Tac   t Gp, Greater
Peoria Aprt   ria IL

113 Tac Ft   Hulman Fld,
Terre Hau

124 Tac B   , Des Moines MAP,
Des Moin

103 Tac   Spt Sq, Willow Grove NAS,
Willow   e PA

4. Each of the fol named offs, ANGUS (on EAD), orgn indc, is
granted the aeronautical rating of Mast   av, per para 1-14d, AFM
35-13. Authority: Para 1-7b(5), AFM 3   :

GRADE, NAME AND SSAN

MAJ GENE J PETTY
                                    NY

LTCOL CARL R BECK
                                    PA

ORGAN   TION

136   Intcp Sq, Niagara Falls
Int   prt, Niagara Falls NY

197   ac Elect Warfare Sq, Olmsted
Fl   Middletown PA

5. CAPT DENNIS M HYATT,   ANGUS (Not on EAD), NY ANG,
136 Ftr Intcp Sq, Niagara Falls In   Aprt, Niagara Falls NY, is
granted the aeronautical rating of Sen Nav per para 1-14e, AFM
35-13. Authority: Para 1-7b(5),   M 35-13.

6. Verbal orders of the Comdr o 1 Aug 72 suspending 1STLT GEORGE W
BUSH,   , ANGUS (Not on EAD), TX ANG, Hq 147 Ftr Gp, Ellington
AFB, Houston TX, from flying st us are confirmed, exigencies of the
service having been such as to preclude the publication of competent
written orders in advance. Reason for Suspension: Failure to
accomplish annual medical examination. Off will comply with para
2-10, AFM 35-13. Authority: Para 2-29m, AFM 35-13.

7. Verbal orders of the Comdr on 1 Sep 72 suspending MAJ JAMES R BATH,
               ANGUS (Not on EAD), TX ANG, Hq 147 Ftr Gp, Ellington AFB,
Houston TX, from flying status are confirmed, exigencies of the service
having been such as to preclude the publication of competent written
orders in advance. Reason for Suspension: Failure to accomplish
annual medical examination. Off will comply with para 2-10, AFM 35-13.
Authority: Para 2-29m, AFM 35-13.

BY ORDER OF THE SECRETARIES OF THE ARMY AND THE AIR FORCE

OFFICIAL

ALDO E. TIMM, Colonel, USAF
Executive, National Guard Bureau

FRANCIS S. GREENLIEF, Major General, USA
Chief, National Guard Bureau

DISTRIBUTION:
15 ea State for ea Off
 1 AFMPC/DPMAJD
 1 NGB-AD
25 NGB/DPM

AO-S7, Dated September 29, 1972: Written order confirming verbal orders that Bush
was suspended from flying for "failure to accomplish annual medical examination." Bush
said he "did not recall being grounded."

APPLICATION FOR RESERV. ASSIGNMENT	(If more space is needed for any item, attach additional sheets indicating applicable item number)

INSTRUCTIONS

1. SUBMIT APPLICATION, IN TRIPLICATE, TO PRESENT UNIT OF ASSIGNMENT. (IF ASSIGNED TO ARPC (ORS, RRPS, NARS, ISLRS, ETC.), SUBMIT APPLICATION EITHER TO THE LOCAL AIR RESERVE UNIT OR TO THE UNIT WITH WHICH ASSIGNMENT IS DESIRED).
2. ALL APPLICANTS MUST ATTACH COMPLETED DD FORM 1844 (CHAP 32, AFM 35-3).
3. IF APPLICANT IS A CIVILIAN EMPLOYEE OF THE FEDERAL GOVT, ATTACH COMPLETED "CERTIFICATE OF AVAILABILITY FOR FEDERAL EMPLOYEE", (CHAP 32, AFM 35-3).

TO:
9921st Air Reserve Squadron
c/o Lt. Col. Reese H. Bricken
2704 Fairmont --- Montgomery, Ala. 36111

1. LAST NAME - FIRST NAME - MIDDLE INITIAL			
Bush, George W.			
2. DATE OF BIRTH ▓▓▓	3. AFRES GRADE 1/Lt.		4. DATE OF AFRES GRADE Nov., 1970

5. ADDRESS AND TELEPHONE NUMBER (*If different from permanent address, indicate both*) ▓▓▓▓▓▓

6A. SERVICE NUMBER ▓▓▓	6B. SSAN ▓▓▓	7. PRIMARY AFSC 1125B
8. ADDITIONAL AFSC'S none.	9. DATE AND TERM OF APPOINTMENT OR ENLISTMENT Sept., 1968	

10. DRAWING DISABILITY COMPENSATION (*If yes, state percent*) ☐ YES ☒ NO   %

11. AERONAUTICAL RATING (*Indicate if on flying status. If requested assignment will authorize flying duty, indicate flying experience by type aircraft and hours in each, date and type of instrument card now held, and date of last physical examination.*)

Flying status

12. CIVILIAN EDUCATION (*Indicate years completed, major subject and degree, if any*)

16 years
Yale University - 1968
BA - History

13. CIVILIAN EXPERIENCE (*In chronological order showing latest experience first, indicate pertinent experience to include employers, positions held, and duration.*)

Red Blount For Senate - Campaign Management
Stratford of Texas - Assistant to Executive
    Vice President - one year
George Bush For Senate - Surrogate Candidate

14. MILITARY SCHOOLS ATTENDED (*Indicate date, course number or title, and location*)

15. MILITARY EXPERIENCE (*Indicate position title, level of command, DAFSC highest grade and duration. List only those experiences that directly substantiate your qualifications for assignment requested.*)

Pilot, Fighter Interceptor
squadron level 1125B, 1/Lt.

16. PRESENT ASSIGNMENT AND ATTACHMENT (*Indicate unit and training category*)

111th F.I.S. (TNG)
P. O. Box 34567
Houston, Texas 77034

17. ASSIGNMENT DESIRED (*Indicate unit if any preferred, training category and pay group or description of type of training desired*)

9921st Air Reserve Squadron
No pay, training category G
Reserve section MM

I CERTIFY THAT THE DATA CONTAINED HEREIN IS TRUE AND CORRECT TO THE BEST OF MY KNOWLEDGE. I ALSO ACKNOWLEDGE THAT UPON MY ASSIGNMENT TO THE READY RESERVE I AM RESPONSIBLE TO NOTIFY MY EMPLOYER OF MY READY RESERVE STATUS AND THAT AS A READY RESERVIST I SHALL BE SUBJECT TO INVOLUNTARY ORDER TO ACTIVE DUTY IN TIME OF WAR OR NATIONAL EMERGENCY DECLARED BY THE CONGRESS, A NATIONAL EMERGENCY DECLARED BY THE PRESIDENT, OR WHEN OTHERWISE AUTHORIZED BY LAW.

DATE 24 May 72	SIGNATURE OF APPLICANT George W. Bush

AF FORM 1288 JAN 69   PREVIOUS EDITION OF THIS FORM IS OBSOLETE.

atch 1

Application for Reserve Assignment—AF Form 1288: Bush applies to be transferred to a postal unit in Alabama. He has already left Texas for Alabama without permission.

Your application for assignment to the 9921 Air Reserve Sq is acceptable and approved herewith. You already understand that this is a Training Category G. Pay Group None, Reserve Secton MM proposition. The continuation of this type unit is uncertain at this time and we may last 3 months, 6 months, a year or who knows! With this in mind, if you are willing to accept assignment under these circumstances, welcome! We're glad to have you.

TO: 1/LT GEO̶R̶G̶E̶ ̶B̶U̶S̶H   FROM: 9921 Air Reserve Sq
2704 Fairmont Road
Montgomery, AL 36111

[X] APPROVED   [ ] DISAPPROVED

REMARKS Your application for assignment to the 9921 Air Reserve Sq is acceptable and approved herewith. You already understand that this is a Training Category G, Pay Group None, Reserve Section MM proposition. MM MMX The continuation of this type unit is uncertain at this time and we may last 3 months, 6 months, a year or who knows! With this in mind, if you are willing to accept assignment under these circumstances, welcome! We're glad to have you.

DATE
26 May 72

REESE H. BRICKEN, LTC, USAFR
Commander

SIGNATURE
Reese W. Bricken

TO: FROM:

[ ] APPROVED (If approved furnish assignment data)   [ ] DISAPPROVED

1. AUTH GRADE	2. AUTH AFSC	3. FUNCTIONAL CODE	4. TRNG CATEGORY	5. PAY GROUP

6. UNIT OR TYPE OF ASSIGNMENT [ ] UNIT [ ] MA [ ] RD [ ] OTHER (Specify)   7. RESERVE SECTION CODE   8. POSITION CONTROL NUMBER

REMARKS

DATE   TYPED NAME AND TITLE   SIGNATURE

NOTE: DO NOT INCLUDE ASSIGNMENT DATA IN SUCCEEDING INDORSEMENTS EXCEPT TO CORRECT ORIGINAL DATA.

TO: FROM:

[ ] APPROVED   [ ] DISAPPROVED

REMARKS

DATE   TYPED NAME AND TITLE   SIGNATURE

TO: FROM:

[ ] APPROVED   [ ] DISAPPROVED

REMARKS

DATE   TYPED NAME AND TITLE   SIGNATURE

REVERSE OF AF FORM 1288   GPO 870-538

Reverse of Form 1288: Alabama postal unit commander accepts Bush's request for transfer, even though the unit may be eliminated, and has nothing to do with aviation.

> Under the provisions of paragraph 30-6 a (4), AFM 35-3, an obligated Reservist can be assigned to a specific Ready Reserve position only. Therfore, he is ineligible for assignment to an Air Reserve Squadron.

DEPARTMENT OF THE AIR FORCE
HEADQUARTERS AIR RESERVE PERSONNEL CENTER
3800 YORK STREET
DENVER, COLORADO 80205

REPLY TO
ATTN OF: DPRMA

SUBJECT: Application for Reserve Assignment, Bush, George ___ Lt, ▇▇▇▇
USAFR

TO: TAG Texas

1. Application for Reserve Assignment for First Lieutenant Bush is
returned.

2. A review of his Master Personnel Record shows he has a Military
Service Obligation until 26 May 1974. Under the provisions of paragraph 30-6 a (4), AFM 35-3, an obligated Reservist can be assigned to
a specific Ready Reserve position only. Therefore, he is ineligible
for assignment to an Air Reserve Squadron.

FOR THE COMMANDER

> Gwen L. Dallin

GWEN L. DALLIN, C___
Reserve Assignments Branch
Directorate of Personnel Resources

1 Atch:
1. AF Fm 1288, 24 May 72 (2) w/ atch

Cy to: 1st Lt Bush
147 Ftr Gp
9921 Air Reserve Sq

DPRMA Letter: Disapproving Bush's transfer to the Alabama postal unit because it has nothing to do with flying and is not a "ready reserve" unit.

September 5, 1972

Col. Jerry Killian
P. O. Box 34567
Houston, Texas   77034

Col. Killian:

     I request permission to perform equivalent duty

with the

          187th Tac Recon Group
          P. O. Box 2584
          Montgomery, Alabama   36105

     This duty would be for the months of September,

October, and November.

     Thank you for your consideration.

               Sincerely,

               First Lieutenant George Bush

Bush Letter: Asking for transfer to Alabama 187th Tactical Reconnaissance unit for the fall of 1972. This appears to be a response to a denial of an earlier request to transfer to the postal unit. Dated September 5, 1972, the letter proves Bush had been AWOL since he left Houston in May and had not bothered to report in from Alabama, even though his request for transfer to the postal unit was denied four months earlier.

1. Approved. Unit Training Assembly schedule is as follows:

       7–8 Oct 72   0730–1600
       4–5 Nov 72   0730–1600

September UTA was held on 9–10 Sep 72.

2. Lieutenant Bush should report to LtCol William Turnipseed, DCO, to perform Equivalent Training. Lieutenant Bush will not be able to satisfy his flight requirements with our group.

5th Ind to 1Lt Gᵇᵘˢ̶ʰ Ltr, 5 Sep 72, Permission to Perform Equivalent Duty with 187th Tᵃᶜ Recon Gp

Hq, 187th Tac Recon Gp (DPM)   15 September 1972

TO: TAG, Ala (AL-AFAB)

1. Approved. Unit Training Assembly schedule is as follows:

        7–8 Oct 72   0730–1600
        4–5 Nov 72   0730–1600

September UTA was held on 9–10 Sep 72.

2. Lieutenant Bush should report to LtCol William Turnipseed, DCO, to perform Equivalent Training. Lieutenant Bush will not be able to satisfy his flight requirements with our group.

FOR THE COMMANDER

[signature]

KENNETH K. LOTT, Capt, AL ANG
Chief, Personnel Branch

6th Ind

TAG Alabama (AL-AFAB)   19 September 1972

TO: TAG Texas

Forwarded.

FOR THE ADJUTANT GENERAL

[signature]

DAVID E. McCUTCHIN, 2d Lt, AL ANG   Cy to: Hq 117 TRW
Air Admin & Tng Off

7th Ind

TAG Texas, P O Box 5218, Austin, TX 78763 (AP) 21 Sep 72

TO: 147th Ftr Intcp Gp, TexANG

Forwarded.

FOR THE ADJUTANT GENERAL OF TEXAS

CHARLES K. SHOEMAKE
Major, TexANG
Chief, Military Personnel (MPO)

Transfer Approval Letter: Accepts Bush into 187th unit in Alabama and orders him to report for duty on specified days in October and November 1972. He was directed to report to Colonel William Turnipseed, who later said he was "dead certain" that Bush never reported for duty.

19. Have you ever been arrested, indicted, or convicted for any violation of civil or military law, including minor traffic violations?

12. PHYSICIANS ONLY
    ☐ I DO ☐ I DO NOT DESIRE TRAINING IN AVIATION

13. CHRONOLOGICAL STATEMENT OF SERVICE AND TRAINING I... ...CE. ARMY, NAVY, MARINE CORPS, OR ANY OF THE COMPONENTS THEREOF, UNITED STATES AIR FORCE, MILITA... ...ACADEMY, OR RESERVE OFFICERS TRAINING CORPS.

DATES		HIGHEST GRADE	ORGAN... (Type a...		DUTY	SERVICE NO.	ACTIVE OR INACTIVE
FROM: 27 May 68	TO: Present	A1N	147th Fighter Gp.		Adm Spec	AF26230638	Active

14. 147th Fighter Group (TexANG) ...ES ENUMERATED IN ITEM 13. ABOVE? ☐ YES ☐ NO. IF SO, STATE:
Ellington AFB, Texas

15. WERE ALL DISCHARGES GRANTED UNDER... CONDITIONS? ☐ YES ☐ NO

16. WERE YOU EVER REJECTED FOR ANY OF THE SERVICES ENUMERATED UNDER ITEM 13. ABOVE? ☐ YES ☐ NO

17. IF ANSWER TO N/A 16 IS YES, S... ...N AND WHERE REJECTED, AND CAUSE.

18. CHRONOLOGICAL STATEMENT OF ... EMPLOYMENT, INCLUDING PART TIME. IF ADDITIONAL SPACE IS REQUIRED, USE A SHEET OF PAPER THIS SIZE A... ...CH TO APPLICATION.

6/6/62 to 21/8/62 (year)	...ker-Botts-Sheppard, Coates, Esperson Bldg, Houston, Tex... (State)		MONTHLY SALARY 60.00
Messenger TITLE Runner ... ...irm		Return to School	
6/8/63 to 21/8/63 (year)	Jack Greeney (Give XX Ranch, Williams, Arizona... State)		MONTHLY SALARY 00.00
Ranch Hand TITLE No... ... Ranch Duties		Return to School	
6/6/65 to 31/... (year)	Circle Oil Co; Lake Charles, Louisiana... State)		MONTHLY SALARY 75.00
Roustabout ... Oil Field Work		Return to School	
6/6/66 to 25/8/66 (year)	Sears Roebuck, 4201 Main, Houston, Texas... (State)		MONTHLY SALARY 2.00
Salesman TITLE Sold Sporting Goods		Return to School	

19. HAVE YOU EVER BEEN ARRESTED, INDICTED, OR CONVICTED FOR ANY VIOLATION OF CIVIL OR MILITARY LAW, INCLUDING MINOR TRAFFIC VIOLATIONS?

██

20. ARE YOU A CONSCIENTIOUS OBJECTOR? ☐ YES ☐ NO

21. ARE YOU NOW, OR HAVE YOU EVER BEEN AFFILIATED WITH ANY ORGANIZATION OR MOVEMENT THAT SEEKS TO ALTER OUR FORM OF GOVERNMENT BY UNCONSTITUTIONAL MEANS, OR SYMPATHETICALLY ASSOCIATED WITH ANY SUCH ORGANIZATION, MOVEMENT, OR MEMBERS THEREOF? ☐ YES ☐ NO. IF SO, DESCRIBE.

22. ARE THERE ANY OTHER UNFAVORABLE INCIDENTS IN YOUR LIFE WHICH YOU BELIEVE MAY REFLECT UPON YOUR LOYALTY TO THE UNITED STATES GOVERNMENT OR UPON YOUR ABILITY TO PERFORM THE DUTIES WHICH YOU MAY BE CALLED UPON TO UNDERTAKE? ☐ YES ☐ NO. IF SO, DESCRIBE.

ITEM 18 Cont'd (Use additional sheet if necessary)
2/6/67 to 25/8/67: James L. Bayless, 901 First City Nat'l Bank, Houston, Texas
$250.00 - Bookkeeper - Return to School

I CERTIFY THAT THE ABOVE ANSWERS ARE TRUE AND CORRECT TO THE BEST OF MY KNOWLEDGE AND BELIEF:

PRINTED GEORGE WALKER BUSH (First, middle, and last names) SIGNATURE (First, middle, and last names)
George Walker Bush

Enlistment Contract: Background information on any criminal behavior. Item 19, asking about previous arrests, indictments, or convictions has been redacted.

. . .   .'.' .   '"ENT FOR ENLISTMENT IN THE NATIONAL GU' .

DATE	PLACE
27 May 68	Ellington AFB, Texas

1. In connection with my enlistment in the National Guard this date, the following is a complete and accurate record of all violations and offenses (including minor traffic violations) for which I have been arrested (regardless of the subsequent dispositions of my case) by civil law enforcement officials. (Prior service personnel list only those violations occurring during and/or subsequent to last period of honorable active service, except for offenses previously revealed. If none, so state.

(For each answer checked YES set forth a full explanation under REMARKS, Item 1e below)

YES NO

    a. Have you ever been arrested, charged or held by Federal, State or other law enforcement authorities for any violation of any Federal Law, State Law, County or Municipal law, regulation or ordinance?

    b. Have you ever been convicted of a felony or any other offense, or adjudicated a youthful offender or juvenile delinquent (Including violations of local ordinance)?

    c. Have you ever been imprisoned, under sentence of any court?

    d. Are you now or have you ever been on suspended sentence, parole, probation or are you awaiting final action on charges against you?

    e. REMARKS: (Enter full explanation for those questions answered "YES").

REFERENCE ITEM	OFFENSE	DATE AND PLACE	DISPOSITION

2. Have you ever been rejected for enlistment or induction in any of the Armed Forces or been discharged from previous service under other than Honorable conditions, under personnel security regulations or by reason of unsuitability or undesirable habits or traits or character, or for medical reasons? YES ☐ NO ☒ (If answer is YES give details below).

SERVICE	DATE AND PLACE	CAUSE

3. I have read or had explained to me the following cited paragraphs of the directives indicated below which sets forth the criteria (or reasons) for discharge and types of discharges and certify that I have ☐ Have ☒ (initial one) engaged in disloyal or subversive activities as defined therein.

CHECK ONE	MILITARY SERVICE	PARAGRAPHS	DIRECTIVES
☐	Army National Guard	14 and 19	AR 604-10
☒	Air National Guard	6 and 7	AFR 35-62

4. Indicate below the number, relationship and age of persons dependent on you for support. If none so state

RELATIONSHIP	AGE

5. I certify that the recruiting officer has informed me that should I willingly conceal any information required above I may later be subject to disciplinary action or discharge upon its discovery.

TYPED FIRST, MIDDLE, LAST NAME	SIGNATURE
GEORGE WALKER BUSH	George Walker Bush
TYPED NAME UNIT COMMANDER OR AUTHORIZED REPRESENTATIVE (WITNESS)	SIGNATURE
WILLIE J HOOPER JR, Capt, Asst Admin Officer	

NGB FORM 21
17 AUG 66

Statement for Enlistment in the National Guard: Asks four questions about any criminal background. "Yes" and "No" answer boxes are redacted, as is the space below where details appear to have been written.

17. Have you ever been arrested, indicted or convicted for any violation of civil or military law including minor traffic violations? *(If "Yes" explain stating nature of offense, date, name and place of the court and dispositon of the case.)*

13. OTHER TYPES OF TRAINING COMPL		ACKGROUND QUALIFICATIONS OF VALUE TO THE AIR FORCE					
None							

14. CHRONOLOGICAL STATEM... AND TRAINING IN THE AIR FORCE, ARMY, NAVY, MARINE CORPS, OR ANY OF THE COMPONENTS THEREOF; UNITED STATES MILITARY OR NAVA... RESERVE OFFICERS TRAINING CORPS.

DATES		HIGHEST GRADE	ORGANIZATION (Type and service)	DUTY	SERIAL NO.	ACTIVE OR INACTIVE
FROM	TO					
27 May 68	Pre...	Amn	147th Ftr Gp (TexANG)	Adm Spec	AF 26230638	Active

15. SELECTIVE SERV...

BOARD NUMBER	BOARD ADDRESS	CURRENT CLASSIFICATION	SELECTIVE SERVICE NO.
294	Room 413, 201 Fannin Street Houston, Texas 77002	I -D	41-62-46-1480

16. KNOWLED... FOREIGN LANGUAGE

L...UAGE	HOW ACQUIRED (School, family, work. etc.)	READ			SPEAK			UNDERSTAND		
		EXC.	GOOD	FAIR	EXC.	GOOD	FAIR	EXC.	GOOD	FAIR
Sp...ish	School		x			x			x	

17. HAVE YOU EVER BEEN ARRESTED, INDICTED OR CONVICTED FOR ANY VIOLATION OF CIVIL OR MILITARY LAW INCLUDING MINOR TRAFFIC VIOLATIONS? (If "YES" explain stating nature of offense, date, name and place of the court and disposition of the case.)

[redacted]

18. EMPLOYMENT RECORD (Start with your present position and work back). DO NOT ENTER PART-TIME EMPLOYMENT OR EMPLOYMENT OF LESS THAN 60 DAYS DURATION

EMPLOYER	TYPE OF WORK	DATES: FROM-TO	SALARY	WHY TERMINATED
Baker, Botts, Sheppard, Coates	Messenger	6/6/62 to 21/8/62	200.00	Return to School
Jack Greenway, XX Ranch Williams, Arizona	Ranch Hand	6/6/64 - 21/8/63	200.00	Return to School
Circle Oil Co.Lake Charles,La.	Oil Field Wk	6/6/65 - 31/8/65	375.00	Return to School
Sears Roebuck, Houston,Texas	Salesman	1/6/66 - 25/8/66	212.00	Return to School
James L. Bayless, 901 1st Natl Bnk	Bookeeper	2/6/67 - 25/8/67	250.00	Return to School

REMARKS:

19. I UNDERSTAND AND AGREE THAT:

A. Upon completion of the training course, I will accept an appointment as an officer in the Reserve of the Air Force in career reserve status. Further, I agree to remain on active duty as a commissioned officer for the period prescribed in AFR 36-22 or 36-51 on the date of this application, unless sooner relieved by competent authority.

B. If, at the time I am about to be appointed an aviation cadet, or officer trainee, I am a member of the Air Force with less than 16 months remaining under my enlistment contract, I will extend my enlistment for the necessary period to include 16 months' service.

C. As an applicant for aviation cadet training, I am unmarried and, if selected for training, will remain unmarried until either my graduation or elimination therefrom.

I certify that the foregoing entries are true, correct and complete to the best of my knowledge and belief; and in signing this application I do so with the understanding that the veracity of all statements made may be investigated and if found incorrect I may be subject to such disciplinary action as appropriate.

DATE	TYPE NAME AND GRADE OF APPLICANT	SIGNATURE
28 May 1968	GEORGE WALKER BUSH, AMN	George Walker Bush

U S GOVERNMENT PRINTING OFFICE . 1966 OF—723-024

Background Form: Item 17 requesting information on arrests, indictments, or convictions has several lines redacted in the space where detail was provided.

I.	IDENTIFICAT	A (Read AFM 36-10 carefully before filling any item.)		
1. LAST NAME-FIRST NAME-MIDDLE INITIAL BUSH, GEORGE W.	2. SSAN ████ FG	3. ACTIVE DUTY GRADE NONEAD	4. PERMANENT GRADE 1st Lt	

5. ORGANIZATION, COMMAND AND LOCATION
111th Ftr Intcp Sq
Ellington AFB, Texas
Texas (ADC)

6. AERO RATING C **CODE** 2

7. PERIOD OF REPORT FROM: 1 May 72 THRU: 30 Apr 73

8. PERIOD OF SUPERVISION

9. REASON FOR REPORT Annual Report

II. PRESENT DUTY

PAFSC 1125D   DAFSC 1125D

Pilot, Fighter Interceptor, Squadron level. Pilots F-102 type aircraft and performs airborne intercepts as required by assigned missions.

III. RATING FACTORS (Consider how this officer is performing on his job.)

1. KNOWLEDGE OF DUTIES — NOT OBSERVED
2. PERFORMANCE OF DUTIES — X NOT OBSERVED
3. EFFECTIVENESS IN WORKING WITH OTHERS — X NOT OBSERVED
4. LEADERSHIP CHARACTERISTICS — X NOT OBSERVED
5. JUDGEMENT — X NOT OBSERVED
6. ADAPTABILITY — X NOT OBSERVED
7. USE OF RESOURCES — X X NOT OBSERVED (MATERIEL / PERSONNEL)
8. WRITING ABILITY AND ORAL EXPRESSION — X X NOT OBSERVED (WRITE / SPEAK)

IV. MILITARY QUALITIES (Consider how this officer meets Air Force standards.)
X NOT OBSERVED

AF FORM 77 JUL 77   PREVIOUS EDITION WILL BE USED.

COMPANY GRADE OFFICER EFFECTIVENESS REPORT

Officer Effectiveness Rating Form: Page one of the form has 55 boxes that commanders use to rate pilots. All are checked "not observed" for May 1972 through April 1973. Bush was in Alabama.

Lt Bush has not been observed at this unit during the period of report. A civilian occupation made it necessary for him to move to Montgomery, Alabama. He cleared this base on 15 May 1973 and has been performing equivalent training in a non flying status with the 187 Tac Recon GP, Dannelly ANG Base, Alabama.

COMMENTS

Lt Bush has not been observed at this unit during the period of report. A civilian occupation made it necessary for him to move to Montgomery, Alabama. He cleared this base on 15 May 1973 and has been performing equivalent training in a non flying status with the 187 Tac Recon Gp, Dannelly ANG Base, Alabama.

REPORTING OFFICIAL

WILLIAM D. HARRIS, JR., Lt Colonel
FG, 111th FIS
TexANG (ADC)

Duty Title: Pilot, Ftr Intcp
Aero Rating: Command Pilot Code: 1
Signature: SIGNED
Date: 2 May 1973

REVIEW BY INDORSING OFFICIAL

I concur with the comments of the reporting official.

JERRY B. KILLIAN, Lt Colonel
FG, 111th FIS
TexANG (ADC)

Duty Title: Squadron Commander
Aero Rating: Command Pilot Code: 1
Signature: SIGNED
Date: 2 May 1973

Officer Effectiveness Rating Form, Second Page: Bush commanders write that he had cleared the base in May 1972 and was "performing equivalent duty" in Alabama. He was not. They did not know.

Total AD/ACDUTRA as of 72 May 26: 1st Lt 22 days

LAST NAME	FIRST NAME			GRADE		DATE OF BIRTH	DATE OF LAST OER	2
BUSH, GEORGE W.	FG3244754			1st Lt	73 APR 30	New Haven, Conn.	73 APR 30	

CHRONOLOGICAL LISTING OF SERVICE

FROM	DATE	DUTY DESCRIPTION	ORGANIZATION AND STATION
27MAY68	to 3Sep68	Unl, HQ	Admin By Apr Adm Spec, RS? (TexANG)
4Sep68	0006	Pilot Tr	111th Fighter Interceptor Squadron, Ellington AFB, Texas (TexANG)
26Nov68	0006	Stu Plt	F-V4A-A, 3550 Stu Sq, Moody AFB, Ga. (ATC)
		Total AD/ACDUTRA as of 26 May 69: 2d Lt, 226 days	
29Dec69	0006	Pilot Trainee, 111th Fighter Interceptor Squadron, Ellington AFB, Texas (TexANG)	
70 Jun 20	1125D	Pilot Ftr Intcp, 111th Ftr Intcp Sq, Ellington AFB, Tx (Tex ANG)	
		Total AD/ACDUTRA as of 70 May 26: 2d Lt 313 days	
		Total AD/ACDUTRA as of 71 May 26: 2d Lt - 43 days, 1st Lt - 3 days	
		Unit redesignated 111th Ftr Intcp Sq (Trng)	
		Total AD/ACDUTRA as of 72 May 26: 1st Lt 22 days	
1 Oct 73		HD TR TexANG Per ANGR 36-05, SO ANG-A 158, State of Texas AG Dept, Austin, Tx, and transferred to ARPC (ORS), 3800 York St, Denver, CO 80205 effective 2 October 1973. (DOS TexANG 1 Oct 73).	

COMBAT REPORT

10. REMARKS Previous Service Numbers: AF26230638
Selective Service Number: 41-62-46-1480
Reserve Status Expires: 26 May 74   Code: AA
Civ Occupation: Securities   Since:
Appointed: ANG:
Unif. Maint. Alws. Entitlement: Last Paid:
Next Payment Due:
Last Physical: Class:
TAFMS: 19/15
TAFCS: 15/05

U.S. GOVERNMENT PRINTING OFFICE : 1965 OF—799-399

Discharge Record: Proves Lieutenant Bush did not do duty after May 26, 1972. This is the last recorded date on this service sheet before his discharge. This means the almost two-year intervening time period is unaccounted for.

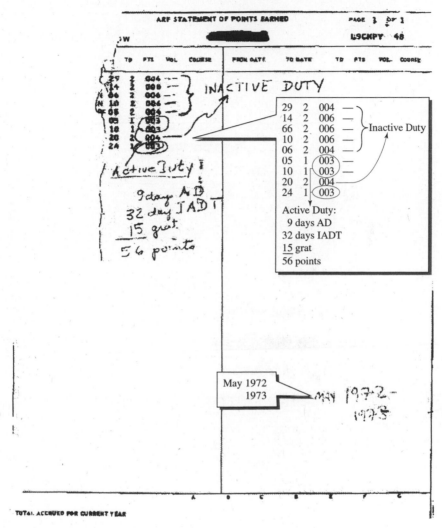

Document 99 with Annotations by Albert Lloyd: Torn points sheet Bush campaign said proved he had served in Alabama. The writing is Lloyd's attempt to add up points. Number 29 is supposed to indicate that Bush served that day in the Alabama 187th unit, though no one can remember him showing up. The document is torn along the left side and abbreviations for months are missing. Points are not totaled at the bottom, which is standard protocol. The document came from the Texas files. No Alabama document exists to prove duty on November 29, 1972. Only the letter "W" is visible on the name line. The Social Security number is redacted. There are two versions of Document 99. An unmarked version appeared in Martin Heldt's FOIA File from the government. The copy with Albert Lloyd's writing was circulated to reporters during the presidential campaign in 2000. For the years 1974 through 1999, there was no activity in the Bush Guard file. In 1999 through 2000, Lloyd said he discovered three new documents, which were then inserted into the Bush file.

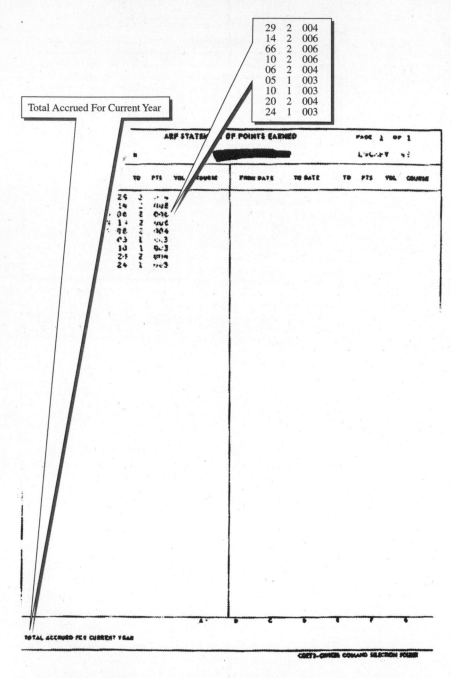

29	2	004
14	2	006
66	2	006
10	2	006
06	2	004
05	1	003
10	1	003
20	2	004
24	1	003

Total Accrued For Current Year

Document 99 from FOIA request by Martin Heldt. Note there is no way to identify months or officer being credited. Total points are not shown. This document, with Albert Lloyd's annotations, was used to convince journalists Lt. Bush was not AWOL.

j. "I have been counseled this date regardiing the provisions of DOD Directive 1215.13, 23 February 1967. I understand that I may be ordered to active duty for a period not to exceed 24 months for unsatisfactory participation as presently defined in Chapter 41, AFM 35–3. Further, I understand that if I am unable to satisfactorily participate in the ANG, and have an unfulfilled military service obligation, that I may be discharged from the State ANG and assigned to the Obligated Reserve Section (ORS), AF Reserve, Denver, Colorado, and subject to active duty for a period not to exceed a total of 24 months considering all previous active duty and active duty for training tours."

k. "However, I also understand that the provisions for invoking the 45 day tour for a member who has a satisfactory attendance record but has failed to progress in specialty training will remain in effect. (Paragraph 41–7a, AFM 35–3.)"

j. "I have been counseled this date regarding the provisions of DOD Directive 1215.13, 23 February 1967. I understand that I may be ordered to active duty for a period not to exceed 24 months for unsatisfactory participation as presently defined in Chapter 41, AFM 35-3. Further, I understand that if I am unable to satisfactorily participate in the ANG, and have an unfulfilled military service obligation, that I may be discharged from the State ANG and assigned to the Obligated Reserve Section (ORS), AF Reserve, Denver, Colorado, and subject to active duty for a period not to exceed a total of 24 months considering all previous active duty and active duty for training tours."

k. "However, I also understand that the provisions for invoking the 45 day tour for a member who has a satisfactory attendance record but has failed to progress in specialty training will remain in effect. (Paragraph 41-7a, AFM 35-3.)"

WITNESSED BY:

WILLIE B HOOPER JR, Capt, Asst Admin Officer   (Signature of Enlistee)
    (Unit Commander or Authorized
        Representative)

                                            George W. Bush
                                              (Typed Name)

Statement of Understanding: Bush signed this document acknowledging that he could be called to active duty, which usually meant Vietnam, if he failed to report or perform satisfactorily. He did not report; he was not called to active duty.

NOTICE OF MISSING OR CORRECTION OF OFFICER EFFECTIVENESS/TRAINING REPORT		DATE 2 Jun 73	SUSPENSE DATE 6 Aug 73

1

TO	INFO	FROM
NGB/DPMO		ARPC/DPABB

LAST NAME - FIRST NAME - MIDDLE INITIAL	GRADE	SSAN	UNIT
BUSH, GEORGE W.	1Lt	▬▬▬▬▬	111 FISq

ATTACHED REPORT IS RETURNED FOR CORRECTION. REPORTING PERIOD	FROM 1 May 72	THRU 30 Apr 73

CORRECTIVE ACTION REQUIRED AS INDICATED BELOW (Check applicable boxes)

1. A rating factor has not been checked in Item _____ , Section ___ .	11. Period of report is incorrect, officer's last report closed on _____ ; therefore, this report must open on _____ .
2. A more comprehensive job description will be entered in Section II.	12. OER must be in one complete original and one complete carbon copy.
3. Rating factors in Section III, Items 1, 2, 3, 4, 5, 6, 7 and 8; Sections IV, V and VI do not agree on all copies.	13. Reporting and/or indorsing official has signed and dated the report prior to closing date.
4. OER will be reaccomplished due to erasure/correction in Section _____ .	
X 5. DAFSC and/or duty title in Section II does not agree with Item 8, AF Form 11.	X 14. Returned for compliance with paragraph 6-7f(3) AFM 36-10.
6. Period of supervision incorrect.	15. Request copy of Page 2, AF Form 11, IAW Para 4-1 f (2) AFM 36-10.
7. Indorsing official must indicate his agreement/disagreement with ratings and comments of reporting official.	X 16. Returned for compliance with figure 6-25 , AFM 36-10.
8. OER is returned for additional indorsement by an official who meets the requirements of Rule _____ , Table ___ , AFM 36-10.	17. _____ official is junior to _____ official. Statement required by rule Table _____ , AFM 36-10.
9. Returned for indorsement by an officer in the grade of _____ or higher, as prescribed by AFM 36-10.	
10. Reporting and/or indorsing official has not signed the report.	X 18. Other (Specify) See Remarks

REMARKS (Reference item numbers)

Item 18. Ratings must be entered on this officer in Sections V & VI. An AF Fm 77a should be requested from the training unit so that this officer can be rated in the position he held. This officer should have been reassigned in May 1972 since he no longer is training in his AFSC or with his unit of assignment.

PLEASE RETURN ORIGINAL COPY OF THIS FORM WHEN RETURNING CORRECTED OER

TYPED NAME AND GRADE OF PERSONNEL OFFICER DANIEL P. HARKNESS, MSgt, USAF NCOIC, Selection Boards Branch	SIGNATURE *(signature)*

2

TO TAG TEXAS	FROM NGB/DPMO	DATED 10 July 73	SUSPENSE DATE Aug 73

REMARKS (If above suspense date cannot be met, furnish anticipated completion date.)

RETURN CORRECTED REPORT DIRECT TO ARPC

TYPED NAME AND GRADE OF PERSONNEL OFFICER	SIGNATURE *Robert L Cole*

(When additional indorsements or remarks are required use reverse or blank sheets.)

ARPC FORM 204 PREVIOUS EDITION DATED JUN 71 MAY BE USED.
      MAR 72

Notice of Missing or Correction of Officer Effectiveness/Training Report: Denver commander sends form to Texas Guard officers wanting further explanation of why Bush was reported "not observed."

Office of Information
147th Combat Crew Training Group
Texas Air National Guard
Houston, Texas   77034

FOR IMMEDIATE RELEASE
spl to The Houston Post
and The Houston Chronicle
w/art

ELLINGTON AFB, Tex., March 24, 1970---George Walker Bush is one member of the younger generation who doesn't get his kicks from pot or hashish or speed. Oh, he gets high, all right, but not from narcotics.

Bush is a second lieutenant attached to the 111th Combat Crew Training Squadron, 147th Combat Crew Training Group, Texas Air National Guard at Houston.

Lt Bush recently became the first Houston pilot to be trained by the 147th and to solo in the F-102 Fighter Interceptor, a supersonic, all-weather aircraft.

In January, the 147th's mission was changed from active air defense of the Texas Gulf Coast to a new mission--to train and make combat-ready all Air National Guard F-102 fighter pilots in the United States.

Lt Bush was the first member of the 147th to be trained by people he will be working with in the future.

After his solo, a milestone in the career of any fighter pilot, Lt Bush couldn't find enough words to adequately express the feeling of solo flight.

"It was really neat. It was fun, and very exciting", he said. "I felt really serene up there. It's exciting to be alone in such a big aircraft and it's a real challenge to fly such a powerful airplane by

MORE

Guard News Release: Bringing attention to Houston media about the swearing in of a congressman's son.

yourself".

Fighter planes are Lt Bush's "thing". He says he has no ambition
to fly any other type of aircraft.

"Fighters are it. I've always wanted to be a fighter pilot and
I wouldn't want to fly anything else", he said. "You have such speed,
such power in a fighter, that it's just fantastic. And the F-102 is
really a good-looking, well-constructed aircraft. It's a really stable
airplane".

Despite the fact that he's flown the F-102 solo for the first time,
Lt Bush isn't letting it go to his head.

"I've got a hell of a lot more to learn," he said. I've got to
learn to respect the aircraft and its capabilities, as well as my own
abilities."

Lt Bush is the son of U.S. Representative George Bush, who is a
candidate for the U. S. Senate seat of Senator Ralph Yarborough. The
elder Bush was a Navy fighter pilot. Lt Bush said his father was just
as excited and enthusiastic about his solo flight as he was.

Lt Bush, who is 23, is due to complete his pilot training June 23.
He will then be released from active duty and assume reserve status in
the Air National Guard. He plans to fly as much as possible with the
Air Guard and work in his father's campaign. Beyond that, he hasn't
any plans.

As far as kicks are concerned Lt Bush gets his from the roaring
afterburner of the F-102.

"Flying, the whole thing, is kicks," he said. "But afterburner
is a real kick."

-30-

LAST NAME-FIRST NAME-MIDDLE INITIAL		SSAN		ACTIVE DUTY GRADE
BUSH, GEORGE W. *(CHECK APPROPRIATE BLOCK AND COMPLETE AS APPLICABLE)*				NONEAD
☐ SUPPLEMENTAL SHEET TO RATING FORM WHICH COVERS THE FOLLOWING PERIOD OF REPORT		☐ LETTER OF EVALUATION COVERING THE FOLLOWING PERIOD OF OBSERVATION		
FROM	THRU	FROM	THRU	

Precede comments by appropriate data, i.e. section continuation, indorsement continuation, additional indorsement, etc. Follow comments by the authentication to include: name, grade, AFSN, organization, duty title, date and signature.

Not rated for the period 1 May 72 through 30 Apr 73.

Report for this period not available for administrative reasons.

[signature]

RUFUS G. MARTIN, Major, ████████ FG, 147th Cmbt Spt Sq, Chief, CBPO, 12 Nov 73

AF FORM 77a JUL 69   PREVIOUS EDITION OF THIS FORM WILL BE USED UNTIL STOCK IS EXHAUSTED.

SUPPLEMENTAL SHEET TO AF FORMS 77, 707. 909. 910. 911 AND 475

AF Form 77a: Texas Guard commanders' response to the Denver request for more information. They repeat that Bush was "not rated" for the period and add that a report on him was "not available for administrative reasons."

Master file

DEPARTMENT OF THE AIR FORCE
147TH FIGHTER INTERCEPTOR GROUP
ELLINGTON AIR FORCE BASE, TEXAS 77030

SPECIAL ORDER   1 May 1973
AE-226-TX

1. Fol named off and/or amn, orgns indicated, this station, are ordered to attend Annual Active Duty Training at the Air National Guard training site Ellington AFB, Texas for the period indicated: (Aero rating and fly status as indicated). Personnel will report to their unit commander for duty on effective date of training. Movement of dependents and household effects at government expense not authorized. Per diem and TPC authorized in accordance with JD 25-69 dated effective 9 July 1969. Rated personnel on flying status are authorized to participate in flying activities during the period covered by this order. Airmen within commuting distance (50mi) are authorized basic allowances for subsistence at the rate of $2.57 per day (Per diem not payable) when rations in kind not available per paragraph 30102c DODPM. The bearer being the agent of an Air Force Reserve member on active duty in excess of 72 hours is authorized commissary privileges only for the period covered by these orders. Individuals not on active duty in excess of 72 hours are not authorized commissary privileges. P/A (Off) 5733850-563-4156-P521.01-S380000. (Amn) 5733850-563-4156-P521.07-S380000. Trans: (Off) 5733850-563-4145-P521.14-408-S414502 (Amn) 5733850-563-4145-P521.18-408-S414502. PD: (Off) 5733850-563-4145-P521.20-409-S414502 (Amn) 5733850-563-4145-P521.24-409-S414502. Authority: ANGM 50-01. Title 32, USC, Sec 503 (Formerly Sec 94, National Defense Act).

111TH FIGHTER INTERCEPTOR SQUADRON	NO DAYS	PERIOD
1ST LT GEORGE W. BUSH	9	22May73 thru 24May73
PAFSC 1125D Non-F'g		29May73 thru 31May73
		5 Jun73 thru 7Jun73

2. SMOP 1 SO AE 176 TX this hqs. dated 13 Apr 73, pertaining to CAPT WAYNE E. WARE   only as reads "NO DAYS" 6, PERIOD: 18 Apr 73 thru 19 Apr 73, 24 Apr 73 thru 27 Apr 73 is amended to read "NO DAYS" 5, PERIOD 18 Apr 73 thru 19 Apr 73; 24 Apr 73 thru 26 Apr 73.

FOR THE COMMANDER

BILLY B. LAMAR, CMSgt, TexANG
Asst Admin Officer

DISTRIBUTION
AE

AE-226-TX

Special Order AE-226-TX: Orders for Bush to report for nine days of duty in the Texas Guard for May and June of 1973. No one remembers him reporting to Ellington AFB in Houston. No Officer Effectiveness Rating Report was filed on Bush for this time period, which was necessary if he had actually served.

Missing Guard Documents

- Pay records: These files are the simplest way for Bush to prove he was on duty for the days he has claimed. If he was, pay records exist at the Defense Finance and Accounting Service in Colorado. In early 2004, the White House released master pay records for the president but not individual pay stubs or receipts for days he performed duty. They can document every day he was compensated for duty, and end the controversy. If no pay record exists, he did not do the duty.

- Retirement Total Points: This document can prove the total number of points Bush earned toward retirement. It would show if he did the minimum required days of duty each year of his six year hitch. The White House did release various "points summary" documents for specific years. However, they do not list the cumulative total nor are they independently verified by pay receipts, tax statements, or the president's W-2 forms. Those were not released.

- Tax and Earnings Statements: The president can authorize the IRS to look for all of his tax records potentially on file from 1968 to 1974. If those exist (e.g., W-2s or tax returns), they can easily be used to determine how many days the president was paid for duty and compared against points records.

- Officer Effectiveness Rating for 1973 through 1974: Bush claimed he did report for duty in Houston this year. If he did, an OER was filed by his commanders, as required. The document has never been produced. No one ever saw him on base.

- Board of Inquiry Report: Pilot suspension was a significant event in the Air National Guard. A Board of Inquiry's written findings on the suspension or the final report of an investigation ought to exist. No such document has ever been produced.

- Medical Records: If Lieutenant Bush were grounded for a medical reason, this would be in his file.

- Microfiche Files from Denver and St. Louis, pay stubs from the Defense Finance and Accounting Service: An authorization to release these complete files to the public and journalists will begin to answer questions about the president's time in the Texas Air National Guard. The "retained records," or hard copy files kept in Austin, which were partially released, are demonstrably incomplete. Microfiche records should be released directly to journalists without White House assessment, as was done by Senator John McCain in the last election.

[Information regarding missing Guard documents is current as of February 18, 2004.]

10

FLYING COLORS

He said that men believe death's elections to be a thing
inscrutable yet every act invites the act which follows and to the
extent that men put one foot in front of the other they are
accomplices in their own deaths as in all such facts of destiny. He
said that moreover it could not be otherwise that men's ends are
dictated at their birth and that they will seek their deaths in the
face of every obstacle.

Cormac McCarthy, "The Crossing"

The day that George W. Bush got word he had been suspended as a pilot in the Texas Air National Guard, August 15, 1972, Richard Cunnare of Alabama was in a helicopter falling from the sky. The commander of the AH-1G Cobra attack aircraft, Chuck Dean, was apparently dead from a bullet to the head, and Cunnare saw the jungle floor in Vietnam rising toward the helicopter. A fourth reconnaissance flight over the same area had exposed Cunnare and Dean to attack by the North Vietnamese. The Cobra's transmission and rotor pin had been shot out, and Cunnare was pulling hard on the ship's controls, trying to find some lift in the blades. He needed luck, more than emergency checklists and heroics.

The helicopter hit the ground hard. Cunnare had found some lift in autorotation procedures, but it only seemed to make the Cobra bounce after impact. The airframe began to disintegrate as the helicopter scraped across the earth. After hurtling up a slope, completely out of control, the Cobra burst into flames. Cunnare, who had been struggling with the operation of the aircraft, had not had time to stow the gunfight he had been using to shoot at the enemy. The crash knocked it into his face, and left him with a huge, penetrating wound to his sinus cavity. The force of the blow to his head was so great that one of Richard Cunnare's eyes was forced from its socket, and hung on a tangle of nerves next to his face. The cornea was lacerated, and he dropped into unconsciousness, almost unaware that his foot had been dislocated by the crash.

When he woke up, Cunnare heard one of the OH-6A Scout helicopters flying near where he had fallen. The other chopper pilots assumed he was dead, but Cunnare felt the rotor wash from the whirring blades.

"I know I got hit in the head real bad," he recalled. "I don't remember a thing until, John Bridgers, who was in the co-pilot's seat in Terry Overton's Cobra, called in to the smaller bird [OH-6A] that there were no survivors. A nonsurvivable crash."

Richard Cunnare, though, had remembered to activate his emergency locator as his helicopter was falling, and the broadcast of the device's frequency began to be heard on radios in the other Cobra and the two OH-6A Scouts circling overhead. The pilots of those helicopters took the signal as a sign Cunnare had lived. About the same time they began hearing the radio beacon, Cunnare realized where he was and what had happened. He heard bullets tearing through the jungle foliage, whacking into trees. From the air, before his crash, he had seen numerous Vietnamese soldiers, and now he figured they were running in his direction to finish the kill. Cunnare reached for his .38 pistol and considered taking his own life.

"I knew they were right behind me," he said. "And I knew they were coming to get me. I just decided to not go through that experience."

Smoke and flame were still rising from Cunnare's flight suit. His hands, arms, and neck had been burned, badly. The Cobra wreckage, which was only five or ten feet from where he lay, was consumed by flame. Chuck Dean had to be dead. Blind, and in agonizing pain, as the North Vietnamese closed on his position, Richard Cunnare figured suicide was a more rationale choice.

"But I couldn't pull my pistol out," he explained. "My hands were burned so bad, and my flight suit is burning off my body, and I couldn't use my burned hand to find my pistol."

Although he was only marginally aware of it at the time, Cunnare had also suffered a broken back, which would have affected his mobility while reaching for his sidearm, and a bullet had torn into his elbow.

Overhead, Terry Overton saw what had happened. Lowering the nose of his aircraft, Overton swept down near the wreckage as his co-pilot John Bridgers fired all of their ship's rockets. The ordnance passed over where Richard Cunnare was spread on the ground, and exploded fifty yards distant, between him and the advancing North Vietnamese.

Cunnare began to scream. "God help me. God help me."

"That's all I could think to do," he explained. "I just kept yelling, 'God help me.'"

An estimated 600 of the enemy were tearing through the undergrowth, trying to reach Cunnare. Onboard the Scouts, two gunners began firing their M-60s and M-79 grenade launchers. No one was certain Cunnnare was even alive. Doug Brown, a pilot in one of the OH-6As, made a high speed pass over the crash site, and told the other crews in the air that he had spotted a body and some burning bushes. On a ridge behind the hill where Cunnare lay wounded, Dexter Florence, the commander of the other OH-6A, sat his ship down. Both gunners with M-60s were now on the ground. Howard Fraley and Thomas Boyd were each armed with 500 rounds.

Climbing up over the ridge, and then racing down the slope, Fraley and Boyd used up all of their ammunition on the North Vietnamese enemy. Standing over the injured Cunnare, the two soldiers laid down protective fire until they were out of bullets. Cunnare's eardrum burst as the two guns blazed near his head. Both men of average height, Fraley and Boyd tossed aside their M-60s, and started to move the injured pilot toward safety.

"I've got a broken back," Cunnare remembered. "My foot is dislocated, and I've got a fractured skull. I'm burned over a huge part of my body, and I'm in shock."

The North Vietnamese were, momentarily, distracted by the helicopters still in the air. Dexter Florence and Doug Brown were buzzing the site, drawing fire, enabling the rescue efforts of Fraley and Boyd. Brown dropped out of sight behind the hill, and, a short time later, approaching enemy soldiers suddenly saw an OH-6A rising above the ridge, before dropping back below the horizon. Each time the helicopter appeared, Vietnamese turned their guns away from Cunnare, and fired at the aircraft. With no ammunition remaining, Brown's only form of assistance was to turn himself into a target.

"Doug Brown was hovering up and down like this behind the ridge," Cunnare said. "He just started popping up and down like a wounded bird."

"And he had nothing to shoot back with?" Cunnare was asked.

"Well, Doug Brown was a man."

So were Howard Fraley and Thomas Boyd. Under increasing enemy fire, the two men began to pull Richard Cunnare toward the protection of the ridge, where one of the helicopters might carry them clear of the North Vietnamese guns.

"Goddamn, Mr. Cunnare." Fraley had slipped his arms under the downed pilot, and was trying to move him up the hill. "You're so damned heavy. How can a pilot weigh so much?"

"Shut up and drag him," Boyd yelled. "We've got to get him out of here."

In the other OH-6A, Dexter Florence was keeping a close watch on the rescue. If Cunnare became too much of a burden, and the enemy got too close, Florence would have to take drastic measures to protect the three men. Fraley and Boyd were unarmed after using up all of the ammo in their M-60s, and were moving only a few feet at a time as they tried to drag the six-foot, 200-pound, limp Cunnare up a jungle incline, and down across a creek to reach level ground. They had to move him almost a hundred yards to find a spot where Florence was able to land the helicopter. The North Vietnamese had gotten to within a few hundred yards of the three, and, according to Doug Brown in the other OH-6A, they looked like "ants coming up the hill in waves."

Cunnare, slipping abruptly in and out of consciousness, began to yell encouragement at his rescuers as they struggled toward a flat spot in a ravine.

"We're gonna make it," he yelled. "We're gonna make it."

"You're goddamned right we're gonna make it," Boyd reassured him.

"You're just too damned heavy, Mr. Cunnare," Fraley screamed above the gunfire.

"Shut up, goddamnit, Howard," Boyd said. "Keep dragging him."

Cunnare's pain had to be unimaginable. Eighty percent of his body was covered with varying degrees of burns, and smoke was still coming off of his flight suit. A broken back, compressed vertebra, a fractured skull, an eye hanging from its socket, and his right foot dislocated during the crash by a control pedal, Cunnare's agony was only beginning.

Forty-five minutes later, bullets still ripping at the jungle, Dexter Florence settled his OH-6A into a flat spot, hovering just above the ground as Fraley and Boyd hoisted the burly Cunnare into the helicopter. Considerably smaller than the Huey or a Cobra attack helicopter, the OH-6A had a lighter payload capacity. The weight of Cunnare, Fraley, Boyd, and pilot Florence put the ship at the edge of its ability to fly. Florence tipped his Scout forward, pointed toward the narrow valley, and traded altitude for air speed. The maneuver gave him the lift needed to climb out of the landing zone.

In the cargo bay, Cunnare's clothes were still on fire. Fraley and Boyd, who had carried him the last hundred yards, began to realize their own arms were also burned. Blood was pouring out of numerous wounds in Cunnare's big frame, and he was calling for his friend.

"Get Chuck," he yelled. "Where's Chuck? You gotta get him."

There had been no time to treat Cunnare's injuries. Florence flew toward the coast, looking for a spot to land and begin giving medical attention to Cunnare. Shortly after his OH-6A touched down, a South Vietnamese medical evacuation helicopter arrived, and Cunnare was given a quarter grain of morphine, intravenously. Fifteen minutes later, he was in a field hospital at Hue, suffering from shock.

"They stabilized me there," Cunnare recalled. "They did something we didn't do. They packed me in ice. And, oh, the horror of being packed in ice when you have that kind of pain, burns, and broken bones."

An American helicopter transferred Cunnare to Da Nang, sixty-five miles to the west. On the flight, a medic kept him focused on surviving, urging Cunnare, "Don't give up. Don't give up." He did not. But for three days, the pilot underwent surgery, open reductions of his dislocated foot and his facial wound. An ophthalmologist treated his cornea, after reinserting his eye into the socket, and a plastic surgeon reconstructed his broken nose. Shrapnel and bullets were picked from Cunnare's body, and then ruined flesh was excised from his most serious burns. In three days, he was placed aboard an air transport to the Brooke Army Burn Center in San Antonio.

From August 21, 1972, until two days before Thanksgiving that year, Richard Cunnare was brought back to health at Brooke. He underwent skin grafts, additional operations on his leg and facial wounds, and, finally, bandages were removed from his eyes. During a convalescent leave to Alabama, he and his wife decided to get a divorce. Cunnare simply said their relationship had become impaired, and he needed to concentrate on his recovery. But his marriage was also a casualty of war.

In ways he was still trying to understand more than thirty years later, the shoot down of Richard Cunnare and Chuck Dean's Cobra continued to affect Cunnare's days. Circumstances that led Cunnare to that hill in Vietnam were not out of his control. He had volunteered, twice, having come from a family with a tradition of service. His father had fought in World War II, and his maternal grandfather was gassed during combat in World War I. The first time he went to Vietnam, as a crew chief on a medical evacuation helicopter, Cunnare's unit had been a part of saving thousands of lives. But he had never forgotten the dead, or those who were in the process of dying.

Other war experiences remained inextricably connected to his living.

Almost as clearly as he recalled his crash, Richard Cunnare cannot let go of what happened a few days before he was shot down. An ARVN fire commander had cleared Cunnare to shoot at a village south of Da Nang. Anti-aircraft guns position near that locale had made night flights even riskier, and the South Vietnamese wanted the enemy weapons destroyed. After the clearance to fire was issued, Cunnare compared the code's initials with his wingman, and then unloaded all of his ordnance on the village. When the bomb damage assessment was conducted the next morning, Scout pilots did not discover a single military age body. The dead were women, children, and elderly.

That memory also survived the war in Vietnam.

And while Thomas Boyd and Howard Fraley dragged a screaming Richard Cunnare through the jungle that morning of August 15, 1972, each of them desperately hoping to live, the young man who was to become president of the United States of America was continuing to ignore direct orders to report for duty to the National Guard. George Walker Bush was exercising family privilege and connections to escape combat in Southeast Asia.

Belief in the principles of duty, honor, and service was what delivered Richard Cunnare to danger. For George W. Bush, though, those concepts were only words, which he, eventually, used in campaign themes.

And, later, in arguments to lead his country to war.

War is something more than simply chaos. It is a series of circumstances and uncontrollable dynamics; the bringing together of resources and people that create the kind of situations best avoided. Moments of bad judgment are amplified, turned profoundly important, when they are made in a war setting. George W. Bush was not exposed to any of combat's absurdities, capricious moments become deadly, because he stayed home in the Texas Air National Guard. He was safe.

Dexter Florence was not.

Three days from going home, Dexter Florence was stationed about fifteen miles from Da Nang. The Arkansan, who was to be awarded the Distinguished Flying Cross for his rescue of Richard Cunnare, was hanging out on the flight line when another pilot passed carrying a flag from the North Vietnamese Army. Florence had an idea.

"Hey, you know, I'm going home in a few days," he told the pilot. "I was wondering if you might cut loose of your flag for a souvenir."

"No." The answer from John Robinson was blunt. "Go out and get your own."

Florence considered the idea. The temptation of capturing a flag was, ultimately, irresistible. His own father, a noncommissioned officer earlier in Vietnam, had captured a Viet Cong flag. Dexter Florence was probably motivated by a desire to equal the old man. He went around the base, and found someone to serve as door gunner, Keven Zane Goodno of Spring Grove, Minnesota, who was willing to join Florence in the hunt. A staff sergeant, Goodno was an armor reconnaissance specialist. No one has determined if Florence ordered Goodno on the mission, or if the young staff sergeant volunteered. Because Dexter Florence was an OH-6A Scout commander, and he was taking a 17th Cavalry recon officer with him, there was no resistance from flight control when Florence reported plans to search for enemy hideouts and weapons. In fact, he did radio back a few observations.

The two were flying in known areas of enemy concentration, skimming above the trees at high speed, hoping to see a flag on a pole, or enemy movement they might report. But their primary objective was a flag. American helicopter pilots had been stealing NVA flags by hovering over the poles while their door gunners or other crew members grabbed the flag and shot loose the rope lines. Unfortunately, NVA soldiers had decided to fight the U.S. souvenir hunters.

When he spotted an NVA flag bouncing on the wind, Dexter Florence brought his OH-6A, often referred to as a "Loach," to a hover just above the top of the pole. Goodno leaned out the door, grabbed the flag, and pulled as he started to shoot loose the ropes. The North Vietnamese, who had recovered a 500-pound American bomb, had either attached it to a trigger on the rope, or remotely detonated the bomb while watching the chopper hover. A huge explosion tore through the helicopter, immediately killing Goodno, and dropping the aircraft.

First Lieutenant Dexter Bush Florence, later to be decorated for heroism, was down, seventy-two hours before his flight home. It was also exactly one year to the day since he and Richard Cunnare, the man he courageously rescued, had graduated together from flight school. In the village of Quang Ngai, the light observation helicopter piloted by Florence, tail number 68-17329 was burning.

Richard Cunnare was still in a hospital in Texas.

"The door gunner was just vaporized," according to descriptions provided to Cunnare. "And somehow, Dexter, being in an armored seat and all that, he survived the crash. And they got to him pretty quickly and pulled him out."

Florence, however, was burned over 98 percent of his body. Cunnare said he had been told only the bottoms of Florence's feet had escaped the flames. He hung on for three more days and died on October 29, 1972, the day he was scheduled to board a flight home.

In his high school graduation photo, Dexter Florence has a short, clipped haircut. His smile is restrained, teenaged self-consciousness inhibiting expression. The earnestness of youth is in his eyes, but there is also something else there, a serious glare, perhaps, or impatience to get on with whatever lay ahead. A talented percussionist, Florence had starred in the Henderson State University band in Tennessee. Cunnare remembered almost shooting him a few times when Florence woke him up by banging out tunes on Cunnare's helmet.

On his enlistment papers, Florence indicated his hometown as Arkadelphia, Arkansas. On October 29, 1998, the twenty-sixth anniversary of his death, the airport in Arkadelphia was dedicated in Florence's name. Prior to the ceremony, John Robinson and Richard Cunnare were reminiscing when Robinson pulled out the North Vietnamese flag he had shown to Dexter Florence, which had prompted him to fly his last mission.

"John, I really don't know what to say about that," Cunnare said.

At the ceremony, Cunnare spoke of the man who had given him a chance at having a future.

"He came to see me in the hospital the next day in Da Nang," Cunnare said. "And I thanked him for saving my life. He said he was just doing his job, and I would have done it for him, or any of the other guys would have done what he did. Anyway, this is a great town, and you raised a wonderful kid. I've got two fine sons, and have got to do a lot because of Dexter."

The airport in Arkadelphia now bears his name: Dexter B. Florence Memorial Field. A scholarship has also been established in his name at Henderson State. A few of the pilots who knew what had happened that day in South Vietnam refused to attend the dedication ceremony. They are still angry over the unnecessary loss of Keven Goodno, and they blame Dexter Florence. The circumstances surrounding the deaths of Florence and Goodno were unknown at the time of the airport's dedication. When Cunnare called Dexter

Florence's brother to tell him the details of his death, Bill Florence was almost relieved. He told Cunnare that he had been angry at the military for many years because he thought Dexter had been sent on a dangerous mission just a few days before going home.

The circumstances of Florence's death did not change Richard Cunnare's feelings for his friend. If it were not for Florence, Cunnare would have never lived to marry again and have sons, earn a master's degree, start a successful business, or fish the Gulf of Mexico with his friends.

As far as Richard Cunnare was concerned, Dexter Bush Florence did not need to die a hero.

He had lived as one.

11

A Congressman's Son

I often feel fairly sick with impotent rage at my inability to make
the authorities show wisdom and efficiency; and the people are
so foolish and uninformed that I am obliged to continually hold
myself in because if I tell anything like the whole truth, they
simply do not believe me, and I do more harm than good. I think
that they are beginning to wake up; but it is very, very late.

Theodore Roosevelt

Bill Burkett was asleep on his couch. Along a dirt road in rural
West Texas, Burkett's ranch house sat about 120 yards back
from a locked gate. Around 10:30 P.M. on a Thursday night
in early April 2001, Burkett was awakened by a sound he recalled as a loud "whap." He then heard what he assumed was a small
piece of glass falling to the floor.

"I didn't know what it was, exactly," he said. "But I knew something had happened."

The light had remained on in the living room where he had
been sleeping. In the morning, while he was trying to figure out
what had caused the window to break, Burkett found a bullet lodged

in the south wall of his home's kitchen. When he looked at the bullet's angle of entry into the wood, he was able to see it pointed straight back to the hole in the window. The trajectory continued out to the dirt road along the edge of his property, about fifteen to twenty-five feet east of his mailbox.

"I was not as scared at the moment as later," he said.

Over the course of the next two years, Bill Burkett claims he received fifteen threatening phone calls at home. According to Burkett, his car's front window had also been shot out, and he had found a bullet with his name on it in his mailbox. Burkett had filed a lawsuit against his former commanders at the Texas National Guard, accusing them of withholding both his pay and health care benefits in an act of vengeance. As state plans officer for the Texas Guard during the administration of Governor George W. Bush, Burkett had written reports detailing a "ghost soldier" scam, which kept troops on the books even after they had left the Guard. This gave the state a chance to keep collecting federal funds on troops it no longer retained on its rolls. When *USA Today* wrote a series of reports in 2001 alleging several states had National Guards that were inflating troop numbers to prevent Congress from transferring units to other states, or to simply keep federal money flowing into Guard operations, Burkett was cited as a source in the article about Texas.

"Bill Burkett, a former lieutenant colonel in the Texas National Guard," reporter Dave Moniz wrote, "says that four years ago, he and a group of officers informed Adjutant General Danny James, the state commander, that 7 percent of the Texas Army Guard's 16,300 troops were ghost soldiers. Burkett and others say that despite promises to fix the problem, the Texas Army Guard continues to include soldiers who shouldn't be on the rolls. According to figures provided by the National Guard Bureau, over the past two years, Texas has had anywhere from 1,300 to 1,800 unpaid soldiers on its rolls, more than 11 percent at its peak."

The only response Moniz got from General James was an e-mail from James' office claiming that 3.7 percent of Texas Army Guard troops were waiting to be discharged. Interviewed in 2004, James said Texas and a number of other states had bureaucratic and procedural problems getting soldiers removed from troop rosters. He said there was no attempt to be deceptive.

Burkett, though, says he had been telling his commanders about the ghost soldier problem for several years, as well as promotions for people with political connections, who did not meet basic educational requirements or had failed officer examinations. He had grown frustrated with leadership's refusal to make changes, and when Dave Moniz of *USA Today* called with questions about the Texas Guard, Burkett decided to go on the record. Whenever he interviewed Burkett, Moniz then called various officials within the Guard to ask follow-up questions. A few days later, Burkett said, he usually got threatening phone calls, which seemed to be a consequence of his speaking with Moniz. In his estimation, each anonymous call was linked to developments in his lawsuit over military health care benefits, or reporters asking questions about the Texas National Guard. For Burkett and his wife Nicki, the most disturbing element of the thirty-second threat was that the caller had detailed information about their private lives.

Burkett says one of the most frightening calls came in April 2003:

> You motherfucker. You've been warned and warned. Ya don't really care if you live or die, do ya, boy? Saw your house again last week. Traded cars, did ya? You like white Cadillacs, don't ya? If they wanted you dead, they would have told me. But I can still break your fucking legs, you know. Or maybe I need to mess up that pretty little wife or those kids. Whatya say, asshole? You think you're sick now? I'd love to really fuck you up and make you wish you were dead. Your time's running out, big boy. I'm going to fuck you till you squeal.

There may have been another reason Bill Burkett was being threatened. As an advisor to General Danny James, Burkett claimed he had been involved, coincidentally, in two conversations relating to the National Guard records of Texas Governor George W. Bush.

During a speakerphone conversation between Bush Chief of Staff Joe Allbaugh and General James, Burkett said he heard Allbaugh tell James to make sure there was nothing "embarrassing" in Bush's Guard files.

And then Bill Burkett said he watched as the "embarrassments" were removed.

As the state plans officer, Bill Burkett had relatively unfettered access to Adjutant General Danny James, the commander of the Texas National Guard. James had agreed to grant Burkett impromptu visits to his office because Burkett was managing the complicated task of figuring out what was wrong with the Texas National Guard, and how to fix it. According to Lieutenant Colonel Burkett, there was nothing uncommon about him showing up at the general's office at Camp Mabry headquarters, and asking his secretary for permission to stick his head in for a brief meeting, or to pose a quick question.

Generally, Burkett tried to schedule appointments because the issues he was dealing with were complex, and required more than just a short meeting. As a career officer in the National Guard, Burkett took great pride in not sticking his nose in where it did not belong or where he was not needed. Burkett's conversations usually involved discussions with the door closed. One day in 1997, however, something came up, and he wanted to speak with General James without a scheduled appointment.

Stepping into the small workspace of James' secretary Henrietta Balderas, just outside the general's door, Burkett says he leaned in and asked if James had a minute to talk. According to Burkett, James motioned for Burkett to wait while he took a call. James punched a button to put his caller on a speakerphone. The conversation was loud and distinct. Bill Burkett said it was easy to hear from where he waited.

He recounted the following conversation:

"General James, this is Joe Allbaugh," the voice on speaker said. "I've got Dan Bartlett on the line with me." Allbaugh was chief of staff for Texas Governor George W. Bush.

"Joe, what can I do for you?" James asked.

"I just wanted to let you know we need to have [Dan] Bartlett and Karen [Hughes] come out there," Allbaugh said. "They're gonna write a book for the governor's re-election bid, and, you know, in case he wants to go further. We need for them to take a look at all the [Guard] files on the governor. Can you make sure all of those are gathered up and there's not anything in there that will embarrass the governor? Just get rid of the embarrassments?"

"Karen Hughes will be out?" James asked. "And Dan?"

"Yeah, that's right," Allbaugh said.

Burkett recalled the conversation as friendly and upbeat, part of a political campaign, no big secret, no big deal.

After the call ended, Burkett said he and James met. The general had made no attempt to close the door, or keep the conversation with Allbaugh private. Burkett knew these types of requests were not unusual within the culture of the National Guard. After almost three decades in the Guard, he had seen files backdated, resumes inflated, and awards recognitions made up to facilitate promotions for the politically well connected. There was a consistent attempt to make officers more marketable. But what he had just overheard gnawed at Burkett's conscience in a way that those other indiscretions had not. The Guard was always about politics. Careers were built more on political ties than on military performance or efficiency. But there was something disturbing to Burkett about a scheme to clean up the service record of George W. Bush. Bush was now an elected official.

"The governor's office just said what they wanted done," Burkett explained. "I'm not sure it ever bothered anyone at the Guard. I know it didn't. I dropped it and didn't say a thing about it. But it bothered me all day long."

According to Burkett's commanding officer, however, the conversation Burkett described never took place. General Danny James, who was the leader of the Texas National Guard during the tenure of Governor George W. Bush, had hired Burkett as a consultant. James said he never put Joe Allbaugh on speaker phone when he spoke with the governor's office.

"I'm sure I didn't have more than a dozen conversations with Joe during my entire time as commander," James said. "Whenever he called, it was private and state business. I sure wouldn't put him on speaker, especially not with my door open. And I can assure you Karen Hughes did not come out to Camp Mabry. It would have been totally inappropriate and unnecessary for the governor's communications director to be out there. [Dan] Bartlett did come out a few times, but it was certainly not to do anything with Governor Bush's files. Burkett's just part of a small group of officers in the Guard during that time who had axes to grind when things didn't go the way they wanted them to."

Accustomed to filing daily reports and keeping track of all Guard developments in his role as consultant to General Danny James, though, Burkett made a notation of what he claimed he had overheard on the speakerphone. In the evening, Burkett said he went to dinner with Chief Warrant Officer George Conn, and told him what he had heard. According to Burkett, Conn's advice was to simply let it go. Burkett said Conn also advised him that the corruption within the Guard was too great for it to be conquered by Bill Burkett. Burkett also said he told the story to another CW3, Harvey Gough. Gough confirmed what had been related to him by Burkett.

When Burkett first began his challenges of the National Guard in 1997, Conn corroborated all of Burkett's claims, including backing a letter to a state senator, which talked about the "cleanup" of Bush's records. Additionally, in an e-mail to the *New York Times* after Burkett's story went public in 2004, Conn told reporter Ralph Blumenthal, "I know LTC Bill Burkett and served with him several years ago in the Texas Army National Guard. I believe him to be honest and forthright. He calls things like he sees them." Conn had already confirmed Burkett's version of events with reporter Dave Moniz of *USA Today* a few years earlier, though Moniz' editors had chosen not to run the story at that time.

The morning after Burkett said he heard the speakerphone conversation, he was scheduled to be part of a staff meeting with General James, and two other senior officers, William Goodwin and Wayne

Marty, among others. According to Burkett, they were all gathered around the coffee machine when a state services employee, later introduced to Burkett as General John Scribner, walked up, and General James informed him of the phone call.

According to Burkett, James said, "Karen Hughes of the governor's office is going to be coming out to look through those [Bush] files. Can you get those together?"

Burkett recalled Wayne Marty adding specificity to James' instructions.

"Make sure to clean it up," Marty said. "We don't want anything in there that will embarrass the governor."

"Yes, sir," was the only response from General Scribner.

Burkett claims the incident occurred in the summer of 1997, a time when Burkett, by his own admission, was angry. As an expert on planning and force preparation, he says he had arranged for a meeting between Governor Bush and U.S. Army General Dennis Reimer a few months earlier. Burkett later characterized the governor as having "blown off" the general's offer to invest Army money in upgrading Texas forces. Because Burkett had devoted endless hours to understanding the failures of the Texas Guard's force readiness, and finding resources to improve the situation, he was angered that the soldiers and airmen of the Texas National Guard and the Guard's mission and role were being used as political fodder.

And now he says he was witness to a scheme to clean up Bush's own Guard files.

"You know, it was just no big deal to them," he said. "They were just taking care of the boss. They didn't even know they were doing anything wrong. And I think they would deny they did anything wrong, even if all of this stuff ever hit the fan."

"Look," General Danny James explained, "It is reasonable to think that the Guard wanted the governor to put his best foot forward when he ran for president. Taking a look at his files is something that was a part of our responsibility. But we didn't do anything like clean them up, or anything else. That's nonsense and it didn't happen."

Working under intense deadlines, and managing the political dynamics of the Texas National Guard, Bill Burkett had begun to have chest pains. Often, his friend CW3 George Conn stopped by to take him for a walk to relax, briefly. About ten days after Burkett claimed he had witnessed the officer conversations concerning cleaning up the Bush files, he says Conn stopped by to say hello.

"Get your hat," Conn allegedly told Burkett. "We're going for a walk."

Burkett, a workaholic, argued lightly before joining Conn. According to Burkett, they walked down a hallway and out the north end of the building in the direction of the Academy on the Camp Mabry grounds.

"Where are we going, George?"

"Colonel, just walk with me."

Taking a rather roundabout course, Burkett said the two men arrived at the old Museum. Inside, General John Scribner was going through the Military Personnel Records Jacket of George W. Bush. Conn introduced Burkett to the General. Next to where Scribner was working, Burkett saw a two-foot tall, gun barrel gray wastebasket, fourteen or fifteen inches in diameter. Conn, whom Burkett said seemed to have a personal relationship with everyone on the base in Austin, began talking with Scribner.

"Well, what are you doing?" Conn asked.

According to Burkett's recollection of the conversation, Scribner confirmed that he was doing as ordered, and was working through George W. Bush's retained records.

"It just seems kind of limited," Scribner answered.

"Oh really?"

"Yeah, there's just a few retirement forms. Some recruiting photos. Really, there's just some trash. There's not as much here as I expected. I think somebody's been through it, several times."

Conn and Scribner began to have a conversation, and walked away, leaving Burkett alone with the file, in an open space about fifty feet from an office. Conn and General Scribner ended up inside of that office. According to Burkett, none of this was planned. However, as Conn and Scribner moved off, Burkett said he "lightly rummaged" through the ten-gallon metal waste can and saw numerous documents, such as statements of points earned by "Bush, George W., 1st Lt." Later, Burkett admitted to not being proud of his behavior, but he was angry over tampering with official records, as well as the way his findings about the Guard were being ignored.

"I just stood there and looked at it," Burkett said. "There was a stack of from twenty to forty pages, somewhere in that range. These were pages of duplicate and primary documents. I saw the primary points documents and they were in the trash. It was just a series of pages taken out of the file and dumped into a trash can."

Burkett also said that he saw Leave and Earnings Statements in the trash. The document on the top had Bush, George W. 1LT on the name line. Burkett reached into the can to move around the stack of papers.

When Conn and Scribner returned, Burkett says Conn asked what was going to be left of the governor's file. "We're just gonna have to try to reconstruct this file out of Denver," Scribner is said to have answered. "They've been through this thing so much. All of the master stuff is on microfiche."

"There was no doubt that the Texas National Guard was providing support for their governor's run for the presidency," Burkett claimed. "It was clearly spoken throughout the conversation." Conn, however, began to deny Burkett's story when national reporters began calling him with questions.

In retrospect, however, Burkett's convictions have grown stronger. He is convinced that one of the sheets of paper in the trash can was a points document. He was certain that it was the record needed to determine whether George W. Bush actually performed any Guard duty between 1972 and 1973, instead of the torn Document 99 provided by the Bush campaign.

"In the back of my mind, I know damned well that I saw a retirement points document that covers the period in question. At the last of his duty, he supposedly went in and did a lot of duty. He needed x number of days to get a year for retirement. I think somebody just tried to cover him on paper so he wouldn't get in trouble.

"So, were the files messed with? Yes, but probably in a different way than most would expect. There wasn't a boiler room conspiracy of sorts to alter the files. I think the objective would have been to make sure that there was very little trace of a file on Bush. Wouldn't that be the smart approach to cover a less than exemplary effort? Wouldn't that be the best way to hide things?"

And there seemed to be much to hide.

But Albert Lloyd, who helped Dan Bartlett of the Bush campaign understand the governor's military record, said no one tampered with the files.

"That's just bullshit," Lloyd said. "It's bullshit. Everything that was supposed to be in that file was in that file. I've worked in military personnel records for over forty years. I know what the hell I'm talking about."

General James also ridiculed Burkett's story. "John Scribner manages the museum," he said. "He doesn't have access to Guard records. It just doesn't make any sense. He would have no reason or authority to go through those records. I can't figure out why Burkett is saying this stuff, other than he's angry at us over his health issues and other things."

Through a public affairs officer, the Texas National Guard said in the autumn of 2004 that Generals Wayne Marty and John Scribner were not available for interviews on Burkett's claims. Phone calls, e-mails, and registered letters to Joe Allbaugh, White House Communications Director Dan Bartlett, and Bush advisor Karen Hughes, never received a response to queries about Burkett's allegations.

"The Texas National Guard will not be responding to any statements made by Mr. Burkett," said Guard spokesman Sergeant Gregory Ripps. Marty, who has become the adjutant general in charge of the entire Texas Guard, and Scribner are both still serving.

Nonetheless, when Burkett's story finally entered into the mainstream media, the White House made Allbaugh available to speak with national news correspondents. He called Burkett's story "hogwash," and John Scribner, who Burkett said was sifting through the Bush file, said, "I have no idea what he [Burkett] is talking about."

George Conn's story also changed. In an interview with the *Boston Globe*, Conn said he did not remember the incident.

"I know George to be an honest, and honorable man," Burkett said. "But he's working for the federal government. He's under a tremendous amount of pressure. I can't ask the man to give up his life for me. He stood behind me on all of the corruption I was making public about the Texas Guard, including my testimony to the State Senate, a letter to a senator talking about the Bush file, and even when he told *USA Today* that I was telling the truth. The truth hasn't changed in all of those years. The only thing that's changed is George's story."

As Burkett's allegations swirled through the national media, the Bush administration began releasing more of the president's National Guard records. The new documents, however, contradicted those made public prior to the Bush run for the White House, and began to raise even more doubt. The first step by the White House was to provide reporters with master pay records and dates that points were earned for service. During the 2000 campaign, Bush said he remembered making up his duty days on November 29, 1972 in Alabama and pointed to the torn Document 99 as proof because it bore that number, though without a month. The new, untorn version indicated that 29 was actually October, and there was neither a witness nor a pay stub to corroborate the new information. Clearly, however, it contradicted the president's campaign explanation for his time in Alabama.

The essential confusion in the new materials was revealed in dates the White House said were the days Bush served duty in Houston in January, March, and April of 1973. The dates are on the untorn version of Document 99, but they are at direct odds with the Officer Effectiveness Rating report issued by Bush's commanders. If Lieutenant Bush was on base for the days listed in the document, his commanders would certainly not have described him as "not observed." More than 30 years later, there was still no documentation that Lieutenant Bush had served any time, as he claimed, with the Texas Air National Guard in Houston during the spring of 1973.

"People need to pay attention to that point," said researcher Marty Heldt. "You can't make the testimony of his commanders go away. He wasn't there, and they have nothing to prove that he was."

As scrutiny of the additional materials increased, an Atlanta businessman went before cameras and claimed he had served several months with Bush in the Alabama guard, and that he remembered seeing him on many occasions. This was reported to be several months during the summer of 1972. However, the White House's own materials showed there is no record of Lieutenant Bush doing anything in Alabama until October 29, 1972, and even that date cannot be verified by pay receipts or other documents.

Releasing the larger file on a Friday evening in Washington to avoid immediate journalistic attention, the Bush administration, nonetheless, found that reporters were discovering new curiosities. The 400 pages were supposed to be the entire record. However, when 160 pages were delivered under FOIA's in 1999 and 2000, they were described as "the complete file" by the Bush campaign. A dental record from Alabama is an example of the seemingly unending contradictions in the record of Lieutenant Bush. He apparently was given a forensic dental exam on the Montgomery air base in January of 1973, a time when he had said during the campaign that he had returned to Houston and resumed serving with the Ellington Air Guard wing. It was not explained why Bush was in Alabama for a dental visit when he had already rented an apartment in Houston. Regardless, the dentist's file did not serve to prove Lieutenant Bush had performed any duty in Alabama.

Journalists are not lawyers, and often overlook critical considerations in the conveyance of information. In the case of the president's National Guard records, nothing was more elemental to their credibility than the chain of custody of the file. Until that is established, there is no way to completely trust released details. Who

printed the entire record off of the microfiche at the National Personnel Records Center in St. Louis? Who had access to it before it
arrived at the White House? Who were the people who examined
the documents on the Bush staff before they were copied and sent to
reporters?

According to Charles Pelligrini, the chief of the records management systems in St. Louis, nothing has changed in the Bush file
since it was committed to microfiche some time after Lieutenant
Bush's discharge from the Texas Air National Guard. (Changing a
federal record requires a detailed application process.) Because Dan
Bartlett of the White House has admitted to flying to Denver to examine the microfiche copy at the Air Reserve Personnel Center, its
historical value is drawn into doubt. However, if nothing was removed from the Bush hard copy file in Austin before it was recorded
to microfiche and sent to St. Louis, there is an accurate, historic
record available. The president needs only to sign a release authorization form, and send it to St. Louis, and reporters can print out the
entire file for themselves. Instead, the White House vets the material, the Department of Defense assesses it, and, undoubtedly, Karl
Rove pores over each page fulminating over possible political impact of each piece of data.

Republicans argued that the president's critics were attacking
him and the honorable service of National Guardsmen and
women. But Bush political operatives knew that the questions surrounding Lieutenant Bush's fractured tenure in the guard were
harming his moral authority as a commander-in-chief. He sent tens
of thousands of members of the National Guard into combat in
Iraq. If they had acted as capriciously about their oath of service,
as did Lieutenant Bush, the U.S. would have been short of troops
needed for the president's attack on Iraq. The Guard matter also
amplifies the debate over whether the president spoke the truth
about intelligence prompting the invasion of Iraq. Bill Burkett's assertions about people tampering with the Bush file indicate that
Lieutenant Bush's performance might have been the first big lie of

the Bush administration. The cooked intelligence related to the war in Iraq was the second.

Will there be another?

George W. Bush was first asked about the Texas National Guard during the 1994 gubernatorial race with Ann Richards. In a televised debate, a panelist asked Bush how he managed to get into the Guard so easily when there were more than 100,000 young men on waiting lists. The reporter wanted to know if Bush's father, then a U.S. congressman from Houston, had used influence to help his son sign up as a pilot. Bush's response was that he knew of no special treatment he might have received, and that he just walked up, raised his hand, and got a pilot's slot at Ellington Air Force Base. Although Bush has long denied any special privileges were afforded him to enlist in the Texas Air National Guard, there is a great deal of evidence that contradicts him.

A source inside the Texas National Guard said, "The minute after that question was asked, they started building their alternative story. They contacted Major Dean Rhome, [Bush apartment roommate during Guard flight school] Colonel Maury Udell, [Bush flight instructor] and Colonel Walter B. 'Buck' Staudt [Commander 147th Fighter Group]. They wanted to make sure who was gonna plug the holes. All they needed was the right people connected to Bush and the Guard to deny the favoritism stuff."

The strongest implication of the use of Bush family influence came during testimony in a lawsuit involving the Texas lottery. After he was fired only five months into his tenure as executive director of the Texas lottery, Larry Littwin, eventually, filed a suit claiming he was victimized by the state's contractor, the G-Tech Corporation. Littwin, who was hired the same day as he was interviewed by the lottery's board, had, immediately, gone to work scrutinizing G-Tech's deal with Texas. According to senior staffers on the lottery management team, Littwin wanted to re-bid the contract because he thought Texas had the leverage to acquire a more favorable agreement. In his court pleadings, Littwin alleged that his dismissal was prompted by a connection between G-Tech lobbyist Ben Barnes and Texas Governor George W. Bush.

Barnes had been hired by G-Tech, and had signed a lifetime contract giving him a percentage of revenues generated by the lottery. In the late 1960s, Barnes was also Speaker of the Texas House of Representatives. As one of the two most influential people in the Texas legislature during those years, Barnes frequently took requests from people interested in getting their sons enlisted in the Texas National Guard. Enrollment in the Army or Air National Guard was considered a legitimate method for avoiding the draft, and not fighting in Vietnam. As a result, there were more than 100,000 young men on waiting lists around the country, hoping to get enrolled. Usually, they were drafted before the Guard called. Waiting lists were often up to five years long. A friend, or family member, who wanted to get George W. Bush into the National Guard, would have had to contact Barnes or someone on his staff.

A Democrat, Barnes became the highest-paid lobbyist in Texas history when he signed the G-Tech contract. Complications arose for Barnes, however, when Republican George W. Bush was elected governor. Harriet Miers, Texas Lottery Commission chair, who later became Bush's personal attorney at the White House, urged the commission's attorney to begin re-bidding procedures on the contract.

"The time has come," Miers wrote in a February 18, 1997, memo to Kim Kiplin, the commission's in-house counsel. "I am convinced the Texas Lottery Commission and the State of Texas will be best served by the re-bid of the Lottery Operator contract as soon as possible."

As early as March 1996, Bush Chief of Staff Joe Allbaugh had been asking for information about the lottery contract. Miers, appointed to the chair by Bush, had sent Allbaugh notebooks of lottery meetings and details on the operator's contract, according to a note from her to Allbaugh dated March 7 of 1996. Allbaugh's interest may have been as political as it was economic. Hundreds of millions of dollars were involved in G-Tech's contract, and two of the key people, Barnes and Executive Director Nora Linares, were both Democrats, who had supported Ann Richards in the race against Bush. Linares was fired, and sued the commission over wrongful dismissal, settling for a statement from the lottery that she had done nothing wrong. Eventually, she sued G-Tech separately for complicity in her dismissal, also resolving that case before it got to court.

Barnes' situation, though, was another matter. If anyone in the Bush family, or one of their friends, had contacted Barnes about getting George W. into the Guard in 1968, Barnes was the possessor of damaging political information, which might be used against the future presidential candidate. In the process of discovery during the lawsuit by fired Lottery Executive Director Larry Littwin, an anonymous letter, addressed to U.S. Attorney Dan Mills in Austin, claimed that a deal had been brokered to keep Barnes silent. Copies of the letter were leaked to a few Texas reporters, but were never published.

"Several months ago many of us felt that the Lottery Commission should re-bid the G-Tech contract when it came up for renewal," the unsigned and undated letter said. "Leaders of the Republican Party strongly supported re-bidding and I believe the chair of the commission also wanted to re-bid. It is now time to disclose at least one reason why it was not re-bid. Governor Bush through Reggie Bashur made a deal with Ben Barnes not to re-bid because Barnes could confirm that Bush had lied during the '94 campaign. During that campaign, Bush was asked if his father, then a member of Congress, had helped him get in the National Guard. Bush said no, he had not, but the fact is his dad called then Lieutenant Governor Ben Barnes to ask for his help to get his son not just in the Guard, but to get one of the coveted pilot slots, which were extremely hard to get. At the time [name redacted] contacted General [James] Rose at the Guard and took care of it. George Bush was placed ahead of thousands of young men, some of whom died in Vietnam.

"Bashur was sent to talk to Barnes who agreed never to confirm the story and the Governor talked to the chair of the Lottery two days later and she then agreed to support letting G-Tech keep the contract without a bid. Too many people know this happened. Governor Bush knows his election campaign might have a different result if this story had been confirmed at the time."

There are several possibilities for the identity of the individual whose name was redacted from the letter, but there is no way to know the writer who mailed the note to the U.S. Attorney. The only reason for the redacted name to be obscured is that it would directly connect the Bush family to the request of a personal favor to treat George W. with privilege. In court pleadings at the time of the lawsuit, Barnes and his attorneys described the notion of a favor repaid as "fanciful and preposterous." Bashur has not commented. Nonetheless, there was great political risk for George W. Bush if the former Lieutenant Governor Barnes went public with a claim that Bush's father had called and asked for help in getting his son into the Texas National Guard. The intercession of a family friend was certain to be less damaging to Bush, politically, especially if that person had contacted Barnes without Bush family knowledge.

After being deposed as part of Littwin's lawsuit, Barnes issued a statement saying that "neither Bush's father nor any other member of the Bush family" asked Barnes for help getting into the Guard. Barnes indicated in his written statement that he was contacted by Houston businessman Sidney Adger, a wealthy friend of George H. W. Bush, who asked Barnes to recommend the younger Bush "for a pilot position at the Air National Guard." Barnes said he called Brigadier General James M. Rose and suggested Bush be considered.

The younger Bush had already sent a personal emissary to Barnes to seek reassurance that his father did not ask for the favor. Don Evans, who was the Bush gubernatorial campaign manager in 1998 and later became commerce secretary, met with Barnes to "knock down a rumor that the senior Bush had solicited Barnes' help during an encounter at the Bluebonnet Bowl in December 1967." Governor

Bush sent Barnes a grateful note when Evans returned with word that the former lieutenant governor had no memory of the elder Bush asking for any such consideration.

"Dear Ben," Bush wrote, "Don Evans reported your conversation. Thank you for your candor and for killing the rumor about you and dad ever discussing my status. Like you, he never remembered any conversation. I appreciate your help."

Political opponents of Bush said the anonymous letter and the governor's note to Barnes smacked of a back room deal. Barnes' client, G-Tech, they argued, got to keep the lottery contract, and Barnes retained his lucrative deal with the company in exchange for not implicating the Bush family on matters of favoritism involving the Guard. But Barnes was already in trouble with G-Tech. The same month that Lottery Commission Chair Harriet Miers was instructing staff to prepare to re-bid the G-Tech contract, Barnes and the company had informed the Texas Lottery Commission that he had agreed to a $23 million settlement to buy out his contract. G-Tech had decided Barnes had become a "lightning rod," in part because he was included in a federal grand jury investigation in New Jersey, regarding accusations that Barnes kicked back a share of his monthly retainer to G-Tech's president. No charges were ever filed.

Regardless, Democrat Barnes, whom Bush Republicans worried might know too much, was gone. And, financially, he had every reason to be happy. Joe Allbaugh and Harriet Miers had begun to ask questions about the G-Tech deal just as it was reported that Barnes was named in the New Jersey federal investigation. If he had become a political liability to G-Tech, for any reason, the Barnes relationship had been successfully excised, and, eventually, Lottery Commission Chair Miers dropped her call for a re-bid of G-Tech's contract. G-Tech's main lobbyists became former Bush aides. Republican Reggie Bashur was hired after Bush was elected, apparently in an attempt by G-Tech to improve connections to the new governor. Cliff Johnson was retained by G-Tech after Barnes was released.

Voters, though, did not seem to care about how Bush got into the Guard. But privilege has been one of the constants in his life, and the facts surrounding his Guard years remain relevant to his leadership as president of the United States. The man who landed on the carrier U.S.S. Abraham Lincoln in a fighter jet, and declared, "Mission Accomplished" in Iraq was twelve days away from losing his student deferment in 1968 and being forced into the draft. When he walked onto Ellington Air Force Base, and told Colonel Walter B. "Buck" Staudt that he wanted to sign up to be a pilot, young American men were dying at a rate of 350 per week in Vietnam.

But George W. Bush did not have to go.

Four weeks before enlisting in the Texas Air National Guard, Bush took the Air Force Officers Qualification Test and got a 25 on the "pilot aptitude" section. According to one of his commanders, this was about "as low as you can get and be accepted." Bush got a 50 on navigational skills, but a 95 on what the test described as "officer quality." The same form had a space where Bush was asked if he wanted to go overseas. Bush checked a box next to "Do not volunteer."

Just before graduating from Yale, Bush was sworn into the Air Guard on the same day he applied. He was jumped over an estimated 500 already on the waiting list. Even though he had been given the oath to join by a captain, Colonel Staudt (who had a reputation as being a very political officer) arranged a second swearing-in ceremony to create a photo opportunity where he was shown taking Bush's oath. When Bush received a special commission as Second Lieutenant, and Staudt was not present for that ceremony, the colonel again staged a repeated event for the camera. U.S. Congressman George H. W. Bush can be seen proudly smiling in the background of the photo as Bush gets his officer's bars.

The 147th Fighter Group, commanded by Staudt, was known as a "champagne unit." The ranks were filled with the progeny of the wealthy and politically influential. In addition to Bush, the sons of U.S. Senator Lloyd Bentsen, U.S. Senator John Tower,

Texas Governor John B. Connally, two sons of wealthy Houston businessman Sidney Adger, whom Ben Barnes said asked him to get Bush into the unit, and seven Dallas Cowboy football players had all served their military duty in Staudt's air wing, which later became part of the 111th "Fighter Interceptor Group."

Before any of these sons of privilege were enlisted, however, their applications had to cross the desk of Brigadier General James Rose, who commanded the air wing of the Texas National Guard. Rose, too, was described by associates as "very political," and he understood the value of putting George W. Bush in a pilot's suit. Jake Johnson, a former chairman of the House Veterans and Military Affairs Committee in the Texas Legislature, said Rose took credit for getting the younger Bush into the Guard. Johnson, who described himself as an ally and close friend of Rose's, said the general told him, "I got that Republican congressman's son from Houston into the Guard."

Staudt, however, told the *Washington Post*, "Lots of people like to take credit. I'm the guy Bush came to see. I don't care who said who called who. We ran the unit. Nobody called me using influence."

Maybe none was needed. Sons of congressmen were taken care of. Bush went through six weeks of basic training for airmen, and then got a special appointment to second lieutenant. The recommendation came from a panel of three senior officers and the commander of his squadron. This is the fastest promotion to second lieutenant on record in the history of the U.S. military. Normally, a second lieutenant commission required eight full semesters of college ROTC courses, or, as a minimum, eighteen months of military service. Air Force Officer Training School was considered essential. Bush had none of these qualifications. Tom Hall, Texas National Guard historian, told the *Los Angeles Times* that he "had never heard of that," except for flight surgeons. An appointment to second lieutenant with Bush's background was considered without precedent.

After 18 months of training, including flight school at Moody Air Force Base in Georgia, George W. Bush flew on duty for 22 months. This was not the type of flying that involved active duty, which is an official call up of reserve pilots needed to serve in a war. What flight time Bush accumulated was all served as a "weekend warrior," though, even that was a commitment he was unable to keep. He took off for Alabama to get involved in politics. Lieutenant Colonel Bill Burkett, who worked for Governor Bush, said no matter how anyone else described Bush's behavior that spring of 1972, it can only be categorized as going AWOL. Burkett was astounded when Bush showed up in a flight suit on a U.S. aircraft carrier.

"As a veteran, as a man that served and saluted George W. Bush while he was governor; as a man of uniform for 28 years, who raised his right hand on an oath to provide protection for the citizens of the United States and the Constitution, I was offended beyond belief.

"This image as a fighter pilot was a crock. It was nothing but a crock. I had men who worked for me under my command, and it brings tears to my eyes when I think about these guys who went to Vietnam. And they volunteered, and two of those guys died. And it brings tears to my eyes. And it hurts me as a commander, and I know that they would have never stepped forward and made these brash claims that Bush made. They simply served quietly and with dignity. And yet here is an individual who steps up and claims an image he cannot support."

Even Albert Lloyd, who was enthused about Bush as a presidential candidate and helped the campaign with Guard records, has changed his mind; not about the Guard, but about George Walker Bush.

"Look, the Guard has always been about favoritism," Lloyd explained. "I don't give a damn about that. It may not be right, but that's how it is. I saw it every day for forty years. But I supported Bush for president because I thought he had some good ideas. He said a promise made is a promise kept. And he was talkin' about us veterans. But he flat out lied. He's broken every goddamned promise he made to us.

"I'll damned sure never vote for the son of a bitch again."

They must have suspected Bill Burkett. He kept coming back to General Danny James with reports on "ghost soldiers," scam promotions, cheating on officers' exams, and failures to improve force readiness and mobilization. Even though he had been hired to find and fix problems within the Texas National Guard, it was becoming clear to Lieutenant Colonel Bill Burkett that his commanders did not want to hear what their consultant had to say. And when a few reporters began to make inquiries about the service records of George W. Bush, Burkett said he was silently blamed for prompting their curiosity.

"At first," Burkett said, "I think I was just tolerated by some of the senior officers and the Bush folks. But I was deemed a threat by most directorate level people because we were examining how effective they were being, and some took it personal rather than professionally."

Eventually, Burkett was loaned out to the U.S. Army for a project in Panama, where he contracted a viral form of encephalomeningitis. As an active duty officer, he was entitled to health care from a nearby base. However, one of his commanders in Austin needed to sign off on his status. And they all refused.

Within four days, Burkett was unable to lie down because of pressure he felt on his brain. Instead of going to an emergency room, Burkett's wife Nicki made desperate calls to the National Guard in Austin trying to understand why her husband was unable to get authorization for treatment. They had no idea what his affliction was. And Hendrick Medical Center, the local emergency room, had already begun collection proceedings on Burkett for an unpaid $4,800 charge related to treatment for a back injury. According to Burkett, his small cattle operation was in serious financial trouble as the result of a long drought, and he did not have the money to pay off the hospital. The back pain had been so severe that he had chosen to go straight to an emergency room rather than wait for a commander's approval.

During the next 140 days, Burkett and his wife wrote eight letters to the governor's office and the National Guard, begging for medical assistance that was legally already his. George W. Bush, however, was busy preparing his 1998 run for reelection, and Burkett got no response. Although Bush officials said they did not see the letters, they were admitted as evidence in a lawsuit against Guard commanders. In addition, Burkett claims that Bush spokesman Dan Bartlett later admitted to Burkett that Chief of Staff Joe Allbaugh had read the correspondence.

"His characterization of all this is just not true," said Major General Danny James, who was promoted to commander of the Air National Guard by President Bush. "We just didn't deny him anything. He could have gotten health care at Dyess [AFB] in Abilene if he would have just picked up the phone and called them."

Burkett's reports and criticisms of the Guard, nonetheless, had prompted a hearing before the State Senate Oversight Committee in Austin. Over three months after he had fallen ill, Burkett was determined to keep his scheduled appointment to testify. Ten minutes before he was to leave, Burkett says the first of a series of threatening phone calls came in on his home number with a caller ID from the State of Texas switchboard.

"Burkett your interests and your health would be served if you just stayed in Abilene. But if you still want to fucking challenge us, then be careful on your trip. We're out there, you asshole. Have a good day, motherfucker."

Dizzy and vomiting from his neurological infection, Burkett made the trip anyway, taking 22 hours to cover the 225 miles between Abilene and Austin. According to Burkett, he nearly passed out during his testimony to the committee. His assessment of the hearing was that the governor's office lied to the committee, and none of the elected members of the Texas legislature were interested in getting involved because Bush was so popular and everyone wanted to see him elected president.

Unable to get treatment approved through state channels, Burkett's family turned to Congressman Charlie Stenholm of Texas and U.S. Senator Hillary Clinton, who got the governor's office to authorize a "release from active duty" physical. Burkett was still so ill months later that the doctors at Brooke Army Medical Center in San

Antonio immediately admitted him for emergency care. His medical report indicated he was still suffering from loss of consciousness, dizziness, headaches, elevated pulse and temperature, ringing in the ears, and a generalized weakness with a loss of sensation on the right side. Ultimately, Burkett lost 60 percent of mobility on his right side.

Financially, the Burkett household situation was worsening. The drought had put them $15,000 behind on their bank note. Burkett had sought payment of $16,000 in salaries and expenses, hoping the money would cover the note and keep his bills up to date. According to Burkett, his paycheck and expense reimbursements were slowed, and then halted, in what he considered a "compounding retaliation." Ultimately, he filed a lawsuit against his superior officers, which was dismissed, because of a legal precedent that military proceedings are not subject to civil claims. Under political pressure from Stenholm and Clinton, Burkett was finally paid in October of 1998, ten months after his check was due.

There may have been another reason he finally got paid. Burkett admitted that he had resorted to blackmail to get the attention of the Bush administration in Austin.

"That's right, I blackmailed them," he said. "I told [Dan] Bartlett that if they didn't do the right thing and get me access to medical care, I would go public with the whole shooting match about the ghost soldiers, the readiness reports, the false findings on what really happened at Waco, the falsification of testimony on two occasions, and, yep, Allbaugh and his call to Mabry to make sure that Bush's AWOL was covered up. That's the way I put it in my phone call."

Ordered medically retired in October of 1999, Bill Burkett had been treated for fifteen months without permanent response. Two medical evaluation boards within the military reviewed his case and put him on temporary disability for five years. This ruling, however, is subject to periodic review, and any time before November of 2004, a solitary physician in the military can overrule the medical board's findings, which would result in the removal of Burkett's pension.

Bill Burkett still cannot sleep lying down, and each day continues to be a struggle. His mother spent the last years of her life trying to sustain him. His two sons dropped out of college to help their father. His wife quit her job. Death seemed likely. And still, according to Burkett, the threats and attempts at intimidation did not stop. Each time he talks to a reporter, or his name turns up somewhere, or there is a development in his medical case, or there is something political and he is suspected of being involved, Burkett's phone will ring.

"Burkett," a voice on the line said in October of 2002. "If you keep this up, you're not just taking chances with your life, but also taking the chance that we will file treason or theft of government secrets charges against you. Back off, I tell you, back off."

But he won't.

In late 2003, Burkett said he found a sign tacked to an exterior wall of his home. In letters cut out from magazine pages, a message was pasted to a piece of paper. It read, "We're still here."

Down his dirt road in West Texas, Bill Burkett sits and waits for whatever is coming next.

12

MEN SUCH AS THESE

War is always the same. It is young men dying in the fullness of
their promise. It is trying to kill a man that you do not even know
well enough to hate. Therefore, to know war is to know that
there is still madness in the world.

President Lyndon Baines Johnson

They gathered in a retirement community; one of those
planned developments where everyone was supposed to
have a golf course view of a fairway or a green. On the
back of each house, there were screened "Florida" rooms,
and fans lazily spun above their heads, stirring the air but not offering relief from the heat. These little attachments at the rear of their
homes helped the owners to realize they were in Florida, done with
work, and relaxing. Out across the Gulf, the south wind of summer
drove more humidity inland, making the night dense and almost oppressive. But these men did not notice.

Thirty-five years ago, in a time and place they will never be able
to forget, the five of them had been brought together by their country's politics, and, perhaps, their own destinies. And since then, a

piece of them had never stopped being soldiers. When Richard Cunnare sent out an e-mail invitation to the reunion, he had referred to "incoming personnel" who were going to be traveling to Pensacola, as though they were all still under the command of the U.S. military. Certainly, they were brothers; their blood having been spilled on the soil of Southeast Asia. But they were closer than siblings.

Across the table, Major Nelson Luce, whenever he spoke, had their attention. Unimposing in stature, Luce, nonetheless, was an unmistakable leader. Smoke rose from a cigarette he kept tapping in an ashtray as he talked. His white hair thick, and his confidence undiminished by the years, Luce was not interested in speaking of his own accomplishments. He wanted the visitor to understand that he was in the presence of greatness.

"These are," he said softly, "two of the bravest human beings who have ever lived." And he nodded through the darkness in the direction of Richard Cunnare and Dennis Telischak.

In 1968, Luce was an aircraft commander in Vietnam. By military standards, he was already an old man in his late 30s. Luce was flying Hueys in an Air Ambulance unit, evacuating combat casualties from the jungles. Often, when he was taking his helicopter into a hot landing zone, he got on the intercom and told Cunnare and Telischak, "The folks at home are never gonna believe this." During the Tet counteroffensive, Luce and his Huey crew lost track of the wounded and dead they had lifted out of the jungles. Although the mantle over the fireplace in Luce's Florida home is covered by an array of military honors, he did not bother to show them to the stranger. Three Distinguished Flying Crosses have been presented to Luce.

Cunnare and Telischak served under his command. Cunnare was the crew chief and Telischak the medic on the "Dust Off" Huey. Every time their ship went up, they were flying into the worst possible conditions of combat. A summons from troops in the field always meant things had turned bad. Whenever Luce went into a landing zone, inevitably, there were Viet Cong firing at his aircraft. Cunnare and Telischak "compacted" themselves into the smallest targets possible, and then set about gathering up the casualties, taking them up to the safety of the sky.

Dennis Telischak, who became a New Jersey business consultant, remained unimpressed with his own experiences, even though he had the most dangerous job in all of Vietnam. If the landing zone was too hot, the fighting too fierce for a Huey to land and extract the wounded, a medic was often lowered into the field of fire, along with a basket, and then he and an injured soldier were hoisted back to the hovering helicopter. Hanging below the ship, rotor wash swinging him on a rope, Telischak was an easy target for Viet Cong gunners.

"I never thought about it," he recalled. "I just figured I had a job to do, and I was going to get it done. I guess I did that. But I always thought I would get through it, go home, and then start my life. That's what happened. I guess I wasn't supposed to die. When I look back on it now, sometimes, I realize how dangerous it was. But I didn't think about it then."

Vietnam sounds like nothing more than a developmental interlude when it is described by Telischak. But he is clearly too smart to have been oblivious to the risks. A man of gentle demeanor, Telischak had to know that the shortest life spans of Americans in Southeast Asia were those of medics and door gunners on helicopters. Men have always found their own private weapons for dealing with warfare, though, and maybe Telischak had an internal mechanism he turned on every time he heard the Huey's turbines. A rational man would not have done what he, Cunnare, and Luce did on a daily basis, as regularly, and unquestioningly, as if they were commuting to jobs in the city. They congregated around death like it was an office water cooler.

While night moved through the Florida panhandle, Richard Cunnare, Dennis Telischak, Nelson Luce, Dave Dillard, and James Bond tried to explain their experiences to an outsider. In spite of what they had seen, the bullets that had zipped past their heads, not one of them considered themselves especially courageous or exceptional. An impression was left that America was full of similar men. Perhaps, it is, and when they are called to serve, whether the war is just or wrong, they answer. Still, they are transformed by the fire they have passed through, regardless of whether they have acknowledged the change.

Cunnare had called them together decades after a battle they had all improbably survived. In 1968, as U.S. ground troops moved to counter the Tet Offensive, a solitary confrontation had connected the five. Above a battlefield, Luce, Cunnare, and Telischak orbited, pulling out the injured "at all cost," whenever there was an opening. On the ground, Dave Dillard worked communications for Paul Bucha, who, on the night of March 18, 1968, was to earn the Congressional Medal of Honor. James Bond, a company commander for the Army, was controlling air and fire support for the troops in contact and was in charge of four rifle companies.

After a long evening of memories, the next morning, instead of into battle, they went fishing on the Gulf of Mexico. Cunnare had arranged for a charter to take them off shore to fish for red snapper. If more than just the five of them had attended the reunion, the fishing boat would not have been large enough because two other groups had hired the captain for the same trip. The boat sat low in the water after everyone had boarded. The gunwales dropped down against the morning tide as the skipper backed his craft from the slip. Fishing was going to be shoulder to shoulder.

The July day was not promising. Cunnare, who refused to acknowledge the sagging clouds and gray mood, was anxious for open water. While the captain briefed his passengers on emergency procedures, Richard Cunnare talked quietly with his two sons. Dave Dillard, who still referred to James Bond as "sir," looked up the canal to the Gulf, and told his former commander he expected the day to be successful. Nelson Luce and Dennis Telischak were quiet, occasionally looking at the dark water. On his face, though, Luce showed he was pleased to be back with people he loved, men who he cared for in a manner he might never be able to explain. A summer rain did not have the power to distract from what was gained by their rejoining.

Swells heaved in the Gulf on the outbound trip, and the horizon pitched and rolled through the glass inside the cabin. On the other side of the settee, Richard Cunnare was trying to tell stories over the noise of the two straining V-8 engines below decks. Color has faded from his hair and his cheeks, but Cunnare has energy and animation, and he wants history to remember his war accurately. Telling the truth about his friend Chuck Dean, who died the day he and Cunnare were shot down, had been painful.

"Three years ago, I got in touch with Chuck Dean's father. He was 87 years old. And I got in touch at one of the reunions with someone from Chuck's family. And the story of our shoot down was kind of a legend because there wasn't supposed to be anyone survive something like that. Anyway, one of these guys at the reunion gave me Chuck's dad's phone number and I called him. He was just so mad about Chuck going back in."

Richard Cunnare understood the anger of Dean's father. Men lose their judgment in combat. The family of Dexter Florence, the man who flew Cunnare out of the crash site, had not been told until after the dedication of the airfield about the exact circumstances of his death. They only knew he had been decorated with the Distinguished Flying Cross for saving Cunnare.

"The Florence family did not know what really happened when Dexter died," Cunnare explained. "All they knew was that he was flying a mission and he was blown up by a land mine. We never told them about the attempt to capture a flag for a souvenir. It was dumb, and Dexter took the other guy with him."

Dexter B. Florence, however, had saved Cunnare's life, so Cunnare attended the airport dedication ceremonies in Arkadelphia, Arkansas. Doug Brown and John Bridgers, who were also decorated for their valor as pilots on August 15, 1972, traveled to Arkansas to honor Florence. Bridgers' father had won the Navy

Cross and the Distinguished Flying Cross at the Battle of Midway, Leyte Gulf, and various other missions in the Pacific Theater of World War II, and Cunnare wondered if there might be something genetic about bravery.

Often, Cunnare's mind is drawn back to the day he almost died, and the improbable risks others took to keep him alive, the fact that there were to be such men available in his neediest hour. In particular, he thinks about the cat-and-mouse game Brown and Bridgers played with the Vietnamese, popping up and down in their helicopter from behind the ridge to draw fire away from Cunnare, Thomas Boyd, and Howard Fraley.

"I'll tell ya," Cunnare said. "That took some stones."

At the stern of the sport fishing boat, Cunnare's two sons stood, heads lowered against the wind and salt spray, talking with their father's friend, Dennis Telischak. Statistically, Telischak ought not to have been alive, either. There were far too many nights of gunfire, thousands of bullets that never found him, aviation acrobatics that ought to have gone wrong. But he was here, contemplating whether the fish will bite and the sky will clear.

"You know, we were just kids," he explained. "I don't think we could really understand all of the dangers. And if we did, maybe we would have been more afraid than we were. None of us thought of ourselves as particularly brave, I can tell you that. I just don't think about Vietnam. Or talk about it. I am right now because our crew is back together, just for this short time."

While they renewed friendships, their country was once more engaged in a foreign war. Iraq was stirring their memories. Guerilla tactics were killing young Americans. There was no end in sight, no real exit strategy. Congress was divided. Americans were protesting. A political solution, which the invasion of Iraq was supposed to deliver, seemed farther away than before America got involved. And the country had been taken into the conflict by a president who had avoided combat in Vietnam.

But George W. Bush's questionable record of military service did not bother Richard Cunnare. Men who found ways to get out of the Vietnam era draft were just liabilities to those who were serving.

"I think James said it last night," Cunnare said. "We didn't want them around. We didn't wanna mess with them. We didn't wanna talk to them. We didn't wanna be affected by 'em. We didn't care about them. And if they came into our units and were trouble, we got rid of them."

"Did you hate guys who got into the National Guard to get out of combat?" he was asked.

"Nope. Nope. I volunteered for what I did. As a matter of fact, the statistics we have from the VHPA [Vietnam Helicopter Pilots' Association] is that 73 percent of all soldiers who went to Vietnam were volunteers."

Cunnare raised his chin, defiantly, as if asking his interviewer to explain that number, maybe argue that those who served were misguided and the men who avoided the guns of Vietnam were smarter. There were, of course, honorable ways to serve in combat, and just as honorable methods of serving the country without carrying a weapon. Whatever answers Richard Cunnare had been seeking, though, he had found them long ago. Some go when their country calls. Others resist. Some believed when American leadership said fighting in Vietnam was necessary to stop communism. Others thought it was a civil war, an internal struggle for power. The Iraqi conflict was no different. Soldiers in the desert believed they were helping to stop terrorism. At home, many people saw the war as a political distraction to help the president avoid criticism for not finding Osama bin Laden, or the real terrorists. Oil was also believed to be one of the causes of the fight with Iraq.

If history wanted to repeat itself, Richard Cunnare couldn't stop it. In Vietnam, he had done what he had thought was right for himself and for his country. That's all he understood, all he needed to understand.

Momentarily, the fishing charter's engines went silent, and the boat began a slow drift in a flattening sea. On the horizon, clouds were losing their dark pitch. One of Cunnare's sons lowered his head into the cabin door.

"Let's go, Dad," he said. "We're baiting lines. Time to get some fish."

Slowly, Richard Cunnare raised himself and walked to the after deck to join his boys and his friends.

"If you ever talk to George Bush again," Cunnare said as he was going outside, "tell him to give us vets all of our benefits. We earned 'em."

The old soldier was still fighting for what he believed was right.

PART

III

COUNTING
CASUALTIES

13

MEMORIAL DAYS

Perhaps passing through the gates of death is like passing quietly through the gate in a pasture fence. On the other side, you
keep walking, without the need to look back. No shock, no
drama, just the lifting of a plank or two in a simple wooden gate
in a clearing. Neither pain, nor floods of light, nor great voices,
but just the silent crossing of a meadow.

Mark Helprin, *A Soldier of the Great War*
(New York: Harcourt, 1991)

He called from the Carl's Jr. Restaurant outside the Marine
base at Camp Pendleton, California. It was their special
place, where they went to talk, and entertain the possibilities of the future. All the way up in Washington
State, she heard the nervousness in his voice on the other end of the
line, and it made her want to laugh. He was such a big guy and so
fearless. All of his accomplishments, and there were many, had come
as a result of his own fortitude, his unwillingness to make excuses or
turn himself into some kind of a victim. And now here he was nervous about talking to the young woman, fretting over her response.

"It was so hysterical," Chelle Pokorney said. "He had this little jitter in his voice, and it was just so funny to hear this big guy because he was never like that. And I was in Washington and then he said if he asked me to marry him what would I say because he was so afraid to ask."

But Frederick E. Pokorney Jr. got up his nerve, and he asked Carolyn Rochelle Schulgen to be his wife. Impatient, the couple made plans to elope and get married before a justice of the peace in Reno, Nevada. Chelle called her best friend to be a witness. They flew to Reno to meet Fred. He had already arrived, and had gone shopping to buy his bride a Mickey and Minnie Mouse "wedding" sweatshirt to give to her after the ceremony.

"We went to the justice of the peace, and I was just going crazy," Chelle explained, "because I was doing this without anyone's guidance. But I just had faith. What the heck. He was a great man."

The justice gave them the option of a thirty-second, one-minute, or two-minute civil marriage, and Fred immediately chose the shortest version. The Pokorneys lived apart while he was stationed at Camp Pendleton and Okinawa. While separated, Chelle finished her bachelor's degree in nursing. Eventually, Fred was accepted into a Marine Corps program to get a college education and prepare him to become an officer. Finally, they were able to live together as he attended Oregon State University in Corvallis.

They also became parents.

"We weren't gonna have kids, while he was going to college because it was too rough," Chelle said. "He came home from OCS [Officer Candidate School] and said 'I wanna have kids.' And I don't know where that came from. I was doing my career and I was really into that and felt like I couldn't be a mom because I was too selfish. He wanted to have kids and boy was he serious."

At Camp Lejeune, North Carolina, they settled into the routine of daily living. Lieutenant Pokorney was often late in getting home, Chelle discovered, because he went to anyone who asked for his help. He was so involved in being a Marine, she said, that Fred frequently was delayed because he went to watch promotion ceremonies or re-enlistments, a habit he had picked up back in Oregon while attending college. Fred Pokorney chose to train in the artillery, and leave the infantry, in order to protect his family. Generally, artillery officers are in the rear, up to thirty miles behind a battle. This was not a lack of courage. Pokorney had seen his daughter, and knew what it felt like to be a father and husband, and he chose to be practical. But he was sent to Iraq attached to a combat infantry unit as an artillery forward observer.

Chelle was afraid.

"He waited until the night before to tell me who he was going with, which unit; that he was going to the front lines as a forward observer. He was the tip of the spear. It was hard to think we were going to war. But that was his job, and he loved what he did, and he did it. And so I had fear. It was a terrible feeling."

Fred was also worried. During training with another officer, Pokorney had told a fellow Marine, "If we go, I'm dead." And then Chelle came home one evening, and her husband told her, "I'm going." He kept his apprehensions private, but Chelle sensed his fears. She had never seen her husband waver, and even now, facing the possibility of death, he did not turn away. He was, though, unable to say goodbye to his daughter, and let her sleep the morning he left for the ship to Iraq.

About two months later, during her Saturday night shift at the hospital in Jacksonville, North Carolina, Chelle was unable to concentrate on her work. She described herself as a wreck, as if she knew, viscerally, that something horrible was happening. Another nurse scolded her for not having control, telling her she was a Marine's wife, and she needed to learn how to deal with these kinds of circumstances. But this wasn't just about coping. Something was wrong, and Chelle knew it. She had a sense of it.

In Iraq, it was already the morning of March 23, 2003. This was an important day in the Pokorney household. It was the date Fred had been commissioned as an officer in the United States Marine Corps.

He was supposed to be promoted to First Lieutenant that afternoon during a ceremony north of Al Nasiriyah. Instead, he had died in a battle on the plains of Persia, most likely a victim of a mistaken American pilot who strafed U.S. troops engaged in a battle with Iraqis.

Chelle knew without being told, her husband was gone. She remembered the letter he had sent home to Taylor.

"I love you very much and miss you so much my heart hurts," Fred wrote. "And I hope I get home to you and mommy soon. And don't forget me. Love always, Daddy."

"He knew," Chelle recalled. "He just knew. But he never wavered. He wrote Taylor to say, 'I'm going to help them [Iraqis] because they need help. Their little kids don't have shoes and they're sick.' I mean, that's what he was fighting for in all of this, a bigger picture. He told her [Taylor] that he was going to Iraq and she'd have to take care of mommy because she was gonna cry all the time. Just tell her it was all going to be okay because he never lost faith."

The battle was being covered on television. CNN was reporting about a bitter fight with the Iraqis in Al Nasiriyah. When she called the base chaplain that night, he kept telling Chelle there was no way she could know Fred's fate. Nobody did. Not yet. But it was quickly confirmed, and the next day, Sunday morning, Chelle called Wade and Suzy Lieseke out in Nevada.

The Liesekes were in Reno where their daughter Angie was having another child. On his drive north across the broad cow counties of Nevada, Wade had been worried over a premonition of Fred's death, which had come in his dreams the night his son died. Suzy had been planning to call Chelle because she had been on her mind all that day. Everyone knew the Marines had moved into Iraq, and reports of the fighting were beginning to make their way back to the states. On Sunday morning, when Wade and Suzy Lieseke got into their pickup to go out for breakfast, Wade noticed a missed call on his cell phone. Chelle had left a message for him to call her as soon as possible.

"And I just went cold inside," Lieseke remembered. "And I'm sure Suzy did, too. And right then I knew something happened to Fred.

And I was praying to God that if something happened to him that he just got wounded. I could hear it in her [Chelle's] voice. I could hear the strain in her voice. I didn't know how to describe it."

Lieseke returned Chelle's call immediately. As he listened to her phone ring on the other side of the country, he prayed that Fred was only wounded, not dead. When Chelle answered, she asked Wade if he were sitting down. Suzy Lieseke did not hear the conversation. Not yet worried, she knew Fred was smart and was not in Al Nasiryah with all the other Marines. She believed that "with all her heart," for a while, even after she had heard otherwise.

"Chelle just said it matter of factly," Wade Lieseke said. "Like she was trying to keep the despair out of her voice. She just said it straight out: 'Fred was killed last night.' And I don't remember what I said after that. I honest to God don't. My whole insides just froze solid like the worst period of fear you could feel. I just felt numb."

Wade Lieseke's sadness was replaced by anger. He thought about his own war, Vietnam, and the absurdities of dying in combat, all the people he had killed, and the friends he had seen die. Lieseke hated to think of his adopted son as nothing more than cannon fodder in a political duel, but that's where his mind kept going. Unavoidably, he found himself hating President Bush, and what he was doing with American Armed Forces in Iraq. It was all wrong, all over again, Lieseke thought.

But Chelle Pokorney did not have time for any of that. She knew what her husband believed, what he stood for, and what he expected of her. Her job was to take care of their daughter, help the wives of other Marines, and be strong. Rick Schulgen, Chelle's brother, drove down from Virginia, and her parents flew across the country from Washington State. They stood beside her as she went before television cameras and the national media to talk of a future without her husband, and what lay ahead for their three-year-old daughter Taylor. Her news conference, only days after her husband had died in combat, was nationally broadcast.

"When she has that first date, there will be five guys [Marines] standing in the door to meet her suitor," Chelle told reporters.

Holding the hand of her mother, June Schulgen, who was crying, Chelle was being the strong Marine wife, maintaining composure, and talking about her final conversation with Lieutenant Pokorney on March 4, 2003.

"It was a blessing," she said to the room full of journalists. "He wished me a happy anniversary. We will celebrate our seventh on Saturday."

Chelle Pokorney said she had felt love from everyone she encountered in Jacksonville, home of Camp Lejeune. She said she expected the Marines to become her family. An estimated 150,000 Marines, both active duty and retired, live on and around the base. Because the Corps is perceived to be made up of people who take their commitments seriously, Chelle was convinced she and Taylor would be cared for until they figured out what was coming next. She believed in Lieutenant Fred Pokorney, and what he believed in: the United States Marine Corps and principles of honor, duty, and service.

But Wade Lieseke was skeptical; not of the Marines, necessarily, just the cause of the war in Iraq. The morning after Chelle's news conference, about 350 people gathered at the high school in Tonapah, Nevada, to honor Pokorney's memory. Lieseke was already letting loose his political disgust with the president. "Bush got his war and our boy's gone," he told the *Reno Gazette-Journal*. "To die in a war is really a waste of a good life."

Suzy Lieseke, who had become Pokorney's adoptive mother, cried when she was asked later about the almost "soulful" connection her husband said she shared with the young Marine.

"He's a son I never had," she said, sobbing. "I've been looking for some special pictures, and I found some the other day, and I didn't get emotional. It just brought me back to the time we made those pictures. I just looked at them, and then when I went to work I just kinda fell apart. My phone rang at work and it was my daughter Angie, and I honestly think Fred knew I was upset, and he had my daughter Angie call me. Sometimes I think it gets better but it doesn't."

Military commitments are common among Tonopah families. In the high middle of the Great Basin, there is not much opportunity for the young graduates of Tonopah High School. Once known as "Queen of the Silver Camps," the mines have now played out, and the Tonopah Test Range for military ordnance has closed down. The historic hotel where Fred had washed dishes, the Mizpah, was also shuttered. Too many travelers had hurried past on their way to Reno or south to shimmering Las Vegas. The children had to leave Tonopah to seek a future. The morning his community honored Fred Pokorney the names of 34 other Tonopah graduates were written on banners hanging in the halls of his old school. Each of them was serving in the U.S. military.

Lieseke had learned to accept Fred's decision to go into the military. But he was unable to deal with the choices made by the president of the United States, which had led to Pokorney's death in combat.

"I cannot describe to you how helpless it makes me feel to know that this man Bush has the power to make decisions to get kids killed. And he did. And he did. It's totally unforgivable. And these people who say it was worth all those American lives because we got rid of Saddam Hussein, my answer to them is what world are you in? That's okay as long as it's not your son or daughter. Until it's your son or daughter, you can't really make that statement."

In North Carolina, Chelle was struggling to contain herself. She wanted to cry, and collapse, and for a short time, she did. But her husband still needed her, even though he had died in the war. She had a promise to keep. Chelle had to make sure her Fred's wish was granted. There was a funeral to prepare for. And she was determined to make sure First Lieutenant Frederick E. Pokorney Jr. was buried with his heroes at Arlington National Cemetery.

Jill Kiehl walked out of the house with a baby in her arms. The door slapped shut behind her. In the Texas sunlight, the child's hair had a reddish cast. She sat in a chair next to an old picnic table in the front yard, and held her infant son closely. A live oak reached over with speckled shade. Around the tree's trunk, a large yellow ribbon had been tied into a bow. Summer in the Texas Hill Country had already faded the color. The cicadas rattled the still air with their distracting chirps. The sounds of July were louder than the soft-spoken young mother.

She was not yet comfortable talking about her husband in the past tense.

"He is 6 foot 8 and I'm 5 foot 2," Jill Kiehl said. "So, I am about at his stomach almost. He has to bend down, and I get on my tippy toes when we kiss. But if we want to kiss on the same level, I have to get up on our couch and we are face to face, which is kinda funny."

The baby grew uncomfortable in the heat, and began to squirm, slightly. Nathaniel Ethan Kiehl came into the world only weeks after his father had left it. James Kiehl had died in the Iraqi ambush of the 507th Mechanized Company in Al Nasiryah on the first day of combat. Kiehl's son showed stout health and brimming eyes. Before their child was born, Jill and James had not thought about meanings behind names. They just chose one that sounded right.

"It's kinda ironic the name we chose," Jill explained. "I looked up Nathaniel and it means 'gift from God.' And you can see, right here, he's got a little birthmark above his eye they call an angel kiss. And I'm wondering who gave him that, huh?"

Jill looked distracted, and the man who was asking her questions stopped for a moment. Her father-in-law, Randy Kiehl, had been standing on the other side of the table listening to the conversation. No one talked. The thrum of the cicadas in the heat was the only sound. When she spoke again, Jill Kiehl was looking down at her son, and her voice was textured with equal parts of sadness and anger.

"The hardest part is just every day the fact that he's not here," she said. "I'm seeing everybody else having a normal life. I know it's kinda petty or mean, but it's like, I don't have my husband, and why are you happy? It's not fair, and you have a normal life and I can't."

She was crying, an angry kind of sadness. Jill wiped at her cheeks with the back of her hand. No one knew what to say to her.

There really was nothing to say. She had hoped for a little house in El Paso where she and James might raise their children while he began his career in technology, and left the military. Instead, she was using his death benefit check to make a down payment on a home in Des Moines, Iowa, to be near her parents.

Comfort High School's basketball coach, Colin Toot, pulled into the Kiehl driveway. He had been asked to stop by and share memories of his former player.

"We retired James' number," Coach Toot said. "We were gonna hang it permanently in the hallway over there at the school, but you know, time goes on and so many new kids pass through a school. There just aren't that many now that remember him, and after all of this news about the war fades away, I expect everyone over there will just look at that jersey behind the glass and wonder who James was. So, we're gonna give the jersey to Randy and Janie [James' step-mother] so they can have it here in the house. There ain't much point in leaving it up there at the school, after a while."

Randy Kiehl, who had disappeared for much of the conversation, was back standing beside the picnic table. In his arms was a sort of iron and limestone cross with the insignia of the United States Army, a gift from the legendary Texas Rangers, lawmen famed in the state for their role in forging a civilization on the frontier. James Kiehl had been laid to rest in the Centerpoint Cemetery next to Comfort, which is the burial site of more Texas Rangers than any other plot of ground in the state.

"Because I wanted to pay James as much honor as I could," Randy Kiehl explained, "I couldn't think of a more honorable place to have my son laying at rest than with the Texas Rangers. And you know what they answered back to me? They said, 'No sir, it's an honor for your son to join us.'"

Randy Kiehl had received national attention when he criticized Private Jessica Lynch's financial windfall from her book. Kiehl thought it absurd that she might gain wealth while the rest of the victims of the 507th ambush had died in relative obscurity, leaving their families with meager military benefits.

Full military honors were accorded to James Kiehl, though, when he was returned to his hometown of Comfort. Echo taps, blown by two buglers, rose through the craggy mesquite and live oak trees, and carried out along the limestone ledges of the Hill Country. His friends drove the 350 miles down from Ft. Bliss, and agonized over how to reconcile the big guy they remembered coming into their house to eat cold pizza with the vision of a box that was being lowered into rocky ground. This casket was not the twenty-two-year-old who allowed his wife to have two ferrets, dogs, and a fish in their apartment; the boy-man who loved video games and created elaborate plans for his characters in weekend games of Dungeons and Dragons; this was not the ravenous friend they hid all their food from whenever he ducked into their apartments, even though they knew he would always find the stash of Grandma's Cookies and eat them all; this was just a box, not James.

Kiehl's best friend, Darrell Cortez, in his dress uniform, snapped a smart salute during the Comfort funeral as his buddy's casket passed.

"The hardest day of my life that I can remember is going to James' funeral," Cortez said, "and trying to mourn his death and be a soldier, and it is so incredibly difficult to hear two bugles in the background play taps, and the person that you are saluting is just as close as your brother, and someone who you considered your brother."

His family and friends, of course, want there to be great meaning to the death of James Kiehl. But their uncertainty about the political purposes of the war has increased. Randy Kiehl, who believes his son has "gone to be with the angels," was unwavering in his belief that James' baptism, just days before dying in Iraq, has had a measurable impact on Christianity, and was part of God's plan for his boy.

"I'm not the only one who thinks this," he said. "I have a lot of pastors who call me and tell me that James' baptism being aired on all of the satellite channels and the newscasts has done more for Christianity than all the ministers and their congregational flocks can do. James was baptized on March the 12th. And, of course, he went to meet God on the 23rd."

When the heat became too much for his daughter-in-law and grandson, Kiehl invited his visitor to join them in the house. He has two videotapes he has played over and over to set events into context for himself. One of them is a copy of the Al Jazeera broadcast showing the bodies of American soldiers after the ambush of the 507th. His son is on that tape, his long frame distinguishing him from the other casualties laid out on the ground. Mostly, though, Randy Kiehl likes to share the tape of his son's baptism, which was recorded by a television crew from Dallas.

In her arms, Jill Kiehl's son pulled softly on his bottle as visions of his father appeared on the screen. James was smiling, always smiling, as he listened to the pastor, and especially when he stepped into the plastic lined hole that served as a baptismal pool. These images of his baptism, the Arab broadcast tape of Kiehl's body, photos on the wall, and his basketball trophies, are how Nathan Kiehl will come to know his father. Jill watched the tape silently, having already seen it so many times that the pain had gone away. Against her will, Jill's husband had already become abstract, hurrying away into memory, making the transition from flesh to image.

And she cannot accept the reason he died.

Jill Kiehl often has to admit that her husband was also killed by the bad planning of American military and political leaders.

"They wanted to get there fast, and get it done, but they didn't take into account the safety of anybody. What good is it gonna do if you are moving fast and you're losing all of your people? It was the race to Baghdad, and that's all they were concerned with, and what are you gonna say, 'Oh yea, we got there in twenty days?' Oooo, big deal. It's a war, you know. He's [Saddam] still gonna be there if you'd taken an extra day or so to get there. And guess what? He ended up gone anyway."

When the tape ended, Jill Kiehl rose from the couch and rocked her son gently in her arms. She stared intently at his face, and the room around her seemed to disappear. The three other people she had been watching the television with were gone from her awareness.

All she saw was Nathanial Ethan Kiehl, his wide eyes and smooth, perfect skin. Jill Kiehl clung to her baby. This boy was all that remained of her husband.

And she hoped for a future for him that did not include war.

The president was coming. Fred Pokorney's funeral arrangements were not yet completed, but Chelle was preparing herself to meet the president of the United States, George W. Bush. Two weeks into the war, the president wanted to visit the Marines at Camp Lejeune, and thank them for their tradition of service to the nation. After his speech, Bush asked to meet privately with family members of the Marines who had been killed in action. Chelle Pokorney was going to meet the leader of the free world.

"Fred would have been so proud," she said. "That was his commander-in-chief, and Fred was just so proud to serve him and the country. He would have been amazed at his wife getting to meet the president."

Wade and Suzy Lieseke had traveled to Jacksonville to be with Chelle, awaiting Fred's funeral. Regardless of the stature of the office of the president, however, Wade did not want to meet with George Bush. He stayed away.

"I just couldn't do it," he explained. "I wasn't sure I could hold myself back. I had no idea what I might say to him, and I didn't want to make anything more difficult for Chelle."

That April afternoon in Jacksonville, Bush spoke before twelve thousand Marines. He was constantly interrupted by applause, and a woman near the stage yelled loudly enough for the microphones to pick up her words, "We love you, Mr. President." American troops were on the move, only days away from the iconic images of soldiers pulling down the statue of Saddam in Baghdad. The president was flush with anticipation of an easy victory. He became a coach addressing his team, congratulating them on their win. In the fifteen-to twenty-minute speech, however, there was only one sentence that referred to the battle that had broken Chelle Pokorney's heart.

"In the tough fighting at Al Nasiriyah," the president told the crowd, "Marines continue to push back the enemy, and are showing the unrelenting courage worthy of the name Task Force Tarawa."

Marines applauded and cheered, as they did on almost every sentence spoken by their commander-in-chief. The president mentioned the "good Marines" who had been lost, and how the nation shared in the Corp's grief. He promised that their families would not be forgotten, nor left behind.

In the private meeting with families of the fallen, Chelle Pokorney waited her turn to speak with the president. She held in her hand the gold lieutenant's bars from her husband's uniform. When George Bush leaned over to say something to the young widow, and shake her hand, Chelle placed the bars in his hand. The president looked at them, and dropped them in his coat pocket. Normally, he is required to hand off to the Secret Service any objects or gifts he has been given. But not the gold bars of First Lieutenant Frederick E. Pokorney Jr.

"Oh, God, I wish Fred could have seen that," Chelle said. "I can just hear him. 'Way to go Chelle. You got the president to take my officer's bars.' You have no idea how proud Fred would have been of that. How proud he actually is of that."

In hushed tones, the president moved through the small group, offering his condolences, meeting the wives and children who would grow up without their fathers. His eyes were watery, but he was composed. He kept returning, however, to Chelle Pokorney. She was almost embarrassed by the attention. Finally, the president had something he wanted to tell Lieutenant Pokorney's wife.

"You are my pillar of strength," he said.

Chelle was moved by the words. They were what Fred expected of her. But it was also validation of her husband's choices, his decision to choose his service and his job over his family.

"My husband believed in the country. He believed in what he gave his life for. Unfortunately, if he came home, if I could somehow bring him back to life, and he could do it again, go and serve in Iraq, he'd do it again. I can't take that from Fred. That's why I try to teach people because as hard as it's been on me, and as terrible as it's been on Taylor, I have to raise this little girl. My husband would do it again, and I don't understand that. I never could understand that when it came to Fred because I loved him so much and he would just do it again knowing he would leave us behind because that's how selfless he was."

The Pokorneys and the Liesekes love each other as a family. Politically, though, they were a house divided. As much as Wade loved Fred, and all that he had believed in and fought for, he felt the president had taken advantage of the commitment and patriotism of the Marines. It was Wade Lieseke's belief that the president of the United States had lied, had made up a rationale for going to war with Iraq, and abused the trust placed in him by the men and women of the Armed Forces. Lieseke was unable to conjure up any patriotic emotions over the war.

"I don't know why I don't feel patriotic," he said. "I guess because what the president is doing is not patriotic. It turns out that our kids are getting killed needlessly. I will never believe this is connected to the safety of the United States. I never believed it when they went there, and I'll never believe it as long as I live."

Lieseke, like a lot of other veterans, thought the meetings with the families were private for political reasons. Eight months after the war had been launched, the president had not attended a single funeral. When the administration banned photos and videotaping of returning caskets at Dover Air Force Base, Bush critics decided he was trying to fight a war without associating himself with the people who were dying. The Pentagon also issued a directive restricting coverage of burials at Arlington National Cemetery, unless families gave permission.

The first Iraq casualty for the U.S. Marine Corps to be buried in Arlington was the posthumously promoted First Lieutenant Frederick E. Pokorney Jr. A Catholic mass was conducted in the chapel at the national cemetery. About 150 people came to the funeral. Pokorney was the first Nevada resident to die in the war in Iraq.

Lieutenant Ben Reid, who had been with Fred on the day he was killed, lined up behind the flag-draped casket to walk the two miles to the grave site with the other mourners. He told Wade and Suzy Lieseke he would tell them what happened to Fred when they were ready to hear. Although she was hardly noticed, Pokorney's birth mother, whom he told the Liesekes he had not spoken to since age six, was reportedly in the church for the mass. Frederick Pokorney Sr. also came to his son's funeral, even though there had been little more than a few phone calls between them in the years since he had left Fred with the Liesekes.

Taylor held her mother's hand as mourners stepped behind the six horses that were to pull the caisson. The mortal remains of the lieutenant were escorted by six Marines in formal dress blue uniforms, a full honor guard, and a twenty-five piece Marine band. A clopping of horses' hooves and audible sobbing were initially the only sounds accompanying the caisson through the narrow blacktop lanes. The procession made its way to freshly opened ground along York Road, which was identified as Section 60, grave number 7861.

"It hurts so much," Wade Lieseke said later, "when you have to walk behind a flag-draped coffin, and you've gotta let it go into the ground and then you walk away. And he's just dead."

In the still spring air, a seven-man rifle team fired a twenty-one-gun salute, and a bugler sent out Taps through the Arlington hills, a sound almost as common as conversation in the National Cemetery. Marine Brigadier General Maston Robeson presented Chelle Pokorney with the precisely folded flag that had covered her husband's casket. Pokorney's dog tags hung from a handle on the casket as his wife reached out to touch the wooden container that held her husband's remains. Taylor put her hand on the flag the Marine officer had given to her mother.

"Where's daddy?" Taylor asked her mother.

The honor guard carefully moved the casket over the grave. First Lieutenant Frederick E. Pokorney Jr., assigned to Marine Headquarters Battery, 10th Marine Regiment, 2nd Marine Expeditionary Brigade, was at rest. A modest stone was placed on the site many weeks later. A cross is etched into the top, just above Pokorney's name and rank. Below his name is the simple inscription; "U.S. Marines Corps, Persian Gulf, Iraq, Aug. 20, 1971, Mar. 24, 2003, Purple Heart, Our Hero."

Just before the ceremony was to end, the motionless air of Virginia was stirred by a brief, stiff breeze that blew across the Potomac River and up the open field to where Fred was to lay. Flowers bent and hats tilted on heads.

"Oh, that was Fred," said Chelle. "It was just one last thing where he wanted to let us know he was okay. It was just Fred saying, 'Okay, Lieutenant Pokorney is here now. Sit up straight. Pay attention. Be proud.' I have no doubt that was him."

Chelle Pokorney left that day with a private vow that she will be at Arlington National Cemetery every year on Memorial Day.

"Arlington was beautiful," she said. "It was the most beautiful thing I could take from this. And I'm absolutely gonna visit him every Memorial Day. It's the least I can do for his little girl because he was so proud on Memorial Day when we were there with those veterans on our first visit. He was just so proud to be a part of that, and that tradition, and thank them for what they did. And he did. Fred never forgot. He never forgot."

Her first Memorial Day without Fred was a month and a half later, and Chelle kept her promise. She was present at the Tomb of the Unknowns when the president laid a ceremonial wreath and spoke to a sprawling, somber crowd of more than 5,000, and an entire nation engaged in war. On a cold, wet day, the president was joined on stage by Secretary of Defense Donald Rumsfeld and Air Force General Richard B. Myers, chairman of the Joint Chiefs of Staff. Behind them, three huge U.S. flags fell limply in the mist. Two years earlier, to the exact day, Chelle and Fred had made their first trip to Arlington, and he had requested that she see he was buried among the soldiers of America's wars.

In his comments, First Lieutenant Pokorney was once more remembered by his commander-in-chief, President George W. Bush:

Beyond the Tomb of the Unknowns, in Section 60 of Arlington Cemetery, we have laid to rest Americans who fell in the battle of Iraq. One of the funerals was for Marine Second Lieutenant Frederick Pokorney Junior, of Jacksonville, North Carolina. His wife, Carolyn, received a folded flag. His two-year-old daughter, Taylor, knelt beside her mother at the casket to say a final goodbye.

An uncle later said of this fine lieutenant, "He was proud of what he was doing and proud of his family, a hard-working guy—the best guy you can ever know. I hope the American people don't forget." This nation does not forget.

The president mispronounced Fred's last name, calling him "Pork-uh-knee." He winked, and offered a short wave to Chelle as he passed her at the conclusion of the ceremonies. Chelle was not concerned about the president's failure to properly say her fallen husband's name.

"Of course not," Chelle said. "We were just so honored that he would remember Fred. The president has so much to deal with, so many lives to worry about. Having him mention Fred at all was just such an honor."

A few hours later, two time zones to the west, thousands of people had filed into the Fort Bliss National Cemetery. Rows of graves appeared to reach all the way to the slopes of the Franklin Mountains on the western edge of the cemetery. The number of people attending the Memorial Day events in east El Paso was well above normal because of the deaths of soldiers from the 507th Mechanized Company, which was stationed at Fort Bliss. The nine troops of the 507th, who had died in the Al Nasiriyah ambush, had left behind ten children under the age of seventeen. Nathan Kiehl, of course, had been born after his father was dead.

On stage, Major General Stanley Green was accompanied by Claude and Eunice Johnson, the parents of Shoshana Johnson, the POW who had survived the battle of Al Nasiriyah. Unknown to Green, the sea of faces in front of him included Ruben and Amalia Estrella-Soto, whose son was killed by the Iraqis in the ambush.

262   COUNTING CASUALTIES

If this day were to honor the soldiers and their families, reporters wondered why the Estrella-Sotos were not standing beside the general as he mentioned their son. The Johnsons had been invited.

"This year's Memorial Day service is filled with special significance," Major General Green said in his prepared remarks. "On March 23, a terrible tragedy occurred when members of the 507th were ambushed by Iraqi soldiers. Buried in this hallowed place, just short of his nineteenth birthday, is Private Ruben Estrella."

Although Green mentioned Private Estrella, journalists suspected military leaders at Fort Bliss of trying to offer up the Johnson family as a reminder of a happy ending and keeping the Estrella-Soto family offstage because it might bring further attention to the sadness of what happened to the 507th. If the Johnsons were on the stage as Blue Star parents, why weren't the Estrella-Sotos, or the parents of Johnny Mata from nearby Pecos, or his wife Nancili and their two children? Did the Army leave them out of view because of the deaths of their soldiers?

Reporters tried to ask Major General Green but were directed to Fort Bliss public affairs spokesperson Jean Offutt.

"She told us they couldn't find the Estrella-Sotos' phone number," said reporter Laura Cruz of the *El Paso Times*. "This didn't make any sense to most of us. They prepared everything far enough in advance that they had a program with the Johnson's name printed on it. They should have had the time to find the Estrella-Sotos."

Major General Green worked his way through the crowd to the grave of his soldier, Private Estrella-Soto, to speak with his parents. He discovered the teenager's mother on her hands and knees, atop her son's grave, almost hysterical with grief. Three of his comrades, Private Patrick Miller, Sergeant James Riley, and Specialist Joseph Hudson, were on one knee next to her with their hands placed on the private's grave.

"This is not my son," Amalia Estrella-Soto cried. "He has to be lost. He has to be among the other soldiers. Please help me look for him."

Hudson hugged the soldier's mother and assured her, "He's looking down on us."

"I can't think of anything," Mrs. Estrella-Soto wailed. "I don't want the memories; I want my son. The only thing on my mind is finding my son."

General Green lowered himself and made an attempt to comfort Mrs. Estrella-Soto. "I cannot say any words that will make you hurt less, but know that we have the greatest respect for your family and your son."

The private's mother, whose son had talked her into signing his enlistment papers against her own intuition, collapsed into her husband's arms.

Ruben Estrella-Soto had been buried eight days before he was to turn nineteen. A thousand people, including his eighteen-year-old fiancée Sonia Romero, had gathered at the San Juan Diego Catholic Church for his funeral mass. In spite of their pain, the El Paso church was filled with the verses of the traditional Mexican birthday song "Las Mananitas." Ruben's sister Cynthia, and his brother Edgar, cried through the lyrics. A picture of Ruben in his uniform was placed alongside the casket, which had been draped in white. Born in Chihuahua, Mexico, he had become a naturalized U.S. citizen, and wanted to serve his country. He had graduated from Mountain View High School in El Paso only one year earlier. After the mass, the Rev. Ed Roden-Lucero urged the school district to name a school after Ruben.

When he was buried at Fort Bliss National Cemetery, Ruben's mother held two carnations in her hand as she sat next to her husband. Amalia Estrella-Soto rose, and stood at attention with a military rigidity as a bugler began to play. Seconds later, her husband did the same, and lifted his right hand to his heart. Ruben Estrella-Soto Jr. was dead as a result of combat in the war in Iraq.

He was just a boy.

Larry Horning was ready to retire. But he had one last challenge he wanted to confront. His professional years had been spent as a sales executive for a soft drink distribution company. A lot of that time he had been on the road, chasing the endless horizons of Nevada for his Reno employer, talking to distributors, finding tactics to improve sales. Horning frequently traveled the lonely miles of Route 95, Veterans' Highway, which runs up the spine of Nevada from Las Vegas to Reno, and he had spent nights in Tonopah when the road became too long to get home.

When Horning heard that a Tonopah man had been among the first Americans to die in the war in Iraq, it jarred loose something in his memory. As an officer of the Sertoma Club [Service to Mankind] in Reno, Larry Horning was one of four founders of an East-West High School Football Classic. For twenty-two years, the Sertoma members had organized an all-star football game between the best senior players from across Nevada and some of the California border towns. A lot of names, business associates, community leaders, politicians, and high school athletes had passed through Horning's memory in his twenty-nine years as a member of the Sertoma Club. But something about the name Fred Pokorney, which he had read one morning in the *Reno Gazette-Journal*, made him wonder about the Marine's background.

"I went and looked up the names on our roster from some of the games," Horning said. "I was fairly certain Fred had played in our game. It was awful finding his name on that roster, and knowing that this fine kid was now gone."

Fred Pokorney was listed as number 91 for the West Team in the 1989 Sertoma Classic in Reno on June 23, 1989, at Reno High School. He played linebacker and tight end. Larry Horning was club president that year, and he made it his habit to attend the practices and get to know as many of the players as possible. Pokorney, with his great size and sure hands, was hard to forget, even from fourteen years earlier.

Pokorney's adopted father, Wade Lieseke, recovering from a serious gunshot wound he suffered while serving as the county sheriff in Tonopah, was unable to travel to Reno. It was the only game of

Pokorney's entire high school football and basketball career that Lieseke missed.

"I wasn't going to miss anything with Fred," Lieseke explained. "I wanted to be a part of his achievements, to help him any way Suzy and I could. He was just a special kid. He deserved everything we could do for him."

Larry Horning also wanted to do something for Fred. The war in Iraq felt almost like it was being fought at the foot of the Sierras. On the same day he had read about Pokorney, Horning also learned that Donald J. Cline Jr., a twenty-one-year-old Marine from the Reno suburb of Sparks, had died in the same battle as Fred Pokorney. Married with two infant sons, Lance Corporal Cline died while trying to protect wounded Marines who were being evacuated. After making the five-hour drive down to Tonopah and meeting with the high school principal, guidance counselors, and coaches, Horning asked the Sertoma membership to honor both young men at the June football game, and to dedicate it in memory of the former star, First Lieutenant Frederick E. Pokorney Jr.

"We also decided to retire Fred's number," Horning said. "We put a jersey in this frame with his 91 on it. No one will ever wear that number again at the East-West Classic."

In the parking lot of his favorite coffee shop in Sparks, Horning held up the framed jersey. Desert sunlight lit up the bright blue color worn by Pokorney during his glory days. Horning's soft face and eager demeanor were betraying his emotion as he showed the framed jersey to two visitors. He had pulled it out of the back seat of his Explorer and held it carefully, offering it up for examination. People feel like they have to do something. This was what Larry Horning was able to do. In his eyes, however, it was obvious Horning did not think it was adequate. It was just a jersey. But this was an act of gratitude, of love even, and he wanted to help, somehow.

"We're also going to be giving a dollar from each ticket to the Nevada Patriot Fund," Horning said. "It was set up by the governor to help the families of soldiers who died. We should have 2,500 people at the game, so that'll be helpful for the fund."

At the banquet to honor all of the 2003 players, Horning had prepared plastic laminated copies of newspaper stories about Pokorney's and Cline's deaths. They were taped to the wall in the back of the hall. Few of the young athletes made their way back to read the articles. None of them were even in kindergarten the year Fred had been honored by being named to play in the East-West Classic. Hardly any of them had probably even heard of his name in the news.

After the all stars had been introduced, Horning called Wade and Suzy Lieseke to the microphone. Wade slowly escorted his wife to the podium. Larry Horning held up the frame containing the jersey with Fred Pokorney's number from his 1989 participation in the East-West Classic. Wade took off his glasses and wiped his eyes. Suzy placed her hand on his back. They wanted to honor Fred. But everything was becoming a reminder of how much it hurt that he was gone. Before the presentation, Horning read from a column by a Reno newspaper writer, and his voice broke on a reference to "unconditional love."

"I never met the boy," Horning read. "But I will always love the man."

He exhaled deeply, and tilted his head forward. No one in the banquet hall made a sound. "This is Fred's family." Horning hugged the Liesekes, and returned to the podium.

"Fred was a giant of a man," he said. "He was large in life, and he's even bigger in death. We can't thank you enough for sharing him with us."

Wade almost did not want to be there. He went through it all for Fred, so that he might be remembered. But he and Suzy didn't have any interest in a framed jersey. They wanted the young man who had become a part of their lives. Every damned day was painful, and Wade could not get a sense that it was ever going to ease up, leave him alone.

"I want to express our family's heartfelt thanks," he said. "Fred stood for everything Sertoma stands for. We'll miss him for the rest of our lives."

There was warm applause, a few concluding remarks, and the players and their families moved toward the double doors.

"I'm still joining the Army," one of the boys said. "I just think it's the right thing for me."

Wade left that night having trouble reconciling his memories with reality. How did a kid who played all of those football games on the plateau up above Tonopah end up dead in an Iraqi desert? Wade's images of Fred included the proud Marine in his dress blues, but the sweetest thoughts were of those nights at Logan Field where the home team bleachers maybe accommodated a hundred people, and T Mountain rose above the goal posts at the north end zone. The field, set in the middle of a quarter mile cinder track oval, appeared to be the only green found in all of Nye County. To the west, communications towers on a mountain showed flickering red lights against the dry autumn nights as Fred ran joyfully through his youth. Eventually, Wade and Suzy Lieseke hoped, their hurt might heal, and they would think of these times more than Fred's faraway death.

During half time of the Sertoma Classic game the next night, Wade and Suzy were escorted to the middle of the field by Larry Horning. While they stood and faced the crowd, Wade's taut facial muscles revealed the conflict between his hatred for the president and his love for Fred, a poem was read over the public address system about how Lieutenant Pokorney and Lieutenant Cline were "standing guard o'er heavens scenes." The stadium announcer then began to read from a brief script, which had been handwritten in Horning's block script.

"Tonight, we take the time to recognize a hero from the war with Iraq. You will notice that both teams are lined up in the middle of the field for this solemn presentation."

In the stands, two teenaged girls were chatting on their cell phones loudly enough that an adult urged them to be quiet. They did not put down their phones. A high school boy stomped his feet on the aluminum bleachers, as if trying to bring attention to himself. Someone scolded him, telling him to "behave." On the field, the all-stars of both teams gathered around Wade and Suzy in what Horning had sketched on paper as a "circle of love." Each of them had Fred's Sertoma Classic number 91 on the sleeves of their jersey.

"First Lieutenant Pokorney lost his life in a battle in Iraq on March 23rd, 2003. He was a Sertroma Classic participant in the 1989 classic played at Reed High School in June of that year. God bless the family, Fred's wife Chelle and his daughter Taylor, and all Americans who played such an important part in the war with Iraq. We are, and will be forever grateful to you. God Bless America."

Larry Horning gave Wade and Suzy the picture frame containing Fred's jersey, and they held it up together to show the crowd. Players lined up, shook Wade's hand, and embraced Suzy. Eventually, the referees in their striped shirts walked up and put their arms around the couple. Afterward, as they walked off the field, Wade almost appeared to be keeping his eyes averted from the framed jersey, as if he did not want to be reminded of Fred's death, what was lost and maybe even what he had missed by not being able to see Fred perform during the Sertoma Classic. Suzy hung closely at his side, more concerned about what her husband was enduring than her own emotions.

The Lieseke's lingered briefly, thanking Larry Horning for what he had done. No Reno reporters came up to ask questions. The big game was their primary interest. A cool wind was moving through the Sierras from the west that night, down the Truckee River valley, and Wade hunched his shoulders against the cold, not knowing what else to say to Larry Horning. He and Suzy left shortly after the second half of the game began, and disappeared anonymously through the gates as teenagers chattered on cell phones, and parents and relatives of players cheered on their stars.

When they got back to Tonopah, Wade hung Fred's jersey on the wall near the door. No one who enters the Lieseke house will miss its broad-shouldered width and bright blue color. It was placed on the same wall as the shadow box of Wade's medals, which Fred had made as a gift for his adopted father. The Lieseke's sixteen-year-old son Jonathan plays for Tonopah's Muckers now, and Wade and Suzy watch him on Friday night home games at a new field across the road from where Fred played. They both hope he will have the long and happy life that was denied to Fred.

In an attempt to somehow make himself feel better, Wade bought a Harley Davidson Road King motorcycle to provide a distraction. He rides it every day, sometimes half way across the state to Pahrump, where he is getting physical therapy for injuries received as a lawman and soldier. Nevada's two lanes are infinite, and Wade can make himself disappear into the highway, where there is nothing but him, the rush of the wind, and the ragged seam the mountains have sewn against the sky. But even then he is forced to think about things he cannot control; what happened to Fred in Iraq; how he is still dealing with Vietnam; his own loss of faith in the people who seem constantly to lead America into unnecessary tragedies. When he rolls the power up on the big bike, Wade Lieseke feels like he is going somewhere, and that, eventually, he will arrive at a time and place where he will be forever left alone by war.

14

AT WAR WITH
MR. WILSON

They deem him their worst enemy who tells them the truth.

Plato

I t had been this way for months. Calls were coming from reporters, columnists, television producers, and correspondents.
All of them wanted former Ambassador Joseph Wilson's opinion, perceptions, and analysis on the White House's claims that
Iraq had tried to acquire "yellow cake" uranium from the African
country of Niger. Wilson, his thick gray hair furling near his collar,
looks more like a gracefully aging California surfer than a diplomat.
But his *New York Times* editorial about Iraq and African uranium created a sensitive controversy for the Bush administration. As autumn
of 2003 colored the leaves along the Potomac, there was a drop off
of interest in the Washington press corps over what Wilson had
been saying.

But Wilson was still angry.

The truth had been ignored. His credibility had been assailed, and worst of all, his wife, an undercover CIA operative, had her cover blown by a leak from a "senior administration official." The White House had spent some time and effort trying to convince political reporters that Wilson was backing away from his belief that George Bush's senior political advisor Karl Rove was behind the leak.

"I think the White House would like people to believe I have backed off on that," Wilson said. "What I said was in response to a question related to the investigation. I said I would like to see the investigation proceed because, after all, wouldn't it be useful to see Karl Rove frog-marched out of the White House in handcuffs? What I can tell you, following Mr. [Robert] Novak's article, which exposed the identity of my wife, Karl Rove, among others, campaigned to push that story on the press, and, so even if Karl Rove was not the leaker, potentially liable or vulnerable for criminal activity, ask yourself if that is the sort of ethical treatment that one expects out of one's federal government; that their senior officials would be dragging the wife of someone they perceive to be an opponent through the public square to administer a beating. After all, this president said he was going to change the tone in Washington, and if he's changed it, it's for the worse."

Wilson's animation on the subject of Karl Rove is well-earned. In February 2002, he was dispatched by the CIA to Niamey, the capital of Niger, Africa, to check on the validity of a series of documents, which purported to prove that Saddam Hussein had made an attempt to purchase low-grade uranium ore from the country. Wilson's qualifications, as a former ambassador to Gabon and the advisor on African affairs to the National Security Council, were unquestionable. After an eight-day investigation, Wilson concluded, as had the sitting ambassador in Niger, Barbro Owens-Kirkpatrick, several intelligence analysts and agencies, and a four-star general, that the documentation was phony.

But the claim still ended up in the president's State of the Union speech more than a year later. Wilson was stunned. There were at

least four reports within the U.S. government, at the state department and the CIA, which had, presumably, been sent to the national security advisor's office, and, Wilson assumed, the office of
the vice president. Wilson drew the inevitable inference that the
Bush administration was trying to make the case for war against
Iraq and was busily suppressing information that did not support
that goal. In an opinion piece published in the *New York Times*
entitled, *"What I Didn't Find in Africa,"* Wilson wrote that the White
House "twisted intelligence to exaggerate the Iraqi threat."

Only eight days after Wilson's July 6, 2003, editorial, syndicated
columnist Robert Novak dropped the name of Wilson's wife into a
column about the ambassador's trip to Africa. A writer with a conservative political disposition, Novak's column was interpreted by many
as an effort to portray the ambassador as a Democratic political hack
out to harm the Bush administration. In Wilson's estimation, and in
the opinion of many CIA operatives, the mention of Valerie Plame in
Novak's column was gratuitous and calculated to do harm.

"Wilson never worked for the CIA," Novak wrote, "but his wife,
Valerie Plame, is an Agency operative on weapons of mass destruction. Two senior administration officials told me Wilson's wife suggested sending him to Niger to investigate the Italian report. The
CIA says its counter-proliferation officials selected Wilson, and asked
his wife to contact him. 'I will not answer any question about my
wife,' Wilson told me."

What Wilson did say later, however, was that Novak had been
told by the CIA not to use Plame's identity in his story. The implication in that request, as far as Wilson was concerned, ought to have
been clear to an experienced journalist like Novak; Valerie Plame's
work was important to national security.

"He [Novak] acknowledges talking to the CIA before publishing her story," Wilson explained. "And the CIA said, don't use her
name. Don't use that bit of information. What part of no doesn't
Mr. Novak understand? We're not talking about information here.
We're talking about national security assets. We're talking about, as

he put it, 'operatives.' What part of no doesn't he understand? You can't get away with a hard no or a soft no. We're talking about people's lives here. We're not talking about bits of information."

Immediately, everyone in Washington began to speculate about the identity of the two "senior administration officials." Wilson, though, who had anticipated some retribution for contradicting the president, was astonished by the severity of the act of vengeance.

"I fully expected after I wrote the story [*NYT* op-ed] there would be attacks on my own credibility," Wilson explained. "I was prepared for that. After all this is a town in which it is fair game to destroy the messenger if you don't like the message he is delivering. What I don't think anyone was prepared for, in my family, or indeed the mainstream Republican party, was that these guys in the White House, not being able to damage my credibility, they would simply drag my wife out into the public square and administer a beating on her to destroy her credibility. That, even by Washington's bare knuckle politics, is just beyond the pale."

It may have also been a crime.

Under the Intelligence Identities Protection Act of 1982, persons having access to classified information about U.S. operatives, and who willfully disclose that knowledge, are subject to fines up to $50,000 and a maximum of 10 years in prison. The immorality of the act, however, appeared to go well beyond the statute's ability to punish. With the nation at war, leaking the name of an undercover operative, who was reputed to be working in the area of weapons of mass destruction, was a sin and a possible act of treason. Novak's use of the term "senior administration officials" is Washington parlance for a source within the White House, or, possibly, the vice president's office. Wilson, though, sounded confident the Bush administration was destined to pay a political price for the leak, as well as, possibly, a legal punishment for the perpetrator.

"I think it's despicable," he said. "And I think, frankly, it's also appalling that the president has been so nonchalant about this; a president who has made some very, very strong statements about leakers in the past, threatened to shut down the informational flows to the jurisdictional committees up on the hill because there were leaks of information, and he has referred to my wife's case, saying, 'Well this town leaks like a sieve, anyway, and maybe, or maybe not, we'll get it.'"

There was something lost by the publication of Valerie Plame's identity; not just to the Wilson family, but also to the U.S. government. Plame worked as an operative with "nonofficial cover" (NOC). Such agents are required to spend years developing a professional career and a kind of pseudo-profile for themselves in order function in the intelligence community. They are also completely on their own should they ever be found out. By practice, the CIA does not acknowledge NOC agents.

According to CIA analysts, NOCs are the "holiest of holies" within the agency. Reports have indicated that Plame, who was working overseas as an employee of a business fronted out of Boston, was dealing with dozens of U.S. operatives on matters of counterproliferation. In short, she was engaged in the very arena, on the precise issue over which the president of the United States took his country to war; she was trying to reduce the spread of weapons of mass destruction. Valerie Plame was a national security asset.

By describing sources as "senior administration officials," Novak proscribed the bounds of where to look for the individuals who gave him information. People fitting into that category are drastically limited in number, regardless of the White House's protestations that there are a few thousand "senior administration officials." Because the consequence of the leak appeared to be political, the first place to look was in the office of Karl Rove, senior advisor to the president on matters of politics. Rove, who has a lengthy resume of disclosures and leaks to Texas and national reporters, has, along with Chief of Staff Andrew Card, kept the Bush White House almost leak proof. To believe that he didn't know what happened, it is necessary to assume that he lost his grip over all things political, an unlikely scenario given his historical performances as a mastermind.

Besides, Rove has a record of slipping the good stuff to Robert Novak.

In 1992, Rove was a direct mail consultant on the Texas portion of the presidential campaign of George H. W. Bush. Campaign manager for Texas, Rob Mosbacher, had angered Rove by not giving him the entire contract for direct mail in the state. During the 1988 campaign, all of the money for direct mail had been spent using Karl Rove & Co., and Rove had assumed nothing was going to change for the reelection effort.

"I thought another firm was better," Mosbacher said. "I had a million dollars for direct mail. I gave Rove a contract for $250,000 and $750,000 to the other firm."

Rove, of course, had wanted it all. Discreetly, he began to tell Texas journalists about how the Bush campaign in the state was being mismanaged. Although Rove refused to go on the record about problems of the Republican candidacy of President Bush, he described failures of campaign leadership. He was, however, generally vague. Eventually, someone did write negatively about the Bush Texas campaign in 1992. But it wasn't a Texas reporter. Robert Novak published a column in which he suggested, "The president's reelection effort in Texas has been a bust."

According to Novak's column, Mosbacher was called to a secret meeting in Dallas, where U.S. Senator Phil Gramm of Texas demanded Mosbacher be "stripped" of his managerial responsibilities. The meeting also reportedly included Fred Meyer, a leader of the Texas Republican Party, as well as George W. Bush. Gramm, who was a client of Rove's, may have even organized the gathering at the behest of his consultant.

"Also attending the session was political consultant Karl Rove," Novak's column indicated, "who had been shoved aside by Mosbacher."

Other than the attendees of the Dallas meeting, not much else about Novak's column was accurate. Neither George W. nor Meyer was of the opinion that the Texas Bush campaign was "a bust," and

Mosbacher was not "stripped" of his authority, nor shoved aside. Rove, however, was suspected of being the source of a leak to Novak about the inner workings of the campaign. Novak has consistently denied Rove provided the information for his piece, but Mosbacher, and President George H. W. Bush apparently believed differently.

"I said Rove is the only one with a motive to leak this," Mosbacher said. "We let him go."

A long-time family friend and professional associate of the Bush family, Rove could not have been fired without the approval of the candidate, President George H. W. Bush, who, obviously, also suspected the direct mail consultant of leaking the campaign-in-disarray story to Novak.

Through the years, whenever the incident has been mentioned, Rove has consistently denied any involvement with that particular Novak column. When he was made the subject of a cover profile by *Texas Monthly*, Rove was asked again whether he had anything to do with the genesis of the Novak article. His answer was no.

"As far as I know," Rove told the magazine, "Mosbacher still thinks I'm the one who did it."

Mosbacher does.

He also believes Rove is too smart to get involved in breaking the law to "out" the identity of a CIA agent. But in Texas, where Rove sharpened his political long knives, his was the first name to enter the minds of journalists. During his career as a political consultant in Texas, Rove was a source of countless leaks of information, documents, and data generally harming opponents of his clients. Always, his release of information was well-timed to do the most political damage.

If Rove was not the source of the original Novak column using the name of Valerie Plame, Wilson is certain Rove was involved in trying to bring attention to the occupation of Wilson's wife. At least one reporter, identified in some reports as Chris Matthews of MSNBC's *Hardball*, called Wilson to tell him that Rove was pushing the story. Wilson also discovered that Andrea Mitchell, a correspondent for NBC News, was on the receiving end of the same pitch.

"I've never publicly said that it was Chris Matthews," Wilson pointed out. "But there was a reporter, a respected reporter, who I have no reason not to believe, and his quote was, 'I just got off the phone with Karl Rove, and he told me that your wife is fair game.' Now prior to that, I had received phone calls on previous days, one from Andrea Mitchell, [NBC News] saying that White House sources tell us that the real story here is not the sixteen words, even though the president acknowledged that those sixteen words didn't belong in the State of the Union, the story is not the sixteen words; the real story is Wilson and his wife."

Those sixteen words, the presidential statement in George W. Bush's State of the Union Speech that Saddam had tried to obtain uranium from Niger, had helped to gain public support for a war with Iraq. Wilson had proved them false. And somebody in the White House was angry, and let Novak know that Wilson's wife was a CIA agent.

Although Rove has avoided any public discourse on his role, if any, in the affair, the White House has used the repetitive skills of spokesman Scott McClellan to issue official denials. When the subject was first raised at a regular briefing in the White House press room, McClellan insisted no one in the Bush administration was guilty.

"I'm telling you flatly," he said, "that is not the way this White House operates. I've seen no evidence to suggest that there's any truth to that."

"That's different from saying it didn't happen," a reporter argued. "Are you saying absolutely it did not happen?"

"I'm saying no one was certainly given any authority to do anything of that nature, and I've seen no evidence to suggest there's any truth to it. I want to make it very clear that is simply not the way this White House operates."

"If it turns out that someone in your administration did do that . . ."

McClellan cut off the scenario before the reporter was able to finish.

"I'm not even going to speculate about that," he said. "I have no knowledge of any truth to that report."

"Don't you want to get some more facts? How do you know that no one in the administration [was involved]? Robert Novak's been around a long time."

"If I could find Anonymous, I would."

It was unclear what the White House was doing to identify the source of its leak. The Department of Justice, under Attorney General John Ashcroft, launched an investigation, and Democrats subsequently demanded an independent counsel. As both a candidate for governor and U.S. senator in Missouri, Ashcroft had used Karl Rove as a political advisor, and, according to published records, had spent $385,000 with Rove's company during his campaigns. Additionally, the White House indicated Bush was willing to exercise "executive privilege," if any of the documents subpoenaed by the attorney general fell under the presidential purview of national security interests. Democrats also complained about the fact that it took investigators 12 hours before they got to the White House to begin acquiring evidence, a sufficient period of time for incriminating material to be gathered and destroyed. When Ashcroft finally recused himself from the case, skeptics believed he was only comfortable stepping aside because he knew critical evidence was not going to be found by his replacement.

Wilson, nonetheless, said he has confidence in the professionals conducting the inquiry. He felt all along, however, that the political relationship between Rove and Ashcroft required the Attorney General to recuse himself.

"But that's sort of out of my lane," Wilson added. "But remember, this is not a crime that's been committed against me, and it's not even a crime that's been committed against my wife; it's been committed against the national security of my country. It just happens to have my wife's name tied to it, and it just happens to have been committed because certain people wanted to defend or protect their political agenda at the expense of a national security asset."

Irrespective of his wife's profession, Wilson was an unlikely target for a partisan assault. The side table of his office is covered with photos of him and leaders of the United States, Africa, and Iraq, including one of him and President George H. W. Bush. Prior to becoming known as the husband of a secret agent, Joseph C. Wilson IV, was expected to be remembered as the last American diplomat to meet with Saddam Hussein before the Gulf War. Although there is a framed picture of Hussein and Wilson in his office, the ambassador may have spent more time confronting the Iraqi dictator than he did involved in polite diplomacy.

Hussein had insisted that the U.S. embassy in Baghdad turn over the names of Americans living in Iraq just before the advent of the Gulf War. U.S. officials, including Wilson, were convinced the Iraqi leader intended to round them up, and use the Americans as human shields at strategic locations around the country. The U.S. military, under George H. W. Bush, was preparing to launch air strikes against Iraq, which were to lead up to an attack on Iraqi forces occupying Kuwait. An estimated 2,000 Americans, who had been working and living in Iraq, were hiding from Saddam Hussein's forces. Wilson said 150 others had been taken hostage and were deployed as human shields around the country, and 65 were being protected in the U.S. embassy compound.

In a highly publicized incident, Wilson, who was the Charge' d'Affaires at the U.S. embassy, showed up at a news conference in Baghdad with a noose around his neck. The act was direct defiance of a diplomatic note being sent around by Iraq to embassies in Baghdad, which demanded all foreign nationals be brought down for registration. Wilson refused.

"They [Iraqis] certainly did threaten capital punishment," Wilson explained, "if I didn't turn over the hostages. But they threatened that to all diplomats. I was the one who said, 'If you wanna hang me, if it comes down to giving you my American citizens so you can take them hostage, or you hanging me, then I will bring my own rope.' I thought early on that chances were pretty good some of us were not going to survive Desert Shield, and we based that on not on whimsy but an assessment in the past of how Iraqi governments had acted under stress. They were typically killing the purveyors of the bad news."

Through difficult negotiations, Wilson was eventually able to evacuate all of the Americans remaining in Iraq. Rowland Evans, who was, at that time, the writing partner of Robert Novak, wrote that Wilson had displayed "the stuff of heroism." President George H. W. Bush offered Wilson a personal commendation for his actions.

"Your courageous leadership during this period of great danger for American interests and American citizens has my admiration and respect," Bush wrote. "I salute, too, your skillful conduct of our tense dealings with the government of Iraq. The courage and tenacity you have exhibited throughout this ordeal proves that you are the right person for the job."

A year later, President George H. W. Bush named Joe Wilson as U.S. ambassador to the African nation of Gabon.

"I must say, I was proud to be the first President Bush's Charge leading up to the Gulf War. I think history will record that Desert Shield, Desert Storm were a diplomatic exercise in how one should manage a diplomatic and subsequent military crisis."

"You apparently feel a bit differently about how his son has handled Iraq?"

"If this could have been done worse," Wilson concluded, "I think we'd be hard pressed to figure out how."

There was much that had gone wrong.

After reaching a consensus among administration officials that weapons of mass destruction were the best rationale for going to war against Saddam Hussein and Iraq, neo-conservatives and Bush spokespeople, including the vice president, the deputy secretary of defense, the national security advisor, and others, began to argue that Hussein was attempting to reconstitute his nuclear weapons program. This was especially surprising news to the International Atomic Energy Agency, which, in October 1997, had declared all such efforts had ended, and that constant monitoring had shown there was no nuclear activity in Iraq. The White House provided no direct intelligence to contradict the IAEA's findings.

Because the justification for the war was to be constructed around WMD, the White House refused to let die the notion that Hussein was in pursuit of nuclear weaponry, and the prerequisite of raw uranium. This argument appeared to be given some credibility when documents, alleging to prove an attempt by Iraq to purchase yellow cake uranium from Niger, ended up in the hands of an Italian tabloid reporter. Elisabetta Burta, a writer for *Panorama*, a glossy Italian weekly, was provided 22 pages of information from a businessman, whom she believed had intelligence connections. From a previous story on the war in Bosnia, Burta knew the man to have access to inside sources. He had, in the past, provided Burta with reliable information. The documents, which have since been posted on the Internet, show letterheads for the Niger government and the Iraqi envoy to the Vatican.

The source of the materials made Burta believe they were probably legitimate. Information on the photocopies also appeared to coincide with a 1999 trip to Niger by Iraq's ambassador to the Vatican, Wissam al-Zahawie. Nothing, however, was secret about al-Zahawie's visit. U.S. ambassador to Niger, Charles O. Cecil, filed a routine report of the visit with Washington, based, primarily, on the fact that al-Zahawie's picture had been published in the local paper. No article had been written to accompany the February 1999 photo publication, and no mention was made of uranium. Nonetheless, Seymour Hersh of the *New Yorker* wrote that shortly after the events of September 11, 2001, Italy's Military Intelligence and Security Service, known as SISMI, provided the CIA with a written summary of the trip, which had taken place more than two years earlier.

The Bush administration used the SISMI report to begin public pronouncements about Saddam Hussein and attempts to acquire nuclear materials. Materialization of evidence, which had just been given to reporter Elisabetta Burta, appeared to be all that the White

House needed to corroborate its case against Iraq. But there have been suspicions about why Burta was given the documents, and what was done with them once in her possession. *Panorama*, the tabloid she writes for, is owned by Italian President Silvio Berlusconi, a close Bush ally, and a supporter of the war with Iraq. The paper's editor, Carlo Rosella, reputedly has close connections to the Berlusconi government. For purposes of verification, Rosella ordered Burta to provide the U.S. embassy in Rome with copies of the papers she had been given. According to Hersh, whose work has uncovered most of the contradictions and falsehoods in the Niger story, the station chief of the U.S. embassy sent the documents onto Washington without even bothering to vet them for accuracy or realism.

Who created the fake documents, and why, has not been determined. Journalist Hersh has quoted an unnamed, retired CIA agent who claimed the forgeries were produced by operatives angry at the Bush administration. According to Hersh's source, the agents wanted to "put the bite" on the White House for pressuring intelligence operatives and analysts to deliver data that supported the push for war. The source told Hersh that the plan was to promote the documents as real until the Bush team embraced them, and then embarrass the White House by showing the flaws in the forgeries. Obviously, if true, the tactic backfired. There was, also, a report that the Italian intelligence agency, SISMI, created the false papers and gave them to a Berloscuni paper to print.

Ultimately, though, the tabloid's editors decided not to publish a story on the documents provided to Burta. Evidence that they were sloppy forgeries was overwhelming. The papers indicated that Iraq had tried to purchase 500 tons of crude uranium ore, known as yellow cake, from Niger. When they were shown to a senior official at the U.N. nuclear agency, according to a Reuters report, his "jaw dropped" over how obviously fake they were. One of the documents, an October 2000 letter about uranium from Niger's foreign minister, bore the signature of Allele Elhadj Habibou, who had not been foreign minister since 1989. A second letter, supposedly from the president of

Niger, was such a bad forgery that Jacques Bautes, the French nuclear scientist who was head of the U.N. Iraq Nuclear Verification office for the IAEA, saw it immediately, as did other officials at the agency. The narrative of the letter referred to the president's authority to make a deal with Iraq under Niger's 1965 constitution, which had been abandoned by Niger for a more modern governing instrument more than four years before the letter had been dated. The IAEA also quickly concluded that Wissam al-Zahawie's signature, too, was a forgery and those letterheads for the correspondences were out of date.

The series of letters, though, appeared to be driving Bush administration claims that Saddam Hussein was attempting to "reconstitute" a nuclear arsenal. Although the data was considered a bit too unsound to even be published by an Italian tabloid owned by a backer of war with Iraq, it did end up as part of the British government's September 2002 dossier. In chapter 3 of the presentation, under the heading, "Current Position: [on Iraq] 1998—2002," the Tony Blair administration asserted, "Iraq continues to work on developing nuclear weapons, in breach of its obligations under the Non-Proliferation Treaty, and in breach of UNSCR 687. Uranium has been sought from Africa that has no civil nuclear application in Iraq."

Of course, there was no proof of the charge, and in absolute disregard of warnings from intelligence operatives in the United States and the United Kingdom, the allegation was published as fact. The three nations most strongly in favor of attacking Iraq, the United States, Britain, and Italy, were part of an international echo chamber adding volume and resonance to unproven assertions that Saddam Hussein was trying to make clandestine purchases of uranium from Africa.

No one in the Bush administration appeared to be listening when, less than two weeks before the United States launched its initial attack on Iraq, Mohamed El Baredei, director general of the International Atomic Energy Agency, declared the Niger letters to be false. On March 7, 2003, as young American men and women in Kuwait readied themselves for a war that was to eliminate Iraq's weapons of mass destruction, El Baredei's proclamation went largely unheard:

> Based on a thorough analysis, the IAEA has concluded, with the concurrence of outside experts, that these documents, which formed the basis for the reports of these uranium transactions between Iraq and Niger, are, in fact, not authentic.

In April, after the invasion, the White House still did not appear to be listening. On its web site, under a headline of "Disarm Saddam," the administration made clear it did not believe the findings of IAEA. The allegations that Saddam Hussein had tried to buy uranium from Niger were reasserted with these words, "He recently sought significant quantities of uranium from Africa, according to the British government."

The Bush administration has not wavered from its version of events. Six months after the Niger papers had been shown to be fraudulent by the IAEA, and U.S. troops were well into their occupation of Iraq, Vice President Dick Cheney appeared on the September 14, 2003, edition of *Meet the Press* with Tim Russert, and continued to insist the Niger story was true.

"This whole question of whether or not the Iraqis were trying to acquire uranium in Africa in the British report," he said, "this week the committee of the British parliament spent 90 days investigating all of this, revalidated the British claim that Saddam was in fact trying to acquire uranium in Africa. What was in the State of the Union speech, and original British white papers, there may be a difference of opinion there. I don't know what the truth is on the ground with respect to that."

Ambassador Joseph C. Wilson IV, however, did know.

He was just ignored.

"I looked at how the uranium business functions," Wilson explained, "whether or not it would be feasible or possible for such a transfer of product to take place without the entire world knowing about it. And secondly, I looked at how the bureaucratic structure within the government of Niger works to cover such a sale. And then how is that decision made; how is that decision registered within their government for the purposes of collecting taxes and revenues on the exports; that was one side of it. And then I looked at the feasibility of such a sale taking place off the books. Was it possible for the military junta leader to affect this transfer with Iraq without everybody knowing about it? My conclusion was that it just wasn't feasible. It just could not have happened."

Wilson had never been completely politically opposed to war against Iraq. Obviously, he had supported President Bush's father in the Gulf War, and he professed to back the use of military force to execute a policy of containment against Saddam Hussein. Ideologically, he had judiciously avoided, as a diplomat, public involvement in partisan politics. During the 2000 election, after retiring as a diplomat, Wilson acknowledged he made a contribution to the George W. Bush for President Campaign because he felt Bush was a better candidate than U.S. Senator John McCain. In the general election, however, he voted for Al Gore, supported him with money, and served on a panel that advised Gore on foreign policy.

But politics, he insisted, had nothing to do with his trip to Africa.

"I undertook this mission at the request of my government. I brought back a report. That report happened to be accurate. The fact that they declined to consider that report, and the other reports on that subject on an issue as important as going to war, and instead used information that was so dodgy that it didn't even find its way into the pages of an Italian weekly tabloid, and did find its way into the president's State of the Union address, begs the question: did we go to war on false pretenses, or as I said in the press if they were lying about this what else were they lying about?"

His decision to write about this was the result of the Bush administration's continued use of the false claims around Niger and Iraq. Wilson remained certain that the disclosure of his wife's identity was nothing more than an act of both vengeance and intimidation by the

White House. According to Wilson, the goal of the leak was to keep intelligence operatives quiet; to send a message they might endure the same public pillorying, if they decided to contradict the Bush administration.

CIA agents, retired and in active service, have been dumbfounded by the public revelation of Valerie Plame's career. Democrats, seeking to take advantage of this outrage, were unable to convince Republican congressional leadership to hold hearings on the leak. Instead, Senator Tom Daschle conducted a form of an inquiry, which looked more like a panel discussion or group news conference where former agents read prepared statements.

James Marcinkowski, who had also been a clandestine operative, was disgusted by the Bush administration's attempts to frame the leak as an accident.

"Anyone who would care to try to portray this action as merely negligent, as opposed to deliberate, should also be prepared to explain how anyone so completely inept as to divulge this information by accident ever became a 'senior official' in any organization, let alone an organization running the country," Marcinkowski said.

Three retired agents spoke to the Democrats. Larry Johnson, who had gone through CIA training with Valerie Plame, denounced the White House for allowing the leak to be dismissed as an act of politics, rather than treachery.

"What sickens me," Johnson said, "is the partisan nature that the White House has allowed [the leak controversy] to take on."

A registered Republican, Johnson said his remarks were drafted in cooperation with two other retired agents. All of them claimed to have contributed money to the Bush campaign, and said they voted for the president.

They sounded as passionate and angry as Joe Wilson.

The ambassador's wife's career had not ended, but it had dramatically changed. Friends and family were being given an explanation of her endeavors, and the need for deception in the course of serving her country. The Wilsons have been forced to adopt security measures because of the nature of Mrs. Wilson's work, and the character of many of the individuals with whom she interacted. The Wilson's lives may have changed. But the former ambassador was worried that America's political process was also undergoing a profound transformation.

"I'm perfectly happy to engage in the political debate," he explained. "And I think all of that is fair game. The debate consists of an argument over ideas, over actions and policies. It is totally inappropriate to bring family members or personalities into that debate, and when that happens to be a national security asset, then I think it's very clear that you've passed the bounds of ethics, and one is, I think within one's rights, to question to whom are you loyal? Is it to the American flag and the American constitution, or is it to a political party. I happen to be loyal to the American flag and the American constitution."

After a full career as a Foreign Service diplomat, Joseph C. Wilson IV had become an international business consultant in Washington, D.C. His office on Pennsylvania Avenue is about a hundred yards from the Oval Office. On this autumn day in 2003, the American flag was snapping sharply over the world's most famous building.

Joe Wilson had no doubt what that flag stood for.

But he wondered what it meant to the people inside of the White House.

15

SOLDIER DOWN

Those who cast the votes decide nothing.
Those who count the votes decide everything.
                                        Joseph Stalin

Former U.S. Senator Max Cleland of Georgia has more energy than might be expected of a man who moves through his days with one arm and no legs; the simplest of life's tasks turning into logistical challenges. Physically, the man Cleland became was the result of an accident. In Vietnam, he noticed a hand grenade lying on the ground and assumed it was his. When he bent over and picked it up, the device exploded inches from Cleland's body. Laid into the hold of a Huey helicopter with three of his four limbs mutilated by the explosion, the communications officer was presumed to be a fatality.

"I was laying there on the ground, smoking, literally," he said. "When they came and gave me first aid and put me on the helicopter, and I just met one of the guys recently who saw that happen. He said I saw them put you on the chopper, and you were a dead man, so I just really shouldn't be here by all logic. But my life was saved, dramatically, and it has changed my life powerfully because I have a powerful feeling about those who are committed to combat, and a powerful feeling and identity with those who have to fight our nation's wars. I'm very reluctant, very reluctant, to commit this country to combat because combat maims and kills people. And it's always a last resort."

Max Cleland did more than just survive. He lived.

"You know," he said. "I went through the Tet Offensive, got blown up, wound up in VA hospitals, in 1970 I came back home and told my mother and father that, 'I got no job, no girlfriend, no car, no future, no apartment, no hope, so now's a great time to run for the state senate.' That's exactly what I did. So, that's the story."

Actually, that's only the beginning of the story. Until 2002, every day of Max Cleland's adult life had been spent in service to his country. His work has included the office of U.S. senator for Georgia, director of veterans' affairs under the administration of Jimmy Carter, and offices of state senate and secretary of state in Georgia. One of Cleland's political advisors said the senator's motivation for living, after the loss of three of his limbs in Vietnam, was to help other people, which is what he did, until he encountered defeat through the politics and strategy of President George W. Bush and his advisor Karl Rove.

"It's a low water mark," he explained. "It's a powerful low water, second only to getting blown up in Vietnam because I've had the same sense of my life being shattered by the experience, and the same sense of the need by the grace of God, and the help of friends, to put it back together in some way that I don't know."

Cleland's electoral demise, like his rise in American politics, grew out of issues of national defense. After the 9/11 attacks, the Democratic senator decided the United States needed a structural, organized approach to matters of domestic security. Working with his colleagues, chiefly U.S. Senator Joseph Lieberman, also a Democrat, Cleland was the co-author of a bill to create a Department of Homeland Security. A massive transformation of almost all of the U.S. government, the measure was designed to simplify funding, processes, and laws to reduce the dangers from terrorism. In the White House, however, the Bush administration argued that the last thing America needed was another gigantic bureaucracy.

Eventually, however, the president's advisors began to discover that there was widespread public support for the idea of a Department of Homeland Security. The Bush political and policy team, lead by Karl Rove, quickly pieced together its own proposal. There were, however, numerous provisions within the administration's version of the homeland security bill that most Democrats considered "poison pills." Language reduced or eliminated the collective bargaining power of federal employees working for the new department; a clause Democrats believed was designed to weaken unions. Cleland supported his own version of the homeland security bill, rather than the president's.

Believing in his own ideas was costly for Max Cleland. During the mid-term elections of 2002, Georgia's television viewers saw a man they knew to be an American hero, the winner of the Silver Star, the second highest military honor awarded by the U.S. government, portrayed as an enemy of his own country. Cleland's face was shown on screen with Osama bin Laden and Saddam Hussein in a political attack ad aired by his opponent, Republican Saxby Chambliss. Chambliss, who got a medical deferment from the draft because of a "trick knee," approved an ad that depicted Cleland as being almost part of a bin Laden and Hussein conspiratorial effort to destroy America.

"The ad became relatively infamous," Cleland explained, "as part of the slime and defend strategy of the White House run against me that showed my picture up there with Osama bin Laden and Saddam Hussein; that I was somehow against homeland security. I thought it was interesting that I was the only veteran, Vietnam veteran, in the race. I was the only person who had fought terrorists, and I actually had been a co-sponsor of the homeland security bill when the president himself had actually been opposed to it. The ad was absolutely false on its face, and to put me up there as someone who lost three limbs in Vietnam fighting terrorists, to put me up there and equate me with Saddam Hussein and Osama bin Laden was absolutely outrageous."

The patriotism of Max Cleland was under attack. Even his political opponents, up until that point, had not dared to ever question the senator's loyalty and devotion to his country. Cleland's media advisor in the campaign, Karl Struble, considered the ad so grotesque and absurd that no one in the electorate would take it seriously. Surely, he thought, such a tactic had to backfire. There was far too much hypocrisy inherent in the ad's message for the public to miss.

"The people making this ad, Karl Rove, [Dick] Cheney, the president of the United States, [Donald] Rumsfeld, all of those people, none of them were in Vietnam," Struble explained. "And many of them, including Saxby Chambliss, his [Cleland's] opponent, tried to avoid fighting for this country, and you've got a guy, who sacrifices his body for his country, and then you've got people making ads, who attack his patriotism, and they didn't serve, ever, in our armed services. They ought to be ashamed."

They were not. In fact, the ad was part of a larger GOP strategy to take control of the U.S. Senate, and, just as had happened in Vietnam, accumulating circumstance set up the injury of Max Cleland. This time the harm was political instead of physical as the political dynamics of Georgia began to follow a precarious course. The state's Democratic governor, Roy Barnes, had made a decision to remove most vestiges of the Confederacy from the Georgia state flag. White males, agitated by the move, were convinced Democrats were trying to destroy Georgia's history and culture. Ralph Reed, a fundamentalist conservative who had worked closely with Karl Rove, convinced the Bush political strategist to spend extra money in Georgia. After Senator Paul Wellstone's plane crashed in Minnesota, Rove transferred $700,000 from that campaign down to the Saxby Chambliss campaign. Democrats estimated 300 busloads of Republicans, 10,000 volunteers, went door-to-door, and increased voter turnout for a mid-term election to resemble presidential election year totals. Republican expenditures in the Georgia senatorial race were reported at $14 million.

Struble, Cleland's media consultant, who won several key races for Democrats elsewhere in the country during 2002, considered the defeat of his Georgia client an awful failure for himself and the democratic process.

"There was no way he could have possibly lost if it was run on positives. Instead, what they decided to do to Max Cleland was character assassination. What the White House and Saxby Chambliss did, I don't know how they sleep at night. They took a man who got the second highest award in this country for bravery, and then they impugned his integrity and courage for this nation. It's one thing to have a difference on policy. It is another to take his name and picture and put it up against Osama bin Laden and suggest he is somehow aiding and abetting."

Max Cleland said his loss was a product of "snake pit" politics; a strategy he characterized as "slime and defend." The former senator believes Karl Rove has adopted an approach that requires "sliming" the opponents of Republicans with distortions and half-truths, and "defending" the president, regardless of whether the political accusations against him are worthy of public debate. That strategy, Cleland thinks, was perfected in the Georgia senate campaign, and the television spot including him with bin Laden and Hussein was a creation of the Rove approach to winning at all costs.

"Was Karl Rove the architect of that strategy?" Cleland was asked.

"Absolutely. There's no question about that. Karl Rove and his minions. There's no question. What does that say about our politics? I think we are in deep trouble. George W. Bush said he was gonna change the tone in Washington, and he has. He's made it terribly worse."

Bush, obviously, did not want Max Cleland to remain in the U.S. Senate. Using his immense post-9/11 popularity as a wartime president, Bush visited Georgia five times to campaign for Republican Chambliss. Those appearances, and the 185,000 additional Republican voters believed to have been generated by Rove and Reed's efforts to get out the vote, were considered the elemental reasons Cleland lost a reelection campaign many had suggested he was going to handily win.

But there is an alternative explanation.

And it has profoundly disturbing implications for American democracy.

The week before the Cleland-Chambliss contest, when pollsters stopped measuring the potential outcome of the race, the final surveys showed the incumbent Democrat leading by two to five points. The same polls indicated Democratic Governor Roy Barnes was comfortably out front of his Republican challenger Sonny Perdue by a margin of 9 to 11 percent of the vote. When the results of the election were reported, pollsters were dumbfounded. Chambliss beat Cleland with a 53 to 46 percent margin, which was a statistical turnaround of as much as 12 points. The swing in the gubernatorial race was even more dramatic. The GOP's Perdue picked up 51 percent of the vote while incumbent Barnes only earned 46 percent. When the results were compared against the final opinion polls before Election Day, Perdue's fortunes had improved by as much as 16 percent in a matter of only a few days. He became Georgia's first Republican governor in 130 years.

Although Cleland is confident he was a victim of a tide of angry white men brought to the polls by Rove and Reed, a report from the Georgia secretary of state's office revealed demographic breakdowns were relatively standard for a mid-term election. Only the number of black women voting showed a slight increase. Strangely, when analysts deconstructed the vote totals, Chambliss did surprisingly well in the Democratic regions of southern Georgia (which account for about half of the state's 159 counties), exceeding Republican party totals from the primary by as much as 22 points, while the Democrat Cleland went up 14 percent in the GOP stronghold of northern Georgia.

The baffling demographic shifts coincided with another political development in Georgia. Under the Help America Vote Act, signed into law by President Bush, Georgia became the first state in the union to conduct an entire, statewide election using electronic touchscreen voting. Diebold Election Systems won a $54 million contract from Georgia to provide the technology, and there were numerous problems. Several county election supervisors said the machines were freezing up, and long lines of voters formed as technicians struggled to reboot the computers. In Fulton County, where downtown Atlanta is located, newspapers reported the heavily Democratic county lost 67 memory cards from the voting machines, which resulted in a ten-day delay of vote certification. (The electronic cards have the record of votes cast on the machines.) When terminals in neighboring DeKalb County broke down and were taken out of service, ten of those memory cards simply disappeared, and were later recovered.

Both the election results, and the electronic stumbles of counting the vote, prompted a great deal of skepticism in the Georgia electorate. Under various state and federal laws, electronic voting machines are required to undergo logic and accuracy testing. Wyle Laboratories was contracted by the Georgia secretary of state's office to conduct certification testing of the thousands of terminals to be deployed for the November 2002 election. After certification, the law does not allow any changes to machines without further testing. As a minimum standard, the company providing the machines must deliver documentation to the secretary of state that any repairs do nothing more than fix the specific problem.

And there were significant problems with Georgia's voting machines.

According to whistleblower Rob Behler, as soon as shipments of the machines began arriving at the Diebold warehouse in Georgia, the terminals had problems booting up, were consistently freezing, often crashing, and many were registering inaccurate times and dates on their clocks. In an interview with *Wired Magazine*, Behler said there were numerous failures of the Diebold systems, and he had no idea of how to respond.

"It's hard to track down a problem," he said, "when you go out to your car, and the first time it starts, the next time the headlights don't work, the next time you start it the brakes are out, and the next time you start it the door falls off. That's really the way they were.

"JS equipment is what we were calling it at the time," Behler added. "Junk shit. Everyone in the warehouse was familiar with the term, to say the least."

Behler, a contractor whose job was to set up the voting machines and ship them out to Georgia's counties, estimated that 25 to 30 percent of the terminals did not properly function. The answer to these kinds of technological malfunctions is for the manufacturer to develop a software "patch," separate lines of code to correct the failures. Behler, who did not speak publicly until after the election, said he was ordered by Diebold to install three different patches on the Georgia voting machines. Behler claimed to have put patches on 1,387 terminals and was still getting an error rate of 20 to 25 percent. He said the software fixes were never examined by any independent third party, and that the machines did not undergo any recertification process. According to Behler, the secretary of state's office wasn't even told about the patches.

"That's the last thing Diebold wanted," Behler said. "They made that very clear. I sat around tables where [they] discussed whether they were going to tell them [Georgia's secretary of state's officials] the truth, the half-truth or a complete lie. I understand if a company has information that they need to keep under tight lip. But when you sit around discussing lying to a client in order to make sure you're getting paid, it's an ethics issue."

Behler said no one other than the Diebold software engineers knew what was in the patches, and they may have been altered even before Behler installed them on the machines. If what he has publicly described is accurate, the code for the patches was posted to an Internet FTP [file transfer protocol] site, along with all of the election software, because that expedited the process of resolving technological issues before the voting day deadline. However, even if the FTP site were password protected, experts said it would have been a relatively simple task to hack into the location and insert rogue code, which might be designed to affect election results. People who downloaded the file were shocked, if only by its name: rob-Georgia.zip.

Dr. Rebecca Mercuri, an expert on voting systems at Harvard's John F. Kennedy School of Government, has suggested changing code on voting machines is not very challenging. "There are literally hundreds of ways to do this," she said. "There are hundreds of ways to embed a rogue series of commands into the code, and nobody would ever know because the nature of the programming is so complex. The numbers would all tally perfectly."

When Roxanne Jekot, a computer programmer and teacher at Lanier Technical College near Atlanta, heard that the Diebold files were available at an FTP site, she downloaded them to take a look at the code. She told Andrew Gumbel, a reporter for the *Independent* of London that there were "security holes" all over the Diebold programs.

"I really expected to have some difficulty reviewing the source code," she said, "because it would be at a higher level than I am accustomed to. In fact, a lot of this stuff looked like the homework my first year students might have turned in."

According to Jekot, the writers of the program had left comments inside of the code, such as; "Not a confidence builder, would you say?" and, "This really doesn't work." After a line-by-line review, Jekot, who has twenty years experience as a programmer, said she found enough to "stand your hair on end."

If the machines were patched, as whistleblower Rob Behler has claimed, and those fixes were not certified by the state, Georgia's 2002 election results are likely not legal. "Having any change to the operating system allows someone to slip in anything to the code," Dr. Mercuri of Harvard said. "If a patch was not run through the inspection process, then there could be a violation of the Georgia state law."

There is no record from the Georgia secretary of state's office that any patches were ever certified for installation.

Diebold has refused all requests to talk about its voting machines, claiming that there is too much proprietary, copyrighted information at risk. The only comment on the alleged patches to the Georgia machines has come from Joseph Richardson, a Diebold spokesman, during an interview with *Salon*. He denied that any patches were installed in Georgia.

"We have analyzed that situation and have no indication of that happening at all," he said.

Diebold's public relations problems had begun well before its problems in Georgia. Seattle researcher Bev Harris, a housewife and the owner of a small PR agency, discovered an earlier set of Diebold's files and software code posted at another open location on the Internet. Harris set about proving flawed security issues in the code, and how simple it might be for the software to be altered. Eventually, insider memos were leaked to her, allegedly from Diebold workers, that indicated a corruption within the machines, and the way they were utilized.

"These memos show a pattern of allegedly breaking the law," she said. "Starting with using uncertified software, Diebold insiders allegedly admit to doing 'end runs' around the voting system, and in one of the most shocking sets of memos, they allegedly admit that a 'replacement' set of vote totals was uploaded in Volusia County, Florida, which took 16,022 votes away from Al Gore in November 2000. The explanation for how a supposedly secure system can have replacement votes put on it, and the whereabouts of 'card #3,' which contained the second vote upload, are missing in action."

According to Harris, the votes were later given back to Gore, but only because a Florida clerk noticed the tally going down and sent out an alert.

Harris has become the de facto leader of a grassroots campaign to stop the installation of electronic voting machines around the United States. In the course of her research, Harris discovered that none of the states she examined conducted anything more than cursory testing of performance during the logic and accuracy exams. To truly understand how the voting machines were tallying votes, Harris has argued, software code needs to undergo a line-by-line analysis. The code, however, is considered copyrighted and proprietary information protected by the Digital Millennium Copyright Act (DMCA), and not even the states that purchase the machines are allowed access to the information on how the results are recorded. DMCA was also used to temporarily shut down Harris' web site. Diebold sued her for posting memos and information it claimed was protected by the law, and forced Harris to pull down www.blackboxvoting.org for 30 days.

Harris' greatest concern, however, is that there is no independent corroboration of results; no printout of a voting receipt or separate sets of data to be compared to machine results. There is no way to audit what happened in Georgia's 2002 elections, or any other state in the 2004 presidential vote.

"An audit," Harris explained, "is simply the act of comparing two independent data sets that are supposed to match. Probably the most important understory to the voting issue right now is this: The voting industry is spending literally millions of dollars, and going through amazing feats of contorted logic that can best be described as marketing gymnastics, to convince us that we should discontinue proper auditing. They want us to eliminate the ballot which you verify, and trust the secret system instead. Even with the optical scan machines, which retain a paper ballot, some states have passed laws to prevent us from looking at the paper ballot to use it for a proper audit."

States Boards of Elections around the country apparently find the costs associated with printed ballots to be unnecessarily high. Although the attachment of a printer to a machine is relatively simple, it increases hardware expenses by as much as 10 percent, and requires more staffing and additional protocols for the custody and counting of paper ballots, should they be needed for verification.

Thomas Swidarski, a senior vice president for strategic development and global marketing at Diebold, has insisted there is no reason to worry about electronic failures in elections. He said that three companies, contracted by the National Association of State Election Directors, do a rigorous examination of every line of code to eliminate any possibility of tampering, and then the machines go to the individual states for logic and accuracy testing. Swidarski also said that the unprotected code, which was discovered by Bev Harris, was no longer relevant because it was outdated and not in use, and all programs were now password protected.

Researcher David Dill, however, was not calmed. A professor of computer science at Stanford University, Dr. Dill has set up his own web site, www.verifiedvoting.org, to generate support for a printout of the electronic ballot cast by each voter. Otherwise, he has argued, no one can ever really know election results because what happens inside the voting machine is unknown.

"If I was a programmer at one of these companies," he explained, "And I wanted to steal an election, it would be very easy. I could put something in the software that would be impossible for people to detect, and it would change the votes from one party to another. And you could do it so it's not going to show up statistically as an anomaly."

Dill's investigation into the inherent flaws of electronic voting prompted the secretary of state in California to require a "paper trail audit" of all votes electronically cast in the state. However, the deadline for implementation is 2006, two years after the first presidential election scheduled to be conducted electronically.

The ground-breaking research of Bev Harris caused Johns Hopkins University's Information Security Institute to perform an independent study of Diebold's source code, which Harris had found on the Internet. Four of the university's scientists, Tadayoshi Kohno, Adam Stubblefield, Aviel D. Rubin, and Dan S. Wallach, reached a startling conclusion.

"Our analysis shows that this voting system is far below even the most minimal security standards applicable in other contexts," the Johns Hopkins researchers decided. "We highlight several issues including unauthorized privilege escalation, incorrect use of cryptography, vulnerabilities to network threats, and poor software development processes. For example, common voters, without any insider privileges, can cast unlimited votes without being detected by any mechanisms within the voting terminal. Furthermore, we show that even the most serious of our outsider attacks could have been discovered without the source code. In the face of such attacks, the usual worries about insider threats are not the only concerns; outsiders can do the damage. That said, we demonstrate that the insider threat is also quite considerable. We conclude that, as a society, we must carefully consider the risks inherent in electronic voting, as it places our very democracy at risk."

Diebold issued a response to the Johns Hopkins analysis, which said the four scientists expressed "an incomplete understanding of the full scope of the electoral process" and that their report was "explicitly based in large part on false assumptions."

"The researchers," Diebold wrote, "reached their conclusions after reviewing an inadequate, incomplete sample of Diebold Election Systems' voting software system. Furthermore, the report was released directly to the press, rather than submitted to standard peer review by presentation to an open academic forum.

"This report, which delivers a multitude of false conclusions based on such inadequate information, is damaging to the community of people working to improve the efficiency and security of the electoral process."

The high profile analysis by Johns Hopkins caught the attention of Maryland election officials, who had just offered a $55.6 million dollar contract to Diebold for the purchase of its AccuVote-TS voting system. The state hired the Science Applications International Corporation (SAIC) to see if there was a cause for concern. SAIC first scrutinized the methodology and findings the Johns Hopkins study, and critical statements made by Aviel D. Rubin, who authored the report. According to SAIC's summary, "The State of Maryland procedural controls and general voting environment reduce or eliminate many of the vulnerabilities identified in the Rubin report. However, these controls, while sufficient to help mitigate the weaknesses identified in the July 23, [2003] report, do not, in many cases, meet the standard of best practice or State of Maryland Security Policy."

The conclusions of SAIC, however, were hardly more assuring than the critical Johns Hopkins study.

"This Risk Assessment has identified several high-risk vulnerabilities in the implementation of the managerial, operational, and technical controls for the AccuVote-TS voting system. If these vulnerabilities are exploited, significant impact could occur on the accuracy, integrity, and availability of election results."

SAIC documented 328 flaws in the Diebold system, and 26 of those were classified as "critical." Unfortunately, 69 pages of the 200 in the SAIC report were heavily redacted, leaving unanswered an endless stream of questions about how the machines actually work, and tabulate vote totals, especially after the available text characterized the flaws as "stunning," and the overall assessment was, "The system, as implemented in policy, procedure, and technology, is at high risk of compromise."

In spite of the worries detailed in the SAIC study, the Maryland State Board of Elections was reassured by Diebold's claims that all of the problems were easily repaired prior to elections. Election officials in Maryland concluded that "an alternative system could not be implemented in time to conduct the March 2004 Presidential Primary election and could jeopardize the November 2004 presidential general election." Diebold retained its multimillion dollar agreement with the state.

Nonetheless, SAIC concluded that many of the risks classified as "low" or "medium" on the Diebold systems were raised to "very high" when the machines were connected to modems. Diebold has argued that there is no need for modems or wireless connections to the AccuVote-TS terminals. Votes are tabulated on memory cards, which are then taken to an elections board location for final tabulations, although totals can be sent via modem. Researcher Bev Harris, however, said she discovered a file among 40,000 posted on Diebold's web site, which indicated there was communication with a machine during the course of Election Day in San Luis Obispo, California. Harris claimed the file included actual votes, which ought not to have been recorded until after the election.

"It is impossible for this file to have existed if there wasn't some sort of illicit electronic communication going on for remote access," Harris said. "What happened, specifically is, now, it's against the law to start counting the votes before the polls have closed. But this file is date and time stamped at 3:31 in the afternoon on Election Day, and somehow all 57 precincts managed to call 'home,' and add themselves up in the middle of the day. Not only once but three times. If you have no electronic communications between the polling places and the main office, how does that happen?"

If what Harris has described is possible, elections could be monitored before polls are closed. Manipulation of results becomes a simple technological function. This kind of a scenario was what generated all of the fears and criticism of both the voting machines and their manufacturers. Transparency is not possible because of copyright protections on the software code. State Boards of Elections are not allowed, under penalty of federal law, to see how the election results were generated. According to Rebecca Mercuri, the secretive functions of electronic voting terminals is why the public is reluctant to embrace the technology.

"These companies are basically saying 'trust us,'" she said. "Why should anybody trust them? That's not the way democracy is supposed to work. It makes it really hard to show their product has been tampered with if it's a felony to inspect it."

Dozens of complications were reported in the 2002 elections caused by the Direct Recording Electronic (DRE) systems. In a central Texas county, three candidates on the ballot all received 18,181 votes, but no investigation or recount was ordered, regardless of the almost statistical improbability of those totals. A single machine in Iowa miscounted a million votes, and in Dallas, Diebold had to remove 18 machines because voters who pressed the Democratic candidate's button found that a Republican's name lit up on the screen. Heavily Democratic precincts in Broward County, Florida, lost 100,000 votes from a software glitch. They were later reinstated. Alabama's gubernatorial race was turned upside down by a late discovery that the incumbent Democrat, Don Siegelman, had been credited with an excess of 7,000 votes. The mistake was discovered after midnight in a rural county and provided enough of a margin to elect Republican Bob Riley as governor. Alabama's Republican attorney general refused to authorize independent ballot inspection or any type of recount.

The political profiles of executives in the largest producers of electronic voting machines, Diebold, Election Systems and Software, Hart Intercivic, and Sequoia Voting Systems, have also created suspicions among public interest groups. An anxiety has begun brewing that corporations are out to hijack American democracy by electronically delivering candidates that best serve business interests. The belief is that these politicians tend to be Republican. Nebraska U.S. Senator Chuck Hagel was both a member of the GOP and an owner of one of the largest manufacturers of DRE terminals in the nation. From 1990 to 1995, Hagel was the CEO of American Information Systems, which later became Election Systems and Software (ES&S). ES&S has captured about 50 percent of the U.S. market for electronic voting machines. Hagel is an investor in McCarthy Group, Inc., which is the holding company that owns ES&S.

When he ran for the U.S. Senate from Nebraska, Hagel disclosed on his Federal Election Commission (FEC) filings that he had an investment of $1 to $5 million in McCarthy Group, Inc. He listed the company as an "excepted investment fund," a category that has, historically, applied to mutual funds. Candidates are not expected to disclose all of the transactions and shares of companies they own through the multiple purchases by mutual funds. Generally, "excepted investment fund" has meant the shares are publicly traded. McCarthy Group, Inc. is privately held.

By listing McCarthy Group as an "excepted investment fund," Hagel was able to avoid listing the underlying asset of the company. The McCarthy Group owns ES&S, and ES&S is owned, in part, by AIS Investors, Inc. Senator Hagel also has shares of AIS Investors, Inc. None of this, however, was reported on his FEC filings during his campaign. The failure to disclose was a deception. When voters went to the polls to pick their U.S. senator in Nebraska during the 1996 and 2002 elections, almost all of the votes in the state were tallied by machines manufactured by ES&S. Chuck Hagel owned a portion of the company that sold the machines that counted 85 percent of the votes in the state where he was elected.

Hagel's conflict of interest was first reported by researcher Bev Harris on her new web site, www.blackboxvoting.com, on October 10, 2002. The information was picked up by Channel 8 News in Lincoln, Nebraska, and the station conducted an interview with a spokesperson for Hagel's office, which was broadcast on October 22, 2002. Through a proxy, Hagel insisted that he had sold his shares of

ES&S prior to being elected. His office also issued a fact sheet claiming he had made full disclosure. However, the *Hill*, a Washington, D.C., publication focusing on politics and government, reported in early 2003 that Hagel's campaign finance chairman, Michael McCarthy of the McCarthy Group, Inc., admitted that Hagel retained his ownership in ES&S' parent company, as well as AIS Investors, Inc., which has money in ES&S. The only information disclosed on Hagel's FEC forms was that he had a $1 to $5 million investment in McCarthy Group, Inc. He did not reveal that the holding company owned ES&S. Hagel's office has made no public pronouncement that he has sold his percentage share of ES&S.

When Bev Harris learned that Senator Hagel was an owner of the company that produced the machines that counted 85 percent of the votes in elections he won, she contacted the Senate Ethics Committee. Chief Counsel of the committee, Victor Baird, met with Hagel's staff on two separate days in late January of 2002, reportedly to make inquiries about the information on disclosure forms. After his second meeting, Baird resigned as the lawyer for the Ethics Committee. Immediately, Baird was replaced by Robert Walker, who offered a less stringent interpretation of "excepted investment fund," which Hagel had claimed when failing to report that McCarthy Group, Inc., owned ES&S. Alexander Bolten, a reporter for the *Hill*, spoke with a former Senate Ethics Committee staffer, William Canfield, who told the publication that "excepted investment fund" was a category designed to cover mutual funds that sell or purchase thousands of various holdings on a regular basis, not private holdings like McCarthy Group.

Charlie Matulka, the man who ran against Chuck Hagel in the 2002 election, wrote a letter of complaint to the Senate Ethics Committee about Hagel's lack of information on the required FEC forms. Victor Baird dismissed Matulka's concerns in a November 18, 2002, letter with the words, "Your complaint lacks merit and no further action is appropriate with respect to the matter, which is hereby dismissed."

Matulka had been suspicious ever since he saw the vote totals from his 2002 run against Hagel. The senator had gotten 83 percent of the vote, the largest electoral victory in Nebraska history, six years after defeating a popular incumbent Democratic governor who had tried to reach the U.S. senate. In his reelection bid, Hagel had even won by large margins in the African American community of Omaha, which was a traditional stronghold for every Democratic candidate for any office.

"This is a big story," Charlie Matulka said. "Bigger than Watergate ever was. They can take over our country without firing a shot, just by taking over election systems."

Senator Hagel has refused to make any public comment to journalists on the controversy. Apparently, though, he does not believe it will have any impact on his political career. Hagel may have designs on the presidency. Internet domain names Hagel2008.com and ChuckHagel2008.com have both been purchased by his company.

There are several perceived political apparent conflicts of interest among the companies producing electronic voting machines. In early August of 2003, Walden O'Dell, CEO of Diebold, Inc., was among a group of George W. Bush supporters visiting the president as he vacationed at his ranch in Crawford, Texas. The event was put together for "Rangers and Pioneers," fundraisers who had organized donors to provide the Bush campaign with $100,000 and $200,000 contributions. When O'Dell returned to his home in Ohio, he wrote a letter to 100 of his friends, asking them to attend a Bush fundraiser at O'Dell's mansion.

"I am committed to helping Ohio deliver its electoral votes to the president next year," O'Dell wrote.

O'Dell's company, at the time, was trying to win the contract to provide voting machines to the state of Ohio for the 2004 presidential election. Federal Election Commission figures indicate that eleven Diebold executives had given the Bush reelection effort a total of $22,000 in donations, the legally allowable maximum. Before his trip to Texas, O'Dell had invited Vice President

Dick Cheney to his home for a fundraiser, which put $500,000 into Cheney's campaign account. No money from Diebold executives has gone to Democrats. In fact, there was no record that any of the major manufacturers of voting systems has donated to a Democrat. W. R. Timken, a Diebold board member, who is also a "Pioneer" for the Bush campaign, gave the president a tour of the company during a visit by the president to Ohio.

Bev Harris, who has used her investigation's results to publish a book, *Black Box Voting: Ballot-Tampering in the Twenty-First Century* (High Point, NC: Plan Nine Publishing, 2003) has said Diebold's influence frightens her.

"Basically what we have is a company that is giving money, hand over fist and helping in campaign strategizing for a particular political party at the same time as making the machines that count the votes," she said.

There does not appear, however, any federal attempt to scrutinize apparent conflicts of interest in the voting machine industry or slow down the transformation of the electoral process to electronic voting. The Help America Vote Act has appropriated over $3 billion dollars for the systems in the wake of the hanging chad fiasco of Florida's presidential recount in 2000. With the technology protected by copyright laws and lacking transparency to assure voters, there is no way to independently corroborate election results. When the "patched" and repaired Diebold voting terminals in Georgia, with their reported failure rate of 20 to 25 percent, showed that Republican Saxby Chambliss had defeated Democratic incumbent Max Cleland, there was no way to contest the results.

Democracy was forced to trust the machines.

There are no windows in Max Cleland's corner office. The Distinguished Adjunct Professor at American University has no privacy, either. He shares his space with two assistants, a dramatic change from the more than 50 staffers who worked for his office in the U.S. Senate. As a Fellow in the Center for Congressional and

Presidential Studies, Cleland has returned to the Washington, D.C. campus that transformed his life's ambitions. When he was a student in American's Washington semester program, the young man from rural Georgia fell in love with government and the democratic process. Speaking to students in the classroom today, the former senator tries to fill them with the excitement that brought him to public service, not the dark cynicism he has begun to experience through the Bush administration and its policy of preemptive war.

"That's the sad part of this," Cleland said. "The coalescing of the permanent war strategy of [Dick] Cheney and [Paul] Wolfowitz, who generally believe, based on a right-wing view of the world that we have power, and only we can do it, and we don't need our allies, and we are gonna go in and reshape the Middle East with the use of force. It ain't gonna happen. The ground truth, as the soldiers call it, is so much different. We're creating more terrorists. We're creating more problems in the Middle East. So, that strategy is backfiring. But that coincides with the political Machiavellian moves of a guy like Karl Rove, who is only interested in winning. He's not interested in policy. It's painfully obvious, and since that keeps the president's numbers artificially up, if the country is in turmoil and trouble, and people rally round the flag, then he goes for it."

That kind of criticism has brought attention to Max Cleland. As a wounded military veteran, his comments bear great weight with journalists and political analysts. Cleland has not been lacking a podium, either. He has served as a Democrat on the commission investigating 9/11, formerly known as National Commission on Terrorist Attacks Upon the U.S. In late 2003, however, Senate Democratic leadership nominated Cleland to serve on the board of the Export-Import Bank, which meant the former senator would have to leave the 9/11 commission. By statute, anyone holding a federal job, such as being on the Export-Import Bank's board, cannot serve on the panel investigating 9/11. His departure from the commission is expected to diminish the volume and impact of the Georgian's political attacks on the president.

But Cleland's worrisome message was already spreading.

"You know what I worry about?" he asked. "I don't worry about the president or Rove. What I worry about is what happened to us in Vietnam. Over time, when the American people get turned off to war, they also get turned off by the warrior. You see, that's the real injustice here. It's one thing to get turned off by the war and take the administration into account. But it's another thing to leave those kids out there for so long that, ultimately, their own generation, and the American people turn against them, and I saw it, and I was part of it, when back home people won't have anything to do with you. That's not right. If you leave the war going for too long for no reason, or with a dead end strategy, that will happen, and that's what I'm trying to forestall."

A documentary television crew, which had been taping an interview with Cleland, began to tear down lights and equipment as the senator was assisted back to his university office. A caller had been waiting. Another reporter was on the phone and wanted to know what Cleland thought about the latest terrorist attack in Iraq. Quickly, he slipped from his wheelchair into the more comfortable seat behind his desk. The energy and determination of a fallen soldier, rising to fight again, was in his voice as he held the receiver to his ear:

> We are not doing the right thing by them [U.S. troops]. We're taking advantage of their patriotism, their commitment, their love and loyalty to this country. We're taking advantage of that while it artificially looks like the president's poll numbers are up but underneath more and more American people are dissatisfied, anxious, and concerned about what in the world is going on over there.

Max Cleland was still serving his country, saying important things America needed to hear.

16

THE POKORNEY GIRLS

Do ye hear the children weeping, O my brothers,
Ere the sorrow comes with years?
They are leaning their young heads against their mothers,
And that cannot stop their tears.

Elizabeth Barrett Browning, "The Cry of the Children"

O utside of their travel trailer, a television crew was setting up a camera and lights. Chelle and Taylor Pokorney had been living in a place called Trailer Park Village in Quantico, Virginia. Seven months after her husband, 1st Lieutenant Fred Pokorney Jr., had been killed in Iraq, Chelle was still emotionally raw and uncertain of what to do next. She told the visitor sitting at her table that leaving the Washington, D.C., area was like leaving her husband, who had been buried at Arlington National Cemetery. Too many issues were still unresolved for Chelle Pokorney to move to wherever it was that came next for her and three-year-old Taylor.

"I'm waiting for the report from the Marines on the investigation of the A-10," she said. "The whole friendly fire thing. People say, 'Is it gonna help if you know every detail?' Well, yeah, that was my husband. I want to know every detail up to the time it happened, and what he said, and who he was with because that's what you hold onto. I never got to say goodbye."

Chelle's husband, who saved the life of Lieutenant Ben Reid and called in critical air strikes while under attack, was originally recommended for a Bronze Star. However, officers have asked that the commendation be upgraded to a Silver Star. Waiting for word on his medal has left Chelle Pokorney feeling more pain was inevitable. After Lieutenant Pokorney died in Al Nasiriyah, all of his mail came home to Chelle in one shipment. It arrived on the same day as his memorial service. None of the letters she had written or photos of Taylor had ever found their way to her husband. A simple thing like the absence of house keys from his personal belongings can leave her aching.

"I keep waiting for closure, you know, keep waiting for closure," she repeated. "I never got the house keys back. Nobody can understand that. It's just that it doesn't mean anything to them, but that was your husband who didn't come home, and that was the key to open the door. And it was home. Nobody can understand that pain. They just think you're silly because you hold on, and you're crazy."

On the settee in the trailer, Chelle has placed a framed photo of her husband, who is wearing camouflage and casting his resolute eyes in the direction of the camera. It is the first thing a visitor sees when stepping into the living space. Taylor Pokorney looks at the photo many times a day.

"See," she says. "There's my daddy. He's looking right at me from heaven."

Chelle rubbed her daughter's back. None of the adults in the room spoke. Chelle and Taylor had just returned from a trip to New York City. By telling her story of the financial confusion and the challenges of grief, Chelle believed she could help other families deal with the complications of their loss. As a guest of the Fallen Heroes Foundation, Chelle had hoped to use her time during an appearance on *The Today Show* to talk about what military families were facing with combat fatalities. Instead, interviewer Matt Lauer spent most of the air time quizzing General Tommy Franks, who sat next to Chelle, about the U.S. military's tactics in Iraq.

By now, it ought to have been getting easier, she figured. But it wasn't.

"Right now," she explained, "I want to tell my story because there's huge financial changes. There's a lot of need. I find out every day there's something new. It's been seven months and I still don't have the answers to what we get and what we don't get. Taylor still doesn't have dental insurance. Wow, Daddy gave his life, and I still have to fight with them [the military] to get it [insurance]. Why, I ask? There is supposed to be somebody to help me but they don't get what help is, so they don't make it happen. I want to help those other families so they don't have to go through what I've had to go through for seven months."

Chelle walked over to the counter and ran water to pour into the coffee machine. She had trouble talking without crying. She said that after Fred died, the first casualty assistance officer the Marines sent to her home was drunk. After telling her she ought to be stronger because she was a Marine's wife and more grateful because her husband got to be buried in Arlington, Chelle said she ordered the officer out of her home. There have been two others assigned to her and Taylor. Insensitivity was something Chelle Pokorney never expected from the Marines or the American public.

"I was real positive from the beginning that this is what Fred did, this is what he gave his life for; he was a Marine, and that is the reality, and people say that, and that's probably the worst thing you could say to a military family; that you knew what you signed up for because nobody wants this to happen, and that's such a terrible thing to say. Including one of the media guys I was on with who said, 'You knew the reality of this. What were you thinking?' How heartless. How heartless. How heartless can you be? But you never want a little girl to lose her daddy. It's the reality, yes. But when it happens, don't stop and tell a family you signed up for this, you knew what you were getting into, because it's horrible."

"We're all set."

The television producer leaned his head into the open door of Chelle and Taylor's trailer. A camera sat on a tripod next to a picnic table. Chelle stepped out into the October light, running a single finger across the wetness beneath each of her eyes. The Virginia air was cool, and stirring, lifting the leaves cluttered along the edge of the blacktop. Taylor followed after her mother, stopping to check on her German shepherd waiting inside his cage for a walk. Her face is the face of her father, rendered in the feminine. The cheeks are full, and her eyes have already become serious with independence.

"How's she doing?" Chelle was asked.

"Oh, she's doin'. She's coming back. She's got his light, and his stamina, and she misses him."

"And she knows what happened?"

"We were talking about it last night. She said, 'Why did those bad people kill my daddy?'"

Taylor caught up with her mother and pulled at her sleeve. "I wanna go find some nuts," she said.

"Well, go find some for me, buddy," Chelle said. "So we can feed the squirrels."

Taylor ran to the edge of the pavement and began digging among the fallen leaves, searching for acorns. Her mother, too tired to constantly hold off the tears, was talking about an encounter with another military family.

"We saw another little boy," Chelle Pokorney said, "And she said, 'Why did his daddy have to go, too?' And she said, 'Is his daddy in his heart like my daddy is in mine?' She knows. We miss him. We have to talk about him to keep him alive because he'll never be able to hold us again, and I wish . . ."

She turned her head, looking away, looking for something.

"He was a wonderful father," Chelle said, finally. "Just wonderful. And a wonderful husband."

Staying near the Marine base at Quantico, Virigina, had been both agonizing and healing for Chelle Pokorney. There are great memories lingering there; her husband in his dress blues leaning down to embrace her for a dance, a first camping trip for Taylor, cookouts and conversations with friends who had chosen a life of military service. If Fred were to be posthumously awarded the Silver Star, Chelle hoped that it might be presented to Taylor on the base at Quantico. But she was on the move now, no longer confident that everyone in the military was possessed of honor and responsibility like her husband. Chelle had already sold their modest house in the neighborhood outside Camp Lejuene in Jacksonville, North Carolina, because she no longer felt a part of the Marine family.

"I thought I could stay in the military town I was in," she explained. "And I'd have some more support, and people would never forget, and I thought, wow, this is my family. But a few months later, after everybody came home, the reality is that Taylor and I were alone. A few people trickled by. But they mostly weren't there, and the days that they weren't there were so empty. People come up to me and say, 'We thought you moved,' and I just sit there and say, 'wow, you never called. You never came over, so how can you say that? Those are just such empty promises and words. How can you say that? You don't know how that affects us.' So we left."

Chelle sat down with the interviewer. Another camera was pointed at her face. This was not the role she wanted to play. All she wanted was her husband, her daughter, and a quiet family life of holidays, vacations, and the contentment of knowing her husband was fulfilled by his service to his country. Instead, she has been consumed with a sense of obligation to speak the truth, honorably, as her husband would, about her loss, and what all the families of those lost in combat are confronting. In a way that she was unable to ignore, Chelle Pokorney had become a symbol. She reminded families, who had soldiers or Marines still in Iraq, that their loved one might not come home, either. No one wanted that reminder. People stayed away from the Pokorney house.

"When you lose your Marine, and you lose your husband, and your best friend, and your daddy," Chelle said, "You hold onto what people say to you, and when they let you down, it's the most horrifying thing. It's worse than just reliving his death over and over again."

Chelle Pokorney's support for the president and the war in Iraq has not wavered. She loves the president and trusts his judgment, just as her husband did. In her opinion, George W. Bush has the most difficult job in the world, and he would not put American troops in danger unless he felt it were necessary to protect the country. The angry polarization of Americans, sharply divided over the war, has not affected Chelle's beliefs. Although she admits to not being political, she worries for the soldiers and their families when she hears people criticizing the American presence in Iraq. She tells herself that debate is precisely what Fred died for, so that people can have free and open discussions, say and do what they want, whether they are in the United States or Iraq. That's what she knows. That her country is beautiful, still, no matter what the political climate might be. And her husband loved it and would die for America a second time, if only he were given a chance.

"I'm going to visit him every Memorial Day." Chelle was sobbing, the unabashed tears of a deep, deep sorrow, an agony she was uncertain would ever let her be. "It's the least I can do for his little girl; take her to Arlington to see him. Because he was so proud on Memorial Day when he was with those veterans. He was just so proud to be a part of that, and that tradition, and thank them for what they did. And he did. Fred never forgot. He never forgot."

Taylor Pokorney reached up and took the hand of her new friend and led him in the direction of the playground while her mother was being interviewed. After filling her knit cap with acorns, she had lost interest in looking for more. She clambered over the plastic playscape, constantly talking about the make-believe situations she was creating. Although the sky was clear, she told her friend the rain was going to begin falling and he needed to climb up the slide for protection. When she jumped on a spring-mounted rocking horse, Taylor asked to be pushed. As the toy animal swung slowly back and forth, she grew quiet, and quit leaning her slight weight into the pitch and roll of the little horse.

"Stop. Stop," she said.

Instead of getting down, Taylor kept her grip on the red handles near the horse's neck. She looked up to the unfamiliar face.

"All my friends are sad," she said.

He did not know what to say. Her short, brown hair began swaying again as Taylor worked the horse back into motion. She had not expected a response. It was just something that had registered with a child, and she had given voice to what she knew. By the time they returned to the trailer, the television taping was concluding. Taylor urged her mother to let her dog out of the cage.

"Can we take him for a walk?" Taylor pleaded.

"Sure." Chelle opened the gate and clipped the leash to the dog's collar. Taylor had named her pet "Stitch," after the movie *Lilo and Stitch*, which had been her favorite movie she had seen with her daddy. The dog pulled hard at his restraints and Chelle hesitated to hand the leash to her daughter.

"By myself. By myself," Taylor insisted. "Sit Stitch. Sit. Come here. Let's take a walk."

While the dog began pulling the little girl, the camera crew followed, and Chelle tried to articulate where she was in terms of healing. She understood grief. She was a nurse. All of the signs were there. It was a process. But it seemed like it was taking too long. She needed to go on. New York had opened doors. She had been offered a position as the honorary co-chair of the Intrepid Foundation. The job meant she would have resources to help other military families deal with their casualties, the absurd bureaucracies, uncertain benefits, loss of health care, and the complications of moving on to another life. But she wanted to go home to Washington first. Be with her parents and her brother. Process things some more. Feel the broken places inside of her start to mend before she went back into the world.

"A part of me thinks people just want to avoid me," she said. "It's too real for them. And who wants to be around somebody who cries all the time? Or somebody who reminds them of what could happen to them? I'm thinking that's okay for me. I can deal with that. But what about Taylor?"

It is difficult for Chelle Pokorney to think that her husband gave his life in service to his country and his daughter's future has become more uncertain. When a Marine dies in combat, he stops getting paid the next day. The death benefit he signed up for is usually enough money to help his survivors make a transition to a future without him. But it is not always sufficient. Chelle expected to return to work as an RN, but was unsure about earning enough to comfortably get Taylor from age 3 to 18. College, without her father's income and commitment, seemed an improbability. Why didn't the government have any mechanism to help military families deal with these issues? Who takes care of the families of servicemen and women who have died in combat? Are they really just tossed aside?

Taylor, frustrated with her mother's distractions, and the intrusive television gear, interrupted the conversation to talk about Stitch.

"He doesn't like the camera," she explained. "He likes walking. Let's walk him. Come on, mom. Stitch, heel. Heel, Stitch."

When her husband was alive, Chelle Pokorney worried about very little. Sure, there were the usual financial challenges of any military family. But she was confident they could handle those. Fred's presence, their love, gave her confidence everything was fine, and getting better. He always assured her that if anything ever happened to him, the Marines cared for their own, and their families. She would be okay. The military was her family. That's the code of conduct Fred Pokorney would have lived up to if one of his own men had been killed in battle, and Fred had come home. But that's not what happened for Fred's wife.

"That's the first thing my mom said to me when this happened," Chelle said. "She said, 'You are going to be alone because Fred's gone, and no one is going to be there for you.' She was right because I thought, at first, when everybody was there, and it was all hot and heavy, and they said, we're your family, we're gonna take care of you. And it wasn't true."

After Stitch was put back into his cage, Chelle showed the television crew an album of photos. Her life with Fred and Taylor was shining across the pages. As each page was turned for the camera, Taylor pointed.

"Oh look, I'm eating cake. Oh, daddy loves me. Oh, I've got a bottle 'cause I'm a baby. See, my Daddy's got something in his hand."

Chelle's eyes were wet again. She was doing this to keep alive her husband's memory, assure that he was not forgotten. He always seemed to do what was right. Fred Pokorney served when called. He made no judgment about why he was sent to Iraq. If there were deceptions or dishonorable men involved in that decision, there was nothing a Marine lieutenant might have done to change things. His only option was to do his job. And he did. Those were the principles in which he believed, fought and died for, and his wife hopes they are what will guide Fred Pokorney's daughter.

"She said the other night, 'Mommy, I don't know if I wanna be a first lady or first president.' Whatever. You choose. I'll be stressed. But I can't stop you. It's just like your daddy, doing what he loved."

A few days later, Chelle Pokorney cranked the handle on the travel trailer and lowered it onto the ball hitch of her Ford truck. Her brother, who had also been emotionally devastated by Fred's death, was joining Chelle and Taylor on a cross-country drive back to Washington State. They planned to stop in Texas to visit relatives and then take Taylor to the Grand Canyon. In Nevada, they expected to see Wade and Suzy Lieseke before turning north, toward home and Washington.

There was something out there in America for Chelle and Taylor. Chelle didn't know what it was. There had to be people who cared and would help, maybe a new job, a different future than the one she had dreamed of with Fred. Whatever it was, Chelle was determined to find it. She would just keep going until she did. And for Taylor's sake, she would never, ever give up.

Fred would not forgive her for that.

Epilogue

Johnny Came Home

The time you won your town the race,
We chaired you through the marketplace,
While home we brought you shoulder high,
As man and boy stood cheering by."

A. E. Housman, "To an Athlete Dying Young"

The little girl sat at the table with her face leaning close to a small piece of paper. Her dark, bobbed hair swung forward, slightly obscuring the soft curve of her cheeks. She did not notice her mother enter the room.

"What are you doing, mija?" her mother asked.

"I'm writing Daddy a note." She answered without looking up, her concentration focused on the careful shaping of words and letters.

"Oh, mija."

Nancili Mata wanted to cry. Instead, she smiled and did not let emotion take control of her. When she surrenders to her sadness, she does so in private.

"I have to be strong because if I'm not my little girl will see me, and then she'll hurt more than I will," she explained.

At age seven, Stephani Mata has the oversized, startled eyes of a child finding amazement in the mundane. A happiness moves across her round face, and it rarely disappears. She has figured out a way to deal with a sadness no child should ever have to confront.

"They are just so sweet when she writes them," Nancili said. "They make me want to cry. But I don't. I won't let myself."

The notes began appearing after the funeral out in Pecos. Nancili found them stuck to pictures of her husband, Johnny. In the hallway of their new home or on shelves, anywhere there was a photo of Johnny Mata, a message from Stephani might be attached.

"Dear Daddy," she wrote. "I miss you. But I know you are happy up in heaven with Jesus. Love, Stephani."

Johnny Villareal Mata and his wife, Nancili, were supposed to grow gray together in the house he had bought for her in the North Hills area of El Paso. In seventh grade, she had told the shy Johnny, "You're going to be mine." He only smiled, unaware that the entire course of his life might be determined by the strong-willed girl with high cheekbones and unabashed honesty.

Nancili got what she wanted, though, because it made Johnny so happy to provide for her dreams. The house at the foot of the Franklin Mountains, however, was also a dream of his. As a chief warrant officer in the U.S. Army, Johnny had managed his money well enough that they were able to build a new home with a two-car garage, and a view of the Franklins out of almost every window.

"In a way, I felt like a queen," Nancili said. "Johnny and I, we had known each other for fifteen years, and I think the longer we knew each other, the better we were. At the end, he was like, 'Okay, this is your dream. I bought you a house.'"

Every day, the mountains across from her new home have a different look. Nancili Mata notices how the light changes the color of the rock and the softening created by a passing cloud obscuring the sun. The desert heat can give the Franklins a frightening sharpness before they are colored and made inviting by the long light of a new morning. She feels this way, too. There are dramatic changes inside of Nancili, and she struggles to be strong, to understand.

"I have my days. I like to go to the cemetery in Pecos and do my talking to Johnny. Most of the time at the cemetery, when I start getting depressed, I pray, and it helps."

Almost a hundred people showed up at the home of Domingo and Elvira Mata the first night news came that their son, Johnny, was missing in Iraq. Each night, a priest performed a rosary, and prayers were offered for Johnny's safe return. The crowds and the candles did not go away until Johnny's casket, being transported by the army, was met at the Reeves County line by police cruisers. Thousands lined the roadways, silently watching the procession, holding up candles in the 3:30 A.M. desert darkness. When he was buried, half of the 10,000 population of Pecos surrounded the church, or stood in the withering desert heat at the graveyard, waiting for the arrival of Johnny's funeral cortege.

Nancili did not get to see her husband for a final time when his body was returned. Brutalized by gunfire, she became convinced what was left was not the man she loved.

"I thought about seeing his body, and then another day I talked to my priest, the chaplain, and it made me realize it wasn't gonna be Johnny any more," she told a visitor. "It was just a body. And the way my husband always was, he was clean, always good-looking, detailed, and he would like to be remembered the way he was. I was speaking to the funeral person, and he said he didn't even get to see him because he [Johnny] was so wrapped up in a blanket. I think we made a pretty good decision, and I'm pretty comfortable with that."

Everything Johnny and Nancili Mata had dreamed about was killed in that Iraqi ambush in Al Nasiriyah. Settling into his duty station at Fort Bliss, Texas, Johnny Mata decided to invest his savings in the new home. In January 2003, Stephani, and her big brother, Eric, moved into their own bedrooms. Before the family had finished unpacking boxes, however, Johnny got orders for overseas deployment.

While his family adjusted to the new house, he was packing bags for a long trip. By March, Johnny Mata was in Kuwait.

"We made a video the night he left, and you could hardly see Johnny because Stephani was all over him. Every time you look at the picture, she's climbing all over her daddy." Nancili drew her index finger across the recesses below each eye, pressing away the tears. "Stephani is such a daddy's girl."

Johnny Mata was movie star handsome. A photo that circulated in his hometown of Pecos, Texas, showed him with his strong, angled jaw tilted slightly upward, dark, wavy hair shining in the sun, and a smile that dominated all of his other distinguishing features. Nothing, his family said, ever deterred Johnny. Even Pecos, suffering a kind of dry desperation on the northern edge of the Chihuahuan Desert, did not wear down Johnny Mata the way it did so many of the other young people. Great commerce and big dreams have never come closer to Pecos than the eighteen wheelers howling past out on Interstate 20. But none of that ever affected Johnny's attitude. He loved his parents, Domingo and Elvira, and his four brothers and sister. He loved his wife and his children. And he loved his country, so much that he was willing to go to war.

"He always wanted to serve his country that way," Nancili said. "The reason that it didn't bother me was because I would see it in his heart. If he wanted to do anything, it was like excitement. You would see that glow."

While Nancili spoke, an old-timers' baseball game was being played on a nearly grassless ball diamond beyond a tall fence. On the outfield wall, carnations, made out of tissue, spelled out the message, "In your honor, Johnny." A blast furnace wind meant that even the shade of a temporary awning did not offer relief from the heat. Flavored ice cones and barbecue were being sold behind the bleachers. Money raised was to be donated to local charities in the name of Johnny Mata. His daughter, wearing a tee shirt, spun around to show the silk screen to a stranger; "In honor of my father and hero,

Johnny Mata." Mata's face, encircled by the text, shines through the cotton fiber.

As a mechanic, Johnny Mata had acquired expertise in all of the heavy vehicles used by the U.S. Army. When his commander-in-chief, the president of the United States, issued orders that the 507th Mechanized Company relocate to Kuwait, Johnny saw his role as that of a soldier doing his job. He and Nancili did not talk about the politics of going after Saddam Hussein. There was no point to such a discussion. Orders were orders. He had to go, and so did all of the other soldiers in his outfit.

No one at Fort Bliss knew about faked documents trying to prove Saddam had attempted to buy uranium from Niger. They didn't know there were no provable connections between Saddam and Al Qaeda terrorists. Their commander-in-chief, they were certain, took his duties as solemnly and seriously as everyone at Fort Bliss. If the president said there were weapons of mass destruction in Iraq, every soldier accepted the statement for fact. As hazy as the politics were, they were irrelevant to everyone shipping out from Biggs Army Air Field at Fort Bliss. A soldier does not debate the politics of a presidential decision. He follows orders.

"We don't think about no politics in our family," said Domingo Mata. Johnny Mata's father is a man whose impressive size reflects an appetite for all of life's pleasures. He had been hovering nearby, listening to his daughter-in-law answer questions.

"Politics is just when someone tells you they'll do something so you'll help them get something they want, and then when they get in there, they forget all about the people who got them in. In our family, we just do what we need to do, what we think is right. That's all Johnny did. When he went up there (Iraq) he just wanted to help all those little children who were hungry, and hurtin', you know?"

Logic told Nancili and all of the Matas that they did not need to fret too much over Johnny's deployment. Even though Johnny was in Kuwait, the president sounded like he was trying to give the situation time to work itself out, peacefully. Surely, he did not want a war. Besides, Johnny was not with a combat unit. He fixed vehicles. His work was done at the rear. By the time the 507th moved through, the Matas reasoned, the Marines, infantry, and air support were certain to have secured the area and chased off, or killed the enemy. Odds of Johnny Mata encountering harm or great danger were considered minimal.

But Nancili Mata knew her husband, and it made her worry while her family expressed confidence.

"I did not think he was safe. I said, 'Johnny, I want you to tell me, if a vehicle is broken down, how are you gonna fix it? Are you gonna go out there and fix it, or are they gonna bring it to you?' And he said, 'Well, sometimes they bring them and sometimes you have to go out there and fix them.' And I said, 'Okay, if they break down you send somebody else to fix it,' knowing well that he wouldn't do that. He would go out there."

She believed in her president, though. This was the United States of America. George W. Bush had grown up just down the highway to the east. He had to have the basic, common sense that comes from learning to live on such a harsh, unforgiving landscape. Nancili Mata shared that with the most powerful man in the world. Her family traced its lineage way back to the days when the state had been called Tejas, and it was ruled by Mexico. She knew the kind of sensibilities a place like this could provide a person, the cold, clear judgment it taught by the desert heat. There was no reason not to trust a president who came from here. Surely, her president would be guided by restraint and honor, a wisdom swept clean by the dry, desert winds of his youth.

Instead, Nancili Mata has new troubles.

"I worry, sometimes, that he [God] will come for me, too. And I'm ready. I want to go be with Johnny. But we . . . I've got these two kids to raise. I have to be here for them. I want to see them grow up. And then I'll go see Johnny."

Eric, who is 16, has already made plans. After high school graduation, he will enlist. "My intentions are to go into the Army," he said. "My father's death has strengthened that decision."

Stephani Mata walked up and touched her mother's arm, needing nothing more than closeness. Just then, Nancili tilted her head back and lifted her eyes toward heaven, as if she were speaking directly to her husband. Her gaze burned through the makeshift awning protecting her from the white, hot Texas sky.

"Wait for me," she said.

And then her voice softened.

"I'll be there. But not yet."

A Letter to the President from the Father of a Fallen Marine

Tonopah, NV.   November 30, 2003

Mr. President,

March 23. That day will be forever a day for my family and I to remember, for two reasons. One, March 23, 2001, our adopted son, a boy who we raised through high school, who called me "dad" and my wife "mom" was commissioned a second lieutenant in the U.S. Marine Corps. He excelled at everything he did, from being a star athlete in football and basketball, an honor roll student, to being a husband and father, and a son. The Marine Corps recognized that he was one of the best of the best, saw what a good person and leader he was, and did something about it.

He was accepted into the Officer Candidate Program, where he excelled again, completing a four-year degree at Oregon State University, and was commissioned a second lieutenant, as I say, on March 23, 2001. It was one of the proudest moments of his life, and for his wife, Chelle, and infant daughter, Taylor, also. We were fortunate to be there to see it, as we never missed the important things in his life. His ball games, graduation from high school, graduation from boot camp as the number one recruit in his company, his wedding to Chelle, and his commissioning. These bright spots in his life, and our life, and the thousands of other memories, are all we have left now. You see, your decision to invade Iraq took what was to be, the future, away from him, and his family.

The second reason March 23 will remain so vivid to us, is that is the day our son was killed in Iraq, two years to the day after he was commissioned a second lieutenant.

First Lieutenant Frederick E. Pokorney Jr., USMC, died a horrible death that day in the desert in Iraq, along with many others, and we will always wonder why, Mr. President. Sure, we have listened to the "reasons" for this war, and have also wondered why you rushed into this so poorly prepared, against all reason, and even against the advice of your own father, who sent troops there before you.

The spin you put on this invasion has caught up with you, or should I use the correct word, "deception"? The lie about Saddam being involved with September 11, the weapons of mass destruction, not following the U.N. accords, et al. But they never held water, and now over 400 dead soldiers have come home, leaving nothing but memories for their families. Can you ever really convince people that Saddam was an immediate threat to the United States when he was basically the Mayor of Baghdad since the 1991 war in the Persian Gulf? Our air power made it impossible for him to be anything else. He murdered his own people. That is the next reason, right? When your father sold out the Shiites in 1991, he, and you, knew the bloodbath was coming, and it did. Millions were killed in Rwanda, and we never lifted a finger, so what is the real reason for this invasion?

I see. We needed to free the Iraqi people and rebuild Iraq. Why did you use such destruction in the first place, when there was little resistance? I am forgetting, the big corporations, such as Halliburton, Cheney's people, who helped you get elected, got multibillion dollar contracts with no bid process to rebuild Iraq, and you stripped cost-control measures so they can exceed the money allotted. Is this the real reason you have used and abused our military, in the name of patriotism and the War on Terror? You used our own anxieties and fears from Sept. 11 to convince people to support this invasion, but not everyone believed you. I am a Vietnam combat veteran, and we remember the lies and deceptions used then as 60,000 of us died in the service of our country while billions in profit from the war was made. We became the scapegoats of a war we won every day, but were never allowed to finish, but we served proudly, leaving politics to others as the body count mounted.

I cry inside every time the news comes on, knowing they will say more U.S. soldiers are dead, and why? You allowed over 400 to die before you would use the weapons that would stop the daily random killing of our troops. Why? An elitist such as yourself was protected from duty in Vietnam by your father, so someone had to go in your place. Maybe this is one reason you have no idea how many lives you have ruined forever, because you and your family were always protected from serving and dying.

More questions, Mr. President. Why are you so concerned, if that is the right word, about Iraq having power and schools, and medical care, to the tune of 166 billion dollars, when most people can't afford medicine, lose power, and have substandard schools in America? Is it a matter of oil, or is that the easy answer? Are you going to appease the crowd that says, "Do something, don't sit around," when it comes to fighting terror, by sending our troops into ill-thought out invasions where they were not properly trained or equipped for this fight? How many dead will it take before you admit this invasion hasn't slowed down terrorists, or that your stupid comment, "Bring 'em on," encouraged our enemies to do just that? How many dead will appease those who want you to "do something," even if it is wrong?

I have many more thoughts, but what I have to say will not change what you do. Many more will die, and maybe someday you will tell the truth about why they died. We want to know. Chelle Pokorney wants to know, and I know Taylor Pokorney will want to know someday. Our son, the best person I have ever known, is gone, a hero who gave his life for his country, and many more followed him to Arlington. You got your war, Mr. President, against all advice, and the cost in American lives mounts every day with nothing changing over there, except more grieving families here. Can you live with that, Mr. President? I hope not.

Wade Lieseke
Tonopah, Nevada

NOTES

Introduction

Chapter 1: No Guns, No Glory

Page 3   "'If we don't take those bridges . . .'" Lieutenant Ben Reid's May 19, 2003 debriefing document.

Page 4   "'We're dead,' . . ." Lieutenant Ben Reid's recall of Pokorney comment during conversation with Chelle Pokorney.

Page 4   "'From what I remember,' . . ." See previous note.

Page 5   "Pokorney and Reid had become . . ." Interview with Ben Reid, June 2003.

Page 5   "'After September 11, . . .'" Interview with Chelle Pokorney, June 2003.

Page 6   "'I remember when Fred . . .'" Interview with Wade Lieseke, Tonopah, Nevada, June 2003.

Page 7   "'Here we are, advancing . . .'" Interview with Reid, June 2003.

Page 8   "On the combat radio . . ." See previous note.

Page 8   "'I still don't know where . . .'" See previous note.

Page 9   "'I hate to say this, . . .'" See previous note.

Page 9   "Very quickly, Reid and Pokorney's men . . ." See previous note.

Page 10   "'Hey, I'm hit, . . .'" Interview with Reid, June 2003, provided exact detail of Pokorney's words at the time of shooting.

Page 11   "Grabbing the maps . . ." Reid debriefing document, May 19, 2003.

Page 12   "'We've got no . . .'" Interview with Reid, June 2003, his detailed memory of exchange with Pokorney.

Page 12   "'Sir, Torres has been hit,' . . ." Reid debriefing document, May 19, 2003.

Page 13   "'I was glad Fred told me . . .'" See previous note.

Page 13   "'Espinoza, come up here . . .'" See previous note.

Page 14   "'I guess that was kinda stupid,' . . ." Reid interview, June 2003.

Page 14   "'Sir, Buessing is dead.' . . ." See previous note.

Page 15   "'I didn't go check on Fred,' . . ." See previous note.

Page 15   ". . . as a 'magical round' . . ." Reid debriefing document, May 19, 2003.

Chapter 2: A Beautiful Lie

Page 17   "'. . . do not leave the Israelis . . .'" Anonymous, August 2003.

Page 18   "'. . . Judge whether good enough . . .'" "Plans for Iraq Attack Began on 9/11," CBSNews.com, by David Martin, September 4, 2002.

Page 19   "'We're takin' him out.' . . ." "First Stop, Iraq" by Michael Elliott and James Carney, *Time*, March 4, 2002.

Page 20   "'Let's look at it simply,' . . ." "Wolfowitz: Iraq War Was About Oil," by George Wright, *Guardian Newspapers*, June 4, 2003.

Page 22   ". . . he harbored terrorists . . ." The White House, "A Decade of Defiance and Deception," September 12, 2002.

Page 22   "'. . . Saddam is the infidel,' . . ." Anonymous, June 2003.

Page 23   "'Their presence there over . . .'" "Deputy Secretary Wolfowitz Interview with Sam Tannenhaus, Vanity Fair," *DoD News*, May 9, 2003.

Page 24   "A Sunday morning story, . . ." "Threat and Responses: The Iraqis; U.S. Says Hussein Intensifies Quest for A-Bomb Parts," by Michael Gordon and Judith Miller, *New York Times*, September 8, 2003.

Page 25   "'In the last 14 months,' . . ." See previous note.

Page 25   "'the aluminum tubes were intended . . .'" See previous note.

Page 26   "'We made many, many calls,' . . ." Interview with Judy Miller, September 2003.

Page 26   ". . . appeared to be talking about . . ." "Depiction of Threat Outgrew Evidence," by Barton Gellman and Walter Pincus, *Washington Post*, August 10, 2003.

Page 27   "'We tried to get other intell . . .'" Interview with Judy Miller, September 2003.

Page 27   "Knowing that the war effort . . ." "Depiction of Threat Outgrew Evidence," by Barton Gellman and Walter Pincus, *Washington Post*, August 10, 2003.

Page 28   "'The media keeps creating . . .'" Interview with Hussain Haqqani, May 2003.

Page 29   "'And what we've seen recently . . .'" Transcript of NBC-TV's *Meet the Press* interview with Vice President Dick Cheney.

Page 30   "The strongest assertions were . . ." Transcript, *CNN's Late Edition* with Wolf Blitzer.

Page 31   "Andrea Mitchell of NBC News, . . ." "The Miller Brouhaha," by Charles Layton, *American Journalism Review*, July 2003.

Page 31   "'An alarming disclosure.' . . ." See previous note.

Page 31   "An Italian rocket, . . ." "Depiction of Threat Outgrew Evidence," by Barton Gellman and Walter Pincus, *Washington Post*, August 10, 2003.

Page 32   "Those plans had been stolen . . ." See previous note.

Page 32   "'It would have been extremely difficult . . .'" See previous note.

Page 33   "The findings showed . . ." "Aluminum Tubing Is an Indicator of an Iraqi Gas Centrifuge Program: But Is the Tubing Specifically for Centrifuges?" by David Allbright, *Institute for Science and International Security*, October 9, 2002.

Page 34   "'This is the problem with . . .'" Interview with Judy Miller, September 2003.

Page 34   "But they did . . ." "Where Are Iraq's WMDs?" by Evan Thomas, Richard Wolffe, and Michael Isikoff, *Newsweek*, June 9, 2003.

Page 35   "In a piece about a third as long . . ." "Threats and Responses: Baghdad's Arsenal; White House Lists Iraq Steps to Build

Banned Weapons," by Judith Miller and Michael R. Gordon, *New York Times*, September 13, 2002.

Page 36   "'People who understood gas centrifuges,' . . ." "The Miller Brouhaha," by Charles Layton, *American Journalism Review*, July 2003.

Page 36   "'We worked our asses off . . .'" Interview with Judy Miller, September 2003.

Pages 37–38   ". . . protesting the belief that the tubes . . ." "Evidence on Iraq Challenged," by Joby Warrick, *Washington Post*, September 19, 2002.

Chapter 3: Boys at War

Page 39   "'. . . and I approached James . . .'" Interview with Randy Kiehl, Comfort, Texas, July 2003.

Page 40   "'My hour of need was . . .'" KTVT-TV, Dallas, interview in Kuwait with James Kiehl, March 12, 2003.

Page 41   "'At first, of course, he was . . .'" Interview with Jill Kiehl, Comfort, Texas, August 2003.

Page 41   "'You always have the threat . . .'" KTVT-TV, Dallas, interview in Kuwait with James Kiehl, March 12, 2003.

Page 42   "'Our danger lies to the . . .'" See previous note.

Page 42   "'Go and make disciples . . .'" See previous note.

Page 43   "'James never wanted . . .'" Interview with Randy Kiehl, Comfort, Texas, July 2003.

Page 43   "On the grounds of the White House, . . ." *NBC News*, Tom Brokaw interview with President George W. Bush, April 25, 2003.

Page 44   "'God told me to strike . . .'" *Haaretz*, Israeli newspaper, June 26, 2003.

Page 44   "Shortly after the president's stroll . . ." *NBC News*, Brokaw interview with Bush.

Page 45   "'I was hesitant, . . .'" See previous note.

Page 46   "'That was the Saudis in touch . . .'" Saudi analyst, anonymous.

Page 46   "Since that tally included . . ." Nicholas D. Kristof, *New York Times*, May 6, 2003.

Pages 47–48   ". . . five lanes of vehicles, . . ." *Attack on the 507th Maintenance Company*, U.S. Army, Draft Predecisional, July 9, 2003.

Page 48   "King was also provided . . ." See previous note.

Page 48   ". . . had not ordered briefbacks . . ." See previous note.

Page 49   "'I don't even know who did . . .'" Interview with Jill Kiehl, Comfort, Texas, August 2003.

Page 49   "Back in El Paso . . ." Interview with Darrel Cortez, El Paso, Texas, August 2003.

Page 49   "'I said, "Son, . . ."'" Interview with Randy Kiehl, Comfort, Texas, July 2003.

Page 50   "This was the kind of service . . ." Interview with Nancili Mata, Pecos, Texas, August 2003.

Page 50   "'Too many mistakes, . . .'" See previous note.

Page 50   ". . . whose mother had to be convinced . . ." "A Time to Remember," by Laura Cruz, *El Paso Times*.

Page 50   ". . . objectives, Dawson, Bull, . . ." *Attack on the 507th Maintenance Company*, U.S. Army, Draft Predecisional, July 9, 2003.

Page 51   "While King's smaller group . . ." See previous note.

Page 51   "As the main group was leaving . . ." See previous note.

Page 52   "King seemed determined to catch up . . ." See previous note.

Page 52   "Mistakenly, King had assumed . . ." See previous note.

Page 53   "'The Marines are at a checkpoint, . . .'" Interview with Nancili Mata, Pecos, Texas, August 2003.

Page 53   "'The soldiers of the 507th . . .'" Interview with Laura Cruz, reporter, *El Paso Times*.

Page 54   "'soldiers fight as they are . . .'" Army closehold predecisional draft reports.

Page 54   ". . . lights began to shimmer . . ." *Attack on the 507th Maintenance Company*, U.S. Army, Draft Predecisional, July 9, 2003.

Page 54   "'I thought it was the convoy in front . . .'" NBC News, *Dateline*, Interview with Joe Hudson, et al., 507th Maintenance Company, August 1, 2003.

Page 54   "Only five drivers had . . ." *Attack on the 507th Maintenance Company*, U.S. Army, Draft Predecisional, July 9, 2003.

Page 55   ". . . with Iraqi civilians manning machine guns, . . ." See previous note.

Page 55   "'We passed them,' . . ." NBC News, *Dateline*, Interview with Joe Hudson, et al., 507th Maintenance Company, August 1, 2003.

Page 57   ". . . issued a basic combat load . . ." *Attack on the 507th Maintenance Company*, U.S. Army, Draft Predecisional, July 9, 2003.

Page 57   "'I personally disagree with . . .'" Interview with Darrell Cortez, El Paso, Texas, August 2003.

Page 58   "Choosing to go northward, . . ." *Attack on the 507th Maintenance Company*, U.S. Army, Draft Predecisional, July 9, 2003.

Page 58   "'Lock and load.'" See previous note.

Chapter 4: A Few Young Men

Page 60   "'I looked at that thing . . .'" Interview with Wade Lieseke, Tonopah, Nevada, July 2003.

Page 60   "'Suzy and I dug them out.' . . ." See previous note. Lieseke's detailed memory of conversation with Pokorney.

Page 60   "'Yeah, there's just one thing . . .'" See previous note.

Page 61   "Wade Lieseke invited the young . . ." See previous note.

Page 61   ". . . never struggled to fit in . . ." Interview with Pokorney classmate, Jennifer Klapper, Tonopah, Nevada, July 2003.

Page 61   ". . . 'always good for at least one touchdown . . .'" Interview with Mike Grigg, August 2003.

Page 62   ". . . 'a piece of paper to make him my son.' . . ." Interview with Wade Lieseke, July 2003.

Page 62   "'We always just assumed . . .'" Interview with Suzy Lieseke, Tonopah, Nevada, July 2003.

Page 62   "'He was a pretty independent . . .'" Interview with classmate Mike Grigg, August 2003.

Page 62   "'He was far beyond my . . .'" See previous note.

Page 63   "When he got out of his patrol car, . . ." Interview with Lieseke.

Page 63   "After an injury . . ." See previous note.

Page 64   "'I said, "Fred, my problem . . ."'" See previous note.

Page 64   "Neither he nor his wife, . . ." Interview with Chelle Pokorney, July 2003.

Page 64   ". . . Air Force Colonel William . . ." See previous note.

Page 65   "'It is not in our nature . . .'" Remarks by the president at the Memorial Day Ceremony, Arlington National Cemetery, The White House, Office of the Press Secretary, May 28, 2001.

Page 65   "Fred trusted his president. . . ." Interview with Chelle Pokorney, July 2003.

Page 65   "Hearing their stories . . ." See previous note.

Page 65   "'I want to be buried here . . .'" See previous note. Chelle Pokorney's detailed memory of conversation with Fred Pokorney.

Page 66   "The consequences of those two facts . . ." See previous note.

Page 66   "'We aren't real political people,' . . ." See previous note.

Page 66   "'What I know now is that it was . . .'" Interview with Wade Lieseke, July 2003.

Page 67   "'If we are gonna let the place fall . . .'" See previous note.

Page 67   "'They've got no feeling . . .'" See previous note.

Page 67   "'President on down, . . .'" See previous note.

Page 68   "'Fred did believe . . .'" Interview with Chelle Pokorney, July 2003.

Page 68   "'Take care of Taylor . . .'" See previous note.

Page 68   "'I did have this feeling,' . . ." See previous note.

Page 68   "The tanks had been ordered . . ." "A Deadly Day for Charlie Company," by Rich Connell and Robert J. Lopez, Los Angeles Times, August 26, 2003.

Page 69   "'Say again,' . . ." See previous note.

Page 69   "Body parts of Iraqis . . ." See previous note.

Page 69   "Close air support appeared . . ." "A Deadly Day for Charlie Company," by Rich Connell and Robert J. Lopez, Los Angeles Times, August 26, 2003.

Page 70   "He did not turn over Pokorney, . . ." Interview with Ben Reid, July 2003.

Page 70   ". . . he told one of his injured men, . . ." Ben Reid's debriefing document, "1st Lt. Reid's Account of 23 March 2003 Battle at Al Nasiriyah," May 19, 2003.

Page 70   "'I was scared,' . . ." See previous note.

Page 70   "'I felt really alone, . . .'" See previous note.

Page 70   "His orders to Garibay . . ." See previous note.

Page 71   "'See if my eye is still . . .'" See previous note.

Page 71   "'I guess I started doing . . .'" See previous note.

Page 71   "The gunnery sergeant saw the A-10 . . ." See previous note.

Page 71   "'It's the first time any of us . . .'" Interview with Ben Reid, July 2003.

Page 71   "The A-10 had made other passes . . ." "A Deadly Day for Charlie Company," by Rich Connell and Robert J. Lopez, *Los Angeles Times*, August 26, 2003.

Page 71   "'I remember gunny . . .'" Interview with Ben Reid, July 2003.

Page 71   ". . . did not get hit by the A-10's . . ." Ben Reid's debriefing document, "1st Lt. Reid's Account of 23 March 2003 Battle at Al Nasiriyah," May 19, 2003.

Page 72   "'Fred was not put on a track,' . . ." Interview with Ben Reid, July 2003.

Page 72   ". . . did not see any massive trauma . . ." See previous note.

Page 72   "At least two published reports . . ." "A Deadly Day for Charlie Company," by Rich Connell and Robert J. Lopez, *Los Angeles Times*, August 26, 2003, and "U.S. Marines Turn Fire on Civilians at the Bridge of Death," by Mark Frichetti, *Sunday Times of London*, March 30, 2003.

Page 72   "Much of his torso . . ." Interview with Wade Lieseke, July 2003.

Page 72   "'I saw an A-10 come in from . . .'" Interview with Ben Reid, July 2003.

Page 72   "A bullet entrance wound, . . ." See previous note.

Page 73   ". . . along with another Marine, . . ." See previous note.

Page 73   "'The earth went black . . .'" "Marines Sure They Were Victims of Friendly Fire," by Art Harris, *CNN*, October 2, 2003.

Page 73   "'I'm turning around . . .'" See previous note.

Page 73   "'I wore what was inside . . .'" "A Deadly Day for Charlie Company," by Rich Connell and Robert J. Lopez, *Los Angeles Times*, August 26, 2003.

Page 74   "Malfunctioning pumps . . ." See previous note.

Page 74   ". . . who had been lying . . ." Interview with Ben Reid, July 2003.

Page 74   "'I'm not an emotional person . . .'" Interview with Wade Lieseke, Tonopah, Nevada, July 2003.

Chapter 5: Pioneers of a Warless World

Page 75   "His soldiers were properly armed, . . ." U.S. Army Report, *Attack on the 507th Maintenance Company*, U.S. Army, Draft Predecisional, July 9, 2003.

Page 76   ". . . 'consolidated and secured,' . . ." See previous note.

Page 76   "'No soldier was issued . . .'" Interview with Darrell Cortez, El Paso, Texas, August 2003.

Page 76   "King ordered all vehicles . . ." *Attack on the 507th Maintenance Company*, U.S. Army, Draft Predecisional, July 9, 2003.

Page 76   "King ordered all trucks . . ." See previous note.

Page 77   "Sergeant Dowdy radioed . . ." See previous note.

Page 77   ". . . 'in the rear with the gear.' . . ." Interview with Darrell Cortez, El Paso, Texas, August 2003.

Page 77   "The limited supply of walkie-talkie . . ." Interview with Nancili Mata on her debriefing with U.S. Military, Pecos, Texas, August 2003.

Page 77   "'These people were technicians, . . .'" Interview with Randy Kiehl, Comfort, Texas, August 2003.

Page 78   "'It's his commander-in-chief. . . .'" Interview with Jill Kiehl, Comfort, Texas, August 2003.

Page 78   "A private, Brandon Sloan, . . ." *Attack on the 507th Maintenance Company*, U.S. Army, Draft Predecisional, July 9, 2003.

Page 78   "'It is unclear . . .'" See previous note.

Page 79   "'This is where we start splitting . . .'" NBC News, *Dateline*, "POWs of 507th Recount Ordeal," August 1, 2003.

Page 79   ". . . at the tail end of the column, . . ." *Attack on the 507th Maintenance Company*, U.S. Army, Draft Predecisional, July 9, 2003.

Page 79   ". . . Dowdy wasn't sure . . ." See previous note.

Page 79   "Just a few months earlier, . . ." Interview with Nancili Mata, Pecos, Texas, August 2003.

Page 80   "'Those devices, they didn't have . . .'" See previous note.

Page 80   ". . . trucks on a dangerous run . . ." *Attack on the 507th Maintenance Company*, U.S. Army, Draft Predecisional, July 9, 2003.

Page 81   ". . . 'inadequate individual maintenance . . .'" See previous note.

Page 81   "King came upon tanks . . ." See previous note.

Page 81   ". . . those same tanks . . ." Interview with Ben Reid, July 2003.

Page 82   ". . . Damien Luten jumped up . . ." *Attack on the 507th Maintenance Company*, U.S. Army, Draft Predecisional, July 9, 2003.

Page 82   "'I was up there, . . .'" ABC News, "The Real Story of Jessica Lynch's Convoy," June 17, 2003.

Page 82   ". . . shot in the knee. . . ." See previous note.

Page 82   ". . . who had been driving, . . ." *Attack on the 507th Maintenance Company*, U.S. Army, Draft Predecisional, July 9, 2003.

Page 82   "The Humvee, with a man . . ." See previous note.

Page 82   ". . . turned around in the midst . . ." See previous note.

Page 83   "'My vehicle was being . . .'" "Thoughts of Family Sustained Soldier," by Laura Cruz, *El Paso Times*, July 17, 2003.

Page 83   "James Grubb, a specialist, . . ." *Attack on the 507th Maintenance Company*, U.S. Army, Draft Predecisional, July 9, 2003.

Page 83   "When the mortar fire . . ." "Thoughts of Family Sustained Soldier," by Laura Cruz, *El Paso Times*, July 17, 2003.

Page 84   ". . . Marines from Task Force Tarawa, . . ." *Attack on the 507th Maintenance Company*, U.S. Army, Draft Predecisional, July 9, 2003.

Page 84   "Hernandez had been ducking . . ." NBC News, *Dateline*, "POWs of 507th Recount Ordeal," August 1, 2003.

Page 84   ". . . ordered his driver . . ." *Attack on the 507th Maintenance Company*, U.S. Army, Draft Predecisional, July 9, 2003.

Page 84   "'Machine gun fire,' . . ." NBC News, *Dateline*, "POWs of 507th Recount Ordeal," August 1, 2003.

Page 84–85   ". . . 'unloading on anything . . .'" See previous note.

Page 85   ". . . slammed into the back of Hernandez' . . ." *Attack on the 507th Maintenance Company*, U.S. Army, Draft Predecisional, July 9, 2003.

Page 85   "'There was one point . . .'" "Ex-POW Tells of Firefight, Capture," by Maribel Villalva, *El Paso Times*.

Page 85   "'. . . all of a sudden,' . . ." NBC News, *Dateline*, "POWs of 507th Recount Ordeal," August 1, 2003.

Page 85   "The Army was unable to . . ." *Attack on the 507th Maintenance Company*, U.S. Army, Draft Predecisional, July 9, 2003.

Page 86   ". . . 'no movement whatsoever' . . ." NBC News, *Dateline*, "POWs of 507th Recount Ordeal," August 1, 2003.

Page 86   ". . . while Hudson struggled . . ." See previous note.

Page 86   "'At this point,' . . ." See previous note.

Page 86   ". . . and pulled out Hernandez, . . ." *Attack on the 507th Maintenance Company*, U.S. Army, Draft Predecisional, July 9, 2003.

Page 86   "'After he got shot in the leg,' . . ." Interview with Nancili Mata, Pecos, Texas, August 2003.

Page 87   "'Just pop, pop, pop,' . . ." NBC News, *Dateline*, "POWs of 507th Recount Ordeal," August 1, 2003.

Page 87   ". . . Riley reached into the wreckage . . ." *Attack on the 507th Maintenance Company*, U.S. Army, Draft Predecisional, July 9, 2003.

Page 87   "'Is anyone alive?' . . ." ABC News, "The Real Story of Jessica Lynch's Convoy," June 17, 2003.

Page 87   ". . . Lynch's foot was twitching . . ." NBC News, *Dateline*, "POWs of 507th Recount Ordeal," August 1, 2003.

Page 87   "'The weapons are jamming up. . . .'" See previous note.

Page 87   ". . . try and commandeer an Iraqi truck . . ." *Attack on the 507th Maintenance Company*, U.S. Army, Draft Predecisional, July 9, 2003.

Page 88   "'Trying to take cover . . .'" NBC News, *Dateline*, "POWs of 507th Recount Ordeal," August 1, 2003.

Page 88   "'I seen [sic] a group . . .'" See previous note.

Page 88   "'None of the weapons were . . .'" See previous note.

Page 89   ". . . 'maneuvered several miles under fire.' . . ." *Attack on the 507th Maintenance Company*, U.S. Army, Draft Predecisional, July 9, 2003.

Page 89   ". . . colliding with the barrel of an Iraqi tank. . . ." See previous note.

Page 90   "'The Estrella-Soto family is . . .'" Interview with Laura Cruz of the *El Paso Times*, El Paso, Texas, August 2003.

Page 91   "'They said just because of the . . .'" Interview with Jill Kiehl, Comfort, Texas, August 2003.

Page 91   ". . . 'kind of kid who was more interested in protecting . . .'" Interview with Colin Toot, Comfort, Texas, August 2003.

Page 92   "'God has a reason,' . . ." Interview with Randy Kiehl, Comfort, Texas, August 2003.

Chapter 6: That Awful Power

Page 93   ". . . in 'nondescript clothing,' . . ." "AFTEREFFECTS: PRO-HIBITED WEAPONS; Illicit Arms Kept Till Eve of War, An Iraqi Scientist Is Said to Assert," by Judith Miller, *New York Times*, April 21, 2003.

Page 94   "'A scientist who claims to have . . .'" See previous note.

Page 94   ". . . the 'major discovery' . . ." See previous note.

Page 94   "'Under the terms of her . . .'" See previous note.

Page 95   "'I had an independent . . .'" Interview with Judy Miller, September 2003.

Page 95   ". . . 'made clear that Judy Miller was aware . . .'" "Scoops and Truths at the Times," by Russ Baker, *Nation*, June 5, 2003.

Page 96   "'I have a photograph . . .'" Interview with Judy Miller, September 2003.

Page 96   "'In terms of information . . .'" Interview with Richard Gonzales, October 2003.

Page 96   "'Has the unit . . .'" "Miller Brouhaha," by Charles Layton, *American Journalism Review*, August/September 2003.

Page 96   "'. . . more than a smoking gun,' . . ." See previous note.

Page 97   "'Reporter Judith Miller' . . ." See previous note.

Page 97   ". . . a scientist had told . . ." See previous note.

Page 97   "'In an interview with Fox today,' . . ." See previous note.

Page 97   "'But those stockpiles that we've . . .'" "Search for Evidence," *The Newshour with Jim Lehrer*, April 23, 2003.

Page 98   "'And that's what the Bush administration . . .'" See previous note.

Page 98   "'He had been ordered to destroy . . .'" "Miller Brouhaha," by Charles Layton, *American Journalism Review*, August/September 2003.

Page 99   "'. . . an edited version . . ." See previous note.

Page 99   ". . . 'politically potent use . . .'" "Pulitzer Prize Winning Reporter Crosses the New York Times' Line of Strict Neutrality," by Daniel Forbes, *Globalvision News Network*, May 7, 2003.

Page 99   "Talk show host Rush . . ." See previous note.

Page 100   "'It's very vague . . .'" See previous note.

Page 100   "'What's surprising and I think . . .'" "Scoops and Truths at the Times," by Russ Baker, *Nation*, June 5, 2003.

Page 100   "'You go with what you've . . .'" Interview with Judy Miller, September 2003.

Page 100   "'You have to accept terms . . .'" See previous note.

Page 101   "'Most pungently,' . . ." "Deep Miller: Did the New York Times Just Change the Rules of Journalism?" by Jack Shafer, *Slate.com*, April 21, 2003.

Page 101   "'Surrounding this whole saga,' . . ." "Still Miller Time: New York Times Circles the Wagons; Paper Criticized for Iraq

WMD Coverage," by William E. Jackson Jr., *Editor and Publisher Magazine*, July 2, 2003.

Page 102   "'Bart Gellman [*Post* reporter] tried as hard as . . .'" Interview with Judy Miller, September 2003.

Page 102   "'I did not come to debunk . . .'" Interview with Barton Gellman, October 2003.

Page 103   "'Did she really say that?' . . ." See previous note.

Page 103   "'To me, it was world-class . . .'" "Search for Evidence," *The Newshour with Jim Lehrer*, April 23, 2003.

Pages 103–104   "According to a military court . . ." "After Saddam: The Controversy over Ahmad Chalabi," by Max Singer, *National Review Online*, June 20, 2003.

Page 104   ". . . a state department audit of his spending . . ." "Ahmad Chalabi and A New Iraq," *The Newshour with Jim Lehrer*, May 7, 2003.

Page 105   "Baghdad Bureau Chief John Burns, . . ." "Intra-Times Battle Over Iraqi Weapons," by Howard Kurtz, *Washington Post*, May 26, 2003.

Page 105   "'I am deeply chagrined . . .'" See previous note.

Page 105   "'I've been covering Chalabi . . .'" See previous note.

Page 106   "'Of course, I talked with . . .'" Interview with Judy Miller, September 2003.

Page 106   "'The White House Iraq Group had . . .'" Interview, anonymous, with CIA analyst.

Page 108   "'Paradigm shift, my ass!' . . ." "Follow That Story: Deep Miller; Is the New York Times Breaking the News or Flacking for the Military?," by Jack Shafer, *Slate.com*, April 23, 2003.

Page 109   ". . . turned MET Alpha into a 'rogue operation,' . . ." "Embedded Reporter's Role In Army Unit's Actions Questioned by Military," by Howard Kurtz, *Washington Post*, June 25, 2003.

Page 109   "'That really pissed me off,' . . ." Interview with Richard Gonzales, October 2003.

Page 109   "'I don't know how either of them . . .'" Interview with Barton Gellman, October 2003.

Page 110   "'Let me just tell you,' . . ." Interview with Richard Gonzales, October 2003.

Page 110   "'I see no reason for me . . .'" "Embedded Reporter's Role In Army Unit's Actions Questioned by Military," by Howard Kurtz, *Washington Post*, June 25, 2003.

Page 111   "'Judith was always issuing . . .'" See previous note.

Page 111   "'We think she did some good work . . .'" See previous note.

Page 111   "'I'll tell you this, too,' . . ." Interview with Richard Gonzales, October 2003.

Page 112   "An eyewitness related to . . ." "Embedded Reporter's Role In Army Unit's Actions Questioned by Military," by Howard Kurtz, *Washington Post*, June 25, 2003.

Page 113   "'If he'd ever bothered to ask me . . .'" Interview with Richard Gonzales, October 2003.

Page 113   "'This was totally out of their lane, . . .'" "Embedded Reporter's Role In Army Unit's Actions Questioned by Military," by Howard Kurtz, *Washington Post*, June 25, 2003.

Page 113   "'These so-called facts . . .'" Interview with Judy Miller, September 2003.

Page 113   "'I don't know why Mr. Kurtz chose . . .'" Letter from Colonel Ted Seel to *Washington Post* ombudsman, author's copy.

Page 114   "'She didn't bring MET Alpha . . .'" "Embedded Reporter's Role In Army Unit's Actions Questioned by Military," by Howard Kurtz, *Washington Post*, June 25, 2003.

Page 114   "'Howard Kurtz' article . . .'" Letter from Richard Gonzales to *Washington Post* ombudsman, author's copy.

Page 114   "'Your article makes several false . . .'" Letter from Zaeb Sethna, Iraqi National Congress, to *Washington Post* editor, author's copy.

Page 115   "'But I did not put those people . . .'" Interview with Barton Gellman, October 2003.

Page 116   "Founded by Daniel Pipes, . . ." "Pulitzer Prize Winning Reporter Crosses the New York Times' Line of Strict Neutrality," by Daniel Forbes, *Globalvision News Network*, May 7, 2003.

Page 116   "'Saddam Husayn [sic] poses . . .'" See previous note.

Page 116   "As far back as 1990, . . ." See previous note.

Page 116   "'West European societies,' . . ." See previous note.

Page 117   "The Middle East Forum (MEF) also . . ." See previous note.

Page 117   "'If I didn't think it was appropriate,' . . ." See previous note.

Page 118   "'I'm declining to answer,' . . ." See previous note.

Page 118   "'My question would be,' . . ." See previous note.

Page 118   "'The Islamic threat,' . . ." "A Devil Theory of Islam," by Edward W. Said, *Nation*, July 25, 2000.

Page 119   ". . . less than conventional obituary . . ." "Commentary of Edward Said," *Wall Street Journal*, September 29, 2003.

Page 119   ". . . a 'weapon(s) in the contest . . .'" "A Devil Theory of Islam," by Edward W. Said, *Nation*, July 25, 2000.

Page 120   "'Just imagine a book,' . . ." See previous note.

Page 120   ". . . blamed for factual errors . . ." See previous note.

Page 120   "'You know what,' . . ." Interview with Judy Miller, September 2003.

Page 121   ". . . ridiculed Miller's tactics . . ." "Embedded Super Reporter Judith Miller Reveals Raiders Won 2003 Super Bowl," by Dennis Hans, Take Back the *Media.com*, February 7, 2003.

Page 121   "'Based on that evidence, . . .'" See previous note.

Page 122   "'It didn't occur to me . . .'" Interview with Judy Miller, September 2003.

Page 122   ". . . 'a wacky-assed piece.' . . ." "Off the Record," by Sridhar Pappu, *New York Observer*.

Chapter 7: Rewards of Service

Dialogue and quotes for this chapter were the result of various interviews and e-mail conversations with Bill Burkett, which took place over the course of several months during the latter half of 2003. Material for the narrative is drawn largely from Burkett's recollection. The author's own experience reporting on the Waco tragedy at Mount Carmel, and the Bush speech at The Citadel, are the source of analysis on those portions of the narrative. Major General Danny James was interviewed by telephone in January 2004 subsequent to the comments made by Bill Burkett.

Chapter 8: Bird of Pray

The interview with Richard Cunnare, which provides most of the detail for this chapter, was conducted over the course of two days in July of 2003. Dialogue was created through Cunnare's memory of events related to his shoot down, as well as his own historical notes. Context related to the history of the Vietnam War was acquired from various sources, and relates commonly accepted histories of American involvement during the time period described in the narrative.

Chapter 9: The Ghost Soldier

Page 149   "Word had reached . . ." Interview, anonymous, Bush associate.

Page 149   "After only 22 months . . ." AO S7, National Guard Bureau document, dated September 19, 1972, "Verbal orders of the commander on 1 Aug. suspending 1st Lt. George W. Bush."

Page 150   "Bush formally asked to serve . . ." Application for Reserve Assignment, Guard document.

Page 150   ". . . last flight at the Ellington air wing . . ." Interview with Lieutenant Bob Rogers, analysis of records, September 2002.

Page 150   ". . . a postal unit in Alabama. . . ." Application for Reserve Assignment, Guard document.

Page 150   "'We met just one week . . .'" "One Year Gap in Bush's National Guard Duty," by Walter V. Robinson, *Boston Globe,* May 23, 2000.

Page 150   "'The continuation of this type . . .'" Alabama National Guard document, dated May 26, 1972, signed by Reese W. Bricken.

Page 151   "'He is ineligible . . .'" Deptartment of the Air Force document Fm 1288, May 1972, from Director of Personnel Resources.

Page 151   ". . . 'would be for the months . . .'" Letter to Colonel Killian, signed by GWB, dated September 5, 1972.

Page 151   ". . . included orders that he appear . . ." AL-AFAB transfer approval document, signed by Kenneth Lott, dated September 15, 1972.

Page 151   "'. . . flight requirements with our group.' . . ." See previous note.

Page 151   "'I'm dead certain . . .'" "One Year Gap in Bush's National Guard Duty," by Walter V. Robinson, *Boston Globe*, May 23, 2000.

Page 152   ". . . also said he has no memory . . ." See previous note.

Page 152   "'Governor Bush specifically remembers . . .'" "Record of Bush's Ala. Military Duty Can't Be Found," by Wayne Slater, *Dallas Morning News*, June 25, 2000.

Page 152   "'I was there on a temporary . . .'" See previous note.

Page 153   ". . . a reward of $1000 offered . . ." "Questions Remain on Bush's Service as Guard Pilot," by Walter V. Robinson, *Boston Globe*, October 31, 2000.

Page 153   "'If he did, . . .'" "Onc Year Gap in Bush's National Guard Duty," by Walter V. Robinson, *Boston Globe*, May 23, 2000.

Page 153   "'Bush is supposed to have orders,' . . ." Martin Heldt interview, September 2003.

Page 154   ". . . 'worthless' and 'not dependable' . . ." Interview, anonymous, September 2003.

Page 154   "'Reason for suspension: . . .'" AO S7, National Guard Bureau document, dated September 19 , 1972, "Verbal orders of the commander on 1 Aug. suspending 1st Lt. George W. Bush."

Page 155   ". . . 'family physician was unavailable' . . ." "Questions Remain on Bush's Service as Guard Pilot," by Walter V. Robinson, *Boston Globe*, October 31, 2000.

Page 155   "'It was just a question . . .'" "Bush's Military Record Reveals Grounding and Absence for Two Full Years," by Lieutenant Robert Rogers.

Page 156   ". . . the Pentagon announced plans . . ." 12-31-69, DoD Directive 1010.4: *Drug and Alcohol Abuse Prevention*, by DoD Personnel.

Page 156   ". . . 'points to a potentially devastating . . .'" "Bush's Military Record Reveals Grounding and Absence for Two Full Years," by Lieutenant Robert Rogers.

Page 157   "'His flying status . . .'" "2 Democrats: Bush Let Guard Down," by George Lardner and Howard Kurtz, *Washington Post,* November 3, 2000.

Page 157   ". . . and knocked over garbage cans . . ." "At Height of Vietnam, Bush Picks Guard," by George Lardner and Lois Romano, *Washington Post,* July 28, 1999.

Page 157   ". . . 'mano a mano' . . ." See previous note.

Page 158   "'Have you ever been arrested, . . .'" Enlistment Contract for Armed Forces of the United States, #32298, dated May 27, 1968, signed by GWB.

Page 158   ". . . four questions about criminal behavior. . . ." Statement for Enlistment in the National Guard document, dated May 27, 1968, signed by GWB.

Page 159   "'. . . arrested, indicted, or convicted . . .'" Request and Authorization for Active Duty Training/Active Duty Tour document, dated May 28, 1968, signed by GWB.

Page 159   "'Not Observed' on all 55 different . . ." Officer Effectiveness Rating, Annual Report, 1 May 73—30 April 73, dated May 2, 1973, Wm. D. Harris Jr., Jerry Killian.

Page 159   "'Lt. Bush has not been . . .'" See previous note.

Page 159   "'He cleared this base . . .'" See previous note.

Page 160   ". . . director of personnel at Ellington . . ." "One Year Gap in Bush's National Guard Duty," by Walter V. Robinson, *Boston Globe,* May 23, 2000.

Page 160   ". . . no record of any duty . . ." Chronological Listing of Services document.

Page 160   "'That's the part I sure . . .'" Interview with Lieutenant Robert Rogers, September 2003.

Page 161   "'We didn't let anyone . . .'" Interviews with Bill Burkett, various dates.

Page 161   "A Riverside, New Jersey . . ." "Reservist Loses Plea," *New York Times,* July 7, 1967.

Page 161   "A similar case . . ." Marine Reactivated, *New York Times,* July 18, 1968.

Page 162   "'I understand that I may be ordered . . .'" Statement of Understanding, Ellington Air Force Base, dated May 27, 1968, signed by GWB and witnessed by Willie J. Hooper.

Page 162   "Paragraph F said . . ." See previous note.

Page 162   "'If I fail to participate, . . .'" See previous note.

Page 163   "'When the two commanders simply said . . .'" Interviews with Bill Burkett, various dates.

Page 163   "Campaign officials clearly believed . . ." "Bush's Guard Attendance is Questioned and Defended," by Jo Thomas, *New York Times*, November 3, 2000.

Page 163   "'National Guard records provided . . .'" See previous note.

Page 164   "This points statement, . . ." ARF Statement of Points Earned, Document 99 from FOIA files [with annotations by Albert Lloyd].

Page 164   "A letter 'N,' . . ." See previous note.

Page 165   "'I had his social security . . .'" Interview with Albert Lloyd, October 2003.

Page 165   "'I found it in a general . . .'" See previous note.

Page 166   " . . . 'very unusual,' . . ." Guard interview, anonymous.

Page 166   "'This is a story that just really . . .'" Martin Heldt interview, September 2003.

Page 167   "First posted on the web site of . . ." "The Real Military Record of George W. Bush: Not Heroic, but not AWOL, Either," by Peter Keating and Karthik Thyagarajan, *George Magazine*, October 10, 2000.

Page 167   "'Yeah, that's my . . .'" Interview with Albert Lloyd, October 2003.

Page 168   "'. . . certain duty days.' . . ." AL-AFAB transfer approval document, signed by Kenneth Lott, dated September 15, 1972.

Page 168   "'We don't even know that . . .'" Martin Heldt interview, September 2003.

Page 168   "Harkness must also have been suspicious. . . ." Notice of Missing or Correction of Officer Effectiveness Training Report, dated June 29, 1973, signed by Daniel P. Harkness.

Page 169   "'Ratings must be entered . . .'" See previous note.

Page 170   "'Report for this period . . .'" Supplemental sheet to AF for 77a, signed by Rufus G. Martin.

Page 170   ". . . top 5 percent of all pilots . . ." "One Year Gap in Bush's National Guard Duty," by Walter V. Robinson, *Boston Globe*, May 23, 2000.

Page 170   ". . . he 'doesn't get his kicks . . .'" Office of Information news release, 147th Combat Crew Training Group, Ellington AFB, March 24, 1970.

Page 170   "'If Bush had come back . . .'" "Questions Remain on Bush's Service as Guard Pilot," by Walter V. Robinson, *Boston Globe*, October 31, 2000.

Page 170   ". . . for duty on specific days: . . ." Special Order AE=226=TX, dated May 1, 1973, document signed by Billy B. Lamar.

Page 171   "'This document,' . . ." "Bush's Military Record Reveals Grounding and Absence for Two Full Years," by Lieutenant Robert Rogers.

Page 172   "Thomas' narrative further confused . . ." "Bush's Guard Attendance is Questioned and Defended," by Jo Thomas, *New York Times*, November 3, 2000.

Page 174   ". . . was not a minor event. . . ." Interview with Lieutenant Robert Rogers, September 2003.

Page 174   "'If a full file . . .'" Interviews with Bill Burkett, various dates.

Page 175   "'Pay records are kept . . .'" Interview with Albert Lloyd, October 2003.

Page 175   "'As I've tried to point out to . . .'" Interviews with Bill Burkett, various dates.

Chapter 10: Flying Colors

Similar to Chapter 8, this narrative was constructed with the recollections of Richard Cunnare, as well as videotapes, his own notes, and records. Dialogue was built through extensive interviews with Cunnare over the course of two days in July 2003.

Chapter 11: A Congressman's Son

Page 210   "'I didn't know what . . .'" Interviews with Bill Burkett, various dates.

Page 211   "'Bill Burkett, a former . . .'" "Ghost Soldiers Inflate Guard Numbers," by Dave Moniz, *USA Today*, December 18, 2001.

Page 212   ". . . and a number of other states . . ." Interview with Major General Danny James, January 2004.

Page 212   "'. . . You've been warned and . . .'" Text of call recorded by Burkett.

Page 213   "'General James, this is Joe Allbaugh,' . . ." Burkett's reconstruction of conversational details.

Page 214   "'The governor's office just said . . .'" e-mail from Bill Burkett.

Page 214   "According to Burkett's commanding . . ." Interview with Major General Danny James, January 2004.

Page 215   "'I'm sure I didn't have . . .'" See previous note.

Page 216   " . . . 'Karen Hughes of the governor's . . .'" Interviews with Bill Burkett, various dates.

Page 216   "'. . . just no big deal . . .'" See previous note.

Page 216   ". . . 'It is reasonable to think . . .'" Interview with Major General Danny James, January 2004.

Page 217   ". . . where Scribner was working, . . ." See previous note.

Page 218   "'There was no doubt . . .'" See previous note.

Page 219   "'That's just bullshit,' . . ." Interview with Albert Lloyd, October 2003.

Page 219   "'John Scribner manages . . .'" Interview with Major General Danny James, January 2004.

Page 219   "'. . . Guard will not be responding . . .'" Interview with Sergeant Gregory Ripps, Texas National Guard Public Affairs Officer, Camp Mabry, Austin.

Page 219   ". . . was first asked . . ." Author's question as debate panelist, Belo Broadcasting gubernatorial debate, 1994.

Page 223   "'The minute after . . .'" Texas National Guard interview, anonymous.

Page 224   "Littwin alleged that his dismissal . . ." "Bush Friend Pushed for Guard Slot, Ex-Speaker Testifies," by George Lardner Jr., *Washington Post,* September 28, 1999.

Page 224   ". . . Barnes frequently took requests . . ." "Bush Reportedly was Helped in Joining Guard Unit in Vietnam Era," by George Lardner Jr., *Washington Post,* September 9, 1999.

Page 224   ". . . Barnes became the highest-paid . . ." "Barnes, Partner to get $23 Million in G-Tech Buyout," by George Kuempel, *Dallas Morning News,* June 19, 1997.

Page 224   "'The time has come,' . . ." Texas Lottery Commission memo from Harriet Miers to Kim Kiplin, dated February 18, 1997, signed by Harriet Miers.

Page 224   ". . . had sent Allbaugh notebooks . . ." Locke, Purnell, Rain, Harrell letterhead memo from Harriet Miers to Joe Allbaugh, March 7, 1996, signed by Harriet Miers.

Page 225   "Linares was fired, . . ." Interview with Nora Linares, July 2003.

Page 225   "'Several months ago . . .'" Author's copy of anonymous letter leaked to reporters.

Page 226   ". . . 'neither Bush's father nor any other . . .'" "Bush Reportedly was Helped in Joining Guard Unit in Vietnam Era," by George Lardner Jr., *Washington Post,* September 9, 1999.

Page 226   ". . . who asked Barnes to recommend . . ." "Draft-Dodge Tale Threatens Bush's Run for Presidency," by Julian Borger, *Guardian of London,* September 29, 1999.

Page 227   "'Don Evans reported . . .'" See previous note.

Page 227   ". . . a 'lightning rod,' . . ." "Lottery to Keep G-Tech Contract," by Ken Herman, *Austin American-Statesman,* April 10, 1998.

Page 227   "G-Tech's main lobbyists became . . ." "Bush Announces Rules to Limit Lobbying when Staffers Leave," by Wayne Slater, *Dallas Morning News,* September 4, 2003.

Page 228   ". . . got a 25 on the 'pilot aptitude' . . ." "At Height of Vietnam, Bush Picks Guard," by George Lardner Jr. and Lois Romano, *Washington Post,* July 28, 1999.

Page 228   "'Do not volunteer.' . . ." See previous note.

Page 228   ". . . the colonel again staged . . ." See previous note.

Page 229   ". . . as 'very political,' . . ." Interview with Texas National Guard, anonymous.

Page 229   "'I got that Republican congressman's son . . .'" "Bush Reportedly was Helped in Joining Guard Unit in Vietnam Era," by George Lardner Jr., *Washington Post*, September 9, 1999.

Page 229   "'Lots of people like to . . .'" See previous note.

Page 229   ". . . recommendation came from a panel . . ." Special Order ANG-A 146, AGTEX, dated August 28, 1968, signed by Brigadier General James M. Rose.

Page 230   "'As a veteran, . . .'" *Democracy Now* interview with Bill Burkett, April 2003.

Page 230   "'. . . the Guard has always been about . . .'" Interview with Albert Lloyd, October 2003.

Page 231   "'I think I was just tolerated . . .'" Interviews with Bill Burkett, various dates.

Page 231   ". . . unpaid $4,800 charge . . ." See previous note.

Page 232   ". . . later admitted to Burkett . . ." See previous note.

Page 232   "'His characterization of all this . . .'" Interview with Major General Danny James, January 2004.

Page 233   "'That's right, I blackmailed them,' . . ." Bill Burkett e-mail response to question from author.

Page 234   "'We're still here.' . . ." Bill Burkett e-mail, November 2003.

Chapter 12: Men Such as These

Narrative, quotes, and dialogue for this chapter are the result of a Gulf of Mexico fishing trip and interview with Richard Cunnare, Dennis Telischak, Nelson Luce, James Bond, and David Dillard. The trip occurred in July of 2003 off the coast of Pensacola, Florida.

Chapter 13: Memorial Days

Page 246   "'It was so hysterical,' . . ." Interview with Chelle Pokorney, Virginia, October 2003.

Page 246   "'We went to the . . .'" See previous note.

Page 247   "'He waited until . . .'" See previous note.

Page 247   "'If we go, . . .'" See previous note.

Page 248   ". . . supposed to be promoted . . ." Interview with Lieutenant Ben Reid, June 2003.

Page 248   "'I love you very much . . .'" Copy of letter to Taylor Pokorney from Lieutenant Pokorney.

Page 248   "'He knew,' . . ." Interview with Chelle Pokorney, Virginia, October 2003.

Page 248   "'And I just went cold . . .'" Interview with Wade Lieseke, Tonopah, Nevada, July 2003.

Page 249   "'. . . matter of factly,' . . ." See previous note.

Page 249   "'When she has that first date, . . .'" "Widow of Tonopah Marine says Corps will Become Her Family," by Estes Thompson, *Associated Press*, March 27, 2003.

Page 250   "'It was a blessing,' . . ." See previous note.

Page 250   "'To die in a war . . .'" "Tonopah Graduate Killed in Ambush," by Martha Bellisle, *Reno Gazette-Journal*, March 26, 2003.

Page 251   "'He's a son I never . . .'" Interview with Suzy Lieseke, Tonopah, Nevada, October 2003.

Page 251   "'I cannot describe . . .'" Interview with Wade Lieseke, Tonopah, Nevada, July 2003.

Page 252   "'So, I am about at his . . .'" Interview with Jill Kiehl, Comfort, Texas, August 2003.

Page 252   "'It's kinda ironic . . .'" See previous note.

Page 252   "'The hardest part . . .'" See previous note.

Page 253   "'We retired James' . . .'" Interview with Colin Toot, Comfort, Texas, August 2003.

Page 253   "'Because I wanted to pay . . .'" Interview with Randy Kiehl, Comfort, Texas, August 2003.

Page 254   "'The hardest day of my life . . .'" Interview with Darrell Cortez, El Paso, Texas, August 2003.

Page 254   "'I'm not the only one . . .'" Interview with Randy Kiehl, Comfort, Texas, August 2003.

Page 255   "'They wanted to get there . . .'" Interview with Jill Kiehl, Comfort, Texas, August 2003.

Page 256   "'Fred would have been so . . .'" Interview with Chelle Pokorney, Virginia, October 2003.

Page 256   "'I just couldn't do it,' . . ." Interview with Wade Lieseke, Tonopah, Nevada, July 2003.

Page 257   "'In the tough fighting . . .'" "Bush Visits Camp Lejeune to Praise Marines," by John Wagner, *Raleigh News-Observer*, April 4, 2003.

Page 257   ". . . and dropped them into his coat . . ." Interview with Chelle Pokorney, Virginia, October 2003.

Page 257   "'. . . I wish Fred . . .'" See previous note.

Page 257   "'You are my pillar . . .'" See previous note.

Page 258   "'I don't know why . . .'" Interview with Wade Lieseke, Tonopah, Nevada, July 2003.

Page 259   ". . . escorted by six Marines . . ." "Nevadan Buried at Arlington National Cemetery," Associated Press, *Reno Gazette-Journal*, April 15, 2003.

Page 259   "'It hurts so much,' . . ." Interview with Wade Lieseke, Tonopah, Nevada, July 2003.

Page 259   "'Where's daddy?' . . ." "Nevadan Buried at Arlington National Cemetery," Associated Press, *Reno Gazette-Journal*, April 15, 2003.

Page 260   "'Oh, that was Fred,' . . ." Interview with Chelle Pokorney, Virginia, October 2003.

Page 260   "'. . . the most beautiful thing . . .'" See previous note.

Page 261   "'Beyond the Tomb of the Unknowns, . . .'" "President Bush Honors the Brave and Fallen Defenders of Freedom," White House press office release of text, WhiteHouse.gov, May 26, 2003.

Page 261   "'We were just so honored . . .'" Interview with Chelle Pokorney, Virginia, October 2003.

Page 261   "Unknown to Green, . . ." "On Memorial Day, ex-POWs Help Ease a Family's Grief," by Laura Cruz, *El Paso Times*, May 27, 2003.

Page 261   "'This year's Memorial Day . . .'" See previous note.

Page 262   ". . . journalists suspected . . ." Interview with Laura Cruz, El Paso, June 2003.

Page 262   "'She told us . . .'" See previous note.

Page 262   "'This is not my son,' . . ." "On Memorial Day, ex-POWs Help Ease a Family's Grief," by Laura Cruz, *El Paso Times*, May 27, 2003.

Page 263   "'I can't think of anything,' . . ." See previous note.

Page 263   "In spite of their pain, . . ." "Mourners Sing Birthday Tribute for Soldier," by Maria Cortes Gonzalez, *El Paso Times*, April 15, 2003.

Page 263   ". . . held two carnations . . ." See previous note.

Page 264   "Horning frequently traveled . . ." Interview with Larry Horning, Reno, Nevada, June 2003.

Page 264   "'I went and looked up . . .'" See previous note.

Page 264   "Fred Pokorney was listed . . ." 1989 Sertoma Classic program and team roster.

Page 265   "'I wasn't going to miss . . .'" Interview with Wade Lieseke, Tonopah, Nevada, June 2003.

Page 265   "'We also decided . . .'" Interview with Larry Horning, Reno, Nevada, June 2003.

Page 266   "'Fred was a giant . . .'" Remarks from podium by Larry Horning.

Page 267   "'Tonight, we take the time . . .'" Program remarks written by Larry Horning.

Chapter 14: At War with Mr. Wilson

Page 271   "'I think the White House . . .'" Interview with Joe Wilson, Washington, D.C., October 2003.

Page 271   ". . . by the CIA to Niamey, . . ." "What I Didn't Find in Africa," by Joe Wilson, *New York Times*, editorial, July 6, 2003.

Pages 271–272   ". . . at least four reports . . ." Interview with Joe Wilson, Washington, D.C., October 2003.

Page 272   ". . . dropped the name of Wilson's wife . . ." "Mission to Niger," by Robert Novak, *Chicago Sun-Times*, July 14, 2003.

Page 272   "'Wilson never worked . . .'" See previous note.

Page 272   ". . . Novak had been told . . ." Interview with Joe Wilson, Washington, D.C., October 2003.

Page 272   "'. . . acknowledges talking to the CIA . . .'" See previous note.

Page 273   "'I fully expected . . .'" See previous note.

Page 273   ". . . Intelligence Identities Protection . . ." "Capital Games," by David Corn, *Nation*, July 2003.

Page 273   "'. . . it's despicable,' . . ." Interview with Joe Wilson, Washington, D.C., October 2003.

Page 274   ". . . 'holiest of holies' . . ." "The Spy Who Was Thrown into the Cold," by Julian Borger, *Guardian of London*, October 22, 2003.

Page 275   "Campaign manager for Texas, . . ." "Karl and Bob: A Leaky History," by Rick Casey, *Houston Chronicle*, November 7, 2003.

Page 275   "'I thought another firm . . .'" See previous note.

Page 275   "'. . . effort in Texas has been a bust.' . . ." See previous note.

Page 275   "'Also attending the session . . .'" See previous note.

Page 276   "'I said Rove . . .'" See previous note.

Page 276   "'As far as I know,' . . ." "Genius," by S. C. Gwynne, *Texas Monthly*, March 2003.

Page 276   "Mosbacher does. . . ." "Karl and Bob: A Leaky History," by Rick Casey, *Houston Chronicle*, November 7, 2003.

Page 277   "'I've never publicly . . .'" Interview with Joe Wilson, Washington, D.C., October 2003.

Page 277   "'I'm telling you flatly,' . . ." "Cheney Claims Again Iraq Tried To Acquire Uranium From Niger," by Amy Goodman, *Democracy Now*, September 16, 2003.

Page 277   "'I'm saying no one . . .'" See previous note.

Page 278   "'If I could find . . .'" See previous note.

Page 278   ". . . Ashcroft had used Karl Rove . . ." "Attorney General Is Closely Linked to Inquiry Figures," by Elisabeth Bumiller, *New York Times*, October 2, 2003.

Page 278   "'. . . out of my lane,' . . ." Interview with Joe Wilson, Washington, D.C., October 2003.

Page 279   "An estimated 2,000 Americans, . . ." See previous note.

Page 279   "'. . . threaten capital punishment,' . . ." See previous note.

Page 280   "'Your courageous leadership . . .'" Personal note to Wilson from President George H. W. Bush.

Page 280   "'I must say, . . .'" Interview with Joe Wilson, Washington, D.C., October 2003.

Page 281   ". . . an Italian tabloid reporter. . . ." "The Stovepipe," by Seymour Hersh, *New Yorker*, December 9, 2003.

Page 281   ". . . filed a routine report . . ." See previous note.

Page 281   ". . . provided the CIA . . ." See previous note.

Page 282   ". . . the tabloid she writes for, . . ." See previous note.

Page 282   ". . . Rosella ordered Burta . . ." See previous note.

Page 282   ". . . 'put the bite' . . ." See previous note.

Page 282   ". . . 'jaw dropped' . . ." "U.N. Official: Fake Iraq Nuke Papers Were Crude," by Louis Charbonneau, *Reuters*, March 26, 2003.

Page 282   ". . . bore the signature of Alle . . ." See previous note.

Page 283   ". . . the French nuclear scientist . . ." See previous note.

Page 283   ". . . more modern governing instrument . . ." See previous note.

Page 283   "In chapter 3 of the presentation, . . ." "Iraq's Weapons of Mass Destruction: Assessment of the British Government," British Government Document, Ch. 3, "Iraq Under Saddam," September 12, 2003.

Page 283   ". . . Niger letters to be false. . . ." "Documents Linking Iraq to Uranium Were Forged," by Jeff Sallot, *Globe and Mail*, March 8, 2003.

Page 284   "'Based on a thorough . . .'" See previous note.

Page 284   ". . . under a headline of . . ." "Disarm Saddam Hussein," WhiteHouse.gov.

Page 284   "'This whole question . . .'" *Meet the Press with Tim Russert*, NBC News, September 12, 2003.

Page 284   "'I looked at how the uranium business . . .'" Interview with Joe Wilson, Washington, D.C., October 2003.

Page 285   "'I undertook this mission . . .'" See previous note.

Page 286   "'Anyone who would . . .'" "Naming of Agent was Aimed at Discrediting CIA," by Edward Alden, *Financial Times*, October 25, 2003.

Page 286   "'What sickens me,' . . ." See previous note.

Page 287   "'I'm perfectly happy . . .'" Interview with Joe Wilson, Washington, D.C., October 2003.

Chapter 15: Soldier Down

Page 288   "'I was laying there . . .'" Interview with Max Cleland, Washington, D.C., October 2003.

Page 289   "'I went through the Tet . . .'" See previous note.

Page 289   "'It's a low water . . .'" See previous note.

Page 290   "'The ad became . . .'" See previous note.

Page 291   "'The people making this . . .'" Interview with Karl Strubble, Washington, D.C., October 2003.

Page 291   ". . . 300 busloads . . ." Interview with Max Cleland, Washington, D.C., October 2003.

Page 291   "'There was no way . . .'" Interview with Karl Strubble, Washington, D.C., October 2003.

Page 292   "'Absolutely. There's no . . .'" Interview with Max Cleland, Washington, D.C., October 2003.

Page 292   "Those appearances, . . ." See previous note.

Pages 292–293   ". . . the final surveys showed . . ." "Special Investigation: Is Democracy Under Threat in America?" by Andrew Gumbel, *Independent* (United Kingdom), October 14, 2003.

Page 293   ". . . revealed demographic breakdowns . . ." See previous note.

Page 293   ". . . won a $54 million . . ." See previous note.

Page 293   "In Fulton County, . . ." See previous note.

Page 294   "Wyle Laboratories was . . ." "Did E-Vote Firm Patch Election?" by Kim Zetter, *Wired News*, October 13, 2003.

Page 294   ". . . there were numerous failures . . ." See previous note.

Page 294   "'It's hard to track down . . .'" See previous note.

Page 295   ". . . ordered by Diebold . . ." See previous note.

Page 295   "'. . . the last thing Diebold . . .'" See previous note.

Page 295   "'There are literally . . .'" "Special Investigation: Is Democracy Under Threat in America?" by Andrew Gumbel, *Independent* (United Kingdom), October 14, 2003.

Page 296　"'I really expected . . .'" See previous note.

Page 296　"'If a patch was not run . . .'" "Did E-Vote Firm Patch Election?" by Kim Zetter, *Wired News*, October 13, 2003.

Page 296　"'We have analyzed that . . .'" See previous note.

Page 297　"'These memos show . . .'" "Will the 2004 Election be Stolen with Electronic Voting Machines?" An Interview with Bev Harris, Buzzflash.com, September 29, 2003.

Page 297　"Diebold sued her . . ." See previous note.

Page 298　". . . 'is simply the act . . .'" See previous note.

Page 298　"Thomas Swidarski, . . ." "Machine Politics in the Digital Age," by Melanie Warner, *New York Times*, November 9, 2003.

Page 299　"'If I was a programmer at one of these . . .'" VerifiedVoting.org, David Dill web site.

Page 299　". . . California to require a . . ." "State Move a Victory for Safe Voting," by Dan Gillmore, *San Jose Mercury-News*, November 26, 2003.

Page 299　"'Our analysis shows . . .'" "Analysis of an Electronic Voting System," by Aviel D. Rubin, Johns Hopkins Information Security Institute Technical Report TR-2003-19, July 23, 2003.

Page 299　"'We conclude that, . . .'" See previous note.

Page 300　". . . 'reached their conclusions . . .'" "Checks and Balances in Elections Equipment and Procedures Prevent Alleged Fraud Scenarios," Diebold Election Systems, July 30, 2003.

Page 300　"'This report, . . .'" See previous note.

Page 300　"'The State of Maryland . . .'" "Risk Assessment Report: Diebold AccuVote-TS Voting System and Processes," Science Applications International Corporation, September 2, 2003.

Page 300　"'This Risk Assessment has identified . . .'" See previous note.

Page 300　". . . 328 flaws . . ." See previous note.

Page 301　". . . 'stunning,' . . ." See previous note.

Page 301　". . . 'an alternative system . . .'" Maryland State Board of Elections, letter to James C. DiPaula Jr., Secretary of Deptartment of Budget and Management, September 23, 2003.

Page 301　". . . raised to 'very high' . . ." "Risk Assessment Report: Diebold AccuVote-TS Voting System and Processes," Science Applications International Corporation, September 2, 2003.

Page 301   "'It is impossible for this file . . .'" "Will Bush Backers Manipulate Votes to Deliver GW Another Election?" by Amy Good-
man, et al., *Democracy Now*, September 4, 2003.

Page 302   "'These companies are basically . . .'" "Machine Politics in
the Digital Age," by Melanie Warner, *New York Times*, November 9, 2003.

Page 302   ". . . all received 18,181 votes, . . ." "Special Investigation: Is
Democracy Under Threat in America?" by Andrew Gumbel,
Independent (United Kingdom), October 14, 2003.

Page 302   ". . . had to remove 18 . . ." See previous note.

Page 302   ". . . in Broward County, . . ." See previous note.

Page 302   "Alabama's gubernatorial race . . ." See previous note.

Page 303   "Hagel was the CEO . . ." "Hagel's Ethics Filings Pose Disclosure Issue," by Alexander Bolton, *Hill*, January 29, 2003.

Page 303   ". . . investment of $1 to $5 million . . ." See previous note.

Page 303   "The McCarthy Group owns . . ." See previous note.

Page 303   ". . . 85 percent of the votes . . ." See previous note.

Page 303   ". . . Channel 8 News . . ." Blackboxvoting.com, by Bev Harris,
March 26, 2003.

Page 304   ". . . admitted that Hagel retained . . ." "Hagel's Ethics Filings
Pose Disclosure Issue," by Alexander Bolton, *Hill*, January 29,
2003.

Page 304   ". . . Victor Baird, met with Hagel's . . ." Senate Ethics Committee Chief Counsel/Director Resigns, by Bev Harris,
March 26, 2003.

Page 304   ". . . Baird was replaced . . ." See previous note.

Page 305   "'This is a big story,' . . ." See previous note.

Page 305   ". . . designs on the presidency. . . ." Hagel May run for President in 2008, by Bev Harris, Blackboxvoting.com, March 26,
2003.

Page 305   ". . . a group of George W. Bush supporters . . ." "Voting Machine Controversy," by Julie Carr Smyth, *Cleveland Plain Dealer*,
August 28, 2003.

Page 305   "'I am committed . . .'" See previous note.

Page 305   ". . . a total of $22,000 . . ." "Machine Politics in the Digital
Age," by Melanie Warner, *New York Times*, November 9, 2003.

Page 306   ". . . $500,000 into Cheney's . . ." "Will Bush Backers Manipulate Votes to Deliver GW Another Election?" by Amy Goodman, et al., *Democracy Now*, September 4, 2003.

Page 306   "No money from Diebold . . ." "Machine Politics in the Digital Age," by Melanie Warner, *New York Times*, November 9, 2003.

Page 306   ". . . gave the president a tour . . ." "Will Bush Backers Manipulate Votes to Deliver GW Another Election?" by Amy Goodman, et al., *Democracy Now*, September 4, 2003.

Page 306   "'Basically what we have . . .'" See previous note.

Page 307   "When he was a student . . .'" Interview with Max Cleland, Washington, D.C., October 2003.

Page 307   "'That's the sad part . . .'" See previous note.

Page 308   "'You know what I worry . . .'" See previous note.

Page 308   "'We are not doing . . .'" See previous note.

Chapter 16: The Pokorney Girls

Quotes, dialogue, conversations, and scenes for this chapter resulted from a Saturday morning interview with Chelle Pokorney in Quantico, Virginia. The interview was conducted for both the author and a television film crew producing a documentary on the Iraq war and the politics leading up to the conflict.

Epilogue: Johnny Came Home

Page 318   "'What are you doing, . . .'" Interview with Nancili Mata, Pecos, Texas, August 2003.

Page 318   "'I have to be strong . . .'" See previous note.

Page 320   "Almost a hundred people . . ." See previous note.

Page 322   "'We don't think about no politics . . .'" Interview with Domingo Mata, Pecos, Texas, August 2003.

Page 324   "'My intentions are to go . . .'" "The Final Gift," by Victor R. Martinez, *El Paso Times*, April 2003.

ACKNOWLEDGMENTS

My first debt is to the people who defend our country. America has always had courageous souls who put protection of our democracy above their own safety. They stand between us and our enemies. But our democracy will not stand long if we betray their devotion and commitment.

In doing the research for this book, a number of families of service men and women killed in Iraq were contacted about participation. Most declined to be interviewed. A number of them believed that the lives of their lost soldiers were deserving of individual treatment. Unfortunately, the story of an American soldier killed in action has become too common. And we are comforted more by our victories than our casualties, so those are the stories that get told.

The families who did share their experiences were profoundly open with both their love and their grief. Chelle Pokorney wanted America to understand what she and her daughter Taylor and America lost with the death of First Lieutenant Frederick E. Pokorney Jr. She has been generous with her feelings, her time, her frustrations, and her hope for the country her husband died for.

Wade and Suzy Lieseke, who brought Fred Pokorney into their lives and their home when he was a teenager, welcomed me like an old friend. I expect to be returning to Tonopah many times during my life. If anyone has a right to voice an opinion on war and have it heard widely, it is Wade, who served two tours as a gunner in a helicopter in Vietnam and lost his adopted son in Iraq. Fred considered the Liesekes to be his parents. They are still crying.

Randy Kiehl, father of James Kiehl, and Jill Kiehl, wife of the fallen 507th soldier, were always cooperative and willing to talk about James, regardless of how much it hurt. A day at Randy's house in the hill country left me more convinced than ever that leaders of all countries must try everything but war to resolve differences. One look at James' son, Nathaniel, who will never know his father, will win that argument.

Friends of James Kiehl, in particular Darrell and Theresa Cortez, as well as Chris and Becky Langley, who shared pizza and memories of their friend, are owed thanks. I felt as if I knew James after I had spent an evening with them gathered around a table one night in El Paso. Colin Toot, James' high school basketball coach, helped me feel the loss of James.

Nancili Mata and her children Eric and Stephani gave a stranger the story of Johnny Villareal Mata. Nancili and her two children have been changed by his death in a way that America ought not to ignore. Nancili gave up her husband, a man she had loved since middle school, and Eric and Stephani surrendered their father because America said he was needed. I recall, during the Gulf War, asking a ten-year-old girl, crying as her father boarded a flight from Fort Hood to Kuwait, if she thought the country needed her daddy. She said, "No, I think I need my daddy." Nancili, and Eric and Stephani still need Johnny.

In El Paso, I was introduced to the story of nineteen-year-old Ruben Estrella-Soto by Laura Cruz, a reporter for the El Paso Times. Young, and extremely talented, Laura is the kind of journalist that makes her profession an invaluable part of the culture of her community. Laura's knowledge of Fort Bliss, home of the 507th, and the families of soldiers, was critical in giving this book context. The work of other reporters at the El Paso Times also provided source material for this book. Laura Cruz did not just understand her town and what the war had done to it; she felt it, and wrote about it with a skill that enabled her readers to know how much was being endured by Private Estrella-Soto's family and others connected to the 507th.

In an effort to see that the truth was served, First Lieutenant Ben Reid of the U.S. Marine Corps courageously shared his experiences during the battle of Al Nasiriyah. His interest, totally selfless, was in making certain Fred Pokorney's family knew what happened to him. Endings in war are not glorious and often are the result of mistakes. But families are owed the facts. Reid's insistence on telling it straight is in keeping with the finest traditions of the Marines and is the kind of honorable act his friend Fred would have appreciated.

What understanding I have of the political and cultural dynamics at work in the Middle East has been refined by Husain Haqqani and Stephen Schwartz. Hussain, of the Carnegie Endowment for International Peace, is passionate about helping Americans make informed decisions. Stephen Schwartz has a depth of intellect that is daunting to average reporters. His seminal work, *The Two Faces of Islam* (New York: Anchor Books, 2002) ought to be required reading for anyone in our country who thinks they know the causes behind the war on terrorism and who is supporting al Qaeda.

Reporting on a question as complex as war, and the intelligence leading to conflict, is the most challenging assignment any journalist can ever get. Judy Miller of the *New York Times* and Barton Gellman of the *Washington Post* helped me write about the logistical and competitive complications of their profession. I have no doubt they were both in pursuit of the same truth. The two certainly had the kind of frankness all journalists seek in their own sources. Chief Warrant Officer Richard Gonzales of the Mobile Exploitation Team Alpha gave me additional understanding of journalistic difficulties confronted when reporters are trying to write about the intelligence community from a war zone. Satirist Dennis Hans, writing about coverage of weapons of mass destruction, made me laugh so hard I pulled a rib muscle.

Still taking risks for his country, Lieutenant Colonel Bill Burkett laid bare everything he says he saw and heard while serving under George W. Bush. His life has been threatened. His health has been damaged. His future is questionable. But he is still talking. Burkett and his wife Nicki ought not to be enduring indignities after all of his years of service. I hope this helps. His story is an important one.

In Florida, I met Rich Cunnare and his friends, Nelson Luce, Dennis Telischak, James Bond, and Dave Dillard. Out in the Gulf, pulling up red snapper, they told about their war. Cunnare's experience, getting shot down while George W. Bush was avoiding his National Guard duties, gave important context to the president's behavior during the Vietnam era. I believe Rich has honored the men who saved his life by telling their stories. If there is any fairness, the heroics of Dexter Florence, Doug Brown, John Bridgers, Thomas Boyd, Howard Fraley, and the fearless Chuck Dean will be remembered for many years. Cunnare is just one of the men still living because of their courage.

Nothing is more inspiring for a writer of politics and current affairs than coming across people who take their citizenship seriously. I discovered this important trait in Martin Heldt of Clinton, Iowa, who taught himself many things, including Freedom of Information laws, to pursue the National Guard records of President Bush. Lieutenant Robert "Hawkeye" Rogers, a former pilot in the Guard, was as intent on the subject as his friend Martin. Together, they are largely responsible for what America knows about the president's record in the Texas Guard. I hope my narrative helps to illuminate their dogged research. Bev Harris, a committed American citizen, has demanded democracy not yield to technology. Her research and unrelenting effort to bring accountability to the electronic voting machine industry is precisely the kind of devotion that has kept alive our republic. Larry Horning of Reno, Nevada, also made me feel good about our country. He had to help the Pokorneys, somehow, and he made me believe we are all like that.

Ambassador Joseph Wilson, who was besieged by reporters and producers, gave up a part of his day to elaborate on what has happened to him and his wife, a CIA agent. Wilson and his family have been wronged, and it will be an even greater injustice if the person who leaked his wife's name cannot be found.

At American University, former U.S. Senator Max Cleland was as insightful and analytical as he has ever been during the course of an interview for this book and a documentary. America will outlive all of the bad decisions of its leaders as long as there are patriots like Max Cleland saying what's actually true.

If this narrative has any conciseness or moments of linguistic clarity, it is because of my friend, who has become my editor, Paul Willcott. Paul has run by my side through the South Texas tropics and has bought me fine whiskey in Manhattan. He loves words, knows stories, and can make sentences shine. I wish I could write like him.

A number of other people have read portions of this manuscript for accuracy and correction of terminology. Ken Vest, who is more a brother than a friend, gave me the first assessment of the book's middle section, and I made changes. Ken, Sue, Jesse, and Jeremy Vest have made every trip to Washington feel like coming home. My brother-in-law John Pagels, and his wife Barb, offered a sunlit room in Virginia for writing during those trips east. Bob Hillman, the only 365-day-a-year journalist I have ever known, opened his doors, and good bottles of wine. Jack Holt, a business associate and friend, who served in the U.S. Marine Corps, made certain I did not commit the grievous error of referring to Marines as soldiers. He's also pretty handy with grammar and an editor's scalpel. James Clingman, a Cincinnati businessman, scholar, teacher, and columnist inspired me to think more critically of George W. Bush.

A collaboration and friendship with Wayne Slater on *Bush's Brain: How Karl Rove Made George W. Bush Presidential* (New York: Wiley, 2003) laid the foundation for this project. I am thankful for the graciousness of Joe Mealey and Michael Shoob, who let me sit in on their interviews as they filmed a documentary. They have believed in my writing in a way that has helped to keep me motivated. Robert Bryce, author of *Pipe Dreams*, commiserated with me on the absurdities of politics whenever he or I were astonished by the situation in our country. Greg Groogan, my brother from another bloodline, has kept me propped up and in fine perspective, and always seemed to know when to call. Nobody is smarter than my real brother, Tim Moore, who is more astute on politics and the economy than all presidential advisors. Whenever my thinking ran down a dry arroyo, he always helped me find a way out. My brother is my best friend. My sisters, Elaine Abo Neaaj, Beverly Hargrove, Becky Sims, and Brenda Britt keep reminding me how lucky I am to finally get to do what I have always dreamed of doing. My mother, Joyce Moore, probably needs to talk a little less about her son the writer.

Mike Moeller and Nora Linares invited me into their home to help me understand the political dynamics of the Texas Lottery. My nephew and friend Tobin Baird gave summer shelter when I was road-worn, and access to the night skies of the California Sierras. Jason Stanford kept showing off insight exceeding his years, hoping, unsuccessfully, to be quoted again. Instead, I just stole some of his ideas. Regular discussions, e-mails, and lunches with Eddie Martinez always yielded notions I had overlooked. Because no author can talk to enough sources, the work of many journalists is cited, both in the narrative and the chapter notes.

This book, like my first one, was sold to John Wiley and Sons, Inc., by Sam Fleishman of Literary Artists Representatives, who took a chance on me. I hope I have lived up to his expectations. Joan O'Neil, my publisher at Wiley, has expressed the kind of enthusiasm that gave me confidence in what I was doing. David Pugh has once more played the role of friend and editor, telling me when I am wrong, even though he knew he might be in for an argument. He always won, and this book is better because of David. Any attention this book has gotten can be credited to the tenacity of Mike Onorato in Wiley's publicity department, and Jesica Church, along with Peter Knapp and Elka Villa in marketing. Almost as if it is routine, Robin Factor and Todd Tedesco have compressed the production process to meet the demands of the marketplace, without sacrificing their standards. Nancy Marcus Land and her team at Publications Development Company of Texas gave the text its appeal, and corrected my punctuation, grammar, and spelling. Helene

Godin has kept me from goofing up, which, she can tell you, even over a phone line, is no minor achievement. She may be the world's most pleasant lawyer. Any mistakes in this narrative are the creation of the author.

The concluding thoughts I had as this manuscript was being completed were of Ambassador Wilson and his family. I agree with him. We all have a simple choice. And it has nothing to do with a political party. My loyalty is to the Constitution and the American flag.

And, of course, to my forever girls: Mary Lou and Amanda.

JAMES C. MOORE

Austin, Texas
January 2004

INDEX